PRAKRIT DHAMMAPADA

BASED UPON

M. SENART'S KHAROSTHI MANUSCRIPT

WITH

TEXT, TRANSLATION & NOTES

PRAKRIT DHAMMAPADA

BASED UPON

M. SENART'S KHAROṢṬHĪ MANUSCRIPT

WITH

TEXT, TRANSLATION & NOTES

BY

BENIMADHAB BARUA, M.A. (CAL.), D.LIT. (LOND.),

POST-GRADUATE TEACHER IN THE DEPARTMENTS OF PALI AND ANCIENT INDIAN HISTORY AND CULTURE, CALCUTTA UNIVERSITY, FORMERLY STATE SCHOLAR TO THE GOVERNMENT OF INDIA, AUTHOR OF 'A HISTORY OF PRE-BUDDHISTIC INDIAN PHILOSOPHY.' 'THE ĀJĪVIKAS.' 'PROLEGOMENA TO A HISTORY OF BUDDHIST PHILOSOPHY,' ETC.

AND

SAILENDRANATH MITRA, M.A.,

POST-GRADUATE TEACHER IN THE DEPARTMENTS OF PALI AND INDIAN VERNACULARS, CALCUTTA UNIVERSITY, FORMERLY RESEARCH SCHOLAR TO THE GOVERNMENT OF BENGAL, PROFESSOR OF PALI, BAPTIST COLLEGE, RANGOON.

PUBLISHED BY THE

UNIVERSITY OF CALCUTTA

1921

PRAKRIT DHAMMAPADA

BASED UPON

M. SENART'S KHAROSTHI MANUSCRIPT

WITH

TEXT, TRANSLATION & NOTES

BY

BENIMADHAB BARUA,

M.A. (CAL.), D. LIT. (LOND.),

POST-GRADUATE TEACHER IN THE DEPARTMENTS OF PALI AND ANCIENT INDIAN HISTORY AND CULTURE, CALCUTTA UNIVERSITY, FORMERLY STATE SCHOLAR TO THE GOVERNMENT OF INDIA, AUTHOR OF 'A HISTORY OF PRE-BUDDHISTIC INDIAN PHILOSOPHY.' 'THE AJIVIKAS.' 'PROLEGOMENA TO A HISTORY OF BUDDHIST PHILOSOPHY,' ETC.

AND

SAILENDRANATH MITRA, M.A.,

POST-GRADUATE TEACHER IN THE DEPARTMENTS OF PALI AND INDIAN VERNACULARS, CALCUTTA UNIVERSITY, FORMERLY RESEARCH SCHOLAR TO THE GOVERNMENT OF BENGAL, PROFESSOR OF PALI, BAPTIST COLLEGE, RANGOON.

GYAN

Published by

Gyan Publishing House
5, Ansari Road
Daryaganj, New Delhi-110002
Phone: 011-47034999, 9811692060
E-mail: books@gyanbooks.com

Distribution Network
gyanbooks.com
India, USA, Canada, UK, Australia, France

ISBN : 978-81-212-2384-3 (PB)
First Published, 1921

2nd Impression 2021

Printed at: Gyan Press, Delhi.

Prakrit Dhammapada
Based Upon
M. Senart's Kharosthi Manuscript with Text, Translation & Notes
Author: Benimadhab Barua

To

The Hon'ble Sir ASUTOSH MOOKERJEE, Saraswati,

Sastra-Vachaspati, Sambuddhagama-Chakravarti,

Kt., C.S.I., M.A., D.L., D.Sc., Ph.D.,

the avowed champion

of

the cause of Buddhistic Researches in this country,

but for whose effort, sympathy and support

Buddhistic studies would not have found place

in the University of Calcutta,

this work is dedicated

in token of the devotion, heart-felt esteem and gratitude

of the authors.

CONTENTS

INTRODUCTION

PART I

SENART'S EDITION OF THE KHAROṢṬHĪ MANUSCRIPT

**

PART II

Present Edition of the Kharoṣṭhī Manuscript

Introduction

1. Discovery of the Kharoṣṭhī Manuscript of the Dhammapada.—The Dhammapada, now edited and translated with improved readings and readjustments, is the only text of which a fragment has been preserved in Kharoṣṭhī, a script in which two recensions of Asoka's Rock Edicts, at Shahbazgarhi and Mansehra, are inscribed, and this is the only Buddhist text which has been hitherto found composed in a Prakrit dialect. The manuscript is one of the earliest finds from Khotan. Among later finds in Khotan, we have to mention a few documents containing "dispositions and reports of local authorities, instructions, regulations, official and private correspondence—all inscribed in the Kharoṣṭhī script and drawn up in a Prakrit dialect."[1] Prof. Lüders says, "the date of the Prakrit documents is fixed by the Chinese wooden tablets which have been mixed with the later, and one of which is dated A.D. 269."[2] The first discovery of the Prakrit text of the Dhammapada in Kharoṣṭhī was made in 1892 by the French traveller Dutreuil de Rhins, who found altogether three fragments in Khotan, which he despatched to Paris. With regard to these fragments Prof. Lüders notes: "In 1897 Senart made known their contents and value.........Senart's communication created a sensation in the Âryan section of the Oriental Congress held in Paris. The find represented a Kharoṣṭhī manuscript.

[1] These we owe to Sir Aurel Stein. See his monumental work, *The Ancient Khotan*, in two big volumes.

[2] Lüders' paper *Uber die literarischen Funde von Ostturkestan*, translated by Mr. G. K. Nariman in his *Literary History*, p. 238.

**

The Kharoṣṭhī character till then had been known only from inscriptions in the outermost boundary of North-West India. Epigraphical comparison proved the date of the manuscript to be the second century. As to its contents, it was a recension of the Pāli Dhammapada in a Prakrit dialect, which was till then unknown in literary compositions. The manuscript was only a fragment. Another portion of the same manuscript was brought to Petrograd."[1] The portion which was taken by a Russian traveller to St. Petersburg (now called Petrograd) was, as M. Senart says,[2] deciphered and adjusted by Serge d'Oldenbourg, who later on placed the documents at his disposal. This courtesy on the part of the Russian servant was all the more welcome to M. Senart at a time when he himself was engaged in daciphering and adjusting the fragments in the Rhins collection. On examination M. Senart found that Serge d'Oldenbourg's documents filled some graps in the fragments of the Paris manuscript at which he was working. In Senart's edition, published in 1897 (*Journal Asiatique*), Serge d'Oldenbourg's documents have been incorporated intact (see B, ll. 1-15, pp. 24-31).

Since the publication of M. Senart's edition in 1897, several European scholars headed by Lüders have taken pains to make improvements on it and discuss the paleographic linguistic and literary importance of the Kharoṣṭhī manuscript. We shall never forget the day when in going together through M. Senart's edition we were struck by some inaccuracies of both identification and adjustment of the fragments as well as of particular verses, the first impression gradually deepening into settled conviction of certain drawbacks in the otherwise excellent work of a scholar whose name is in the very forefront of Oriental scholarship. At an opportune moment we chanced upon two incomplete couplets in his arrangement, numbered as line 1 in his plate A[2] and as

---

[1] Nariman, *Literary History*, p. 227.

[2] Le Manuscrit Kharoṣṭhī du Dhammapada, Preface.

PREFACE

This work of which the first instalment is now published, grew by way of a digression from our monograph—'Asoka's Dhamma, a landmark of Indian literature and religion', which is still in course of preparation. The digression took place at a point where the question of the bearing of Asoka's inscriptions and teachings on the Dhammapada class of Buddhist literature had to be discussed. The original plan was to re-adjust the verses and fragments and correct the readings in M. Senart's edition, wherever necessary and possible, chiefly in the light of the extant Pāli and the Sanskrit parallels. The idea of a complete edition with notes, translation and introduction was not conceived until after an interview with the Hon'ble Justice Sir Asutosh Mookerjee, President of the Post-Graduate Councils, who was kind enough to discuss with us the detail of the plan of the work, inspiring us to undertake the work and finish it by all means. We are happy that the undertaking is now fulfilled, although we do not doubt that the execution of the work would have been far more satisfactory, if placed in better hands.

It is especially gratifying to us that we have been able to re-edit a work which excited so much interest since its first publication about a quarter of a century ago and publish a greater portion of it fortunately during the lifetime of the illustrious M. Senart who ushered it into existence. The world will also remember with gratitude the labours of the Russian and French travellers—Petroffsky and Dutreuil de Rhins—who had discovered the fragments of the Kharoṣṭhī Manuscript and taken them to Europe. It is to Serge d'Oldenbourg that we owe the adjustment of a few fragments of the few verses, incorporated in M. Senart's Plate marked B.

In order to facilitate comparison, we have felt it necessary to reproduce in Part I of our work M. Senart's edition with his valuable notes translated into English. His parallel quotations have been omitted in Part I, but reproduced in Part II, marked with a †. The few alphabetical types used by him in paleographic discussion had to be omitted in our translation for the simple reason that they would be quite out of place without the fac-simile of the plates. So much about the reproduction of his work. Our part in the work consists in a radical shuffing and re-arrangement of his plates, fragments and, in some cases, verse-lines, consistently with the colophons indicating the total number of verses contained in a group, with the result that the whole work has been divided into so many distinct chapters. No fragment has been left unadjusted and no verse left incomplete, although there are one or two doubtful cases. Numerous new identifications and parallels have been supplied from all possible sources corroborating our adjustments and readings. The verses have been commented on by notes explaining their position in a chapter, and bringing out their literary, linguistic and historical significance. Part III contains the text as adjusted and restored in Part II, with translation. Part IV contains a short dissertation on the genesis, development and historical importance of the Dhammapada class of texts, while in Part V an attempt has been made to construct a comparative grammar of the language of the Prakrit text and that of the Kharoṣṭhī inscriptions and documents. In the Introduction will be found an account of the various recensions of the Dhammapada with special reference to their history, place and significance in Buddhism, while the

Glossary contains an index of words with their meanings and Pāli and Sanskrit equivalents.

It will be seen that the plan of the chapters appearing in Part II of this instalment was worked out independently of the very valuable suggestions of R. Otto Franke in his article *Zum Manuskript Dutreuil de Rhins* contributed to the *Z. D. M. G.* (60), 1906, and of Sylvain Lévi in his Study of the Recensions of the Dhammapada (J. A. September-October, 1912). We have the satisfaction to note that our readjustments and identifications coincide in numerous instances with theirs. The names of scholars who have contributed in manifold ways to the knowledge of the Dhammapada texts will be found in the Bibliography of references which follows.

Our obligation to Sir Asutosh is too great for words, and we shall ever remain grateful to him for the personal interest he has taken in the progress of the work. Our thanks are also due to Kabibhaskar Srijut Sasankamohan Sen, B.A., the Gopaldas Chowdhury Lecturer in Bengali, who has offered us from time to time important suggestions particularly with regard to the interpretation of the text. We have profited a great deal by some useful suggestions from Prof. Sylvain Lévi who was good enough to read the proofs of the latter portion of the Introduction. We are no less thankful to Mr. Ramaprasad Chanda, B.A., Superintendent, Indian Museum, Calcutta, Mr. B. C. Majumdar, B.A., Lecturer in Indian Vernaculars and in Comparative Philology, Dr. D. R. Bhandarkar, M.A., Carmichael Professor of Ancient Indian History and Culture, Dr. I. J. S. Taraporewala, Professor of Comparative Philology and Dr. F. W. Thomas, Librarian, India Office Library, who have also shown interest in the preparation of an edition like the present, and to Mr. Ramaprasad Chaudhury, M.A., and Mr. Prabodhchandra Bagchi, M.A., who were kind enough to assist us in various ways.

It must be said to the credit of Mr. A. C. Ghatak, B.A., Superintendent, Calcutta University Press, that but for his able management the work could not have been printed in the form in which it is now brought out. Lastly, we cannot close this Preface without a word of thanks to Babu Probodhchandra Chakravarti of the University Press who was entrusted with the work of setting up and who has acquitted himself of his task so well.

Senate House, Calcutta:	B. M. Barua
The 20th February, 1922.	S. N. Mitra

BIBLIOGRAPHY

The list of important texts and articles consulted :—

1. Dhammapada edited by V. Fausböll, 1900.

2. Dhammapada (P. T. S.)

3. Dhammapada—the English translation by Samuel Beal of the Chinese *Fa-keu-pi-u* (Trübner's Oriental Series, pocket edition).

4. Udānavarga—translated into English by W. W. Rockhill from the Tibetan (Trübner's Oriental Series).

5. Die Turfan-Recensionen des Dhammapada edited by R. Pischel in the Sitzb. d. K. Pr. Ak. d. Wiss, Berlin, 1908, p. 968 ff.

6. L'Apramādavarga edited by Sylvain Lévi with a valuable study of the Recensions of the Dhammapada in J. A., T. XX, 1912,

7. Documents Sanskrit De La Seconde Collection M.A. Stein edited by de la Vallée Poussin in J. R. A. S., 1912. These together with the three folios in the Pelliot collection comprise the following chapters and stanzas : (1) Anityavarga, st. 24-42 (fols. 3-4) ; (2) Kāmavarga, st. 1-19 (fols. 4-5) ; (12) Mārgavarga, st. 18-20 ; (13) Satkāravarga, st 1-11 a-b (one folio) ; (21) Tathāgatavarga, st. 8-18 ; (22) Śrutavarga, st. 1-2, 19 (Pelliot) ; (23) Ātmavarga, st. 1-26 (Pelliot) ; (24) Sahasravarga, st. 1-2 (Pelliot) ; (29) Yugavarga, st. 39-53 (fols. 52) ; (30) Sukhavarga, st. 26-52 (fols. 55-7) ; (31) Cittavarga, st. 1-38 (fols. 57-9) ; (32) Bhikṣuvarga, st. 3-14 (Pelliot), 15-29 (fols. 62-3).

8. Lüders' *Bemerkungen zu den Kharoṣṭhī Manuskript des Dhammapada* in the Nachrichten der K. Ges. d. Wiss. Zu Gottingen, Phil.-Hist. Klasse, 1899, p. 474 ff.

9. R. Otto Franke's article—*Zum Manuskript Dutreuil de Rhins* in Z. D. M. G., B. 60, 1906, p. 477 ff.

10. T. W. Rhys Davids on *the Gosinga Kharoṣṭhī Manuscript* in J. R. A. S , 1899, p. 426 ff.

11. de la Vallée Poussin's *Essai D'identification des Gāthās et des Udānas en prose de l'Udānavarga de Dharmatrāta* in J. A., T. XIX, 1912, p. 311 ff.

12. Jules Bloch on *Le Dialecte des Fragments Dutreuil de Rhins* in J. A., T. XIX, 1912.

13. Sten Konow's *Bemerkungen über die Kharoṣṭhī-Handschrift des Dhammapada* in the Festschrift Ernst Windisch, 1914, p. 85 ff.

14. A. Stein's Ancient Khotan, Vol. I., particularly Appendix E.

15. Max Müller's Introduction to his translation of the Dhammapada (S. B. E., Vol. X., Pt. I).

16. T. W. Rhys Davids—Buddhist India, p. 128 ff.

N. B.—So far as our information goes (J.R.A.S., 1899, p. 429) there is still a portion, perhaps a larger portion, of the Kharoṣṭhī Ms. under the disposal of Serge d'Oldenbourg and we can never doubt that when the contents thereof are made known, they will serve to enrich our knowledge of the Dhammapada. Nothing could be more regrettable to us than the fact that the prospect of seeing the portion in print has to be indefinitely deferred. It also pains us to confess that Beckh's edition of the Tibetan version of the Udānavarga, so much praised by Lévi and other Tibetan scholars, is a sealed book to us. In going through Rockhill's translation of the Tibetan work one is apt to feel embarassed by the tentative character of it, and the first suspicion is strengthened when it is compared with the portions of the Sanskrit original now within our reach. But by far the most bewildering is Beal's translation of the

Fa-kheu-pi-u, although the original translators in Chinese are very largely responsible for a violent distortion of the contents and sense of the Indian original. If the Fa-kheu-pi-u or its text portion the Fa-kheu-king be the specimen of the Chinese rendering of Indian texts, the student of Indian literature will surely labour in vain in grappling with the super-human and almost unsurmountable difficulty of mastering a knowledge of the Chinese alphabet and diction—a pursuit which, to put in the words of a witty Bengalee friend, will amount to breaking one's teeth in cracking the nut for so scanty and strange a kernel.

Grünwedel, Stein and Pelliot have placed humanity under a deep debt of gratitude by their successive missions into Central Asia, or more correctly to say, the Chinese Turkestan, for bringing together numerous fragments of the manuscript of the Udānavarga which is undoubtedly a Buddhist work of the Dhammapada class. We cannot but agree with M. de la Vallée Poussin in thinking that the text of this Ms. is a recension of the original of the Tibetan text attributed to Dharmatrāta and bearing the name of Udānavarga. But one must naturally be tempted to join issue with him when he describes the language of the text as "quasi-Sanscrit," for although in certain verses the older Pāli or Prakritic forms are retained, obviously for the sake of metre, the attempt at Sanskritisation appears to have reached in this text a stage well-nigh perfection as compared with previous attempts.

line 17, or the last line, in his plate A³. These lines, considered by him as two separate verses, appeared to us to be but integral parts of one single verse. To be clear, let us quote the lines as manipulated by him :

> .. madenamakabha devanasamidh(i)gat .
>
> ....
>
> (A², 1)
>
> apra .... u
>
> apramada praśajhati pramadu garahitu sada
>
> (A³, 17)

He has taken A², 1 to be the remnant of a verse for which he could find no parallel in Pāli or in Buddhist Sanskrit. It is obvious that in commenting upon it he completely lost sight of the Dhammapada verse 30, which reads :

> Appamādena Maghavā devānaṁ seṭṭhataṁ gato
> Appamādaṁ pasaṁsanti pamādo garahito sadā

—or else he would not have been led into equating *kabha* of *makabha* with a Sk. *garbha* (see pp. 5-6), but would have easily suggested that the Prakrit *makabha* is the counterpart of the Pāli *Maghavā*. But coming to A³, 17 he made a right hit on the aforesaid Pāli parallel, forgetting, however, to enquire whether A², 1—which he had already come across—with the reading *madena makabha devanasamidh(i) gat.*, which sounded so close to the Pāli *(appa)mādena Maghavā devānaṁ seṭṭhataṁ gat(o)*, could be referred back to in order to fill up the gap. But he could not possibly do so without putting the Plate A² immediately after A³, and thereby impairing his adjustment of the plates arranged in the order A², A³. His failure to combine A³, 17 and A², 1 into one verse is, it seems, due to a fatal oversight, and this oversight on his part led us to examine the fac-similes appended to the text edited by him, and we found that the top of the fragment A² was broken in such a way that it could be exactly fitted into the bottom of the fragment

A^3, so as to give us a complete Prakrit counterpart of the Pāli verse 30, quoted in the last page. Thus we were tempted to place A^2 immediately after A^3 and complete the Prakrit verse, by linking together A^3, 17 and A^2, 1, as follows :—

apra[madena makabha devanasamidh(i) gat]u
apramada praśajhati pramadu garahitu sada ○

We felt further justified by the fact that, for the commencement of the first foot, we had in A^3, 17 exactly two letters, *a pra*, answering to the two dots of omissions in A^2, 1, and for the last letter of the second foot, we had *u* in A^3, 17, answering to a dot of omission in A^2, 1. Proceeding to test the result of this preliminary examination, we had to satisfy ourselves whether the proposed inversion of M. Senart's Plates A^2 and A^3 could justify the unreconciled colophons "ga 25" (at the end of Plate A^1), and "ga 30" (in the middle of Plate A^3), which indicated that the four plates, arranged by M. Senart in the order A^1, A^2, A^3 A^4, contained two groups of Dhammapada verses, one consisting of 25 stanzas, and another of 30 stanzas. It was indeed a very happy moment when we found that by completely reversing M. Senart's order the verses and the four plates could be systematically arranged in two groups or chapters, consistently with the colophons "ga 30" and "ga 25"—a procedure ensuring a logical sequence of thought in the teaching of the groups and the verses alike. Taking our cue herefrom, we have made bold to dispute the whole arrangement of M. Senart's edition, which leaves colophons unexplained. Nay, we have ventured to reconstruct a number of hopelessly mutilated verses, particularly those at the end of Plate B, and to adjust and readjust a host of fragments and verses, testing almost every case in the light of a Pāli or a Sanskrit parallel; and the results of our investigation have been embodied in the following pages, to be judged for what they are worth.

2. **The title "Prakrit Dhammapada".**—M. Senart's edition, entitled "Le Manuscrit Kharoṣṭhî du Dhammapada" is

commonly known as 'the Kharoṣṭhī Recension of the Dhammapada,' which is a misnomer. The title chosen by the French scholar implies a meaning quite different from that which is conveyed by 'Kharoṣṭhī recension,' a name which suggests at once to the mind the idea of a copy of the Dhammapada in the Kharoṣṭhī 'language,' while, as a matter of fact, Kharoṣṭhī is only the name of a *script* in which the text has been preserved. They also speak of a 'Turfan Recension' since the publication of a specimen of the Sanskrit *Udānavarga*, of which a manuscript in fragments has been found in Turfan. As Prof. Pischel, who was the first to bring this specimen to light, explains, the title "Die Turfan-Recensionen" refers only to a manuscript, found in Turfan, of a Sanskrit recension of the Pāli Dhammapada.[1] 'Turfan Recension' must be regarded as a misnomer until it is definitely proved that there was a redaction made of the Udānavarga in Turfan. When, for instance, we speak of the Bengal, Benares and Bombay recensions of the Rāmāyaṇa we understand no more than so many editions of a single epic in Sanskrit, varying with one another according as they are based upon different readings in the different provinces, that is to say, upon texts as altered or modified by the scribes and repeaters of the three localities. The same holds true of the recensions of the Mahābhārata and other texts. But the case of 'the Dhammapada recensions' is somewhat different; for, in speaking of the Dhammapada recensions we cannot mean so many redactions of the same text in the same language, but so many different texts with different titles, composed in different languages, but belonging to a common literary type. To name one Dhammapada recension, in this special sense, after the script (*e.g.*, Kharoṣṭhī recension) and another after the place of find (*e.g.*, Turfan recension) cannot but be misleading and unscientific. This way of naming the Dhammapada texts would go to unnecessarily add to the number of recensions in the case of every new find in a new script or in a new place. The best way to have a consistent

[1] *Die Turfan-Recensionen des Dhammapada*, para. 1

method of naming them would be, we think, to apply to them the name of the language in which they are composed. So far as the Tibetan or Chinese versions of some of these Dhammapada texts are concerned, they are to be considered as translations of one or other recension of the Dhammapada. The Chinese *Fa-kheu-king*, as may be judged from Beal's English translation of its commentary, the *Fa-kheu-pi-u*, is neither a faithful translation nor entirely a new compilation, but bears the character of both. A special case is therefore to be made out for it. It may be put down as a 'Chinese Recension in translation' and considered along with a Pāli, Prakrit or Sanskrit recension, upon which its translation portion is based. If, in the case of a particular Dhammapada recension, or text, as we should also call it, *e.g.*, the Sanskrit Udānavarga, the faithful translations differ in expressions or in ideas, if it happens that there are two or more Tibetan translations of certain originals in Indian language which generally agree in contents and differ slightly here and there, we cannot but admit that their originals were only so many recensions of only one text. If, applying this consideration to the study of two or more translations of a particular Dhammapada text, it appears that they differ either in regard to the arrangement of chapters, the number and arrangement of verses and expressions, then we have to regard them as different versions based upon different recensions of the same text, leaving a sufficient margin for the errors of the translators as well as for the blunders in the original manuscripts of the text from which the translations were made.

Now, coming to the question of the title of our text, it is clear and admitted on all hands that it is composed in a Prakrit dialect, and, as will be shown anon, it is on the whole an original compilation, having some verses and ideas in common with other Dhammapada texts that are now known to us in Pāli, in Mixed Sanskrit or in Classical Sanskrit. It is this common substratum of the Dhammapada texts and the uniform plan and literary principle which they conform to wherein lies the justification of classing our text as a Dhammapada Recension, although the fragments of the Kharoṣṭhī Manuscript on which it is based, leave us in the dark about its title. Further, we prefer to call it a 'Prakrit Dhammapada' inasmuch as the logical differentia of the text as a copy of the Dhammapada can be derived from its linguistic characterization.

3. **Recensions and Copies of the Dhammapada.**—In order to determine the place of our text in the history of the Buddhist literature it is essential that we should have a closer acquaintance with the various 'recensions' and 'copies', of the Dhammapada that are now extant. Strictly, we can speak only of four recensions, *viz.*, the Pāli, the Prakrit, the Mixed Sanskrit and the Sanskrit, to which a fifth might be added, *viz.*, the *Fa-kheu-king*, which is a Chinese Recension in translation. The four Indian recensions comprise not less than six copies of the Dhammapada and three commentaries incorporating the text.

(i) *Pāli Dhammapada.*—Of the existing copies of the Dhammapada this is the best known and most complete. We have several editions of it in Singhalese, Burmese, Siamese, Devanāgari, Roman and Bengali characters, of which the latest and best is the one published by the Pāli Text Society. The excellence of this edition is in a large measure due to Fausböll's edition, so well-known to the students of Buddhist literature. Fausböll was perhaps the first to collect numerous references containing parallels from Buddhist works in Pāli, Prakrit, Mixed Sanskrit, Sanskrit and from a few important Brahmanical works like the Manu, the Rāmāyaṇa and the Mahābhārata. Fausböll occupies the foremost place alike as an editor and a Latin translator. But Max Müller was the first to translate it into English. We have another English translation of the text by James Gray, three German translations by Profs. Weber, Schröder and Neumann, and a French translation by M. Fernando Hû. The text contains 423 stanzas distributed into 26 groups, each of which is named according to the main theme of its component verses. It represents a book of the

Khuddakanikāya of the Theravāda (Sthaviravāda) canon preserved in Ceylon, Siam and Burma. There is a commentary which tradition attributes to Buddhaghosa, though, judging by its style, one cannot help doubting if Buddhaghosa was its real author. It is stated in the opening verses that the existing commentary in Pāli was based upon an older commentary in Singhalese and that the author undertook the work at the instance of a Thera Kumāra Kassapa (of Ceylon). The commentary itself consists of 26 chapters, each one of which appertains to a chapter of the text. One or more verses of a group are encased in a prose story setting forth the occasion on which the Buddha uttered the verse or verses. A prose exegesis forms a sequel to the moral verse or verses and is itself followed by an identification of the Buddha with the hero of the story if it happens to be an account of his previous birth, and by a statement of the psychological effect of the discourse on the mind of the hearer. Indeed, the method of the Dhammapada Commentary is precisely like that of the Jātaka Commentary, edited by Fausböll. We have three editions of the Dhammapada Commentary, one in Singhalese character, published in Ceylon, another in Roman, published by the Pāli Text Society and a third in Devanāgari, published by the Buddhist Text Society, the last one containing the text and the prose exegesis

(ii) *Prakrit Dhammapada.*—Of this copy we have preserved only one fragmentary manuscript in Kharoṣṭhī, found among the ruins of the Gośṛinga-vihāra, 13 miles from Khotan in the circle of Indian colonies. In the absence of a complete record it is impossible to say exactly how many chapters and verses the text contained. It is equally difficult to ascertain the arrangement of its chapters from detached plates and fragments on which M. Senart's edition is based. The chapters and verses, as they occur in our arrangement, are as follows :—

Order of Chapter	Name of Chapter	Number of Verses
1	Magavaga	30
2	Apramadavaga	25
3	Citavaga	5 (chapter incomplete)
4	Puṣavaga	15

Order of Chapter	Name of Chapter	Number of Verses
5	Sahasavaga	17
6	Panitavaga or Dhamaṭhavaga	10
7	Balavaga	7 (Chapter incomplete)
8	Jaravaga	25
9	Suhavaga	20 (Chapter almost complete)
10	Taṣavaga	7 (Chapter incomplete)
11	Bhikhuvaga	40
12	Bramanavaga	50 (?)
	Total number ...	251

We do not know if there is any Tibetan or Chinese translation of it. Its author's name is unknown. No information is yet forthcoming if any commentary was written on it. The utmost that we can say is that this copy of Dhammapada is compiled in a dialect of the Gandhāra region, having a close kinship, in orthography and other linguistic traits, with the dialects of Asoka's Rock edicts at Shahbazgarhi and Mansohra.

(iii) *The Mixed Sanskrit Original of the Fa-kheu-king.*—It is stated in the preface of the Chinese translation, known as the *Fa-kheu-king*, that its original, consisting of 500 verses and 22 chapters, was carried by Wai-chi-lan from India to China "in the third year of the reign of Hwang-wu (A. D. 223)," and was translated into Chinese by the same Indian Shaman with the help of another Indian named Tsiang-im.[1] From a comparison of the *Fa-kheu-king* with the Pāli Dhammapada, Samuel Beal is led to suppose that "the original manuscript brought to China was the same as that known in Ceylon, the differences which occur between the two being attributable to special reasons existing at the time of the translation."[2] He has sought to explain away the difference as to the total number of the verses,—423 of the Pāli text and 500 of the original of the *Fa-kheu-king*—by the assumption that "in the Buddhist calculation the next highest round number is frequently used to denote the exact number intended."[3] We cannot surely venture to

---

[1] Beal's Dhammapada, p. 34.

[2] *Ibid*, p. 13. [3] *Ibid*, p. 14.

dispute Mr. Beal's surmise until the original of the Chinese translation is discovered or an authentic tradition makes it known that the text used by the Chinese translator was other than the Pāli. But we find it difficult to subscribe to his opinion when it is expressedly stated in the preface to the Chinese translation that the original consisted of 500 verses distributed into 26 chapters, and in the 'Memoirs of Eminent Priests' (*Kāo-sañ-kwhāñ*, A. D. 519) that the original was a Sanskrit text.[1] Remembering, moreover, that the original of the *Fa-kheu-king* is said to be a work of a Dharmatrāta or Dharmarakṣita, a name so famous in the tradition of the Sārvastivāda sect of Buddhism, it does not seem improbable that the Indian text, a book of the Kṣudraka-nikāya of the canon, was a Sarvāstivāda work. We are, however, aware that such an opinion as this cannot be shown to harmonise with the account of the development of the entire Dhammapada literature. Reserving this important point for discussion in a separate section, we may do well to give, on the basis of Beal's study, a tabular statement of the chapters and verses composing the Pāli Dhammapada and the Fa-kheu-king Original respectively with a view to facilitate comparison between the two.

Title of Chapter	No. of Verses	
	Pāli Dhammapada	Fa-kheu-king Original
1. Yamakavagga (Twin Verses) ...	20	22
2. Appamādavagga (Chapter on Earnestness)	12	20
3. Cittavagga (Mind Verses) ...	11	12
4. Pupphavagga (Flower Verses) ...	16	17
5. Bālavagga (Chapter on the Fool) ...	16	21
6. Paṇḍitavagga (Chapter on the Wise)	14	17
7. Arahantavagga (Chapter on the Arahant)	10	10
8. Sahassavagga (Number Verses) ...	16	16
9. Pāpavagga (Chapter on Evil) ...	13	22
10. Daṇḍavagga (Chapter on Punishment)	17	14

[1] Nanjio's Catalogue, No. 1365.

Title of Chapter	No. of Verses	
	Pāli Dhammapada	Fa-kheu-king Original
11. Jarāvagga (Chapter on Old Age) ...	11	14
12. Attavagga (Chapter on elf) ...	10	14
13. Lokavagga (Chapter on the World) ...	12	14
14. Buddhavagga (Chapter on the Buddha)	18	21
15. Sukhavagga (Chapter on Happiness)	12	14
16. Piyavagga (Chapter on the Agreeable)	12	12
17. Kodhavagga (Chapter on Anger) ...	14	26
18. Malavagga (Chapter on Impurity) ...	21	19
19. Dhammaṭṭhavagga (Chapter on the Just)	17	17
20. Maggavagga (Chapter on the Way) ...	17	28
21. Pakiṇṇakavagga (Miscellaneous Verses)	16	14
22. Nirayavagga (Chapter on Hell) ...	14	16
23. Nāgavagga (Elephant Verses) ...	14	18
24. Taṇhāvagga (Chapter on Desire) ...	26	32
25. Bhikkhuvagga (Bhikkhu Verses) ...	23	32
26. Brāhmaṇavagga (Brāhmaṇa Verses) ...	41	40
Total number ...	423	502

The Fa-kheu-king Original had a commentary of the Avadāna type, which was translated into Chinese "by two Shamans of the western Tsin dynasty (A.D. 265 to A.D. 313)" under the title of "Fă-kheu-pi-ü,—*i.e.* parables connected with the book of scriptural texts."[1] With regard to this work Beal says: "......it contains certain parables, or tales, connected with the verses which follow them, and which prompted their delivery... ..The method adopted in this work is to give one or two tales, and a verse or more, as the Moral. The chapters are identical with the Fă-kheu-king—the only difference being that the verses or gāthas are fewer—they are, in fact, only a selection from the whole to meet the requirements of the story preceding them. This arrangement is in agreement with the original design of the work. Buddhaghosha, we are told, gives for each verse a parable to illustrate the

[1] Beal's Dhammapada, p. 25.

meaning of the verse, and believed to have been uttered by Buddha in his intercourse with his disciples, or in preaching to the multitudes that came to hear him. And so here we have a tale for each verse, delivered by Buddha for the benefit of his disciples, or others. As to the character of these stories, some of them are puerile and uninteresting. But if I mistake not, they are of a description not opposed to the character of the age to which they are assigned by the Chinese "[1]. Beal's English version is made from the Chinese Fa kheu-pi-u, which is a commentarial selection from the Fa-kheu-king, differing from the Pāli commentary by the absence of prose exegesis.

(iv) *Dharmapada quoted in the Mahāvastu.*—A whole chapter, *viz.* the Sahasravarga, containing 24 stanzas, has been quoted in the Mahāvastu (III., pp. 434-36) expressly from a Dharmapada text (" dharmapadeṣu sahasravargaḥ," *ibid*, p. 434). Besides, in the same work a few consecutive verses, numbering not less than 15, have been cited apparently from the Bhikṣuvarga of the same Dharmapada text. Here we may leave out of consideration the isolated verses which are quoted throughout the Mahāvastu and of which the parallel can be traced in other copies of the Dhammapada. The Mahāvastu edited by M. Senart professes to be a Mid-land Recension of the first Book of the Vinaya Piṭaka and belongs to the Lokottaravāda sect, an off-shoot of the Mahāsaṅghika.[2] The language of the Sahasravarga quoted has no claim to be called pure classical Sanskrit but deserves, on the other hand, to be just what M. Senart called Mixed Sanskrit. It remains to be seen if this copy of the Dhammapada, so much cherished in the Lokottaravāda or Ekavyavahārika literature, can be identified with any one of the three copies of the Dhammapada (one with 500 verses, another with 750, and another with 900), which were known to the authors of the *Fa-kheu-king* (3rd cent. A.D.).[3]

---

[1] Beal's Dhammapada, pp. 25-26.

[2] Mahāvastu, I., p. 2: " Āryamahāsaṅghikānāṁ Lokottaravādināṁ Madhyadeśikānāṁ pāṭhena Vinaya-piṭakānāṁ Mahāvastuye ādi ". See also the colophon at the end.

[3] Beal's Dhammapada, p. 33.

(v) *The Fa-kheu-king, a Chinese Recension in Translation.*—The *Fa-kheu-king* is, according to the Chinese translators' admission,[1] not a faithful translation of the Indian text which the Shaman Wai-chi-lan carried from India to China in 223 A.D. It is to be regarded as more than a translation, because the Chinese translators had not only tampered with the number and distribution of the verses in the original, but added 13 new chapters in Chinese, making up a total of 39 chapters, 752 verses, and 14,580 words. Similar additions and alterations are also to be met with in the Chinese version of its commentary, the *Fa-kheu-pi-u* (A.D. 265-313), although in the absence of an English translation of the former, it is difficult for us to compare the text with the commentary and find out how far they agree or differ. It is clear from the Preface to the *Fa-kheu-king* that the Chinese translators were acquainted with three copies of the Dhammapada,—one with 900 verses, another with 700, and another with 500.[2] The arrangement of the thirteen additional chapters with their titles and verse-numbers is shown in the following table :

	Title of Chapter	No. of Verses
1.	Impermanence	21
2.	Insight into Wisdom	29
3.	The Srāvaka	19
4.	Simple Faith	18
5.	Observance of Duty	16
6.	Reflection	12
7.	Loving Kindness	19
8.	Conversation	12
...	...	...
33[3].	Advantageous Service	20
...	...	...
36[4].	Nirvāna	36
37.	Birth and Death	18
38.	Profit of Religion	19
39.	Good Fortune	19

[1] Beal's Dhammapada, p. 35. [2] *Ibid*, p. 33.

[3] Chapters 9-32 of the *Fa-kheu-king* correspond, with regard to arrangement of chapters, to Pāli chapters 1-24.

[4] Chapters 34-35 correspond to Pāli chapters 25-26. See *ante*, pp. x, xi.

We may here point out that instead of one chapter containing reflections on Impermanence or Old Age, the *Fa-kheu-king*, as appears from its commentary, contains two chapters with titles that can be restored in Sanskrit as *anityavarga* and *jarāvarga*. Counterparts of most of the verses contained in these two chapters can be found in the Prakrit *Jaravaga* as well as in the first chapter of the Udānavarga, dealing with Impermanence. The last chapter of the *Fa-kheu-king* is nothing but a Chinese translation of some Indian recension of the Maṅgalasutta. Similarly, chapter 38 appears to be a translation of some Indian Recension of the Mahāmaṅgala-Jātaka. As to the remaining chapters, one cannot but be struck by a few chapters in the Udānavarga, bearing similar titles though not containing the same number and identical verses, *e.g.*, the chapters dealing with Words, ('Speech' in the Udānavarga), Srāvaka ('The Hearer' in the Udānav.). Thus it appears that the *Fa-kheu-king* is no mere translation of an Indian text, but a recension by itself in translation.

(vi) *The Sanskrit recensions* :—

(*a*) *Original of the Chinese version of the Dhammapada incorporated in the Chuh-yau-king.*—Beal says that the *Chuh-yau-king* is a third copy of the Chinese version of the Dhammapada which is so much expanded as to consist of 7 volumes, comprising 20 *kiouen* or books. The translation was made by Chu-fo-nien (or, Fo-nien=Buddhasmṛiti), the Indian who lived during the Yaou-tsin period, about 410 A. D. "In the preface to this version we are told that Dharmatrāta was uncle of Vasumitra, and that he was the original compiler of the stanzas and stories known as Fă-kheu-king. It informs us, moreover, that the old term '*pi-u*', *i.e.* Avadânas, was the same as 'the Dawn,'...... The preface goes on to state that Shaman Saṅghbhadanga of Ki-pin (Cabul) came to Tchangan (Siganfu) about the nineteenth year of the period Kien-Yuen. Having travelled back to India and returned with a copy of the present work, it was evidently translated by Fonien, with the assistance of others...the whole number of chapters in this work is thirty-three, and that the last is, like the Pâli, on 'the Brâhmāna.' There are ample commentaries attached to many of the verses..."[1]

Rockhill is inclined to identify the Dhammapada text in the *Chuh-yau-king* with the Udānavarga. "The Udānavarga," says he, "is found also in the Chinese tripitaka. The title of the work is there 'Chuh-yau-king,' or Nidâna sûtra.[2] It is also divided into thirty-three chapters, the titles of which agree with those of the Tibetan, with the following slight differences:—Chap. IV. is 'Absence of Careless Behaviour'; Chap. V. 'Reflection'; Chap. VI. 'Intelligence'; Chap. XXIX. 'The Twins (Yamaka)'. The contents of the two works, as far as has been ascertained, are identical. Both the Chinese and the Tibetan versions attribute the compilation of Udânavarga to Dharmatrâta."[3]

Dr. Nanjio, on the other hand, notes: "In A. D. 383, there was a *S*râma*n*a of *K*i-pin (Cabul) Saṅghabhûti by name, who came to *Kh*âṅ-ân, the capital of the Former Tshin dynasty, A. D. 380-390 (bringing with him the Ms. of this work?) According to the *K'*-yuen-lu (fasc. 9, fol. 26 a), this work is wanting in Tibetan."[4] Dr. Nanjio also says that the original was a Sanskrit text.

The *Chuh-yau-king*, as its title implies, is an avadāna-sūtra, *i.e.*, a Dhammapada commentary rather than a Dhammapada text.

(*b*) *The Udānavarga, another Sanskrit Dhammapada.*—This is another Dhammapada text in pure classical Sanskrit, of which a fragmentary manuscript in a later variety of the Gupta script has been found at Turfan. Prof. Pischel was the first to edit portions of this manuscript under the title 'Die Turfan-Recensionen des Dhammapada.' That this manuscript is

---

[1] Beal's Dhammapada, pp. 27-29. Nanjio's Catalogue, No. 1321.

[2] According to Nanjio, the Sanskrit equivalent of the Chinese title is 'Avadāna-sūtra'.

[3] Rockhill's Udânavarga, p. x.

[4] Nanjio's Catalogue, see under No. 1321.

of a recension of the Dhammapada of which the Tibetan version has been translated by Rockhill under the name of 'Udânavarga', will be evident from the close agreement between the Sanskrit manuscript and the Tibetan version, in regard to the arrangement of chapters and the number of verses, as shown in the following table taken from Pischel's edition :

Pāli			Sanskrit			Tibetan	
—		=	II	20	=	II	20
XVI	12	=	V	27	=	V	28
—		=	VIII	15	=	VIII	15
XXI	16	=	XVI	24	=	XVI	23
XVII	14	=	XX	22	=	XX	21
I	20	=	XXIX	57 (66[65])	=	XXIX	59
XV	12	=	XXX	51 (52)	=	XXX	53
III	11	=	XXXI	60	=	XXXI	64

The Tibetan translation was made by Vidyāprabhākara probably, as Rockhill suggests, during the reign of King Ral-pa-chan (A.D. 817-842).[1] There is a Tibetan version of its commentary, which was composed by Prajñâvarman, who lived in Kashmere in the 9th century A.D.[2] There is a fourth or last copy of the Chinese version of a Sanskrit Dhammapada, known as the Fâ tsi Yâo-*k*iṅ (Dharmasaṅgraha-mahārtha-gāthā), compiled by Dharmatrāta, and translated by Thien-si-tsâi (A.D. 980-1001) of the later Sun dynasty (A.D. 960-1127.) According to Dr. Nanjio, it is a compilation of the verses of the *Kh*u-yâo-*k*iṅ. Beal has nothing more to say regarding this Chinese version[3] than that the authorship of its original is assigned to Dharmatrāta, and that it shows no resemblance to the earlier translation, *i.e.*, to the Chu-yâo-king. Having regard to the fact that this Chinese version is almost synchronous with the Tibetan version of the Udānavarga, it remains to be seen if there is any closer similarity between their originals.

(vii) *Miscellaneous.*—There are a number of small collections of maxims or apopthegms 'conceived wholly in the spirit

---

[1] *Udānavarga*, Introd., pp. xi-xii.

[2] *Ibid*, p. xii; cf. Tāranātha, p. 204 (Schiefner).

[3] Nanjio's Catalogue, No. 1439.

of the Dhammapada'. Vasubandhu's *Gāthāsaṅgraha* may be regarded as the prototype of the same. There are two Chinese versions of this Gāthāsaṅgraha, besides two Tibetan versions, in one of which the text is reproduced with the commentary. The collection consists of just 24 stanzas, and what these stanzas are like can be ascertained from Rockhill's English translation of them, appended to his 'Udānavarga.' With regard to this Gāthāsaṅgraha, Mr. Nariman says: "It is a collection of maxims with an intelligent commentary, excerpts from which have been cited by A. Schiefner . . . . the commentary shows us the philosopher Vasubandhu also as a humourous evangelist."[1] Vasubandhu, who flourished in the 4th century A.D. is famous in the history of Buddhism not only as a compiler of a standard Sarvāstivāda work, the Abhidharma-koṣa, but also as the writer of a standard manual of Yogācāra philosophy. But we must remember that the compilation of such a Gāthāsaṅgraha was in no way peculiar to Vasubandhu, or now in Sarvāstivāda tradition of Vasubandhu's time. It appears from Takakusu's analysis of the Jñāna-prasthāna-śāstra (which is the most authoritative of the seven Abhidharma books of Sarvāstivāda, and dated 2nd century B.C.) that its closing section was a collection of similar maxims, composed in a Mlecchabhāṣā, say, Tāmil. Similar isolated collections of maxims can equally be traced within the four corners of the Pāli Nikāyas.

4. Chronology of the Dhammapada Texts.—The Pāli Dhammapada is one of the recognised books of the Khuddaka-Nikāya which represents one of the five divisions of the existing Sutta Piṭaka. The oldest known Pāli work in which the Dhammapada is expressly referred to is the Milindapañho. The traditional date of this work is placed 500 years after Buddha's demise[2], *i.e.*, in 43 B.C., while Professor Rhys Davids places the

---

[1] Literary History, p. 268.

[2] Milinda, p. 3.

date a considerable time before Buddhaghosa.[1] The Kathāvatthu which according to tradition belongs to the 3rd century B.C. contains many quotations of verses, some of which can be found only in the Dhammapada, and not in any other canonical texts, but none of the sources of the quotations are mentioned. The same remark holds true of the Nettipakaraṇa and the Peṭakôpadesa, which like the Kathāvatthu abound in quotations from the canonical works with this difference that in the former two works some of the sources are mentioned by name, although the verses there that are peculiar to the Dhammapada are quoted without any mention of their source. The Netti and the Peṭakôpadesa are the two companion works of exegetic type which are ascribed to Mahākaccāyana, the putative author of all the earlier works of the Nirutti and Niddesa class. Prof. E. Hardy is inclined to place the composition of the Netti in the 1st century, A.D.,[2] but we have reason to believe that the date can be pushed back to the 2nd century B.C. The Mahāniddesa which is a canonical commentary on the Aṭṭhakavagga, now found incorporated in the Suttanipāta and forming its Fourth Book has been modelled upon Mahākaccāyana's exposition found in the earlier Nikāyas,[3] and is not wanting in similar quotations of verses which cannot be found anywhere else in the canon than the Dhammapada. But even an earlier work, the Cullaniddesa, which must have been a pre-Asokan book of exegesis, older than the Suttanipāta and later than the canonical Jātaka Book,[4] contains similar quotations of verses not to be found in any other text than the Pāli Dhammapada. Considering that the closing date of the Pāli canon is not later than the 2nd century B.C., the latest date for the Mahāniddesa can not be later than the closing period of the canon. Further, in one of Buddhaghosa's commentaries, *viz.*, the Sumaṅgalavilāsinī, there is reference to two schools of enumeration, the

[1] Questions of King Milinda, S. B. E., Pt. I. p. xxv.

[2] Netti, p. xxvii.

[3] Mahāniddesa, p. 198.

[4] See *passim*.

Dīghabhāṇaka and the Majjhimabhāṇaka, of the books of the Khuddakanikāya, which, though different in some respects, agree in so far as they distinctly mention the Dhammapada among the books of the Lesser Collection.[1] These two schools along with the Saṁyutta Aṅguttara and the Khuddakabhāṇakas point to a time earlier than the inscriptions at Bharhut which cannot be dated ealier than the 3rd century and later than the 2nd century B.C. The tradition that *Appamādavagga* was recited to king Asoka justifies the presumption that the Pāli Dhammapada existed in the 3rd century B.C. So much about the lower limit of the Pāli Dhammapada.

As regards the lower limit of other copies and recensions, we have seen that the Chinese Fa-kheu-king, dated A.D. 223, presupposes three different Dhammapada selections in Sanskrit: one, its Indian original, with 500 verses, another text with 700 verses, and a third with 900 (p. ix). It has already been shown (pp. x-xi) that the Fa-kheu-king original in Sanskrit was a text different from the Pāli as regards language and number of verses, though agreeing with it in its general form, name, number and succession of chapters, Again, the agreement of the Prakrit Dhammapada with the Pāli and the Fa-kheu-king original in respect of the number of verses and succession of chapters is by far closer than that of the Udānavarga (pp. viii-ix). But there are a number of verses in the Prakrit Dhammapada, notably the 'Uraga' verses at the end of the chapter on the Bhikṣu and some in the Sahasa and Jara Vagas, which are to be found neither in the Pāli nor in the original of the Fa-kheu-king, but occur in the Udānavarga in the chapters on Bhikṣu, Number and Impermanency. The Prakrit Dhammapada stands distinct from the rest in one respect, *viz.*, that its first chapter is devoted to Mārga—the Buddhist Eightfold Path, combining into one group two separate chapters of the Pāli as well as of the original of the Fa-kheu-king, *viz.*, the Magga and the Pakiṇṇaka (Miscellaneous). The first eight of

[1] Sum. Vil., I. p. 15.

[2] Mahāvaṁsa, V. 68.

the additional chapters of the Fa-kheu-king have their counterparts in the Udānavarga, as will be clear from the following table :—

Fa-kheu-king			Rockhill's Udānavarga	
Ch.	I Impermanency ...	...	Ch.	I Impermanency
"	II Insight into wisdom	...	"	IV Purity
"	III The Disciple ...	...	"	XI The Śramaṇa
"	IV Simple Faith ...	...	"	X Faith
"	V Moral Duties ...	...	"	VI Morality (śīla)
"	VI Reflection ...	...	"	XV Reflection (Smṛiti)
"	VII Words ...	...	"	VIII Speech
"	VIII Nirvāṇa ...	...	"	XXVI Nirvāṇa

These additional chapters of the Fa-kheu-king force us to look for an earlier Dhammapada text other than the Pāli, its Indian original and the Prakrit, and we are driven in the last resort to trace their immediate background to one of the two Dhammapadas with 700 and 900 verses, known, in 223 A.D., to Wai-chi-lan, the author of the Fa-kheu-king. The text must be one closely resembling the Udānavarga, if not identical with it. It is the text portion of the original of the Chuh-yau-king which alone can satisfy this test. We have reason to believe that the text portion was extant before the time of Wai-chi-lan, *i.e.*, roughly speaking, before the 3rd century A.D. For the Chuh-yau-king which is a Chinese version, dated 383 A.D., presupposes an Indian commentary in Sanskrit that in its turn presupposes an earlier work, *i.e.*, the Sanskrit text comprising 33 chapters similar to those of the Udānavarga. Here we have got to make allowance not only for the interval of time separating the Chinese version from its original, *i.e.*, the Sanskrit commentary, but also for another interval separating the latter from a still earlier work, which is no other than the Sanskrit text. In ascertaining the latter interval one must also consider that before the commentary was written, the text must have enjoyed some amount of popularity and made its importance sufficiently felt in the community. At any rate, the interval of just 160 years (383 A.D.—223 A.D.)

is the shortest possible time which is needed to make the text earlier than Wai-chi-lan's visit to China.

Even if this surmise as to the possibility of Wai-chi-lan's acquaintance with the Sanskrit text portion of the Chuh-yau-king be correct (as we believe it is), one must yet enquire whether the total number of its verses justifies its identification with the text with 900 verses above referred to. Unfortunately, as we are informed by our colleague Mr. R. Kimura, the task of ascertaining the total number of verses in it is far from easy for the simple reason that the verses in the existing Chinese edition are not numbered, nor properly kept distinct from one another. But counting the verses in so far as they are separated by the commentary portion intervening in each chapter, he finds himself in a position to assure us that whatever the exact total, it certainly exceeds 900, though it is by no means over 1000. If so, of the two texts with 700 and 900 verses, known to Wai-chi-lan, the latter must be said to approximate the text portion of the Chuh-yau-king.

Now, arguing from the close resemblanee which exists between the text portion of the Chuh-yau-king and the Udānavarga, so far as is known to us in its entirety through Rockhill's translation from the Tibetan, we can accept the information supplied by Mr. R. Kimura regarding the total in the former as correct. For, although the latter is dated 982-1000 A.D., the total in it does not exceed 989 verses, or, 1000 in round numbers. But it must be noted that the total in Rockhill's Udānavarga cannot be regarded as a precisely correct number, and that for three reasons : (*i*) that there is a slight difference as to the number of verses in almost each chapter common to Pischel's edition of the manuscript fragments of the Udānavarga and Rockhill's translation of the Tibetan version of the same text; (*ii*) that at least in two instances we notice that a verse which would be counted as one in the Pāli Dhammapada, has been counted as two (cf. Rockhill, III. vv. 12-13, XXIII, vv. 82-83); (*iii*) that there are in it a few repetitions of which six have been noticed by Rockhill. Thus its total 989 can be reduced to 981 [989—(2+6)]. How far this process of reduction can preceed in the text itself it is difficult to say. There are no doubt a number of mechanical multiplication of verses which has practically no *raison d'être*, and has a marked tendency to swell up the volume without bringing out any new idea. We have no right to deduct the verses thus multiplied from the Udānavarga, but must on the other hand count them as they occur in it. General reduction is however possible in relation to earlier texts, if any, where certain verses forming a sub-group in a chapter of the Udānavarga are found less in number. The case in hand could be fairly proved, if by the process of reduction, just mentioned, the total 981 could be further reduced to a number approximating 900.

Dr. Nanjio says that the fourth or last Chinese version of the Dhammapada, the Fâ-tsi-suṅ-yâo-kiṅ, dated A.D. 982-1000, is no other than the text portion of the Chuh-yau-king (p. xvi). But from a comparison of a few chapters of the two Chinese versions with the kind help of our friend Mr. R. Kimura, we are constrained to admit some differences between them, though we can only so far readily concede to Dr. Nanjio that they show a general agreement in many respects. Remembering that a similar agreement can also be shown to exist between the text portion of the Chuh-yau-king and Rockhill's Udānavarga, as well as judging by the dates of the Tibetan version and the fourth Chinese version, we may be justified in holding that their originals were the same, making due allowance for slight variation as may exist between two manuscripts of one and the same text. With regard to the date of the Sanskrit Udānavarga, one can definitely say that it was compiled some time before the time of its commentator Prajñāvarman, who lived in the 9th century A.D., while this much is certain as regards the text portion of the Chuh-yau-king that it was extant before the 3rd century of the Christian era. Not knowing any other copy of the Dhammapada than one with 900 verses which Wai-chi-lan could avail himself of in adding a few chapters resembling those in the Udānavarga, we are naturally tempted to identify the same with the text portion of the original of the Chuh-yau-king, and we are confident that we shall not be found far too wrong in doing so.

Turning to the copy of the Dhammapada with 700 verses, known to Wai-chi-lan, we at once see that it was different from the Pāli with 423 verses, the Fa-kheu-king original with 500 verses and the text portion of the Chuh-yau-king just identified with the text with 900 verses. Thus only two texts are left to be examined, *viz.*, the Prakrit and the Dhammapada in Mixed Sanskrit of which a complete chapter has been quoted in the Mahāvastu (p. xii). As regards the Prakrit Dhammapada, it is impossible for us, in the absence of a complete manuscript thereof or of a tradition supplying a definite information about it, to say exactly how many verses it altogether contained. But judging by the proportion of verses in the chapters common to the three recensions, *viz.*, the Pāli, the Fa-kheu-king original and the Prakrit, we feel inclined to think that the total of the Prakrit verses stood midway between 500 and 700. The following table will make our position clear :—

Pāli	Original of Fa-kheu-king	Prakrit
II 12	II 20	II 25
IV 16	IV 17	IV 15
VI 14	VI 17	VI 10
VIII 16	VIII 16	V 17
XI 11	XI 14	VIII 25
XV 12	XV 14	IX 20
XX 17	XX 28	I 30
XV 23	XV 32	XI 40
XVI 41	XVI 40	XII 50
Total ... 162	Total ... 198	Total ... 232

Bearing in mind that the total number of verses in the Pāli Dhammapada is 423 and that in the Fa-kheu-king original 500, we can test whether the above three totals are in keeping with the ratio of 500 : 423.

(1) $\frac{423 \times 198}{162}$ = 517 which roughly gives the total verse-number of the Fa-kheu-king original.

(2) $\frac{423 \times 232}{162}$ = $605\frac{7}{9}$, *i.e.*, 606 which rougly gives the total verse-number of the Prakrit text.

The totals obtained (Pa. 423; F. O. 517; Pr. 606) might be further tested by a standard ratio provided by the verse-numbers of the *Sahasra*-group in the 5 recensions mentioned in the sub-joined table :—

Pāli	Fa-kheu-king original	Prakrit	Dhammapada quoted in the Mahāvastu	Udānavarga
16	16	17	24	34

Taking in succession the total of the Pāli text and that of the Fa-kheu-king original as the standard number, the relative position of the recensions will appear as follows :—

(1) $\frac{423 \times 17}{16}$ = $449\frac{7}{16}$, *i.e.*, 450 (Pr.);
$\frac{423 \times 24}{16}$ = $634\frac{1}{2}$, *i.e.*, 635 (M. V. D.);
$\frac{423 \times 34}{16}$ = $898\frac{7}{8}$, *i.e.*, 899 (U. V.).

(2) $\frac{500 \times 17}{16}$ = $531\frac{1}{4}$, *i.e.*, 532 (Pr.);
$\frac{500 \times 24}{16}$ = 750 (M. V. D.);
$\frac{500 \times 34}{16}$ = $1062\frac{1}{2}$, *i.e.*, 1063 (U. V.).

Comparing these two series of totals and taking all the recensions of the Dhammapada into consideration, we cannot but persuade ourselves to believe that there were no less than six Indian copies of the Dhammapada with 423, 500, 600, 700, 900 and 1000 verses, and that these copies are no other than those represented respectively by the Pāli, the Fa-kheu-king original, the Prakrit, the Mahāvastu Dhammapada, the text portion of the Chuh-yau-king and the Udānavarga. Of these copies, the first five were well-known before the 3rd century A.D., while the date of the Udānavarga falls in between the 4th and the 9th century A.D. Applying the verse-total as a test of priority and posteriority, we feel justified in concluding

that the Pāli with the minimum total 423 is the oldest copy of the Dhammapada and the Udānavarga with the maximum total 1000 (in round numbers) the latest. The copy which stands close to the Pāli is the Sanskrit original of the Fa-kheu-king; the copy which is one degree removed from the latter is the Prakrit, while the Mahāvastu Dhammapada and the Sanskrit original of the text portion of the Chuh-yau-king occupy in order two intermediate positions between the Prakrit text and the Udānavarga. This chronology cannot, however, be taken to be conclusive until it is further tested in the light of other evidences and harmonised with the general history of Buddhist literature and thought. We propose to examine these evidences under the following heads :

(a) argument from the number and succession of chapters.;

(b) argument from the multiplication of particular verses;

(c) argument from traditions.

(a) *Argument from the number and succession of chapters*—The four Indian copies of the Dhammapada of which the tables of contents are definitely known to us fall into two pairs, each showing a complete agreement in regard to the number and succession of chapters : (1) the Pāli and the Fa-kheu-king original containing altogether 26 chapters, and (2) the text portion of the original of the Chuh-yau-king and the Udānavarga containing 33. All these copies' agree in so far as the succession of two closing chapters is concerned. For in each of them the last chapter is the Brāhmaṇavagga and the last but one is the chapter on the Bhikkhu. Further, they must be said to resemble one another, inasmuch as they have many chapters bearing same titles. The two pairs differ, however, widely from each other regarding the order of succession of the remaining chapters, particularly that of the first three. As regards the first pair of texts,

their first three chapters are arranged in the following order :—

1. Yamakavagga forming the 29th chapter in the 2nd pair.
2. Appamādavagga forming the 4th chapter.
3. Cittavagga forming the 31st chapter.

On the other hand, the first three chapters in the second pair of texts are arranged as shown below :—

1. Anityavarga corresponding with the Jarāvagga—the 11th chapter in the 1st pair.
2. Kāmavarga having its counterpart in the Piyavagga—the 16th chapter of the 1st pair.
3. Tṛṣṇāvarga being an amplified version of the Taṇhāvagga of the 1st pair, placed immediately before the Bhikkhu.

It is impossible to make a definite statement regarding the number and succession of chapters in the Prakrit text and in the Mahāvastu Dhammapada, though we are on a somewhat surer ground as regards the former work. As we have already noticed, the Prakrit Dhammapada shows a far closer kinship in its general form with the 1st pair of texts than it does with the 2nd pair, particularly the arrangement of three chapters in it, *viz.*, 2-4, is exactly on a par with that in the Pāli and in the Fa-kheu-king original. Moreover, whatever the precise succession of the Tasavaga, the Bhikhu and the Bramana in it, M. Senart's Fac-simile of the Plate B of the Kharoṣṭhī Ms. goes to prove that they are closely bound up in thought as in the texts of the 1st pair. Arguing from the arrangement of the 1st three chapters, the two pairs of texts can be shown to represent two distinct periods of literary growth within Buddhism, the earlier period being represented by the Pāli Dhammapada and the Fa-kheu-king original. For the sequence of thought in the first three chapters of these two texts is so much in line with that in a Chāndogya passage that one can not but think the former was merely a systematic carrying

out of the latter. In other words, the sequence can be regarded as a proof of these Dhammapada texts standing close to the Chāndogya Upaniṣad and representing an earlier stage of Buddhism. The first chapter of Twin-verses (Yamakavagga) teaches that *mana* in the sense of *cet nā*—volition or intention—is psychologically the motive for action and determines its moral effect according as the intention of the agent is good or bad. It is followed by a chapter on 'Earnestness' (Appamādavagga) which inculcates the necessity of an active exercise of the will or religious aspiration for the attainment of the highest good which is the quintessence of the older Indian conception of faith (*saddhā*). This naturally leads to another chapter, the Cittavagga, where the nature of mind, as commonly known, is described in order to bring out the idea that the necessity of constant striving, mindfulness and self-control implied in 'earnestness' arises from the very constitution of mind. How this trend of thought was anticipated in the Chāndogya passage will be clear from the quotations below :—

I (*a*) "Mano vāva vāco bhūyo...... vācaṁ ca nāma ca mano' nubhavati—sa yadā manasā manasyati mantrān adhīyīyeti, athâdhīte karmāṇi kurvīteti, atha kurute putrāṁśca paśūṁśca iccheyeti, athêcchata imaṁ ca lokaṁ amuṁ ca iccheyeti, athêcchate mano."

(Chāndogya, VII. 3. 1.)

(*b*) "Manopubbaṅgamā dhammā manoseṭṭhā manomayā,
manasā ce paduṭṭhena bhāsati vā karoti vā,
tato naṁ dukkham anveti cakkaṁ va bahato padaṁ.
Manopubbaṅgamā dhammā manoseṭṭhā manomayā
manasā ce pasannena bhāsati vā karoti vā
tato naṁ sukham anveti chāyā va anapāyinī."

(Dhp. I. vv. 1-2.)

II (*a*) "Saṁkalpo vāva manaso bhūyān, yadā vai saṁkalpayate atha manasyati, atha vācam īrayati, tāmu nāmnîrayati, nāmni mantrā ekaṁ bhavanti, mantreṣu karmāṇi...... Sa yaḥ saṁkalpaṁ brahmêti upāste, kliptānvai sa lokān dhruvān dhruvaḥ pratiṣṭhitān."

(Chāndogya, VII. 4. 1-3).

(b) " Appamādo amatapadaṁ, pamādo maccuno padaṁ,
appamattā na mīyanti, ye pamattā yathā matā.
(Dhp., II. v. 1).

III (a) "Cittaṁ vāva saṁkalpād bhūyo, yadā vai cetayate atha saṁkalpayate, atha manasyati, atha vācam īrayati, tāmu nāmnîrayati, nāmni mantrā ekaṁ bhavanti, mantreṣu karmāṇi."
(Chāndogya, VII. 5.1.)

(b) "Na taṁ mātāpātā kayirā aññe vâpi ca ñātākā
Sammāpaṇihitaṁ cittaṁ seyyaso naṁ tato kare."
(Dhp. III. v. 11).

This sequence of thought is entirely lost sight of in the second pair of texts—the text portion of the Chuh-y u-king original and the Udānavarga—the first three chapters of which deal respectively with impermanence, vanity of human wishes and desire. The trend of thought is that when a man reflects upon the fact of impermanence all around, he cannot but realise the vanity of human wishes and discover its root in a natural craving for pleasure and enjoyment. Thus the two pairs of texts present a radical change in tone from the optimism of earlier thought to the ascetic or pessimistic outlook of later reflection. But was this change sudden or it came about gradually ? The Prakrit Dhammapada bears out the fact that the change did not come about surreptitiously. As we have already noticed above, its first chapter is devoted to the praise of the Buddhist Eight-fold Path, while the succession of the following two chapters is the same as that of the Pāli. The trend of thought implied is that Nirvāṇa or the Supreme goal of Buddhism is reachable by the Eight-fold Path which is but a symbol of 'earnestness' which aims at complete control over mind. Viewed in this light, the Mahāvastu Dhammapada seems to fall in line with the Prakrit text, though nothing can be definitely stated regarding the former work. If, however, this surmise is found to be correct, the six copies will fall into three pairs representing three successive periods or stages of literary

growth. A happy result of such a classification will be that it will enable us to form a definite idea about the contents of all the Dhammapada texts by the aid of those which are now accessible to us. If we know the Pāli Dhammapada, we are expected to know almost the whole of the Fa-kheu-king original; a knowledge of the Prakrit text will help us in knowing the contents of the Mahāvastu Dhammapada; lastly, if we have read the Udānavarga, we have really known the whole of the text portion of the Chuh-yau-king original.

In order to justify the chronology of the three pairs we must enquire as to whether or no the Prakrit text serves as a link of transition between the Pāli and the Udānavarga as regards the multiplication of the number of chapters. The following investigation will make it clear that it does serve as a connecting link. It is a curious fact that the additional chapters of the Fa-kheu-king, *i.e.*, the chapters which were added by the Chinese translators to the translation of a text of 26 chapters similar to the Pāli, presuppose a Buddhist anthology like the Pāli Suttanipāta as the subjoined table will set forth :

	Fa-kheu-king		Suttanipāta.
Sec.	I Impermanency	... ...	III 9 Salla Sutta
,,	II Insight into Wisdom	...	II 10 Uṭṭhāna Sutta
,,	III The Disciple	... ...	I 5 Cunda Sutta
,,	IV Simple Faith	... ...	I 10 Āḷavaka Sutta
,,	VII Love ...	... ...	I 8 Metta Sutta
,,	VIII Words ...	... ...	III 3 Subhāsita Sutta
,,	XXXIX Good Fortune	... ...	II 4 Mahāmaṅgala Sutta

In the same way we can account for the additional chapters in the Udānavarga and *a posteriori* for those in the text portion of the Chuh-yau-king original. If we scan their additional chapters, we at once discover that they are modelled upon certain poems of a work similar to the Sutta Nipāta, and that so far as their component verses are concerned, they are nothing bnt a combination of a Sutta Nipāta, a Dhammapada and a Jātaka Book. We subjoin a table in illustration of the point :—

	Udānavarga		Other texts
Chap.	I Impermanency	...	Salla Sutta (S. N. III. 9) + Dasaratha Jātaka + Mugapakkha Jātaka + Jarāvagga (Dhp.)
,,	II Kāma ...	...	Kāmasutta (S. N. IV. 1) + Kāma Jātaka + Piyavagga (Dhp.)
,,	VIII Speech ...	...	Subhāsita Sutta (S. N. III. 3) + Kokāliya Sutta (S. N. III. 10) + Pupphavagga (Dhp.) + Nirayavagga (Dhp.)
,,	XXXII Bhikṣu ...	...	Uraga Sutta (S. N. I. 1) + Bhikkhuvagga (Dhp.)

Similarly the Sutta Nipāta and the Jātaka Book can be pointed out as canonical sources of most of the additional verses in Prakrit, *e.g.*, the additional verses in the Bhikhuvaga are similar to those in the Uraga Sutta (S. N. I.,), while those in the Jaravaga presuppose the Salla Sutta (S. W. III. 9) and such Jātakas as the Dasaratha, the Ayoghara and the Mugapakkha.

The Pāli Dhammapada (and *a pasteriori* the Fa-kheu-king original) differs from the Prakrit text and the Udānavarga, inasmuch as it does not contain a single verse of which the canonical source is no other than the Sutta Nipāta as we now have it. For instance, its Brāhmaṇavagga is mainly constituted of verses from the Vāseṭṭha Sutta which is incorporated not only in the Sutta Nipāta, but also in the Majjhima Nikāya. The Nāgavagga contains a few verses which can be traced in the Khaggavisāṇasutta, but seeing that this particular sutta has been commented upon in the Cullaniddesa along with the poems of the Pārāyaṇa Group, one may be justified in thinking that it existed as a separate poem before its incoporation in the 1st book of the Sutta Nipāta. At any rate, as we proceed from the Pāli Dhammapada towards the Udānavarga, it becomes increasingly clear that the Sutta Nipāta came to occupy a more and more prominent place in the later texts.

(*b*) *Argument from the multiplication of particular verses* :—Besides the common verses, each copy of the Dhammapada contains some that were evidently drawn upon canonical sources, left untouched by the compilers of other copies. Further, each copy contains a number of verses peculiar to itself, and these, in the absence of evidence proving the contrary, must be regarded as compositions of its compiler. In discussing the question of chronology we have to leave out of consideration the verses that were either newly added or composed on a new model, because chronological data can be derived only from those verses which were multiplied, rather mechanically, on a common basis. The process of multiplication just referred to is twofold : (I) the insertion within one original verse or group some new lines constructed out of some set Buddhist expressions, and (2) the substitution of new expressions. Three instances may suffice to illustrate the first process :—

I Pāli—Mā pamādam anuyuñjetha mā kāmaratisanthavaṁ
Appamatto hi jhāyanto pappoti paramaṁ sukhaṁ.

Prakrit—apramadi pramodia ma gami ratisabhamu
apramato hi jhayatu chaya dukhasa pramuni ○
apramadarata bhoda khano yu ma uvacai
khanatita hi soyati niraeṣu samapita ○
apramadarata bhoda sadhami supravedite
drugha udhvaradha atmana pagasana va kuñaru ○
nai kalu pramadasa aprati asavachaye
pramata duhu amoti siha ba muyamatia ○
nai pramadasamayu aprati asavachayi
apramato hi jhayatu pranoti paramu suhu ○

One must note how the counterpart of one Pali verse has been multiplied in Prakrit to five by the insertion of 8 extra lines. But a more apposite instance is afforded by the second set of verses (p. 208)—

II Pāli—Yānimani apatthāni alāpuneva sārade
Kāpotakāni aṭṭhīni tāni disvāna kā rati ?

Prakrit—yanimani avathani alapuniva śarade
saghavarnani śiṣani tani diṣṭani ka rati ○
yanimani prabhaguni vichitani diśodiśa
kavotakani aṭhini tani diṣṭani ka rati ○

Fa-kheu-pi-u—"When the dody dies, and the spirit flees, ...[1] the flesh and bones lie scattered and dispersed. What reliance, then, can one place on the body ?" "When old, like autumn leaves, decayed and without covering, life ebbed out and dissolution at hand, little good repentance then !"

Divyâvadāna—Yānimānyapaviddhāni vikṣiptāni diśo daśa
Kapotavarṇānyasthīni tāni dṛṣṭvêha kā ratiḥ ?
Imāni yānyupasthānāni alâburiva śārade
Saṅkhavarṇāni sīrṣāni tāni dṛṣtvêha kā ratiḥ ?

Gāthāsaṅgraha—"They (the bodies) are thrown away and scattered in every direction, like those pigeon-coloured bones; what pleasure, then, is there in looking at them."

Udānavarga—"Those pigeon-coloured bones are thrown away and scattered in every direction; what pleasure is there in looking at them".

It is clear that in place of one verse in the Pali Dhammapada we have two verses in the Prakrit and in the Divyâvadāna, while only one of the two verses occurs in Vasubandhu's Gāthāsaṅgraha and the Udānavarga. We at once notice that the Prakrit text has driven two lines in between the two lines of a counterpart of the Pāli verse, thus making altogether four lines and two complete verses. The order in the Prakrit is not followed in Divyâvadāna verses, but inverted. We are unable to determine the order of verses in the original of the Fa-kheu-king and in that of its commentary for these two reasons: (i)

---

[1] The portion omitted reads, "as when a royal personage rejects a (broken) chariot, so do", The Chinese translators have apparently confused a counterpart of the second Prakrit verse quoted above and that of the first foot of the Pāli verse (Jarāva 6)! "*Jīranto ve rājarathā sucittā*"

that the Chinese versions, as confessed by the translators themselves, are far from being faithful[1]: (ii) that as appears from Beal's translation of the Fa-kheu-pi-u, some of the verses of the Pāli Jarāvagga are hopelessly confused and the order of some has been violently tampered with.[2] It is quite likely that the order was tampered with even in the original commentary. The number of 'Jarā'-verses in the Fa-kheu-king is said to have been 14, *i.e.*, 3 in excess of the Pāli, while comparing Beal's translation with the Pāli Jarāvagga, we suspect that the right number is not 14, but 12, *i.e.*, just 1 in excess of the Pāli. The total number of verses in the Fa-kheu-king original was, according to the translators' own statement, 500, whereas we have seen on p. xi that by adding up the additional number of verses as distributed in the chapters corresponding to the Pāli we get a total of 502. If the above calculation of the 'Jarā'-verses be correct, we at once get the traditional total of 500 by subtracting 2 from 502. The total number 12 of the verses of the Jarā-group can be accounted for by the fact that the one verse resembling the Pāli was expanded into two distinct verses. If we can rightly suppose that the Divyâvadāna verses were quotations (perhaps a little more sanskritised form of quotations) from an older Avadana work such as the original of the Fa-Kheu-pi-u, the order of the verses must have been inverted in the older work itself, and this conjecture is fully borne out by the grouping in the Chinese translation The fact of inversion itself requires a word of explanation. One must admit that it

---

[1] Beal's Dhammapada, p. 34: "......the words of Buddha are naturally hard of explanation. Moreover, all the literature of the religion is written in the language of India, which widely differs from that of China.........So to translate them faithfully is not an easy task". (Translators' Preface).

[2] The order of first 3 verses is exactly the same as in Pāli. The 4th verse is a combination of the first foot of the Pāli verse No. 6 and the counterpart of a verse like the first in Prakrit. The order of the next 3 verses does not differ from that of the Pāli. The next 2 verses correspond with the 10th and 11th of the Pāli. The verse No. 10 is nothing but a counterpart of the second Prakrit verse. The last 2 verses correspond with the Pāli, Nos. 8 and 9.

presupposes an earlier process of multiplication and improvement on an older verse similar to the Pāli. We have seen that the Prakrit verses amply attest and illustrate the required process. Two distinct verses resulted from an attempt to expand the ideas of the two Pāli lines, taken separately, thereby improving the simile of the pumpkins and the decaying bones in the first line (pp. 209-210). Even then, the direct source of the Prakrit verses would not be fully determined by the model of the Pāli verse. For there are very many dialectical forms which have a tinge of Mixed Sanskrit. At the same time we cannot hold that the Prakrit had drawn upon the Divyâvadāna and the Avadāna original of the Fa-kheu-pi-u, as in these two works the order of the two verses, betraying a process of their growth from one verse by thrusting two lines into it, has been inverted. Failing to obtain the much-needed order in Mixed Sanskrit in these two works, one must in the last resort look for it in the Fa-kheu-king original. The Udānavarga verse seems to represent a stage later than the inversion of the verse-order, that is to say, later than the Fa-kheu-pi-u original and the Divyâvadāna verses. Seeing that the Udānavarga verse occurs in the same form in Vasubandhu's Gāthāsaṅgraha, itself but a selection from a Dhammapada in Classical Sanskrit, we are led to think that the verse similarly occurs in the original of the text portion of the Chuh-yau-king (the Sanskrit Dhammapada with 900 verses).

Thus the entire process of multiplication and reduction suggests the following links of change and points of enquiry: (1) the origin of a Mixed Sanskrit counterpart of the Pāli verse, (2) the manipulation of two distinct verses in Mixed Sanskrit by thrusting two new lines into one original verse, (3) the transliteration of these verses into Prakrit, (4) the inversion of their order in Mixed Sanskrit, (5) the further Sanskritisation of the verses in their inverted order, (6) the inclusion of the Classical Sanskrit form of the first verse in inverted order, (7) the quotation of it in Vasubandhu's Gāthāsaṅgraha, and (8) its final incorporation in the Udānavarga. If this process be applied as a test of chronology, the Pāli Dhammapada will appear to be older than the Fa-kheu-king original in Mixed Sanskrit, the latter than the Prakrit text, the Prakrit text than the Avadāna original of the Fa-kheu-pi-u, the Avadāna original than the Divyâvadāna verses, these verses than the Sanskrit text with 900 verses, this Sanskrit text than Vasubandhu's Gāthāsaṅgraha, and the Gāthāsaṅgraha than the Udānavarga which is the latest copy of the Dhammapada. The chronological position of the Mahāvastu Dhammapada in Mixed Sanskrit, with the text of 700 verses, remains yet to be ascertained. Now we shall examine the third instance.

III Pāli—yo ca vassasataṁ jantu aggiṁ paricare vane
Ekañca bhāvitattānaṁ muhuttam api pūjaye
Sā yeva pūjanā seyyo yañ ce vassasataṁ hutaṁ.

Prakrit—ya ja vaṣaśata jatu agi pariyare vane
chirena sapitelena divaratra atadrito ○
eka ji bhavitatmana muhuta viva puae
sameva puyana ṣebha ya ji vaṣaśata hūta ○

Fa-kheu-pi-u—(Se VI Metta, p. 71). "If a man lives a hundred years, and engages the whole of his time and attention in religious offerings to the gods, sacrificing elephants and horses, and other things, all this is not equal to one act of pure love in saving life."

Mahāvastu Dhammapada—Yo ca varṣaśataṁ jīve agniparicaraṁ caret
Patrâhāro chavāvāsī karonto vividhaṁ tapaṁ
Yo caikaṁ bhāvitatmānaṁ muhūrtamapi pūjayet
Sā eka pūjanā śreyo na ca varṣaśataṁ hutaṁ.

Udānavarga—"If a man live for a hundred years in forest, wholly relying on fire (Agni), and if he but for one single moment pays homage to a man who meditates on the self, this homage is greater than sacrifices for a hundred years."

In this instance we observe that the Pāli is the same as its Sanskrit counterpart in the Udānavarga, while there are two complete verses in Prakrit as well as in the Fa-kheu-pi-u and the Mahāvastu Dhammapada. The two verses seem to have been constructed out of one older verse of three lines by thursting one extra line within its first two lines. The added line differs in each case as regards its expressions. But seeing that the verse occurs in one of its additional chapters, we have reason to think that the model presupposed, in this particular case, by the Prakrit text, is rather the Mahāvastu Dhammapada or the text with 700 verses which was commonly used by the people, according to the Chinese translators' statement, in their time. If so, the Prakrit text must be taken to be later in point of date than and a combination of the Fa-kheu-king original and the Mahāvastu Dhammapada. Now let us examine the second process of multiplication in order to see whether any fresh light could be thrown on the point at issue.

The second process differs from the first by the fact that it has served to multiply the common verses by the substitution of certain set Buddhist expressions as well as by the construction of a new group of verses on the model of an older one. Its historical importance mainly consists in bringing into prominence some moral qualities or virtues implied in an older verse or in a group of verses, thereby setting forth a greater and greater analytical faculty and power of manipulation exercised by the later compilers. In illustration of it, we can first examine the famous 'Supraudhu'-group (p. 105-6). We notice that the Pāli group consists of six verses and the same is the case with the Fa-kheu-king original as can be inferred from Beal's translation of its commentary (Sec. III. "Śrāvaka", pp. 64-55).

The Prakrit group, as it now survives, is an exact counterpart of the Pāli, but 17 verses being absent from the existing Kharoṣṭhī Ms. immediately after the sixth verse, it is difficult to ascertain the number of verses contained in the whole group. Having regard to the fact that the group in the Udānavarga contains no less than 17 verses, *i.e.*, 11 in addition to the six that are common, it is natural to think that multiplication of the number passed through some intermediate stages, and it is clear from the arrangement of the Udānavarga that these stages were no less than four. Probably in the first two stages, the number was multiplied by constructing some additional verses within the original group, and in the third stage some additional verses were constructed by the substitution of one or two synonyms of Nirvāṇa, while in the Udānavarga a few more synonyms came to be substituted.

Turning to the Number-group (Sahasavaga) (p. 154-6.), we detect that it comprises some four sub-groups, typified by the following four catch-words indicated below by their Pāli forms :

(*i*) Sahassam api ce vācā,
(*ii*) Māse māse sahassena,
(*iii*) Yo ca vassasataṁ jīve,
aud (*iv*) Yo ca vassasataṁ jantu.

We have seen (p. xxiv.) that there is a complete agreement as regards the number of verses in the Number-group between the Pāli Dhammapada and the Fa-kheu-king original, that the Prakrit chapter contains 17 verses, the Mahāvastu Dhammapada 24 and the Udānavarga chapter 34. In the absence of a faithful translation of the Fa-kheu-king original,it is impossible to state as to what verses were really contained in its Number-group. Beal's translation of the Fa-kheu-pi-u shows that the chapter in the Chinese version contains a few verses of the second sub-group, specified above, of which the counterparts are met with in all the copies except the Pāli. The comparison of the Prakrit verses with those in the Mahāvastu Dhammapada reveals a very close agreement between them. Considering that some of the verses of this sub-group occur in one of the additional chapters of the Fa-kheu-pi-u, we cannot but suppose that they were derived from a text other than its original. The Pāli text supplies a counterpart of the first line of each of these verses and that of the second line of one verse in Prakrit:

(*i*) Māse māse sahassena yo yajetha sataṁ samaṁ,
(Sahassav., v. 7, 1st line).

(*ii*) Māse māse kusaggena bālo bhuñjetha bhojanaṁ,
Na so saṅkhatadhammānaṁ kalam agghati soḷasiṁ.
(Bālav., v. 11, note 2nd line).

Judging by the arrangement of the Prakrit verses (6-16), we at once perceive that the multiplication passed through no less than two intermediate stages, in the first of which the number multiplied by the first process and in the second by the second.

The chapter on the Bhikkhu contains a sub-group which will seem highly important in determining the relative position of the Dhammapada texts. We quote it below with a view to facilitating comparison :—

Pāli—Mettāvihārī yo bhikkhu pasanno buddhāsasane
Adhigacche padaṁ sāntaṁ saṅkhārūpasamaṁ sukhaṁ
Pāmojjabahulo bhikkhu pasanno buddhasāsane
Adhigacche padaṁ sāntaṁ saṅkhārūpasamaṁ sukhaṁ.

Prakrit—Metravihari yo bhikhu prasanu budhaśasane
tunati pavaka dharma drumapatra ba marutu ○
Metravihari yo bhikhu prasanu budhaśasani
paḍivijhu pada śata sagharavośamu suha ○
Udagacitu yo bhikhu abhivuyu priapria
adhikachi padaśata akavuruṣasevita ○
Pramojabahula yo bhikhu abhivuyu priapria
adhikachi padaśata aseyane ya moyaka ○

Mahāvastu—Maitravihārī yo bhikṣu prasanno buddhaśāsane
Dhammapada Adhigacchati padaṁ śāntaṁ asecanaṁ ca mocanaṁ.
Karuṇāvihārī yo bhikṣu prasanno buddhaśāsane
Adhigacchati padaṁ śāntaṁ apṛthagjanasevitaṁ.
Muditāvihārī yo bhikṣu prasanno buddhaśāsane
Adhigacchati padaṁ śāntaṁ akāpuruṣasevitaṁ.

Upekṣāvihārī yo bhikṣu prasanno buddhaśāsane
Adhigacchati padaṁ śāntaṁ nirvāṇaṁ padam acyutaṁ.

Udagracitto sumano abhibhuyya priyâpriyaṁ
Tato pramodyabahulo bhikṣu nirvāṇasantike.

Udānavarga—Maitravihārī yo bhikṣuḥ prasanno bnddhaśāsane
Adhigacchet padaṁ śāntam saṁskārôpaśamaṁ śivaṁ.
Maitravihārī yo bhikṣuḥ prasanno buddhaśāsane
Adhigacchet padaṁ śāntam asecanaka mocanaṁ.

* * * * * * *

Pramodyabahulo bhikṣuḥ duḥkhakṣayam avāpnuyāt.

Rockhill's translation.—"The Bhixu who is kind, who has perfect faith in the teaching of the Buddha, will find the perfection of peace (amatam padam), of which one can never be weary."

"The Bhixu who is kind, who has perfect faith in the teaching of the Buddha, will find the perfection of peace, the peace from the Saṁskāra (body)."

"The Bhixu who is kind, who has perfect faith in the teaching of the Buddha, will arrive by degrees at the complete destruction of all attachment."

"The Bhixu who is kind, who has perfect faith in the teaching of the Buddha, will pull himself out of the evil way, as the elephant does himself out of the mire,"

"The Bhixu who is kind, who has perfect faith in the teaching of the Buddha, will shake off all wickedness, as does the wind the leaves of a tree."

"The Bhixu who is kind, who has perfect faith in the teaching of the Buddha, is so near nirvāṇa that he cannot possibly fall away from it."

"The Bhixu who has subdued what charms the heart, what is agreeable to the mind, what delights and what does not delight (*i.e.*, passions), is full of delight, and will find the end of suffering."

In this particular instance, we have four Prakrit verses in place of two in the Pāli, while the Mahāvastu Dhammapada and the Udānavarga verses are not exact counterparts of any previous group. They are on the contrary a combination of verses found in all the previous groups, supplemented by a few which were newly constructed by the compiler of the Sanskrit text. Though the counterparts of any of the groups is not to be found in the Fa-kheu-king and its commentary, it is very likely that some sort of transformation also took place in their originals. Nevertheless, the Prakrit verses cannot be satisfactorily accounted for otherwise than by the hypothesis that they are a combination of elements from two older texts, *viz.*, the Fa-kheu-king original and the Mahāvastu Dhammapada.

Thus applying the twofold process of multiplication of common verses as a test of chronology, we are led to think that the Prakrit text occupies a central position, it being later than the Pāli, the Fa-kheu-king original and the Mahāvastu Dhammapada, and earlier than the text portion of the Chuh-yau-king and the Udānavarga. The Prakrit text with some 600 verses was a combination of two older texts with 500 and 700 verses, just as the Fa-kheu-king, considered as a Chinese recension in translation, was a combination, with its 752 verses, of three older texts with 500, 700 and 900 verses.

(c) *Argument from traditions*—The reader has already been referred (on p. xix) to a tradition in the Chronicles of Ceylon proving that the Dhammapada was a well-known Pāli work in the time of King Asoka[1]. The internal evidence of the work does not help us much in determining its date of compilation. The Nāgavagga contains an interesting verse[2] moralising upon the behaviour of a state elephant, named Dhanapālaka, when the animal was first caught and put under training. It appears from the commentary that the elephant

---

[1] M. Sylvain Lévi says, "The tradition that the Appamādavagga of the Pāli was constructed in the time of Aśoka cannot but be a fiction, and the extraordinary variety of the verses in different recensions of the chapter proves it clearly" (J. A., xx. 1912, p. 226).

[2] Nāgav. v. 5 Dhanapālako nāma kuñjaro kaṭukappabhedano dunnivārayo,
Baddho kabalaṁ na bhuñjati sumarati nāgavanassa kuñjarī.

was in possession of the King of Kāsī.[1] Subsequently the elephant came into the possession of King Bimbisāra, probably as part of the wedding gift from Mahāpasenādi, the King of Kāsī-Kosala. The elephant is no other than one called Nālāgiri[2] in the Pāli Nidānakathā, set upon the Buddha by Prince Ajātasattu at the instigation of Devadatta. The earliest trace of the legend about the taming of this elephant by the Buddha can be found in a bas-relief at Bharhut, bearing the inscription "Dhanapāla hatthināgadamana". The legend must have come into existence sometime before the construction of the railing of the Bharhut Stūpa, *i.e.*, before the 2nd or 3rd century B.C. But the Pāli Dhammapada has nothing to do with this particular legend which seems to have resulted from an after-thought on the part of the Buddhist theologians. The chapter on the Buddha goes, however, to prove that at the time of the compilation of the Pāli Dhammapada the Buddha was sufficiently deified and that the legends about the machinations of Māra and his daughters were yet in the making. As shown elsewhere,[3] the process of deification of the Buddha through the Birth-stories was synchronous with the history of schisms within the Buddhist Order. Seeing that the date of composition of the Jātakas in their oldest form cannot be earlier than the first century of Buddha's demise, one must admit that the date of the Pāli Dhammapada falls within the 4th and the 3rd century B.C.

Tradition attributes to one Dharmatrāta the compilation of each one of the three copies of the Dhammapada, *viz.*, the original of the Fa-kheu-king or the text with 500 verses, the original of the text portion of the Chuh-yau-king or the text with 900 verses, and the Udānavarga or the latest Sanskrit copy with 1000 verses. In the Chinese preface to the Chuh-yau-king

---

[1] "Tattha Dhanapālako nāmâti tadā Kāsirañño hatthâcariyaṁ pesetvā ramanīya nāgavane gāhāpitassa hatthino etaṁ nāmaṁ."

[2] In the Tibetan translation, the elephant is called, "Ratnapāla" or "Vasupāla," which is the same as Dhanapāla. *See* Rockhill's Life of the Buddha, p. 9.

[3] Our Monograph on Asoka's Dhamma.

Dharmatrāta is said to have been the uncle (rather maternal uncle, as M. Sylvain Lévi points out,) of Vasumitra.[1] According to Tāranātha, there were two Dharmatrātas, a Sthavira and a Bhadanta.[2] The Sthavira was a contemporary of the Brāhman Rāhula and one of the four teachers of the Vaibhāṣikas, the remaining three teachers being Ghoṣaka (Aśvaghoṣa), Vasumitra and Buddhadeva (?).[3] Candrakīrti, too, mentions two Dharmatrātas, *viz.*, a Sthavira and a Bhadanta.[4] But Tāranātha emphatically says that one must not confound the Ārya or Sthavira Dharmatrāta with the Bhadanta, for the latter was really the compiler of the Udānavarga.[5] Beal, however, points out that the compiler of the Dhammapada is all along spoken of in the Chinese versions as Ārya Dharmatrāta.[6]

It will be going far away from the historical truth to suppose that one and the same individual compiled all the three copies of the Dhammapada, the first of which differed so widely from the rest in some important respects. The attribution of the texts with 900 and 1000 verses to one individual might be justified on the ground that they are substantially the same.

But even the Udānavarga as a distinct copy must have been the work of an individual other than the compiler of the Sanskrit text with 900 verses. The two epithets, Sthavira and Bhadanta, applied to the name of Dharmatrāta, must, therefore, be taken to imply a real historical distinction in the individual and in time. But the question is whether these epithets refer to two individuals or to three. If Tāranātha's testimony is at all to be trusted, Bhadanta Dharmatrāta must be regarded as the compiler of the Udānavarga. Beal is inclined to think that Ārya Dharmatrāta, a contemporary of Vasumitra, was the compiler of the original of the Fa-kheu-king, recognised as a canonical

---

[1] Beal's 'Dhammapada', p. 9.
[2] Rockhill's 'Udānavarga', p. xi.
[3] Beal's 'Dhammapada, p. 9, f. n. 1.
[4] Burnouf's Introd. a' l' Hist., p. 566.
[5] Rockhill's 'Udānavarga', p. xi.
[6] Beal's 'Dhammapada', p. 9.

work of the Vaibhāṣikas at the Council held under the presidency of Vasumitra during the reign of Kaniṣka.[1] He says, "It would not be surprising if we found that the edition of Dhammapada prepared by Dharmatrāta, belonged to the Vaibhāshika school, whilst that known in Ceylon was compiled by the Sautrāntikas."

Beal is the first to suggest that the terms Sautrāntika and Vaibhāṣika represent two distinct stages of a Buddhist canon, but his mistake lies in identifying the Sautrāntika with the Sthaviravāda. The name Sautrāntika in its generic sense was derived evidently from that of the Suttavāda school or sect which was the sixth in descent from the Theravāda through a schismatic line: Theravāda > Mahiṁsāsaka > Sabbatthivāda > Dhammaguttika > Kassapiya > Saṁkantika > Sutta-vāda.[2] Even if the term Suttavāda or Sautrāntika be taken as a generic name for the Mahīśāsaka or the Sarvâstivāda canon in its final redaction or stage of development, it must always be kept carefully distinct from the Sthaviravāda on account of its schismatic associations. The contents and arrangement of a Sautrāntika work might eventually be found almost identical with those of a Sthaviravāda, and yet, if we are to respect at all the tradition in the Dīpavaṁsa,[3] there must remain a sharp distinction between the two works with regard to their languages. If in the case of a book of the Sthaviravāda canon we find that its language is what we now know as Pāli, then we must expect that the language of a corresponding Sautrāntika work will be something other than Pāli, say, Mixed Sanskrit. Granted this, we have got to answer which copy of the Dhammapada is technically a Sautrāntika work and which a Vaibhāṣika.

Beal seems to think that the Fa-kheu-king original with 500 verses was received into the Vaibhāṣika canon during the reign of Kaniṣka and that it was compiled by Ārya Dharmatrāta, the

---

[1] Beal's 'Dhammapada', p. 9.

[2] Mahāvaṁsa, Chap, V. vv. 6—9. Suttavāda = Vasumitra's Sautrāntika.

[3] Dīpavaṁsa, Chap. V. v. 32 f., quoted in the Kathāvatthu-Comy., p. 6 f.

author of the Saṁyuktâbhidharma Śāstra. His opinion is mainly based upon Hiuen Thsang's account of the Buddhist Council in Kaniṣka's time which is no less open to dispute. In the Chinese traveller's list of the Buddhist celebrities of Gandhāra[1] Dharmatrāta, the author of the Saṁyuktâbhidharma Śāstra, is associated with Pārśva, Manoratha, Asaṅga, Vasubandhu and Nārāyaṇadeva, most of whom flourished in the 4th and 5th centuries A.D., while in another list of Vaibhāṣika teachers, quoted by Beal (*supra*), Dharmatrāta enjoys the company of Aśvaghoṣa and Vasumitra. If the tradition in the Chuh-yau-king deserves any credence, Dharmatrāta, the compiler of the Fa-kheu-king, was the maternal uncle of Vasumitra. According to Hiuen Thsang, Vasumitra, a native of Mid-India and a contemporary of Pārśva presided over the delaberations of the Vaibhāṣika Council which was convened in Kashmir under the auspices of king Kaniṣka[2] and he was the compiler of the Abhidharmaprakaraṇapāda Śāstra.[3] How can we believe that one and the same Vasumitra was the compiler of the Abhidharma treatise and the president of the Vaibhāṣika Council in Kaniṣka's time? The three standard commentaries in Classical Sanskrit, compiled at the above council, presuppose an older redaction of the Sarvâstivāda canon consisting of three Piṭakas, *viz.*, the Upadeśa or Sūtra, the Vinaya and the Abhidharma. Of the seven Prakaraṇas or treatises composing the Abhidharma Piṭaka, one[4] is said to have been compiled 100 years and four[5] 300 years after Buddha's demise. It is the four treatises attributed to Kātyāyana and Vasumitra that are placed by tradition in the Chinese three centuries after the demise of the Buddha. Prof. Takakusu finds reasons to think that Kātyāyana's

---

[1] Beal's 'Records of the Western World,' I. p. 98 f.

[2] *Ibid*, I. p. 151 f.

[3] *Ibid*, I. p. 109.

[4] Abhidharma Vijñānakāyapāda Śāstra by Devaśarman.

[5] Abhidharma Jñānaprasthāna Śāstra and Prajñapatipāda Śāstra by Kātyāyana (Beal's Records. I. p. 195) and Vasumitra's Abhidharma Prakaraṇapāda Śāstra and Dhātukāyapāda Śāstra.

Jñānaprasthāna Śāstra, which is the most important of seven Abhidharma treatises was composed in the 2nd century B.C. (*i.e.*, four centuries after Buddha's demise) and that its language was a local Sanskrit dialect of Kashmir[1]. We cannot but admit that there is a discrepancy of at least one century in the Chinese tradition which can as well be detected by the aid of Vasumitra's own work, the treatise on 'The Points of Controversy among the Buddhist Schools.' This important treatise, now translated in three European languages from the Tibetan[2] and the Chinese,[3] goes to show that Vasumitra flourished at least four centuries after Buddha's demise. He was acquainted with the views of some of the schismatic schools and sects that sprang up during the 4th century B.E. These are the schools and sects which, according to the Chronicles of Ceylon, arose in post-Asokan times. The names of these schools, as also those of the Andhaka, the Āvantika, the Uttarāpathaka and the Vājiriya,[4] are significant as pointing to a time when not only Buddhism was propagated outside the geographical limits of the Middle Country or 'Mid-India,' but so many influential local schools of thought were formed throughout India. King Asoka is justly credited with having sent Buddhist missions for the first time in history to various regions outside the Middle Country,[5] and there must have elapsed some time before it was possible for so many local schools to come into being. From this it will appear quite reasonable to think that the closing date of the Abhidharma Piṭaka of the Sarvâstivāda or Sautrāntika canon was about a century after Asoka, *i.e.*, the reigns of Puṣyamitra and Menander which might also be premised as a closing date of the entire Sarvâstivāda

---

1 J. P. T. S. 1905, p. 67 ff.

2 Wassilief's 'Buddhismus' of which there is a French translation.

3 English translation by Mr. J. Masuda in the Journal of the Department of Letters (C.U.), Vol. I.

4 Mahāvaṁsa, V. vv. 12-13; Dīpavaṁsa, V. v. 54; Kathāvatthu Comy, p. 6 f. and Index; Mahāvyutpatti, 275.

5 Dīpavaṁsa, VIII; Mahāvaṁsa, XII.

canon on the ground that in the Chinese version of one of the books of the Sūtra Piṭaka, *viz.*, the Ekottarâgama or Aṅguttara Nikāya, there is mention of king Puṣyamitra. Rightly or wrongly, Puṣyamitra figures in the Savâstivāda literature, notably in the Divyâvadāna,[1] as a persecutor of the followers of Buddhism. The date of Puṣyamitra's accession to the throne of Magadha is, according to Vincent Smith, 184 B.C. The Chinese version of the Sarvâstivāda canon contains the translation of only four Āgamas which are in many respects the same as the first four Nikāyas of the Pāli Sutta Piṭaka. The Divyâvadāna, too, does not refer to more than four Āgamas.[2] Prof. Sylavan Lévi has, on the contrary, shown that there was a Kṣudraka Nikāya or Lesser Collection consisting of some books similar to the Pāli.[3] That there were five Nikāyas and persons who got them by heart in the time of Puṣyamitra is conclusively proved by the votive inscriptions at Bharhut and Sanchi containing such personal epithets as Pañcanekayika, and Peṭaki.[4] As regards the proof of a close resemblance between the Sarvâstivāda works of the Kṣudraka Nikāya and the Pāli; one can profitably compare the Fa-kheu-king original with the Pāli Dhammapada and see how much agreement there is between them. All this may suffice to show that the Fa-kheu-king original with 500 verses and written in Mixed Sanskrit belonged to an older redaction of the Sarvâstivāda canon, prepared probably during the reigns of Puṣyamitra and Menander. This is not to deny that a new redaction of the Sarvâstivāda canon was made during the reign of Kaniṣka along with the compilation of three Vibhāṣā Śāstras or extensive commentaries which subsequently gave rise to the name Vaibhāṣika replacing the older name Sautrāntika. The new redaction was no more than a later Sanskrit recast of the Sautrāntika

[1] Divyâvadāna, p. 1434.

[2] *Ibid*, p. 333.

[3] T'oung Pao, p. 116 f.; Winternitz's 'History of Indian Literature' in German, Pt. II. p. 187.

[4] Buddhist India, pp. 167-8.

canon in Mixed Sanskrit. But the difference between the two redactions was not merely that of language. The two redactions differed in manner as well as matter, so much so that the names of the texts of the Vaibhāṣika canon had to be changed in order to keep them distinct from their Sautrāntika originals. This fact is countenanced by the evidence of the original of the text portion of the Chuh-yau-king which was but a Sanskrit copy of the Dhammapada with 900 verses and 33 chapters, compiled on the basis of the Fa-kheu-king original with 500 verses and 26 chapters and as M. Sylvain Lévi seems to think, its title was Udānavarga.[1] We cannot persuade ourselves to believe that Ārya Dharmatrāta who wrote the Saṁyuktâbhidharma Śāstra was really the compiler of the original of the Fa-kheu-king for the simple reason that he was a native of Gandhāra, while the latter, described as maternal uncle of Vasmutra, was probably a native of the Middle Country. We are also tempted to think that the Sanskrit text with 900 verses was amplified, though slightly, in the Udānavarga by an individual—Bhadanta Dharmatrāta or whatever the name may be, who flourished about the time of Asaṅga and Vasubandhu, *i.e.*, during the 4th or 5th century A.D. Thus we incline to regard the Buddhist Council in Kaniṣka's time as a landmark in the history of Sarvâstivāda Buddhism indicating a twofold transition: (1) that of the Sarvâstivāda literature from a Sautrāntika or Canonical stage to a Vaibhāṣika or Scholastic, and (2) that of the Sarvâstivāda canon from a Mixed Sanskrit redaction to one in Classical Sanskrit.

Beal is doubly wrong in regarding the Pāli Dhammapada as technically a Sautrāntika work and the original of the Fa-kheu-king as a Vaibhāṣika text, compiled during the reign of Kaniṣka. Our contention is that the latter work was technically a Sautrāntika text in Mixed Sanskrit, substantially the same as the Pāli. If its author Ārya Dharmatrāta was uncle to Vasumitra, its compilation must be referred to a

[1] L'Appramādavarga, p. 11 f. (J.A., xx, 1912, p. 209 f).

date some four centuries after Buddha's demise, and this date is no other than the closing period of the Sautrāntika canon which is not earlier than the 2nd century B.C. The Fa-kheu-king was subsequently recast in Classical Sanskrit by the Vaibhāṣikas during the reign of Kaniṣka and the text prepared was a Dhammapada with 900 verses, *i.e.*, the text portion of the Chuh-yau-king original. The Udānavarga was but a second edition of the Vaibhāṣika text—the Udānavarga of Kaniṣka's time, and its date does not seem to be later than the 5th century A. D. One must anxiously await the discovery of the stone receptacle containing the copper plates on which the Vaibhāṣika canon and commentaries were engraved by the order of King Kaniṣka. Hiuen Thsang tells us that King Kaniṣka had built a stūpa over this stone receptacle.[1] After the examination of the traditions we feel convinced that the 2nd century B.C. was the closing date of the Sautrāntika canon. We have reasons even to believe that about this time the canon of each of the earlier schools was closed. It has been shown in our monograph on Asoka's Dhamma that a number of books were added to the Pāli canon in post-Asokan times, *e.g.*, the Kathāvatthu, the Petavatthu, the Buddhavaṁsa, the Cariyā Piṭaka, the Apadāna and the Khuddakapāṭha. Vasumitra speaks of a second Mahādeva Council, convened, no doubt, during a post-Asokan period, on the lines of the Mahāsaṅghika.[2] Two Mahādevas are important personages in the history of Buddhism, one who is said to have been sent as a missionary to Mahisa-maṇḍala (Mysore) during the reign of King Asoka[3] and another who was invited to Ceylon from the Pallava country in the time of King Duṭṭhagāmanī.[4] There are two inscrip tions on the railing of the Bharhut Stūpa recording the feats of miracle performed by a Mahādeva. It cannot, therefore, be doubted that there lived a great Buddhist leader, named

---

[1] Beal's 'Records of the Western World, I. p. 156.

[2] Journal of the Department of Letters, Vol. I., p. 6. *Cf.* J. R. A. S., 1910, p. 413ff.

[3] Mahāvaṁsa, xii. v. 3.

[4] *Ibid*, xxix. v. 38.

Mahādeva, in about the 2nd century B.C., and if Vasumitra's account of the Mahādeva Council be true, we can equally believe that a redaction of the Mahāsaṅghika or Lokottaravāda Canon was prepared in Mixed Sanskrit and formally recognised at this council. If so, the compilation of the Mahāvastu Dhammapada can be referred to the date of this council.

As regards the Prakrit Dhammapada, one must look for its place of origin either in Khotan where its manuscript in the Kharoṣṭhī alphabet of the 2nd century A.D. was discovered among the ruins of Gośṛṅga or Gośīrṣa Vihāra or in a North-Western region of India, round about Peshawar, where an Indo-Iranian dialect was current[1]. So far as the tradition goes, the Buddhist missionaries cannot be supposed to have penetrated into these regions before the time of king Asoka. The Prakrit verses go to prove that they could not be read or intoned without waiving one's head, that, in other words, the manner of reading was akin to the Tibetan. If we can rightly suppose with Prof. Sten Konow that the place of find of its manuscript was the place of its origin, we must admit that its compilation in the local dialect of Khotan[2] was not possible much before the time of Kaniṣka. Rockhill has prepared an interesting account of Khotan on the basis of Hiuen Thsang's travels and the local annals, preserved in Tibetan translation.[3] It goes to show that not long after the reign of Dharmāśoka Khotan became the settlement of a population, half Chinese and half Indian, whose habits resembled those of China and whose dialect was neither Indian nor Chinese, but a mixture of the two. Buddhism was first introduced from Kashmir into Khotan

---

[1] According to M. Jules Bloch the language of the Kharoṣṭhī Ms. was a dialect of the Western part of the Punjab or that of the North-Western Hills. His views are accepted by Lévi (J. A. xx. 1912, p. 214).

[2] Festschrift Ernst Windisch, 1914, p. 94 ff.

[3] Life of the Buddha, Chap. VIII.

in the 5th year of the reign of king Vijayasambhava who ascended the throne 165 years after the establishment of the kingdom in 234 B.E.[1] It is during the reign of the eighth successor of this king that the doctrines of the Mahāsaṅghika school were brought into the country by the eldest son of the king who entered the Buddhist order under the name of Dharmānanda and went to India.[2] The doctrine of the Sarvâstivāda school of the Lesser Vehicle was introduced into the country by the venerable Mantrasiddhi[3] who was called from India during the following reign. Thus Khotan became a meeting ground of the doctrines of two Buddhist schools shortly before the invasion of India by Vijayakīrti, the 11th successor of Vijayasambhava and Kaniṣka, the king of Gu-zan. These traditions are important as showing how it became possible to compile a Dhammapada in Khotan as a synthesis of two older texts in Mixed Sanskrit, one belonging to the Mahāsaṅghika school and another to the sarvâstivāda or Sautrāntika. The probable date of its compilation must be referred to a time about five centuries after Buddha's demise, say, the 1st century B.C. or A.D. The result obtained is supported by the fact that the Prakrit Dhammapada differs from the Pāli and the original of the Fa-kheu-king by the inclusion of many verses from the Suttanipāta, the Mahābhārata and the Jātaka Book. Curiously enough, most of the verses from the latter source are to be found in the Jātakas illustrated by bas-reliefs at Bharhut. Here we

---

[1] Life of the Buddha, p. 237.

[2] *Ibid*, p. 239. Dr. F. W. Thomas says that Dharmānanda was the second son, *see* his notes on Rockhill's summary of the Annals of Khotan in Stein's Ancient Khotan, Vol. I, App. E, p, 581. cf. Sten Konow's views in the Festschrift Ernst Windisch, p. 95 ff.

[3] According to Thomas, his name was Samantasiddhi. He seems to have brought about a reconciliation between the adherents of the Mahāsaṅghika and Sarvaâstivāda doctrines.

must briefly state the results obtained from the foregoing investigation :

Text.	Probable date of compilation.
(1) Pāli Dhammapada ... ... (a Sthaviravāda work).	Between the 4th and 3rd century B.C.
(2) Fa-kheu-king original in Mixed Sanskrit. (a Sautrāntika work).	2nd century, B.C.
(3) Mahāvastu Dhammapada ... (a Mahāsaṅghika work).	2nd or 1st century, B.C.
(4) Prakrit Dhammapada ... (another Mahāsaṅghika work).	1st century B.C. or A.D.
(5) Text portion of the Chuh-yau-king original or the older edition of the Udānavarga (a Vaibhāṣika work).	1st or 2nd century, A.D.
(6) Fa-kheu-king (a Chinese recension).	*Circa* 223 A.D.
(7) Udānavarga or ... ... the later edition of No. 5.	4th or 5th century, AD.

Concluding Remarks.—The total result stated above can be further tested by a general history of the Tripiṭaka dealing particularly with the genesis and importance of the Dhammapada texts. This important subject has been separately dealt with in a supplementary section of this work. There it has been shown that M. Senart's inference as to the existence of a Dhammapada text older than the Pāli from a particular verse in Prakrit which, in his opinion, contains expressions better or more appropriate than those in the corresponding Pāli verse, is historically incorrect. The legitimate inference in such cases would be rather to say that that particular verse in Mixed Sanskrit or in some such language is older than its counterpart included in the Pāli Dhammapada. We need not be surprised to find that the Dhammapada or the Udānavarga is associated with the Jātakas and Avadānas or that the works of the Jātaka or Avādana class came to be included in the Vinaya Piṭaka of a certain Buddhist school, such as the Mahāsaṅghika or the Sarvâstivāda, since from the very beginning, as the Mahāpadāna Suttanta of the Dīgha Nikāya goes to prove, these three classes of work were closely connected with one another. As a matter of fact, in this important discourse, called an Avadāna but classed as a Jātaka in the Cullaniddesa, two typical Dhammapada verses are intended to serve as model for the Pātimokkha par excellence (pātimokkha-uddesa). In going through this discourse one cannot but be struck by the fact that the Dhammapada as a type of literary composition, alike the Jātaka and Avadāna, grew up in the Buddhist literature by way of a protest against the orthodox code of morality—the Pātimokkha.

Among other important points, we have sought to show that the existing Pāli Tripiṭaka incorporates counterparts of several doctrines and treatises which had originated with other Buddhist schools and sects. It is not so much important in a discussion of the relative position of Pāli, Mixed Sanskrit, Prakrit and Sanskrit within the Ancient Buddhist literature of India to ascertain the dialect or dialects which the Buddha or his disciples generally used as the medium of instruction as to determine the language in which the original materials of the Buddhist canon were prepared during the life-time of the Buddha. We have specified throughout Part II of this work that Dhammapada verses lead us ultimately back to a number of prose discourses in the Dīgha or in the Majjhima Nikāya, constituted of some stock passages or highly crystallised exegetical fragments, which, as their names, *Vibhaṅga*, *Niddesa* and *Khandha* imply, appear as so many solid pieces of brick or blocks of stone with which the first fabric of the canon was constructed. Those who have ever cared to be acquainted with the language and phraseology of these fragments will always shrug their shoulders at the slightest suggestion that Pāli was derived from a *Pallībhāṣā* or popular dialect locally current in Magadha or in the Middle Country. The progress of researches into linguistic developments within Buddhist literature has been much hampered in this country by a thoughtless and most absurd speculation about what we now call and know as Pāli language on the basis of the identity of the name Pāli with the word *Pallī* meaning a village. This school of philologists, quite innocent of the literary history of India, always appear to err on the wrong side. The word Pāli has never been used in the Ceylonese Chronicles and Buddhaghosa's commentaries in a sense other than the canon as distinguished from the commentaries. The significance of the name Pāli or Pāḷi as denoting the text is that the canon consists of the discourses of the Buddha and those of his disciples, characterised by a connected sequence of thought, (*pariyāyena bhāsitaṁ, dhammapariyāyaṁ*) having a good beginning, a good middle and a good end. The primary meaning of *Pallī*, *Paṅkti*, *Pāñti* or *Pāṭi* is no doubt the same. Taken in this sense, *Pallī* denotes a group of houses arranged according to a plan. The Bengali word '*Paṅkti*' denotes a well-arranged row of seats and '*Pāñti*' denotes a well-reasoned opinion in a matter of dispute by a body of experts well-versed in the *Śāstras*. Thus if there is any Bengali word which can be philologically connected with Pāli or Pāḷi, it is *pāñti* in the sense of a well reasoned view, expressed in words.

There is no reason to dispute the tradition, recorded in the Dīpavaṁsa, that the literary language of the Buddhist Order until the breaking out of the first schism about a century after Buddha's demise and the formation of the Mahāsaṁghika School was the same or uniform and that the history of the schisms is bound up with a violent tampering with the language and arrangement of the texts. The schismatic developments in language and literature followed two lines deviating from the Sthaviravāda and three recensions of the canon were closed, in about the 2nd Century B.C.—the Sthaviravāda canon in a language which is now commonly known as Pāli and the Sautrāntika and Mahāsaṁghika recensions in two types of Mixed

Sanskrit. The Sthaviravāda line has continued in Ceylon, Burma and Siam until to-day, while the Sautrāntika and Mahāsaṁghika lines culminated in Classical Sanskrit. The various recensions of Asoka's Rock and Pillar edicts, distributed over a vast geographical area, from Gandhāra to Kaliṅga and from Nepal to Mysore, appear in history as so many indelible records of a reaction against the standardisation of Buddhist scriptural languages. The repeated attempts of the Buddhist emperor to adapt the language of each edict to local dialects were fruitful in more than one way. These suggested a possibility of translating the Buddhist Canonical texts into local dialects, outside the Middle Country and it was really left to his missionaries to accomplish the task. The compilation of a Dhammapada text, such as the Prakrit, in a local dialect of Khotan or in that of the countries round Peshawar, broadly the Gandhāra region, may be singled out as the first visible fruit of the reaction implied in Asokan edicts. Since Asoka the Buddhist missionaries penetrated into dark regions within and outside India with the torch-light of the truths of Buddhism. It is these missionaries and their successors and disciples who translated the sacred texts into several local dialects and thus raised those dialects to the status of literary languages and laid the foundation of many national literatures, characters, languages, arts and civilisations. The history of the subsequent Buddhist literature goes to show that the development of Prakrit became an undercurrent to manifest itself again in about the 10th Century A.D. in the songs and treatises of Sahajiyā and other schools of Buddhist Tāntriks. The history of the Dhammapada literature covers some twelve centuries, from the 4th century B.C. to the 9th century A.D. The Dhammapada texts have an international importance, for it is through them that the lofty massages of Buddhism could be appealed to the various nations of Asia who were less imaginative and by far the less speculative, although in some respects more practical, than the Hindus or Aryanised peoples of India. They are no less important for the fact that they afford us a clue for understanding the process of the origin and growth of poetry as well as of Nīti literature in India and other countries where Buddhism has spread.

I

The Kharoṣṭhī Manuscript of the Dhammapada

As read by M. Émile Senart, together with his Notes translated from French.

A[1]

. . . pratasuhino apramadaviha . .

Apramadaviha is, I suppose, the remnant of *apramadaviharino*, which we again find, for instance, in *Itivut.*, ed. Windisch, p. 74, 1, 25, equally in the genitive. *Pratasuhino* must be in the same way a genitive singular=*prāptasukhinaḥ*. It is clear that the two words might also be some nominative forms in the plural.

2 apramadi pramodia[a] ma gami ratisabhamu[b]
apramato hi jhayatu[c] viśeṣa adhikachati[d] O

Cf. Dhammapada, 27.

a. *Pramodia*=Pâli *pamodeya*, with the *y* dropped (cf. *niraeṣu*, l. 4, *sevea*, A[2], 2, etc.), and with the change of *e* into *i*, which is so frequent in locatives like *apramadi* (A[3], 13), and not only at the end of words.

**

b. This reading appears to me to be in every way better than that of the Pâli Dhammapada. *Sambhrama* is better than *saṁstava,* but especially *gami* is so obviously preferable to *kāma* (for the Prâkrit text the hypothesis of a gross mistake is done away with by the absence of *mā* in the first pâda) that I can only doubt if the Pâli reading is not the result of a mistake. Probably this is an old error, and it may be thought that the Pâli redaction is based upon some version expressed in a Prâkrit, analogous to that of the present text, where the substitution of the tenues for the sonant (cf. *adhikachati,* etc.) was frequent.

c. Above the letter read *ja* remains some trace of a horizontal stroke, which, according to an observation of M. d'Oldenburg, marks the aspiration of *j* in our manuscript.

d. One might be inclined to read *viśeṣaṁ;* but the lower part of the spear in ṣ or in analogous characters is so often twisted in the cases which exclude the interpretation *ṁ* (cf. *gami* of the following line, the ṣ of *ṣavaka,* A⁴, 6, etc.), and the probable notation of the *anusvâra* is so rare in our manuscript (I do not know of any sure instance of it in our fragments of Paris) that I do not hesitate to transcribe as I have done.

3 apramadi pramodia ma gami ratisabhamu
apramato hi jayatu[a] chaya dukhasa pramuni[b] ○

Cf. the Dhammapada verse referred to in the preceding line.

a. This time the sign of the aspirate is wanting above the *j,* as often elsewhere. But this curious peculiarity will be brought home to us by a paleographic examination.

b. The Sanskrit will be *kshayaṁ duḥkhasya prāpnuyāt. Pramuni*=Pâli *pāpune.* In lines 6 and 7 we shall meet successively with *amoti* for *āpnoti,* and *pranoti* for *prāpnoti.* The nasalisation of *p* into *m* does not appear solely due to any memory of the compound *pn* surviving its disjunction into *pun,* for B, 24 has *mano*=*punah,* Pâli *pana.*

4 . . . . rata bhodha[a] khano yu ma uvacai[b]
khanatita (h)i śoyati niraeṣu samapi[c].

Cf. Dhammap., 315.

a. No doubt it is almost restored: *apramadarata* as in the next verse. *Bhodha* for *bhotha*, as generally in this manuscript.

b. Yu=*vaḥ*. In A², 7 we shall find *bhadrañu*=*bhadraṁ yu*=Sk. *bhadraṁ vaḥ*. Accordingly it should be written *vo* instead of *ve* (=*vai*) in the text of the Dhammapada. We shall again come across *uvacai*= *upaccagā* in B, 3; *uvacai*, that is to say, *uvacaya*, *ya* being frequently written *i*; cf. ll. 6, 7 *nai*=*nāyaṁ*; *prahai*= *prahāya*, A², 6 (A², 7?), etc. The *g* is sometimes totally dropped between two vowels: *roa*= *roga* (Cᵛᵒ, 3), and may, with stronger reason, weaken into *y*.

c. *Samapi* is, of course, to be completed into *samapita*.

5 apramadarata bhodha sadhami supravedite
drugha udhvaradha[a] atmana pagasana va kuñ[b] ....

Cf. Dhammap., 327.

a. All the analogies demand the reading *udhvaradha* for *uddharadha*. We shall find elsewhere *utvari* for *uttari* (B, 37). As, in the two cases, the compound commences with an initial *u*, one may think that it is this nearness which accounts for this strange orthography, and that, in reality, it corresponds to a pronunciation *vudharadha*, *vutari*, the *v* having been transposed in writing in the Prâkrit text, like the *r* of *drugha*.

b. In spite of partial mutilation, the last letter is certain; it is *kuñ*[*aro*] that ought to be read, or, what recurs in the same way, *kuñaru*, which we shall presently find again in A², 4.

6 nai kalu[a] pramadasa aprati[b] asavachaye
pramata duhu amoti[c] siha ba muyamatia[d] ○

a. This, as I have just pointed out, should be understood in Sanskrit as *nāyaṁ kālaḥ*.

b. *Aprāpte*. Cf. Dhammap., verses 253, 272.

c. For *amoti*, cf. v. 3 above. The usual omission of the anusvāra does not permit us to decide if we are in the presence of the singular or the plural, if *pramata* =*pramattaḥ* or *pramattāḥ*, and *siha*=*siṁhaḥ* or *siṁhāḥ*. I, however, adhere to the first solution on account of the next verse where the singular is assured and on account of the comparison, which, to all appearance, stands on the sense "a certain lion." The termination *o* is often represented by *a*. In l. 5, we have *pagasana va kuñ[aro]*. The reading *mo* cannot be doubtful, although the vowel appears to have been written in an exceptional way. We had *dukha* in l. 3, but the spelling *duha* is much more in use.

d. A comparison with C^{vo}, 2 will prove that it is right, as I believe, to read *mu*. It must be admitted, however, that *m* presents a form which is scarcely ordinary. It is true that if it is read *kha*—another interpretation easily suggesting itself, the form of the *kh* will not be any more regular, the bend of the ring towards the right being generally much more prominent. If *ba* is taken=*va*, *iva*, as elsewhere (e.g., A^2, 4), the two expressions *khayamatia* or *muyamatia*, both possible in Kharoṣṭhi writing, remain equally obscure to me, perhaps because I do not know or remember any story to which there might be an allusion here. According to the first hypothesis we should have *kshayamatyā*, according to the second, I think, *mṛgamatyā*. In the second case, one might imagine, for instance, a story where the lion killed himself by his negligence, in fancying to have to deal with a gazelle instead of some formidable enemy. In the absence of a parallel verse, which I have not hitherto been able to discover, I can only leave all conclusions suspended. The rest of the strophe is easily rendered: "One should not relax until one should have destroyed the passions in oneself."

7 nai pramadasamayu aprati asavachayi
apramato hi jayatu pranoti paramu sukhu ○

Cf. Dhammap., 27.

8 .... ga[a] 25

a. *Ga*, that is to say, *gā(thāḥ)*, of course. The chapter contains 25 stanzas.

I cannot make anything useful out of the three small fragments that figure on the left of the Plate and do not seem to tally with any part of the principal fragment. The one in the middle gives some sure characters:

. . . . kama ciṭhatu . . . . .

where *ciṭhatu* may be = *tiṣṭhantaḥ*.

A²

1 . . madenamakabha devanasamidh(i)gat .

....

Not remembering any parallel passage either in the Dhammapada or elsewhere, I do not see I have, for the present, anything really useful to say on this fragment. The very mutilation of the words is doubtful. I should only like to remark that the letters *t* and *d* are so very similar that one can never be positive over the transcription of the one or the other, as long as the sense of the context is wanting there to guide the reading. The vocalization of the *dh* of *samidhi* is only likely. *Kabha* may very well represent *garbha*. I should only like to dwell upon the reading of the last character. It is usually read *ph* (cf. Bühler), and I myself have read it so in the name *Guduphara̅sa* in the inscription of Takht i Bahi (*Notes in Epigr. Ind.*, III). But it is, I believe, a transcription that requires to be revised. It is not the normal form of *ph*, nor its slight variant which is used in this manuscript, e.g., in the word *phalana* (C^vo^, 8) and elsewhere. Is it a double *ph* or a double *bh*? Besides the present passage where the interpretation of the sign remains doubtful, it reappears in *abhai* (B, 7), in *salabhu* (B, 20, 21), in *ṣebho=śreyaḥ* (C^{ro}, 7, 18, 21) and in *prabhaṁguna* (C^{vo}, 3, 16, 17); in all these words it is *bh* that we expect, more particularly in *ṣebho* which we also find clearly written as *ṣehu*, where a hardening into *ph* would be quite odd. I have to add that in one case at least, viz. B, 21, we find the *bh* of *apalabho* written in a character different from that which is in question and in which the *bh* of *salabhu* is written side by side. To speak without being positive, the orthography, so inconsistent in this manuscript, seems to indicate that our dialect generally preserved the *bh*. A sure solution would be possible only after all the monuments, where appears the character in question, will have been verified from this point of view. Meanwhile, I have decided to read it everywhere as *bh* and not *ph*. I have transcribed in conformity with this conclusion, but I have not failed to note, in every special case, the sign represented in the transcription.

2 . na dhama na sev . a[a] pramadena na savasi
michadiṭhi na roy . a[b] na sia lokavaḍhano[c]

Cf. Dhammap., 167.

a. The comparison with Dh. 167 enables us to complete [*hi*]*na* and, probably, *sev*[*e*]*a*.

b. For *rocayati* equivalent to *sevayati*, cf. Dhammap., p. 122, l. 15: *kassa tvaṁ dhammaṁ rocesi*: "whose law dost thou approve, dost thou follow?" We had *śoyati* for *śocati* (A^1, 4). It is likely that the manuscript had *royea*.

c. Childers (q. v.) declared that he had not any idea of the precise meaning of *lokavaddhana*. M. Fausböll transcribed the etymological signification: "mundi amplificator", and the rendering of M. Max Müller: "a friend of the world", is quite vague. I suspect that the term rests upon the expression *kula-* or *vaṁśa-vardhana*, and that our verse counsels not to increase the number of beings, that is to say, to renounce desire, on the one hand, and to attain to the perfection that closes the circle of *saṁsāra*, on the other.

3 yo tu puvi pramajati[a] pacha su na pramajati
so ita loku ohaseti abha muto va suriu[b] ○

Cf. Dhammap., 172.

a. There is no doubt as to the reading *tu*. The *ca* of Dhammapada has, as often, an opposite meaning, entirely equivalent. The fold of the bark has rendered the reading of the last two letters very indistinct; it seems certain that the final *t* is accompanied by an *i*; what is on the top of *j* is, on the contrary, very doubtful; I have accordingly decided to transcribe *pramajati*. On the whole, this reading affords a construction equivalent in meaning to *pamajjitvā* of the Dhammapada, but more correct; for it does not leave the relative *yo* alone and without a finite verb. Meanwhile, the right reading might well be *pramajiti* or *pramajeti*=*pramajitva*; not that the form is justified without difficulty, for it would be necessary to allow a spelling *ti* for *tvā* which ill becomes analogy, but that it seems that in line 8, *parivajeti* may likewise be =*parivajetva*.

b. We have several times already met with *i* for *e* in the middle of words. Although *imaṁ* may be more natural, *etaṁ* has nothing surprizing; the substitution of *obhāseti* for *pabhāseti*, and of the sun for the moon does not require any observation.

4 arahadha nikhamadha yujatha budhaśaśane[a]
dhunatha macuno sena nalagara[b] ba kuñaru ○

Cf. Theragāthā, verses 256, 1147.
Cf. Divyâvadāna., pp. 68, 138.
Cf. Burnouf, *Lotus*, pp. 529-530.

a. The incorrect spelling *śaśana* is invariably reproduced in this manuscript.

b. The second and third letters of *nalagara* are indistinct. The parallel passages alone permit of a restoration of the word, and the traces of the letter which I restore as=*la*, seem to me less favourable for a reading *ḍa*, which, in itself, would be equally plausible. I have already pointed out the spelling *ba* for *va* =*iva* (A[1], 6).

5 apramata smatimata suśila bhotu bhichavi[a]
susamahitasagapa sacita anurachadha ○

Cf. Dhammap., 327.

a. The vocative *bhichave* in B. 53 (cf. Pâli, *bhikkhave*) appears to support here the form *bhichavi.* But though the construction is differently modified in either hemistich, I do not find any means to make out anything of *bhichavi* else than a nominative; unless the fault of the copyist be admitted, *bhotu* (=*bhontu*) cannot be interpreted as a second person: "Let the bhikkhus be intent, conscientious, virtuous. The mind well-collected, guard your thought."

6 yo ima sadhamavinau[a] apramatu vihaṣiti[b]
prahai jatisaṅsara[c] dukhusatâ[d] kariṣa[t]i.

Cf. Divya Avad., p. 68.

This verse in the Div. Avad. comes immediately after our verse 4 above.

a. *Vinau*=*vina*[*y*]*aṁ* fits well. But there seems to be, before *ri*, a trace of the remnant of another letter. Besides that it gives a syllable too many for the pâda, I scarcely imagine what it could be. *Viharati* is construed with the accusative, probably on the analogy of *carati*.

b. *Vihaṣiti*=*vihariṣyati*, with syncope of *ri* (*i* ?), and *i*=*ya*, as in *prahai*=*prahāya*, and frequently. Similarly *vihaṣisi*, B, 19.

c. I do not see how the compound which I read *ṅsa* can be interpreted otherwise. It is not difficult to find out the *s* there; as regards the *ṅ*, we have not, I believe, any instance of it in the inscriptions; it is, then, not easy to state precisely the analysis of the constituent elements. The value of the sign is attested by several instances.

d. The *u* of *khu* is perfectly clear; I can only see here a mistake of the scribe, which is explained by the *u* of the preceding syllable; it is, of course, *dukhas'a*[*ṁ*]*ta*[*ṁ*].

7 ta yu vadami bhadrañu[a] yavatetha samakata[b]
apramadarata bhodha sadhami supraveditі[c] ○

Cf. Dhammap., 337.

a. We have already met with *yu=vo, vaḥ* (A¹, 4), and *bhadrañu* is again=*bhadraṁ yu=bhadraṁ vaḥ*. We see that the reading in the Pâli text should not be *vovadāmi=vyavavadāmi*, but separated into two words. The two *vaḥ* s are not a double use; *bhaddaṁ* does not qualify *taṁ*: *bhadraṁ vaḥ* is, in some sort, the plural of *bhadraṁ te*, *bhadante*, and forms an independent expression. It is a different question, which I do not pretend to decide, namely, whether it is convenient to attribute to it all its etymological value or to consider it as a mode of address, and whether to render either simply "Lords!" or "welfare to you!".

b. For *samakata*, cf. *adhikachati* (A¹, 2, etc.).

c. Cf. Dhammap., 78: *ariyappavedite dhamme* . . . For *supravedita* compare, more particularly, one of the frequent epithets of the Dharma: *svākhyata*.

8 pramada parivajeti[a] apramadarata sada
bhavetha kuśala dhama yokachemasa prataa[b] ○

a. I have, in line 3, already suggested that *parivajeti* might be=*parivajetva*. The *t* and the *i* are clear; we cannot, then, look for the second person plural here, which would be expected side by side with *bhāvetha*.

b. This expression is met with, for instance, in the *Suttanipāta*, 425: *Yogakkhemassa pattiyā*; "Estranged from all relaxation, true to a constant application, practise virtue to attain to Nirvāṇa."

Here is the transcription of what remains visible of the two verse-ends, that figure on the fragment reproduced up on the left of Plate A ²:

. . . . loke athatha dhiravenea dicha .[a] ○
. . . . lana sabrayano pratismato[b] ○

a. It does not seem, as one would expect here, that the last letter is *ti*, which would give *dichati*, and, supposing the separation of the words to be precise, it would permit of a transcription in Sanskrit: . . . *loke 'rthārthaṁ dhīro *vaineyo ditsati*. But we are simply hypothesizing. The surest course is to wait till a parallel Pâli text is found.

b. That is to say, *samprajānaḥ pratismṛtaḥ*. The two epithets are likewise contiguous in *Suttanipāta*, v. 413 (425?). Our dialect tends particularly to weaken the tenues that follow the nasal: we have had *sa(ṅ)gapa* = *saṅkalpa* (l. 5 above); we shall have (B, 35) *sija*=*siñca*, and (C[ro], 16) *anuabisa*=*anukampi[sya]nah*, etc.; similarly *sabrayano*; cf. C[ro], 43.

A[3]

1 savi saghara anica ti yada prañaya paśati
tada nivinati[a] dukh..

Of the two small fragments that follow, the first one applies well to this verse; there are to be found traces of the following: *eṣo magu vi[śodhia]*; the second surely belongs to another passage, since the verse ends with *viśodhia*.

Cf. Dhammap., 277.

a. One of the peculiarities attaching to the dialect of this manuscript is that the compound *nd*, dental or cerebral, is written *n*, that is to say, if its appearance as it is written is to be believed, is changed into *nn*: *panita* for *paṇḍita*, etc. *Nibbindati dukkhe*, as Childers has rightly understood it: "Only does he conceive disgust for [existence which is nothing but] pain."

2 savi saghara dukha ti yada prañae gradhati[a]
tada nivinati dukha[b] eṣo magu viśodhia[c] O

Cf. Dhammap., 278.

a. In *prañae*, *ya* is written *e* more than once (for instance, in l. 9), though much less frequently than *i*.

Gradhati=granthati, in keeping with the observation just made on the A² fragment of the principal Plate. I understand the word here in the sense of "to deduce, to reason, to conclude."

b. Our manuscript gives, here and in the next verse, *dukha*, that is to say, *dukhaṁ*, the accusative as opposed to the locative of the Pâli. It is, very likely, the same in the preceding verse. This construction is, however, difficult to explain.

c. *Viśodhi* for *viśudhi* is not surprising in this manuscript where the *u* and the *o* are constantly used, the one for the other. As regards the final letter, it is not impossible that it may be *e* instead of *a*, but there is no more certainty, the less so, as the next verse clearly has *viśodhia*.

3 sarvi dhama anatma ti yada paśati cachuma[a]
tada nivinati dukha eṣo mago viśodhia ○

Cf. Dhammap., 279.

a. Above the letter *chu* appear traces of a sign, which is hardly distinct. I can only explain it as a *kh*, some reader having felt the necessity to note that, for *chu*, *khu* could also be written; in fact, the compound *kṣ* is changed equally into *ch* and *kh* in this manuscript. And the conjecture is so much the more plausible, as, just in the verse following, the word is written *cakhuma*. If it is verified, it will have this interesting character that this superadded *kh*, written, consequently, after the original execution of the manuscript, displays a form more archaic than what figures there ordinarily.

4 magana aṭhagio śeṭho sacana cauri[a] pada
viraku śeṭho dhamana pranabhutana cakhuma ○

Cf. Dhammapada, 273.

a. *Catvāri*, *cattāri* is in the Buddhist dialects readily used for the masculine. I do not believe that our *cauri* may be the direct reflex of *catvāri*, but it may be rather of *caturo*; the change of *o* into *i* may strictly be mechanical. Meanwhile, it is difficult to imagine that the analogy of the use of *cattāri* should not have floated in the mind of those using *caturi*, and influenced this spelling, just as the memory of a Māgadhism *bhicchave* has similarly aided the orthography *bhichavĕ*, *bhichavi* (cf. A[2], 5). As regards the elision of the *t*, see l. 10, *phaṣai* side by side with *bhaṣati*, etc.

5 ....ga 30

6 utiṭha[a] na pramajea dhamu sucarita cari
dhamacari suhu śeati[b] asmi loki parasa yi[c] O

Cf. Dhammap., 168.

a. The omission of the final *e*, *utiṭha* for *utiṭhe*, may only be due to the negligence of the scribe, not to any dialectic peculiarity.

b. The traces of the final *u* of *suhu* are not quite distinct; it is perhaps *suha* which the copyist wished to write. *Śeati* appears to rest, not on the usual form *śeti*, but on the form *śayati*, *aya* being written *e*.

c. This last pâda is found again likewise in C[ro], 29, with the genitive *parasa* for the locative *parasmin*. Similarly, *namaruvasa*, B, 30, *sagaranḍasa*, C[ro], 3. A mistake, simply clerical (*parasa* for *parasi*=*parasmi*) is hardly probable side by side with *asmi loki*. It is more natural to admit a perversion, a confusion in the use of cases, of which the following (l. 9. fg) will supply many instances, and of which the language of the Mahâvastu affords us so many evidences. For *ca* we find in this manuscript a regular scale of clerical modifications: *ja*, C[ro], 17; *ji*, B, 35; *ya*, A[4], 4; *yi*, here and elsewhere; *i*, C[ro], 37; *i* for *ya* is explained well, and the orthography *yi* may be strictly understood as equivalent to *ya*; but in *ji*, for *ja*, it is difficult not to admit an abnormal action of the analogy of *i*-*yi*.

7 uṭhanena apramadena sañamena damena ca
divu[a] karoti medhavi ya jara nabhimardati[b] ○

Cf. Dhammap., 25.

a. The weakening of the medial *p* (and also initial) into *v*, is most frequent in this manuscript.

b. The comparison which this variant of the last pâda involves with that of the Pâli recension, is in itsēlf certainly less satisfactory. For an island, age is a factor of destruction less menacing than the surge (flood) to which it is a prey. I wonder why it should not be understood as *jharā*, and why, on the analogy of *jharī* meaning "river" (PWB q.v.), the word could not be taken, not in the precise acceptation of "cascade, waterfall," but in a generic sense bordering upon that of *ogha*. Cf. the Kharoṣṭhī inscription where Bühler thinks he is able to read *jharanī* and interpret it in the sense of "well." Whatever that may be, the substitution of the verb *abhimardati* is probably inspired by the desire to do away with the metrical inaccuracy of *abhikīrati*.

8 uṭhanamato smatimato suyikamasa[a] niśama-[carino
sañatasa hi[b] dhamajivino apramatasa yaśidha [vaḍhati ○

Cf. Dhammap., 24.

a. *Suyi°*=*śuci°* as in *suyigan(dh)a*, C^{ro}, 3, not to speak of other analogous cases.

b. *Hi* is pretty nearly as good as the *ca* of the Pâli text.

9 uṭhane alasa anuṭhahatu[a] yoi bali alasieuvito[b]
saṅsanasagapamano smatima[c] prañai maga alasu [na vinati ○

Cf. Dhammap., 280.

a. The manuscript has clearly *uṭhane*, which would not permit of any other division of words. It is certain that we have here before us a confusion of the scribe and that the original reading was *uṭhana-alasa*, that is to say, *uṭhanakalasmi*. Compare note *c* to l. 6, where I have cited *sagarauḍasa*=*saṁkārakūṭe*. I do not see how it can be read otherwise than as *anuṭhahatu*; yet it must be admitted that the *ṭha* has a somewhat unusual form, which, the context permitting, might be read *ṭhe*.

b. *Yoi*=*yo ayaṁ*. This reading is assuredly preferable to *yuvā* of the Pâli—little matters youth, since moral force, and not physical activity, is only concerned—which must be due to a confusion of the redactors. There is another confusion lurking, I believe, in *ālasiyā* or *ālasiyaṁ* (cf. Fausböll's notes), neither of which can be well construed with *upeta*. In a dialect where the spelling—and perhaps the pronunciation—*e* could be substituted for *ya*, as is the case with the language of our manuscript, the compound *alasieupeta*=*ālasiya-upeta* would save the metre; the Pâli redactors have sought to restore it by an arbitrary expedient.

c. *Smatima* can only be explained as=*asmatima*, the negative *a* being dropped after the final *o* which precedes. It is, if I am not mistaken, the only instance of sandhi our fragments afford.

10 na tavata dhamadharo yavata baho[a] bhaṣati
yo tu apa bi ṣutvana[b] dhamu kaena phaṣai[c] O
11 sa ho[d] dhamadharo bhoti yo dhamu na pramajati O

Cf. Dhammap., 259.

a. *O* for *u* is in this manuscript particularly common after *h*, cf. for instance, *bahojano*, C^{ro}, 31 (30?); C^{vo} (C^{ro}?), 12, etc. But we have already pointed out some parallel cases, after other consonants.

b. *Bi*=(*a*)*pi* is met with elsewhere, as in C^{ro}, 9. The spelling *ṣ* for *śr* is by far the most common in this manuscript.

c. .... The reading *phaṣai* is certain......... The Pâli has *passati,* that is to say, *paśyati.* *Ṣ* might here be interpreted in the same way as *ṣ* (=*ś*) in *phuṣamu* (B, 25) from *spṛś,* and, as I find that in the verse of the St. Petersburg manuscript which corresponds to Dhammapada 398, *phalia* is= *paligha,* we might strictly bring back our *phaṣai* to *paśyati.* But a double anomaly must have to be admitted in the word itself and immediately beside its exact spelling. I prefer by far to hold that *ph* is for *bh* and *phaṣai*=*bhāṣati.* I have myself sought to discard a whole series of apparent instances of this transformation (cf. A², 1). That it is not produced from sporadic cases, is no reason, especially as the hardening of the sonant into tenues is more frequent in our text. The very resemblance which is manifest here between the letters *bh* and *ph,* might have caused an accidental mistake. With *bhāṣati* the sense is excellent: "it does not suffice to make fine speeches, he must speak by his acts (*kāyena,* in keeping with the classification of kāya-, vāk- and manaḥkarma)", or, if you like, "to teach by example." At the most we may question if *bhaṣai*=*bhāsati,* as *abhai*=*ābhāti* (B, 7), or= *bhāṣaye, bhāṣayet.* Anyhow it is curious to think that such a substitution of *ph* for *bh* in the version which has served as the basis of the Pâli redaction, has been quite the cause of the confusion that has introduced *passati* in the text, and quite naturally, misled the interpreters.

d. *Ho*=*kho, khalu,* as in C^{ro}, 6.

2 apramadu amatapada pramadu mucuno pada
apramata na miyati ye pramata yadha mutu [a]

Cf. Dhammap., 21.

a. The singular *mutu, mṛtaḥ,* may strictly be understood as: "those who live in relaxation are as a dead man"; but it is very probable that our scribe has made a slip and that the original text read *muta*: "they are as those dead," that is to say, sure to die, so as not to escape transmigration.

13 eta viśeṣadha[a] ñatva apramadasa panito[b]
apramadi pramodia ariana goyari rato ○

Cf. Dhammap., 22.

a. I take *viśeṣadha* as formed by the suffix *dhā*, which may in this case very well supply the suffix *taḥ* of the Pâli.

b. *Apramadasa* for the locative; cf. *parasa* in l. 6 above. I had at first read *paniti*=*paṇḍito*, but I do not think that we are here forced to admit this sort of Māghadism. The vowel stroke is not lengthened upwards, and, if it crosses the transverse bar of the letter *t*, it is, I think, only a simplification due to cursive writing, which has united, in the form of a ring, the top of the vowel stroke and the left hook of the consonant. It is certain, at all events, that the phrase is here construed in the singular and not in the plural as in Pâli.

14 pramada anuyujati bala drumedhino[a] jana
apramada tu medhavi dhana śethi[b] va rachati ○

Cf. Dhammap., 26.

a. *Drumedhi*, just as we have had already *drugha*. Other analogous instances will be found afterwards.

b. The reading *śethi* appears to me decidedly better than the Pâli *seṭṭhaṁ*, which gives here but a vague and colourless epithet. *Śethi* is the nominative of *śreṣṭhin*, and the half-verse should be rendered: "But the wise clings to diligence as a banker to his treasures." Although the vowel stroke does not descend below the lower transverse bar of *tha*, several instances prove that it is *i* and not *e* that should be read. I am content with referring to *dithi*, A[4], 2. It is quite the reading *śethi* or *śreṣṭhī* which, in his text, the Tibetan translator of the Udānavarga had before his eyes, as is shown by the version of M. Rockhill (*Udānavarga*, IV, 18): "the wise man must be careful, as is the head of a caravan watching his treasures."

15 apramatu pramateṣu suteṣu bahojagaru
avalaśa[a] va bhadraśu hitva yati sumedhasu

Cf. Dhammap., 29.

a. This is, if I am not mistaken, the only instance, in our fragments, of the substitution of *v* for *b*. It is true that in verses A^4, 4 fg., we find *b* completely suppressed between two vowels : *supraudhu*, etc. In the same way, the compound *śv*, reduced here into *ś*, is in several cases preserved in the form of *śp* : *viśpa*, B, 26 ; *viśpaśa*, B, 25.

16 pramada apramadena yada nudati panitu
prañaprasada aruyu[a] aśoka śoino jana
pravataṭho va bhumaṭha dhiru bala avechiti[b]

Cf. Dhammap., 28.

a. The *y* is sometimes more square, sometimes more angular at the top ; materially, it will be perfectly lawful to read *aruśu* ; but it is allowable also to read *aruyu*, and this is the only transcription which appears to me to give an intelligible form. We want, in fact, an equivalent for *āruhya*. *Yu*=*hya* is peculiar. I must say that it is specially the *u* that astonishes me. As regards the consonant, there are several instances which reveal a particular affinity, in the language of this manuscript, between *h* and *j*, which is readily written *y* [cf. *sabrayana* (A^2 fragment) etc.] ; in B, 34 we find *daj(h)amona* for *dahyamāna*, and in the St. Petersburg fragments I have found *y(i)samano*=*hiṁsamānaḥ*, and *parvahita* =*pravrajita*. We may also compare these instances with *ṣehu*, C^{ro}, 8, *ṣeho* C^{ro}, 9, etc. (*śreyaḥ*), where *y* is represented by *h*. As for the vocalisation in *u*, if I cannot explain it, I am at least in a position to cite another instance of it, altogether similar : *abhivuyu* =*abhibhūya* (B, 30, 31). In both cases, the vowel in the preceding syllable is *u*. It seems then that it may be this nearness, which, by somewhat of an effect of vowel harmony, may have coloured our *a*.

b. Must we explain the first *i* of *avechiti* for *avechati* similarly, or just take it to be a simple slip of the copyist having been influenced by the *i* of the following syllable ?

17 apra...tu
apramada praśajhati[a] pramadu garahitu sada

Cf. Dhammap., 30.

a. The *j* is surmounted by a horizontal stroke, which, as I have said above, appears to mark the aspirate; we have, then, *śajhati*=*śaṁsati*; and there is no doubt about the reading, for exactly likewise we find again *praśaj(h)ati* in B, 21.

A[4]

1 .juo namo[a] so magu abhaya namu sa diśa
radho akuyano[b] namu dhamatrakehi sahato[c] O

Cf. Saṁy. Nik., I, V, § 6, v. 2.

a. This verse is closely bound up with the two following, and completes with them a sort of allegory founded on the imagery which likens Buddhist teaching to a "vehicle", *yāna*. The restoration must be: *uju(k)o*. The reading of the vowel in the syllable *mo* of *namo* is not fully certain; it is so much the more probable that in the next pâdas we have, of a surety, *namu*. We will find plenty of other cases where *m* labialises a following vowel into *u*.

b. Our *akuyano* confirms the reading *akujano* adopted for the Pâli by the editor, M. Feer. To me the explanation appears to be *a-kujana*, "where the wicked are none."

c. *Saṁhata* is as good as *saṁyutta* of the Pâli. The word that precedes is perhaps more doubtful. Fortunately, the Pâli text continues the comparison, which serves as the theme to these verses, speaking, as it does, of

the "wheels of the Law." But here our reading can only be *dhamatrakehi* or *dhamadrakehi*. The second form gives us nothing intelligible; on the contrary, the first may be interpreted as "*dharmatarkaiḥ*, that is to say, "the reasonings, the thoughts of the Law." The *Suttanipāta*, 1101 rightly speaks of *aññāvimokhaṁ*, which is *dhammatakkapurejavaṁ*; the dhammatarkas are thus likewise represented as affording a quick impulse to religious progress. We are going to have, in the next verse, the expression *samedithipurejava*, which, on the other hand, has its counterpart in the Suttanipāta, and the first two terms clear up each other: *samyagdṛṣṭi* denotes "true, just ideas"; *dharmatarka*, in the same way, "the reasonings, the ideas conformable to religion", consequently just and right. It is probable that the reading *tarka* is older than the reading *cakra*, which, being more ingenious and piquant, could, once established, no more have been displaced. I translate therefore: "The path is the straight road, the country, the region of felicity, the chariot, the resort of honest people firmly established in truth."

2 hiri tasa avaramu[a] smati sa parivarana[b]
dhamahu[c] saradhi bromi samedithipurejavu[d] O

Cf. Saṁy. Nik., I, V, § 6, v. 3.

a. For this verse and particularly for the meaning of *apālamba*, cf. Morris, *Journ. Pâli T. Soc.*, 1886, p. 128. The form *avarama* is, I believe, the only example, found in our fragments, of the substitution of *r* for *l*; as for *m*=*mb*, we may compare *udumareṣu* =*udumbareṣu* in B, 40.

b. *Smati sa*=*smati asa*. It seems to me that *parivāraṇa* ought to denote rather a part of the car than, as M. Morris would have it, the escort which accompanies it; this is perhaps the roof which covers and protects it.

c. Although the character *read 'hu'* appears cut off by the transverse stroke of *i*, I doubt, as it seems to bear well the sign *u* at the foot, if this stroke, at all events shorter and less prominent than ordinarily, should be taken into account, and I am of opinion

that it is *dhamahu* that should be read, that is to say, *dhamaṁ ahaṁ*, as in Pâli.

d. *Samyak* is, in this manuscript, always written *same* =*samya*. For the expression, compare note (*c*) of the foregoing verse. This verse is rendered : " Modesty is its skid ; consciousness, the roof which protects it ; and I call the Law, the driver that impels and quickens the truth."

3 yasa etadiśa yana gehi parvaitasa va [a]
sa vi etina yanena nivanaseva satie O

Cf. Saṁy, Nik. I, V, § 6, v. 4.

a. It must be *gehino*, in order that the construction might be correct. I venture only to affirm that the scribe may not have meant to write *gihi*, for the bar (*i.e.*, the vowel stroke) passes slightly down the ring of the letter *ga*. This detail is of so little importance that the confusion between *i* and *e* is here complete, as can also be seen from *vi*=*vai*, *ve* and *etina*. The inversion *parva*° for *pravra*° is not rare ; I have several times noted *parvahita* in the St. Petersburg fragments, where we moreover find the *j* replaced by an *h*, which perhaps has no other rôle than to prevent hiatus, like the *y* of the Ardhamāgadhī orthography. I translate : " Whoever possesses such a car, layman or monk, proceeds to Nirvāṇa in that car."

4 supraudhu praujati [a] imi [b] gotamaṣavaka
yeṣa divá ya rati ca nica budhakata smati O

Cf. Dhammap., 296.

a. I do not see here any trace of the upper stroke intended to mark aspiration, which the following verses present in that word. I have already pointed out this complete elision of *b* between two vowels (A^3, 15).

b. The reading *imi* of our manuscript is evidently much better than *sadā* of the Pâli version. " These disciples of the Buddha are roused truly to the understanding which......" The theme is an exhortation, not a hackneyed praise, of all the disciples of the Buddha indiscriminately.

5 supraudhu praujhati imi gotamaṣavaka
yeṣa diva ya rati ca nica dhamakata smati O

Cf. Dhammap., 297.

6 [s]upraudhu praujhati imi gotamaṣavaka
yeṣa diva ya rati ca nica saghakata[a] smati O

Cf. Dhammap., 298.

a. The form of the second letter (*i.e.*, as much of it as is on a level with the line) does not denote *gh* (aspirated). In fact, the upper stroke which mounts the letter is intended to mark aspiration. We see then that the letter itself does not express it. Cf. B, 3, below.

7 [sup]raudhu praujhati imi gotamaṣavaka
yeṣa diva ya rati ca nica kayakata smati O

Cf. Dhammap., 299.

8 supraudhu praujhati imi gotamaṣavaka
yeṣa diva ya rati ca ahiṅsai rato mano O

Cf. Dhammap., 300.

9 supraudhu p[r]aujati[a] imi gotamaṣavaka
yeṣa diva ya rati ca bhamanai[b] rato mano O

Cf. Dhammap., 301.

a. I do not see any trace of the upper stroke. It is not, however, certain that it had not existed, the ink in this passage being a little effaced.

b. We shall again meet with other instances of the change of *v* into *m*, as *namu*=*nāvaṁ* (B, 35).

FRAGMENTS OF A

Of these, I have collected twenty-seven in all, mostly very small. I attempt only to transcribe those which have preserved at least some complete characters.

I. These are four commencements of line.

[d]ur.(?)ga. e ....

vario[a] va thale chi ....

anuvaṭhitacitasa[b] ....

anuvaṣutacita ....

Cf. Dhammap., 37 :

dūraṅgamaṁ ekacaraṁ ....

Ibid., 34 :

vārijo va thale khitto ....

Ibid., 38 :

anavaṭṭhitacittassa ....

Ibid., 39 :

anavassutacittassa ....

a. *Vario* for *varijo*, like *pavvaita* for *pavvajita*, as I have pointed out above (A⁴, 3).

b. The *u* of *anu* is perfectly certain, as much in this word as in *anuvaṣuta* of the next verse. In the Pâli, however, it has no place either in the one or in the other word; it is *anavasthita* and *anavasruta* which the sense requires and which are in the Pâli version. The scribe has, perhaps, been drawn into this blunder by the thought of *anuvaṭhita=anupasthita*, which floated in his mind.

II.

........................unapanucirah........................

III. A verse-end, written on the darkest surface of the leaf [cf. p. 197 (?) —perhaps p. 19 *i.e.* A² Fragments of verse-ends].

..........ma(?)tvadadatasava ?ya ○

To me the letters, almost all, are too doubtful for transcription.

IV. The letter *no* marks the end of a pâda.

..........uhaṣino yokama . e..........

The two fragments that follow belong to the leaf B, where they will be in their proper places in verses 42-45. They were found, when I was unfolding the the manuscript, mixed up with sheet A. Nothing can show better the disorder in which these fragments have come into my hands.

V. Cf. B, 42 fg.

..........??? so bhikhu jahati o..........
..........mahoho sa bhikhu jahati..........
..........s. bhikhu jahati o..........

VI.

..........vikaya so bhikhu jahati o..........
..........ṣaitha s . . . kh..........

VII. A commencement of line.

samadhimu . i..........

VIII.

..........la cita druracha drunivarana[a]
u ....

Cf. Dhammap., 33.

a. This reading is certain, and of the rest, *durnivāraṇa* seems to me to be least so well as *dunnivāraya.*

IX. A verse-end.

..........ṣu gachati ○

B

The top of this leaf exactly fits in with the end of one of the leaves of the manuscript, which have found their way to St. Petersburg; so that our first sixteen lines meet with their complement there, partially at least. I have thought not to exceed the reserve, imposed upon me by the very courtesy with which my learned colleague and friend M. d'Oldenburg placed his documents at my disposal, by adding any copy of the verse-pieces which have been joined to our own fragments; both of them form an inseparable whole. I have taken care to enclose within brackets what are thus borrowed from the St. Petersburg fragment.

1 yo cutiu veti satvana ?vati ca[a] —[śana[b]
budhu atimaśarira tam aho bromi bramana[c] O]

Cf. Dhammap., 419.

a. It is not possible to distinguish *a priori* the *t* from the *d* in our manuscript. We might as well read *vedi*. Yet the present appears to me here much more probable than the past, and I should be more disposed to admit that the reading of the Dhammapada proceeds from some old confusion, based, perhaps, exactly on the similarity of those two characters. Of the letter which I have replaced by a sign of interrogation, the bottom of the stroke only remains. It has no significant hook permitting of reading it as *u* in order to represent *uvavati*, the *upapatti* of the Pâli. At all events, I believe that the last letter, though the vowel stroke may be a little clipped, bears well the notation of *i*.

b. M. d'Oldenburg transcribes the beginning of his fragment as [*sa*]*rvaśana*. In the facsimile, there is nothing but the end, of which the reading *śana* is surely possible, but not certain, so much the less because it is difficult to see how this form *sarvaśana* would be related to the form *sarvaśaḥ*, *sarvaśo* which the Pâli permits us to expect. On the other hand, with this reading, a syllable is wanting for the metre, and the facsimile, to a certainty, permits us to think that a small piece of the leaf is dropped between the end of our fragment and the commencement of the other. The exact reading of this pâda-end remains, therefore, necessarily doubtful until further settled.

c. *Atimaśarira = antimaśarīraṁ.* Cf. Dhammap., 400.

2 akrodhu anuvayasa vipramutu p . n . .[a]
[budhu vatamala dhira[b] tam aho bromi bramana O]

a. *Anuvayasa = anupāyāsaṁ.* The last letters are half cut off; but the traces tally well with a restoration *punabhava = punarbhavāt.*

b. With this pâda we may compare Dhammap., v. 261: *sa ve vantamalo dhīro thero ti (thaviro ti) pavuccati.* I translate: "The man without anger, without despondency, released from all future birth (= *antimaśarīraṁ* of the preceding verse), wise, stainless, and firm, it is that man whom I call [truly] a brâhman."

3 yo tu puñe ca pave ca[a] uhu ṣaga uvacai[b]
[aṣaga viraya budhu tam ahu bromi bramana O]

Cf. Dhammap., 412.

a. Let it suffice to note in passing the Mâghadhisms *puñe* and *pave* i.e., *pāpe,* for *puññaṁ* and *pāpaṁ.*

b. We should note the letter *hu, uhu = uho, ubhau* [*h = bh,* as often; cf. *ohaseti* (A², 3), etc.]; the interpretation cannot be contested. It is decisive for the transcription of *ahu = aho, ahaṁ,* which recurs so often in our St. Petersburg fragments. *Ṣaga,* here as well as in the following pâda, presents a double peculiarity: *ṣ* for *s,* and the particular form of *g.* One might be tempted to interpret this form as = *gh* aspirated; but, besides that the aspirate would not be justified here, we have already (A⁴, 6, note) met with an instance of a variant equivalent to the letter, with a stroke above, expressing aspiration. It is then much more natural to explain this base of the character as an accidental stroke of a habitual writing, which is very much generalised in certain numismatic alphabets. As regards *uvacai* = *upaccagā,* I refer to A¹, 4.

4 jai parakata[a] budhu jitavi akatagati[b]
[pruju devamanuśana[c] tam ahu bromi bramana O]

a. The initial *j* has not the upper mark of aspiration; it is, however, *jhai*=*dhyāyin*, that we must understand, and *parakata*=*parākrānta*.

b. *Akatagati*, that is to say, *agatāgati*, "who is not drawn into the four agatis", for which cf. Childers. A graceful scribbling without any special signification will here be noticed, whereby the scribe has finished off the spear of *ga*, and which he has reproduced in the lower part of the vowel-stroke of *mi* in the last pâda.

c. The reading *pru* seems certain. For my part, I cannot account for the *r*, and until a better interpretation should be found, I propose to understand *puju devamanuśana*=*pūjyaṁ devamanuṣyaiḥ*. The expression *devamanuṣyapūjita* is, with its various equivalents, current in Buddhist phraseology. The change of *manuṣya* into *manuśa* is, as will be seen later on, constant in our manuscript. I translate: "The man who applies himself to meditation, heroic and wise, who is a vanquisher [of passions], who does not force himself into evil ways, and who is worthy of the respect of gods and men, it is that man whom I call [truly] a brâhman."

5 jai[a] parakata budhu kitakica anasavu
[budhu daśabaluvetu[b] tam ahu bromi bramana O]

Cf. Dhammap., 386.

a. This time again the *letter read j* is well=*j*, without any sign of aspiration.

b. This pâda appears here to be quite out of place, inferior certainly to its Pâli counterpart: *budhu* is twice repeated, figuring already in the first pâda, and *daśabalopeta* is an epithet that only suits the "Buddha" in the technical sense, which cannot be aimed at here. "The man who applies himself to meditation, heroic, wise, true to his duty, and free from passions, the Buddha endowed with ten powers, it is that man whom I call [truly] a brâhman."

6 gamirapraña medhavi marga[ma]rgasa koi ?[a]
[utamu pravara vira tam ahu bromi bramana]

Cf. Dhammap., 403.

a. I have already noted some spellings like *gamira* =*gambhīra*. The end of this pâda presents some difficulty. It is hard to believe that our text does not correspond to that of the Pâli. In the syllable which I transcribe as *i*, we could, it is true, admit the elision of *v*, just as we have ascertained that of the *b* in *supraudhu* and *praujhati*, A[4], 4, 9. It does not yet appear to me certain, a little probable though it may be, that the reading should be *bi*, with the frequent change of *v* into *b*; although half of the last letter is destroyed, what remains of it does not seem to warrant the letter *da*, and I do not yet see any other reading to suggest, that may at the same time be plausible to the sense and consistent with the trace of the manuscript.

7 diva tavati adicu rati abhai[a] cadrimu
sanadhu [chatrio tavati jhai tavati bramano
adha sarva ahoratra budhu tavati teyasa 50[b]]

Cf. Dhammap., 387.

a. The *bh* of *abhai* is written by the same character as the *bh* in A,[2] 1 (cf. note). For the elision of *t* between two vowels, cf. *phaṣai*, A[3], 10, note *c*.

b. The cipher is here added on the margin, at the end of the line, and without the addition of *ga*[*tha*]. The scroll-mark that denotes the end of chapters is thrown into the next line, as can be seen from our fac-simile.

8 kaena savruto bhikhu atha vayai[a] s.v.to
[manena savruto bhikhu sarva drugatio jahi ○]

a. *Savruto*=*saṁvṛtaḥ*. For the change of *ṛ* into *ru*, we may compare l. 25 : *apru*[*tha*]*jana*. I restore *vayai*=*vācāya* (although the transverse line of *i* may have disappeared in the break), because of the sure reading in the next verse; *i*=*ya*. Cf. *vayaya* in l. 10 (?). "The monk who is master of himself in his actions and in his words, the monk who is master of himself in his thoughts, would not fall again into any of the evil paths."

9 kaena sañamu sadhu sadhu va[yai[a] sañamu
manena sañamu sadhu] [sadhu savatra sañamu
sarvatra sañato bhikhu savadugatio jahi]

Cf. Dhammap., 361.

a. That which, in this verse and in those following, is enclosed between the first brackets, belongs to the detached fragment on the left of Plate B, and ought to have been connected with the principal fragment. "It is good to be master of self in one's actions, good to be master of self in one's words, good to be master of self in one's thoughts; it is good to be master of self in all circumstances; the monk who is, in all circumstances, master of his self, would not fall again into any of the evil paths."

10 hathasañatu padasañatu [vayasañatu savutidrio
ajhatma][rato samahito eko satuṣito tam ahu
bhikhu ○]

Cf. Dhammap., 362.

11 yo muhena sañato bhikhu mana[bhani[a] anudhato
artha dhar][mu ji[b] deśeti masuru[c] tasa bhaṣita ○]

Cf. Dhammap., 363.

a. This reading suggests the form *mandabhāṇin*, "who speaks little," as understood from the Pâli texts; it is much more probable than the form *mantabhāṇī*, which the scholiast takes great pain, though in vain, to explain.

b. The *r* is distinguished by the elongation of the right branch of the *m* (frag. of Plate B). I should not decide, with certainty, if the text has *rmu* or *rma*.

c. The reading *masuru* seems very clear on the fac-simile of M. d'Oldenburg. There has been a confusion on the part of the scribe, but this confusion is easily explained; in the Kharoṣṭhī writing it is indeed a form of *s*, which is only distinguished from *dh* by the terminal hook being drawn to the right. This hook is turned towards the right in *s* and towards the left in *dh*. This detail seems to prove, as one would expect, that the copyist was working on a manuscript written in a hand similar to his own.

12 śuñakare [a] pravithasa śatacit.. [bhikhuno amanuṣa rati] [bhoti same dharma [b] vivaśatu ○]

Cf. Dhammap., 373.

a. I do not attempt to decide, at least for the present, if the final *e*=*aṁ*, or, what seems at first more probable, if we have to deal with an extension of the use of the locative.

b. The extremity of the tail of the *r*, attached—as one may see in verse 14—to the right arm of *m*, still remains visible below the gap.

13 yato yato sammaṣati [a] kan(dh)a[na udakavaya [b] lahati priti][pramoju amutu ta vianatu [c] ○]

Cf. Dhammap., 374.

a. I should linger awhile over the reading I suggest for this word; for the conclusion I have come to regulate a whole series of parallel cases; I would speak of the second character. It is certain that the *u* is usually marked in this manuscript by a hook placed at the foot of the consonant and more or less inclined towards the right, besides more or less closed, so as to appear occasionally as a small circle, somewhat oblong. The sign which we have here below our *m* is also a hook, but more rounded and more open than the other and, particularly, placed more towards the right of the consonant. If we consider this circumstance, viz., that the sound *mu* is usually noted by a special character, it must be avowed, in spite of a certain similarity, that the sign scribbled below should be distinguished from the sign *u*, and that therefore it is not *mu* that ought to be read. Given the form of the anusvāra in the epigraphic alphabet, we might incline to find it here again; but surely, the anusvāra is not generally noted in our manuscript; and in the only case, absolutely certain, which I may have cited already—it is in the St. Petersburg fragments—it presents, on the contrary, the exact form of *m*; I cannot, therefore, see in our hook an anusvāra, but simply an *m* final, written below, as often in the epigraphic texts in Dévanâgarî. The reading *samaṁṣati* will, in itself, be unlikely; it is especially in the word *brāhmaṇa* that our sign reappears; the transcription *bramaṁna* is equally inadmissible. The comparison which is forced with the anusvāra of the inscriptions is, however, instructive. Everyone admits that this form of the anusvāra is nothing but the *m* turned round. I think that, in the same way here, our hook is nothing but the *m* turned round, but preserving its normal value. The sign will be thus =*mm*. In all the cases where I have pointed it out, this analysis is absolutely satisfactory. Had it appeared only in the word *brāhmaṇa*, one might surmise a compound *mh*; but, apart from the unlikelihood in writing, there is no room for an *h* in the present case. There is an example which appears to me to be decisive for the interpretation I propose, and which I for my part am finally convinced of; it is in the St. Petersburg fragments, in the verse which corresponds to Dhammap., 82, where the word cannot but be read as *gammiro*=*gambhīro*. Cf. also the two verses in the same fragment, which correspond to Dhammap., 81, where we are authorised in the same way to read *sammijati* (i.e., *mmi* instead of *miṁ*)=*sammiñjati* of the Buddhist Sanskrit and also of Pâli. .... As regards the *ṣ*=*ś* of *sammaṣati*, it is explained perhaps by the nearness of the *r*, somewhat like *ṣ*=*śr* (cf. *ṣutvana* A[3], 10). Nevertheless, the ordinary transcription of Sanskrit *rś* is *ś*, as in °*daśima*, l. 32.

The compound *ndh* is generally written *n* with the stroke of aspiration above, so that it might almost be interpreted as *ndh* or *nh*, as *bañana*=*bandhana* in l. 49 (?) and elsewhere. Here the mark of aspiration is wanting. Precisely in the same way, the *k* is for *kh*=*sk*. The spelling *udaka*= *udaya*, which is quite peculiar, is reproduced in C^ro^, 18. Similarly we will find *dhoreka*° (C^vo^, 37).

c. Neither do I construe nor understand this last pâda like the previous interpreters ; I cannot believe that placed as it is, the pronoun *tam* may refer to *priti-pramoja*. I am of opinion that it is necessary to cut off the sentence at the end of the third pâda, and that the fourth should be translated literally : "liberation from death is [the lot] of him who knows [of those who know] it", that is to say, of those who, knowing it, practise it and destroy the skandhas. For the suppression of the medial *j*, suffice it to refer to *parvaitasa* of A_4, 3.

14 śuñakari pravițhasa śataci[tasa bhikhuno
ama][nușa rati bhoti same dharma vivaśatu ○]

This line is exactly identical with line 12. There is some confusion here of the copyist who must have repeated a line by mistake or neglected some partial variant, which in his text distinguished the two verses. Cf. p. 251-2.

15 ....[.......... ....
......................][............................same dhama vivaśatu○]

In spite of the traces that remain of the first three pâdas, I have not succeeded in restoring the probable reading of it.

16 nathi jhana aprañasa praña nathi ajhayato
[[1]yasa[a] jana ca praña ya so ho] [nirvanasa satia[b]○]

[*Foot-note :* [1] Fr. B VII.]

Cf. Dhammap., 372.

a. This verse and the two following are completed by means of a detached fragment which I designate as fr. B VIII. *Yasa* is genitive doing the function of the locative, as often in this manuscript. I cannot decide, on account of the break, if the letter read *j* of *jana* bears or not the stroke of aspiration. *Ho*=*khalu*, for *vai*, *ve* of the Pâli.

b. The lower part of the last character is tolerably indistinct on the fac-simile. I dare not affirm if the true reading may not be *satii* ; it would be nearer to the Pâli and grammatically more justifiable.

17 tatrai adi bhavati tadhaprañasa[a] bhikhuno
['idriagoti satuṭhi pratimukhe i[b]]..................

[*Foot-note* : [1] Fr. B VII.]

Cf. Dhammap., 375.

a. The *t* is clear. We have, then, opposite to *idha*, *iha* of the Pâli, another variant *tatha prañasa*, whether *tathā* refers to the description in the previous verse [" the monk who thus, that is to say, by meditation, is in possession of the wisdom"], or whether this expression *tathāprajña* goes back to the general analogy of Buddhist phrases as *tādṛś* (*tādi*, *tāyin*), *tathāgata*, etc., with one of which I have dealt elsewhere, *JRAS*, Oct., 1898, p. 866.

b. *I*=*ca*, as we have seen already. For the expression *pātimokkhe ca saṁvaro*, cf. *savuta prātimukhasa*, fr. C,I[ro], 2.

18 mitra bhayea[a] paḍiruva śudhayiva a[b]..................
['paḍisa?ra.tisa. aprak][c]..................

19 datu ayarakuśalo suhu bhikhu vihaṣisi[d] ○

[*Foot-note* : [1] Fr. B VIII.]

Cf. Dhammap., 375 :

mitte bhajassu kalyāṇe suddhajīve atandite

Ibid., 376 :

paṭisanthāravuttassa ācārakusalo siyā

Ibid., 379 :

so attagutto satimā sukhaṁ bhikkhu vihāhisi

a. On account of the break the reading of the character *ye* (=*je*) is not quite certain ; but to me at least the reading seems infinitely probable.

b. The commencement of the pâda can only be read in the light which the comparison with the Pâli lends us. The half-verse of the Dhammapada forms the end of a hypermetric stanza of six pâdas. Ours on the contrary forms, as can be seen, the first third of a stanza of that kind. It is obvious that the arrangement of our text is the best : the half-verse *mitte bhajassu*, etc., connects itself, as badly as possible, with the śloka that precedes.

c. The lower part of the letters having disappeared, the reading in the first pâda, is not sure for all the characters ; after *paḍi* we may allow *sadhara* which will be well=the Pâli *santhāra* ; but the top of the next character has not at all the appearance of a *v*, but rather of a *g*. Did our text read *paḍisadharaguti* ?

d. *Datu* is, of course=*dāntaḥ*, and *ayara*=*ācāra*. We have already met with *vihaṣiti* (A^2, 6). Our form is midway between that of Sanskrit and that of Pâli *vihāhiti*. In Pâli, besides the change of *r*(*i*)*ṣ* into *h*, which seems to surpass the middle level of phonetic degeneration in that dialect, we should notice the spelling *i* for *ya*, which appears also to have been derived from a habit of writing, more free and less regular than has generally prevailed with its literary fixity. Likewise has this only normal form been partly supplanted by spellings like *kāhasi*, *kāhati*, *kāhanti* side by side with *kāhisi*, *kāhiti*, *kāhinti*, which appear isolated and peculiar.

20 salabhu [a] natimañea nañeṣa smihao sia [b]
añeṣa smihao bhikhu samadhi nadhikachati O

Cf. Dhammap., 365.

a. For the character *bh* of *salabhu*, cf. A^2, note *a*. I need hardly remark that *atimaññati* should be understood in the sense of " to despise, to disdain ". Childers and M. Max Müller have already corrected the slight oversight of M. Fausböll.

b. I have discovered no means to distinguish *a priori* the *m* from the conjoint *v* in compounds like *tv*, *tm*, *sm*, *sv*. It is perhaps *svihao*=*spṛhayaṁ*, that ought to be read. The instances we have already cited, where *p* is changed into *m* (A^1, 3, note *b*,) have induced me to think that it might be the same here. But I do not see that it would be to any positive purpose to decide between the two transcriptions. In verse 25, we will meet with the usual change of *sp* into *ph*. For the change into *o* of the final syllable of the present participle, we may compare *anuvici(ṁ)tao* and *anusmaro* (ll. 22, 23).

21 apalabho tu yo bhikhu salabhu [a] natimañati
ta gu deva praśajhati [b] śudhayivu atadrita O

Cf. Dhammap., 366.

a. In the plate one might doubt if it is *apalapho* or *apalabho* that ought to be read; I should say that the original leaves no doubt, and it places us quite face to face with the character *bh*. In *salabhu* we again find the same form of the character *bh* (as in l. 20).

b. For *praśajhati=praśaṁsanti*, cf. the note on A[3], 17. I take *gu* for *ghu* (with loss of aspiration as in *kadha =skandha*)=*khu* i.e., *khalu*, which is also represented by *ho* and *hu*.

22 kamaramu [a] kamaratu kamu anuvicitao
kamu anusmaro bhikhu sadharma parihayati O

a. This verse only differs from the next, which alone is represented in the Pâli Dhammapada and of which it forms the antithesis, by the substitution of *kāma*, "desire," for *dharma*, "law, virtue," and by the corresponding suppression of the negative.

23 dhamaramu dhamaratu dhamu anuvicitao
dhamu anusmaro bhikhu sadharma na parihayati O

Cf. Dhammap., 364.

24 na śilavatamatrena bahoṣukena va mano [a]
adha samadhilabhena vivitaśayanena va O

phuṣamu [b] nekhamaṣukhu aprudhajanasevi.
bhikhu viśpaśa ma?? a?te asavachaye [c] O

Cf. Dhammap., 271-272.

a. *Bahoṣukena* is well explained as=*bahussukkena, bahu autsukya*, and "energy, activity" is a satisfactory meaning. One would, however, expect *s*, rather than *ṣ*, for *ts*. To make amends, the Pâli *bāhusaccena*, if it is, with Fausböll, to be derived from *bahu*+*sata* (=*smṛta*), ought to double the *s*: *bāhussacca*. As the compound *śr* is usually changed into *ṣ* in our dialect, one may almost ask if the original reading should, as Childers seems to suppose (*Dict.*, q. v.), have been *bāhusacca*=*bāhuśrutya*, so that our two variants would be parallel deformations from it. It is so much the more difficult to decide it, as, after all, our text *bahoṣukena*, such as it is, is irreproachable for the sense, and—in view of the confusions between the sibilants, of which the only verse that follows exactly gives us two examples — very much acceptable for the form. *Mano* for *pana*(*ḥ*), *punaḥ* with *p* changed into *m*.

b. The plural *phuṣamu* is certainly preferable to the singular, by the more general turn it gives to the thought. For the substitution of *ṣ* for *ś*, cf. *sammaṣati* (verse 13).

c. Our text would confirm, if there were need of it, the correction that Childers (*J. R. As. Soc.* n. ser. V, p. 225) has rightly introduced in the Pâli text, *vissāsaṁ māpādi* for *vissāsam āpādi*; for, the cases where the final *m* is, in this manuscript, preserved by Sandhi, are quite rare, however *a priori* the division *viśpaśa ma°* may be by far the most probable. I scarcely doubt that the two letters, half lost, may have been *padi*; but I am not quite sure, so as to represent them in the transcription. The medial compound in *viśpaśa* hardly appears clear here. For the different aspects of the compound letter, cf. *viśpa* in the next line, and *v*(*i*)*śpaśa*, Cvo, 24 (23 ?). Striking is the resemblance of the normal form of the compound with the compound figuring on the monuments of Spalagadames, Spalahores, Spalirises, which is generally transcribed as *sp* and *śp* (Bühler, pl. I. l. 29); I dare not declare myself in a decisive way between the two readings. Meanwhile, there cannot be any doubt about the word, which is *viśvāsa*, to be sure; the second dental (i.e., *s*) is then unduly palatalised into *ś* in this text; and this irregularity is explained beyond doubt, as in *śaśana* (ll. 28, 29; A,[2] 4), by the nearness of another palatal *ś*; there is thus but little appearance that this palatal *ś* could have been supplanted in the preceding syllable, where it is justified by the etymology. I therefore incline to the reading *śp*, and introduce it in my transcription. This compound figures here only as representing a Sanskrit *śv*. It does not appear to me to be a sufficient reason to transcribe it as *śv* and risk the disappearance of a dialectic peculiarity which likens itself to a well-known peculiarity of Zend. To be sure, *aprate asavachaye* = *aprāpte āsavakṣaye* is what our manuscript read—a stereotyped verse-end which we have already met with (A^1, 6, 7) and which I reckon more genuine than the turn adopted by the Pâli.

6 na bhikhu tavata bhoti yavata bhichati para[a]
viśpa dharma samadai bh . khu bhoti na tavata ○

Cf. Dhammap., 266.

a. There can be no hesitation in reading it as *para*; I cannot explain the elongation of the stroke of the *r* below the small lower hook, which generally ends the letter in this manuscript. It is clear that *tena* of the Pâli text should be substituted by *tāvatā*, as it does not give the necessary measure nor furnishes the usual correlative face to face with *yāvatā*.

7 yo tu baheti pavana[a] vatava brammayiyava[b]
saghai carati loku[c] so tu bhikhu tu[d] vucati ○

Cf. Dhammap., 267.

a. I do not decide if the copyist has, in *pavana*, forgot the stroke of the *i* = *pāpāni*, or if we have to do with a genitive, which the Buddhist style presents often after a transitive verb and in the function of the accusative (cf. Mahâvastu, *passim*).

b. For *vatava* cf. *vatavantaṁ*, Dhammap., 208, 400. *Brammayiyava* = *brahmacaryavan*; I have already pointed out the spelling *yi*=*ca* (A[3], 6, note *c*); as for *ya*=*rya*, the verse C[ro], 17 will give us side by side *virya* and *hinaviyava*. In the same way, I find *brammayiryena* in a passage of the St. Petersburg manuscript.

c. I have already pointed out the tendency of compounds commencing with the nasal to soften the surd into the sonant (cf. A[2] Frag., note *b*) whence *saghai*= *saṅkhāya*. For *carati* construed with the accusative, cf. above, A[3], 6, and *Mahâvastu*, I, 410.

d. *Ve* of the Pâli is preferable to our first *tu*, which by an unhappy redundance is repeated from the first pâda; as for the second, it is a mistake for *ti*, a mistake to which, it appears, our copyist had a natural proneness (cf. v. 38), always under the influence of a *u* close by.

28 metravihari yo bhikhu prasanu budhaśaśane
tunati[a] pavaka dharma drumapatra ba maturu ○

Cf. Dhammap., 368, for the first half-verse.

a. If we read *tunati*, I can make nothing out of it but *tundati*=tudati (cf. the Middle Vedic *tundate*); but the sense "to strike" is vague, and the expression middling. It is also easy to read *dunati*, and one might believe that it is an accidental inversion of *nudati* "to drive away, to suppress", which suits very well, just as at the end of the verse, *maturu*, which is certainly a gross error of the copyist, is for *marutu*=*mārutaḥ*. It is perhaps a great deal to own two mistakes of the same nature in the same line. The general sense is in every way clear: "The monk who lives charitably, adhering to the teaching of the Buddha, chases the evil as the wind a tree-leaf."

29 metravihara yo[a] bhikhu prasanu budhaśaś—
paḍivijhu[b] pada śata sagharavośamu suha[c] ○

Cf. Dhammap., 368.

a. *Metravihara*, that is to say, *maitravihāro*, can very well be used as equivalent to *maitravihārin*. This form of speech is added as grammatically possible and from a comparison with the verses following, so as to command the disjunction °*vihārī yo* in the Pâli text.

b. *Paṭivijjhati* is understood in Pâli to mean "to penetrate"; it is then a very good synonym of *adhigacche.* The termination only is surprising; in short, I can only see in it a present participle of *paḍivijhaṁ,* which should be completed by the substantive verb understood.

c. In *sagharavośamu* also, I cannot help admitting an inversion, but of the vowel only, for *sagharovaśamu* which exactly corresponds to the Pâli.

30 udagacitu yo bhikhu abhivuyu priapria[a]
adhikachi pada śata akavuruṣasevita ○

For the third pâda, cf. Dhammap., 368.

a. A similar case has already (cf. *aruyu,* A[3], 16) given me the occasion to cite this *absolutive* in *yu* for *ya.* But I have not hitherto found any other example (save, of course, the repetition in the next verse) of *v* for *bh.* Be that as it may, *abhivuyu* cannot be anything but *abhibhūya. Abhivahya,* which one might also think of, on the precedent of *aruyu,* would give neither sense nor any allowable construction. "The monk who feels happy having dominated pleasure and pain, reaches the region of peace, inaccessible to the weak-minded."

31 pramojabahulu[a] yo bhikhu abhivuyu priapria
adhikachi pada śata aseyane moyaka[b] ○

For the first pâda, cf. Dhammap., 381.

a. Note the regular form of the character *hu.*

b. A syllable is wanting in the last pâda, and this irregularity is complicated with the somewhat unforeseen Māghadism *aseyane=asecanaṁ,* so that I scarcely dare to suggest anything by way of firm conjecture. If we admit that the copyist might have omitted a letter, and restore it as *aseyanekamoyaka*, that is to say, *asecanaekamocakaṁ*, we would suppress at least the oddness of the final *e*; but I have no parallel examples for *ekamocaka* "the only deliverer." The general meaning is not affected by this uncertainty of detail: "The monk who feels plenty of joy having dominated pleasure and pain, reaches the region of peace, the region (which is) delicious, (and which is a) liberator."

32 apramadaratu yo bhikhu pramadi bhayadaśima[a]
abhavu parihanae nivanaseva satii O

Cf. Dhammap., 32.

a. Between the character read *śi* and the character read *ma*, an oblique stroke will be noticed. If the case were not, to my knowledge, so isolated, I would propose to see in the form *ma* with the oblique stroke an example of the analogous variant of *ma* to which I have had occasion to call attention elsewhere (*Inscriptions de Piyadasi*, I, pp. 23-24). This is, at least provisionally, the only explanation I can offer on this peculiarity.

33 apramadaratu yo bhikhu pramadi bha ....
.... [a]

Cf. Dhammap., 31.

a. The traces of letters at the end of the line do not fit in exactly with the two lips of the break, and therefore I cannot read them with certainty; but it is very likely that our verse ends like the Pâli by *agiva gachati*. As to the preceding pâda, nothing is certain except that the last letter but one was accompanied by a *u* which well corresponds to *thu* of *thulaṁ*. I have, in the Pâli text, substituted the correction *ḍahaṁ* for *sahaṁ*, rightly pointed out by M. Max Müller (Transl. of the Dhammap., S. B. E., p. 10).

34 jai bhikhu ma yi pramadi[a] ma te kamaguna [bhameṁsu cita[b]
ma lohaguḍa gili pramata kana dukham ida ti ḍa-[jhamano[c]

Cf. Dhammap., 371.

a. The construction of the nominative *pamādo* is not happy, and a finite verb would be more proper; but it appears to me difficult to take *pramadi*, which might be *pramaji*, for the Potential, and I am inclined only to find in it the exact counterpart of the Pâli with a Māghadism in the termination *i*=*e*.

b. Our text furnishes a sure correction of the Pâli, the incongruity in which had justly embarrassed the interpreters. The compound *ṁs* in our (*i.e.*, the Prakrit) alphabet has so much the appearance of a doubled *s* that one would be tempted to imagine that it was on a text written in the same alphabet that the deformation of *bhameṁsu* into *bharassu* must at first have been produced. The identity, in the dialect, of the nominative and the accusative plurals, both in *ā*, facilitates on the other hand, the change of *kāmaguṇā* into *kāmaguṇe*, rendered necessary by the first alteration.

c. *kana*, *kanda*, that is to say, *krandan*. The form *dajjhai*=*dahyate* is explained in Hemacandra IV, 246. "Meditate, O Monk, have done with relaxation! Let not the attraction of desire make thy spirit stray. Do not make the folly to swallow a (red-hot) iron ball to groan afterwards and be burnt with the thought, "what a suffering!"

35 sija bhikhu ima nama[a] sita ti lahu bheṣiti
chetva raka ji doṣa ji tato nivana eṣiti[b] O

Cf. Dhammap., 369.

a. I have already pointed out this change of *v* into *m* in *nama*=*nāvaṁ* (A[4], 9).

b. I need not go back to *ji*=*yi*=*ca* (cf. A[3], 6, note *c*; B, 27, note *b*.). The third person *eṣiti* can be strictly defended if we admit that with the second half-verse the turn becomes general and indeterminate. To be brief, however, the second person of the Pâli is more natural.

36 krodhana akitaña i drohi ni[a]..
?mayiya cara bhikhu..................................śaśani[b] O

a. Of the traces at the end of the second pâda there remains too little to be restored with certainty. Nevertheless, the last letter but one appears to have been a *ja*. I suppose then that the pâda had ended in *jahi*.

b. This last verse may, I think, be re-established with much certainty. I translate, therefore, omitting the short gap of the third pâda : "Spurn the man of anger, the ungrateful, the hateful, the............ observe purity, O Monk, true to the teaching of the Buddha."

37 paja china paja jahi[a] paja utvari[b] bhavai
pajaṣagadhio[c] bhikhu ohatino ti vucati O

Cf. Dhammap., 370.

a. Above the *ja* of the second *paja* can be discerned a small stroke ; but it is short and thick, and does not appear to have been intended to mark aspiration.

b. I had occasion above to point out this transposition of *v* : *utvari*=*vuttari* (A[1], 5, note *a*).

c. Although I may have expressed before (l. 3) that I do not think it right to transcribe as *gh* the form of the letter read *ga*, which we have here, it is not the less singular that this form is met with again precisely in the same word, here and in l. 3, and that, in the two passages, the word (*ṣaga*) should have been written incorrectly with *ṣ* for *s* dental. It goes without saying that our compound is *saṅgādhiko* and that it well answers to the Pâli in sense,—" who is above the five bonds ",—though not in form.

38 savaśu namaruvasa yasa nathi mamaita
asata i na śoyati so hu bhikhu tu vucati[a] O

Cf. Dhammap., 367.

a. *Namaruvasa*, genitive for the locative, as frequently ; *hu=khalu* ; *tu* for *ti*, cf. v. 27 above.

39 alagito[a] ya vi carea dhamu datu śatu sañatu
[brammayari
saviṣu bhuteṣu nihai dana so bramano so[b]
[ṣamano so bhikhu O

Cf. Dhammap., 142.

a. Strictly, it is rather *alageto* that the manuscript has ; nevertheless, the vowel stroke appears to pass a little beyond the hook of *g*. It is, besides, very difficult, in most cases, to decide with certainty if the copyist wished to write *e* or *i* ; to judge of it by a host of examples would not attach to it any importance save a quite relative value.

b. The *o* is comprised in the upper hook of the *s*.

40 yo najakamo bh.v.ṣ. s.r(?)[a]..............................
bhikhu jahati o..............................viva udumareṣu[b]

Cf. Suttanipâta, 5.

a. There is no trace of the stroke of aspiration above *ja*. I am, I believe, sure of the reading *mo*. We have already met with several proofs of the tendency of this dialect to labialise the *a* into *u* after *m*. It quite seems that our manuscript must have had a reading wholly equivalent here to that of the Pâli. Meanwhile, it is impossible to restore *bhaveṣu saraṁ* ; the stroke of the vowel is wanting above the *v* ; as the *ṣ* which follows is certain, we are allowed to ask if it is not a gross error of the copyist.

b. Our text appears to have transposed the second and the fourth pâdas. It is all the more singular that the second half of the stanza forms, in this verse and those following, a sort of stereotyped cadence. I do not see what sense the comparison might have at the end of the verse, where it seems to have been transported from the second pâda. Be that as it may, we may, on the likeness of C^ro^, 1, 2, admit that it should be completed as *puṣ*[*u*]*viva u*°.

Here we come to a series of stanzas, which find their Pâli counterparts in the first chapter, *Uragasutta*, of the Suttanipâta. Unfortunately, the lines that are about to follow are still more fragmentary than these. Some fragments, several of which can be reconciled with certainty, enable us to fill up only a part of the gap; no line can be completed entirely. These restorations concern especially the end of verses, and this end is here uniform for all; what remains of the commencements is short and occasionally doubtful; lastly, although the threads along the margin may be preserved, the scraps which still adhere thereto in the principal leaf B, could not with certainty be re-instated in their proper places and with their respective intervals. In the circumstances, it will be understood that I have not been able to reunite in a decisive manner the beginnings and the ends of line.

It seems at least certain that the eight line-ends, as far as and including that which ends in the cipher on the margin, succeed one another without interruption. Above and below, the leaf is broken; some gaps are then, *a priori*, allowable; but, as to the lower gap, the visible tension of the thread on the left appears to exclude it. The cipher on the margin marks, besides, the end of a chapter; with the line that is prolonged, the last of our eight lines,—ends then the series of stanzas of uniform frame.

If now we looked at the beginnings, it would not appear that, between the line *yo upa*° and the line *yasa vana*°, there are missing more lines than one, viz., that of which the beginning *yo eca sari* is preserved by the Fragment B VI.

This being granted, the fragment B XIII, which fits in surely above the end of line 42, preserves the remainder of a previous stanza of the same structure. A line, then, is certainly dropped after the one which we number 40. Is one only dropped?

To consider the beginnings of line, gaps scarcely seem to be noticeable. If we fill up with a line (to each), we will have eight commencements as against eight ends, and all will appear to agree.

But the fragments A vi and A v, which hold together, apply with certainty to the ends of lines 42-45. It will be necessary then that the beginning *yo upat* should belong to verse 42. Now, if *vikaya* and *ṣaitha* correspond well, which I cannot doubt, to *vigayha* and *osadhehi* of the Suttanipâta, the commencements *yo upa*° and *yo mana*°, indisputably continued by Fr. B x, can only belong to ll. 43 and 44. This adjustment is, it will be seen, confirmed by the lines that follow.

It implies the omission not of one but of at least two verses. The fragments B iv and B iii, which make up the rest, should be joined to the commencement *yasavana*°. The uncertainty which the comparison with Pâli might raise on this last point and on the connection of the end of line *kapa*...with the commencement *yo necasari* of l. 48, does not appear to me to counterbalance the possibilities which I have pointed out. The real difficulty lies elsewhere.

The figure on the margin of l. 49 gives 40 as the number of the stanzas in this chapter. In our arrangement we should have 42. It is not probable that a figure marking the units should have been dropped. By supposing the loss of a single verse this contradiction can be partly reduced. It has been seen that verse 14 occurs twice. It might be said that our copyist has committed a very gross mistake and that the cipher was right. But the hypothesis of a gap of two verses does not support this explanation; for it must be 41. It only remains for us to take the cipher as a mistake. I understand how extreme this procedure is. But I have found no means as yet to avoid it. It is important, at all events, to remember that the agreement of Fr. B x with the commencement of lines 43-44, that of Fragments B vi and B xiv with the commencement of lines 45-47 and 48-50, and that of Fragments B xiii, A vi, A v, B ii, B v and B vii with the ends of lines 41-48 are equally unassailable.

I beg to be excused for having entered into such long details in connection with fragments which are very incoherent and of middling interest; but it should be the duty of an editor not to neglect them.

41 ....

..............[[1] orupa. urako jinav(i)va (t)vaya purana[a]]

[*Foot-note*: [1] Fr. B XIII.]

Cf. Suttan., 1 fg.

a. The first four letters that are readable can hardly be anything but *orapara*; but the *u* is quite visible at the foot of the second letter which has all the appearance of an *r*; the next one may be, though there is no certainty, the remainder of a *p*. As for the final *r*, it has left no trace in our fragment. The regular change of the final *m* of *jinam=jīrṇam* into *v* will be noticed in all these passages. It is the counterpart of *bhamana=bhāvana* (A[4], 9), *nama=nāvaṁ* (B, 35).

42 ....[[1]vikaya so bhikhu jahati] orapara urako[2] jinaviva tvaya [purana[a]

[*Foot-notes*: [1] Fr. A VI.
[2] Fr. B. XIII preserves the traces of the top of the letters *orapara ura*, whereby it agrees with Plate B.]

Cf. Suttan., 2.

a. I suppose that our *vikaya=vigayha, vigāhya*. The equation here is not constrained. At all events, this is the only serial verse of the Suttanipāta with which ours appears fit to be connected.

43 yo upat——[[3]ineti kodhu visara[a]]............[[4] ṣaitha[b]] [[5]so bhikhu jahati] orapara urako jinaviva [tvaya purana

[*Foot-notes*: [3] Fr. B X.
[4] Fr. A VI, and fr. A V, which are adjusted below bear traces of the lower parts of the characters *ṣaitha s. bh. kh.*
[5] Fr. A VI.]

Cf. Suttan., 1.

a. This last letter cannot be a *ṭ*, and has rather the appearance of an *r*, although the foot of the vertical line has not the hook which generally accompanies it. If such then is the true reading, it only remains to admit that the *r* is for the cerebral *ṭ*, *visara* for *visaṭa* = *visṛta*.

b. The reading *ṣaṭha* appears with certainty to result from joining the two fragments. The striking similarity which these characters have with (*o*)*sadhehi* of the Pâli and, at the same time, the difference which renders the interpretation thereof so doubtful, are misleading. If at least we had *ṣathai*, we could believe in a hardening of *dh* into *th*, and in a spelling *i*=*hi*. It is useless to risk conjectures for which we possess only too narrow a basis.

44 yo mana udavahi[a] a[[1]śeṣa bisa]............[[2]mahoho[b]
so bhikhu jahati] orapara urako jinaviva tvaya
[purana

[*Foot-notes :* [1] Fr. B x.
[2] Fr. A v.]

Cf. Suttan., 4.

a. Morris (*Journ. P. T. S.,* 1887, p. 136) was of opinion that it should be read *udabbahi* in Pâli, and derived the word from *ud-vṛh* " to extirpate." Our text can only favour this conjecture. It seems that the mistake in Pâli rests upon a false interpretation of a more corrupt Pârkrit which must have ordinarily weakened *dh* into *h*.

b. *Mahoho*=*mahogho,* just as we have *ohatino* in l. 37. I would have some difficulty to discern the first two characters without the comparison with the Suttanipāta.

45 yo taṣa [[3]udachai aśeṣa sa][a]............
[[4]so bhikhu jahiti o]rapara urako jinaviva tvaya
[purana[5]

[*Foot-notes* : [3] Fr. B VI.
[4] Fr. A V.
[5] Fr. B VII bears traces of the foot of the characters at this line-end, after *rako*.]

Cf. Suttan., 3.

a. I take *udachai*=*udachida*, with elision of the *d* (in Pâli itself we come across *khāyati*, *khāyita*) and an approximate orthography *ai* for *iya*, somewhat as we have *uvacai*=*upātyagāt*, *upaccagā*.

46 yo sa[[1] rvakeleśa dalaitha[a] na]............[[2]ku[b]
so bhikh][[3] u jahati orapara u][[4] rako jinaviva
[tvaya purana]

[*Foot-notes* : [1] Fr. B VI.
[2] Fr. B II.
[3] Fr. B V.
[4] Fr. B VII.]

a. The Suttanipāta does not furnish any counterpart to this verse. *Keleśa* is for *kileśa* ; *dalaitha* from *dālayati* : " He who has smashed all evil passions."

b. The consonant *k* is quite doubtful.

47 [[5] yo ecasari[a] na precasari sa][[6] rva]............
[[7] so bhikhu jahati orapara u][[8]rako jinaviva tvaya
[purana]

[*Foot-notes* : [5] Fr. B VI.
[6] Fr. B XIV.
[7] Fr. B V.
[8] Fr. B VII.]

a. The correction *neca*° seems absolutely necessary.

48 yo necasari na pre[1 casari sarva vi] [a] .... [2 ? p. [b]
so bhikhu jahati orapara ura][3 ko jinaviva tvaya
[purana]

[*Foot-notes*: [1] Fr. B XIV.
[2] Fr. B V.
[3] Fr. B VII.]

Cf. Suttan., 8-13.

a. The formula which constitutes the first pâda, here and in the preceding stanza, and which is reproduced in verses 8-14 of the Suttanipāta, is embarrassing. This time we have *neca*; as surely as we had *eca* in the previous line. In both cases we have *preca*, to be sure. This ill agrees with the Pâli text such as M. Fausböll's edition gives us. That text is in itself very doubtful and obscure. M. Fausböll analyses *na-ati-sarati*, *pratisarati*. According to this hypothesis, neither the long *ā*, which however is contrary to metre, nor the long *ī* which the metre demands, is explained. As regards the rendering "he who did not go too fast forward nor was left behind" (S. B. E, X², p. 2), it only affords, over and above the difficulties too evident to dwell upon, a very vague meaning, which hardly satisfies me. Unfortunately, it is more easy to criticize than to substitute a clear version for it. The persistence of the vowel *e*, and of the reading *preca* in our Ms., appears to me at least decisive against the reading of the Pâli. On the other hand, the persistence of the *n* in the Pâli, face to face with the divergences of our text, makes me inclined to admit for both the cases *necca*, so that the antithesis between *na eca* and *na preca* might be established, that is to say, *na etya na pretya*. But what is to be done with *sari*, for such is the spelling which the measure seems to require? *Sarin* occurs in Pâli in certain compositions, as *avaṁsarī* (*Suttanip.*, 685), to mean "he who guides himself, who takes his course towards." In *etyasarin* and *pretyasarin* I propose to see some expressions formed on this type and opposed to each other, to mean "he who is never on the way to come to this world or to leave it," in other words, "he who is freed from the round of rebirth and death."

b. The letter *p*, though cut off mid-way, seems certain; as regards that which precedes, it *might* be the remainder of a *p*. This reading *kapa*, at the end of the second pâda, would make us think of verse 16 of the Suttanipāta, of which the second pâda finishes with *netukappā*; it is true that the first pâda does not contain the formula *yo neccasarī*, etc. This is still one of the reasons that leave some doubt in me about the precision of agreement which I have attempted to show between the beginnings and the ends of lines. It is in some measure aggravated by the circumstance that the beginning of our line 50 appears to agree with the first pâda of verse 16 of the Suttanipāta, so that if the two adjustments were justified, it is to the commencement of line 50 that it would be suitable to join the present line-end. I have pointed out the difficulties with which a similar adjustment would be confronted; it would render impossible the combinations proposed for the preceding lines, several of which appear surer and more convincing than this one. Besides the uncertainty lurking in the reading *kapa* and the possibility, quite open, of variations between our text and the Pâli version, it will be seen that the identification of our l. 50 with the Pâli beginning of stanza 16 is far from clear.

49 yasa anośea na [[1] sati keyi o] [a] ....

.... [[2] urako jina] ...... [[3] tvaya purana]

On the margin: 40.

[*Foot-notes*: [1] Fr. B XIV.
[2] Fr. B XI.
[3] Fr. B VII.]

Cf. Suttanip., 14.

a. *Anośea*, for *anuśea*, affords again a particular spelling, *ea*=*aya*. We see by the initial *o*, which is certain, that our redaction was deviating from the Pâli.

50 yasa vanaśia[a] na [[1] sati keyi]........................[[2] śala[b]
so bhikhu jahati orap][[3]ara urako jinaviva tva]
..........u....... [c] O

[*Foot-notes*: [1] Fr. B XIV.
[2] Fr. B IV.
[3] Fr. B III.]

Cf. Suttan., 16:

yassa vanathajā na santi keci

and Suttan., 17:

..............(anīgho tiṇṇakathaṁkato) visallo.....

a. It is natural to think that the commencement corresponds well to the first pâda of the Pâli[4], and *vanadhia* = *vanathajâ* should have nothing surprising in such cases, where the *j* is more than once eliminated between two vowels; *ś* for *th* would, on the other hand, have for its defence, the comparison of *śiśila* for *śithila*. The letter read *a* which follows, has a slightly abnormal aspect and the upper hook is much more rounded than ordinarily. If the fac-simile is compared, it may be ascertained that *vanaśia*, such as it is written, is not different from *vanadhia*. Perhaps the scribe had committed a mistake in the reading, which must necessarily have been reflected in his copy.

[*Foot-note*: [4] The fac-simile might make us believe that it must be read *yase vana*°; this would be a mistake. A very small piece of bark sticks above the *s*, and it is the shade that is reflected from it which, in photograph, appears as ink-mark.]

b. The character *vi* in half is still discerned before *śa*. Therefore, I can but little doubt that our two letters represent the end of the word *visallo* which occurs in the next verse of the Suttanipāta. If it is so, our text would represent, for the Pâli, a variant which must have more or less completely associated a pâda of verse 16 with a pâda, or part of a pâda, of verse 17. I have stated farther above (l. 40, note *b*) the motives which, in spite of this difficulty, and although the fragments B IV and B III may not be connected with the fr. B XIV by any external evidence, have persuaded me to tie up these diverse remains into a single stanza.

c. I like to remark, without attaching to the observation any more certainty than is proper, that fr. B III seems to agree quite conveniently with the little that remains of this line in the principal leaf. I have already said farther above (l. 40, note *b*) why the figure 40, which marks certainly the end of a chapter and the number of verses it contains, appears inaccurate. It is, I am of opinion, 41 or 42 that ought to have been written, and the margin is so little affected that I dare not venture to admit that the index of these units was eaten away.

51 ....

....o. vanas . . . ru [a]

a. I can make nothing out of what remains of the last pâda. I regret all the more that the tail of the *s*, which is clearly recognizable, is traversed by a semicircular stroke, which undoubtedly formed with the auxiliary letter a compound, of which it might have been interesting to fix the value.

52 ....

..........................pasadha muto ban(d)hanam eva jayati [a]

Cf. Dhammap., 344: yo nibbanatho [1] vanâdhimutto, etc.

[*Foot-note:* [1] This is Childers' correction, *J. R. As. Soc.*, n. s. V, p. 226.]

a. We have already met with, and will come across several times as we proceed, the *n* surmounted by the stroke of aspiration to express *ndh* of Sanskrit. I do not here decide what exact pronunciation this orthography corresponds to. The reading *jayati* appears very certain. We cannot think of *javati*, written by *y* for *v*, since the first syllable would be short. I can only see in it the equivalent of the Pâli *yāyati* which I find, for example, in *Mahāvagga*, v, 9, 4, and which I interpret as a term derived by extension from *yāti*. The *j* is for *y*, just as we have often in this manuscript the inverse, *y* for *j*.

53 ....

....yi nivana[a] bhodha bhichave ○

a. *Nivana*=*nirvanā*. This word connects this stanza well with the preceding one. *Niḥ-vana*, "without concupiscence," is the synonym of *nibbanatha* of the Pâli in the previous verse. "O monks, liberate yourselves from concupiscence!"

54 ....

....? cheravayo ? . tara[a]

a. These few characters do not suggest to me any plausible restoration. We must wait for the discovery of the Pâli counterpart.

Fragments of B.

I have collected under this head twenty-seven fragments in all. I transcribe here only those which contain at least some certain letters. Although the most important ones already figure above in the partial reconstruction of lines 41 fg., I think I ought, in order to be clearer, to reproduce them here separately.

I. A few remnants of four lines; there is no pâda-end to furnish even a rough indication of the place which the remaining words, more or less visible, occupy in the stanza, and out of which I regret not to be able to draw anything satisfactory.

..........................ta[a] dhamidati ña(t)va..........................

..........................ruakamanaipracea u..........................

..........................vinavanaukavaihadu..........................

..........................????ga(?)ti ?..........................

a. This letter is doubtful; I dare not decide if the trace which appears at the top, on the right, belongs to it or goes with the preceding letter which has disappeared. I need not repeat that for want of an intelligible context all the *t*'s or *d*'s may be taken, one for the other.

II. Cf. line 46.

..........ku so bhikh..........

III. Cf. line 50.

..........ra urako jinaviva tv..........

IV. Cf. line 50.

..........viśala so bhikhu jahati orap..........

V. Cf. lines 46-48.

.... ??u..........

..........bh. .u jahati orapara ur..........

..........o bhikhu jahati orapara ur..........

..........[ka ?]pa s . bhikhu jahati orapara urak..........

VI. Cf. lines 45-47.

. . . . . udachai aśeṣa sa ?..........

. . . rvakeleśa dalaitha na..........

yo ecasari na precasari sa..........

VII. Cf. lines 45-49.

..........?ko ? ? ? ? (t)v-u..........

..........rako jinaviva tvaya purana

..........rako jinaviva tvaya purana

..........ko jinaviva tvaya purana

..........tvaya purana

VIII. Cf. above, lines 16-18.

..........yasa jana ca praña ya so ho (ni)r(va)[a] ....
..........idriagoti satuṭhi pratimukhe i[b] ....
..........paḍisa ? ra ? tisa ayarak[c] ....

IX.

..........gamagasa..........

X. Cf. lines 43-44.

..........ineti kodhu visara..........
..........aśeṣa bisa..........

XI. Cf. line 49.

..........urako jina..........

XII.

..........sañoya..........

XIII. Cf. above, lines 41-42.

..........orup(?). urako jinaviva tva ????
..........orapara u..........

XIV. Cf. lines 47-50.

..........sarva..........
..........casari sarva vi ....
..........sati keyi o..........
..........sati keyi..........

XV.

..........visa?..........

C[ro]

1 .... [[1] yamaloka ji] ita[a] sadevaka
ko dhamapada sud.śita kuśala puṣaviva payeṣiti

[*Foot-note*: [1] Fr. C vi.]

Cf. Dhammap., 44.

a. *Ita*, that is to say, *etaṁ*: the world of Yama and the world of the Devas. *Eta*, as used here, is preferable to *imaṁ* of the Pâli, which is not happily associated with *paṭhaviṁ*. The change of *puṣpa* into *puṣa* is to be noticed. For the sandhi *puṣaviva*, cf. *jinaviva* of verses B, 40 fg., and for *payeṣiti* compare *vihaṣisi* (B, 19), etc.

2 budhu pradha[a]..........ṣiti yamaloka ji eta sadevaka
budhu dhamapada sudeśita kuśala puṣaviva[b]
[payeṣiti ○

Cf. Dhammap., 45.

a. It is certainly to this line and to the next that the commencements belong which, in the present condition of the leaf, appear lower on the right. The spelling *pradha*[*vi*] = *pṛthivi* is to be noticed.

b. I dare not affirm if it ought to be read *puṣaviva* or *puṣuviva*. Meanwhile, I incline to the belief that the scribe had the intention to efface the *u* which he had at first traced. I incline thereto all the more, as in the same word in the preceding line, a somewhat miscarried intention to write *ṣu* seems also to be discovered.

3 yadha saga?uḍasa[a] ujhitasa mahapathi
padumu tatra jaea suyigan(d)ha manoramu ○

Cf. Dhammap., 58.

a. To complete, *sagarauḍasa* = *saṅkārakūṭe*, with elision of the medial *k*. For the equivalence of *saṅkāra-kūṭa* and *saṅkāradhāna*, cf. Childers s.v. *saṅkāro*. The genitive here performs the function of locative. The stroke of aspiration is well visible on the top of the *j* of *ujhita* and of the *n* of *gandha*.

4 .. saghadhadhamaa andhah.te prudhijane[a]
abhi.o.ti[1] prañai samesabudhaṣavaka[b]

[*Foot-note*: [1] In every part of the line, Fr. VII helps us to complete the characters, the lower portions of which it has preserved in part. The initial *a* of the third pâda is wholly preserved there also.]

Cf. Dhammap., 59.

a. The reading *sagadhadhamaa* appears to me certain, except the last letter which might be *e* or *i*; the lower part is not visible. The word remains difficult. I can only get out of the trouble by admitting that the scribe has, through mistake, written *saghadha* for *sagara*=*saṅkāra*. This is what follows from a comparison with the previous verse. *Saghara* =*saṁkhāra* would, in itself, not be inexplicable. Cf., however, line 14. As regards the second part, it only remains for me to take *dhamae*=*dharme*, just as we have in the inscription of Takht i Bahi *śatatimae*, etc. The expression "which is in the condition of dunghill," "which is like the dunghill" can be justified. It seems that the reading is almost *hote*, which should be=*bhūte*. If it is not certain, it is at least highly probable. The transcription *prudhi*=*pṛthak* is remarkable.

b. The *bh* appears certain; *abhirocati* may very well be used=*atirocati*. *Same*=*samya*[*k*] is the usual orthography in our manuscript.

5 [[2]..ga 15]

[*Foot-note*: [2] Fr. C VII.]

6 yo .[[3] hasa sahasani sagami[a] manuṣa jini
eka ji]..........................atmana so ho sagamu[b] utamu ○

[*Foot-note*: [3] Fr. C VII.]

Cf. Dhammap., 103.

a. The *g* of *sagami* has once more the form which one might, had it appeared only here, be tempted to interpret as=*gr*. To be right nearer the Pâli, it should be admitted that °*sahasani* is an inversion for °*sahasina*. But the variant *sahassaṁ sahassāni* "thousand thousands" is at least as plausible as the other expression.

b. I am not at all convinced that the Pâli reading *saṅgāmajuttamo* may be something else than the result of a confusion of writing, skilfully arranged. At all events, there is nothing to look for in our text but the nominative *saṅgrāma uttamaḥ*.

7 saha[[1]sa bi ya gaśana[a] anathapa][[2]..................
e]..................ṣebha[b] ya ṣutva uvaśamati

[*Foot-notes:* [1] Fr. C VII.
[2] Fr. C XI.]

Cf. Dhammap., 100.

a. I should not dare, on the appearance of the character alone, to decide positively if it must be read *śa* or *ya*. But in several cases we find *ś* for *th*, for instance, in *śiśila*, C[vo], 32 (C, 30 ?).

b. The character which I read *bh* is again the same as before.

8 ....[[3]śata bhaṣe anathapadasahita[a]]
e..................ṣ.hu ya ṣutva uvaśamati

[*Foot-note:* [3] Fr. C XI.]

Cf. Dhammap., 102.

a. Although there is nothing left but a faint part of the characters, the agreement of the main leaf puts the restoration of the verse beyond doubt. As regards the gaps, it is less certain that they can be filled up almost exactly from the Pâli; for in that case the present verse will be repeated, without variation, together with line 10. It is probable that some differentiation of detail may have been intended, sufficient to justify, in the not very scrupulous judgment of the Buddhists, the repetition of the stanza in two formulae very much bordering on each other.

9 ....sa bi ya gadhana anathapadasahita
eka gadhapada ṣeho ya ṣutva uvasamati O

Cf. Dhammap., 101.

10 . ja gadhaśata bhaṣe[1] anathapadasahita
eka gadhapada ṣeho ya ṣutva uvaśamati O

[*Foot-note*: [1] These first letters are partly completed by the lower portions in Fr.C IX.]

Cf. Dhammap., 102. Cf. line 8 above.

11 [[2]masamasi sahasina yo yaca] śatena ca[a]
nevi[b] budhi prasadasa kala aveti ṣoḍaśa O

[*Foot-note*: [2] Fr. C IX.]

a. This verse and the next are cast in the same mould, the elements of which we recover, disjointed and loosely differentiated, in verses 106: *mâse mâse sahassena yo yajetha sataṁsamaṁ*, and 70: *na so saṅkhāta-dhammānaṁ kalaṁ nagghati solasiṁ* of the Dhammapada. The equivalent of our six stanzas is found again exactly in the *Udānavarga*, translated by Rockhill, chap. xxiv, where it seems that the text must have been closely nearer ours. The first half-verse, however, is there translated: "Whoever performs month by month, a thousand sacrifices, for a hundred years", which corresponds exactly to the Pâli text. I understand our reading *sahasena śatena ca* in the sense which the text, by multiplying the ciphers, imposes upon the indefinite or infinite number of sacrifices.

b. In the verses following we have *neva* which is the only correct form, because, whether *neva* or *navi*, it must be = *nāpi*. "He who would, month by month, offer sacrifices by hundreds and by thousands, does not earn a sixteenth part of the merit that procures faith in the Buddha."

12 [[1].samase sahasena yo yaea śatina ca
neva]..........prasa.sa kala aveti ṣoḍaśa[a] O

[*Foot-note:* [1] Fr. C VIII.]

a. It is evidently to be completed as [*dhama*]*prasadasa*, and this stanza corresponds to Udânav., xxiv, 27.

13 masamase sahasina yo yaea śatena ca
neva saghi prasadasa kala aveti ṣoḍaśa O

Cf. Udânav., xxiv, 28.

14 masamasi sahasena yo yaea śatena ca
neva saghasadhameṣu[a] kala aveti ṣoḍaśa O

a. This verse is to be compared with stanza 70 of the Dhammapada, which reads, according to the right correction of Childers: *saṁkhātadhammānaṁ*. Here the reading *saghata°* is excluded, and one can only hesitate between *saghadha* and *saghasa*; the last letter has suffered indeed. It seems very well, however, that the black point which still appears below, marks the end of the hook turned from left to right, which characterises the *s*. On the other hand, we have, in line 4, met with *saghadhadhama*, where the *dh* is as certain as difficult to explain, and I was in that case obliged, for want of something better, to take *dh* for *r* as a copying mistake. I do not see any other alternative than to suppose an error similarly here, *s* for *t*. If it could be read *dh*, this peculiar transformation of *t* into *dh* should at least have a counterpart in *samadha* of line 37 (16 ?) and, not to go so far, in *kusidha*=*kusīda* in line 17. At all events, in spite of their close exterior resèmblance, it is quite unlikely that the two qualificatives should be identical in both verses: the sense required by the context is, in the one case, as unfavourable as it is necessarily favourable in the other. It may be admitted here that the use of an oft-occurring expression like *sadhama* has inclined the scribe, hardly learned, to a mistake, so as to render him guilty of it. To this verse corresponds stanza 33 of the Udânavarga, of which the rendering "he who explains well the holy law" appears to reflect the expression *saṅkhyātadharma*.

15 masamase sahasena yo yae[[1]a śatena ca]

.................................?eṣu[a] kala aveti ṣoḍaśa ○

[*Foot-note:* [1] Fr. C XLII.]

a. The mutilated consonant to which is attached the *e* may be *t* or *r*. I know no means to decide between the two, any more than complete the line. The Udâna-varga has four stanzas, 29-32, which may strictly correspond to the spirit of this; yet, as the numbers 29-31 are composed on a unique formula, slightly differentiated in each case, which is in keeping with the turn of the next stanza, and as, on the other hand, the termination *eṣu* suffices to prove that our present verse was not imitated from the next, it is likely that it was to verse 32 of the Udânavarga that this formed a pendant.

16 masamase sahasena yo yaea śatena ca

ekapananuabisa[a] kala naveti ṣoḍaśa ○

a. As I have just said, this stanza forms a pendant to the idea expressed, with slight variations, in the stanzas 29-31 of the Udāna. *Ekapananuabisa* is indeed = *ekaprāṇānukampinaḥ*: "he does not acquire a sixteenth part of the merit that belongs to him who takes pity on a single living being."

17 ya ja vaṣaśata jivi kusidhu[a] hinaviyava

muhutu jivita ṣebha virya arahato driḍha[b] ○

Cf. Dhammap., 112.

a. For *kusidhu* = Pâli *kusīto*, Sk. *kusīda*, cf. l. 14 above, (note *a*).

b. We will find *driḍha* and *vriḍha* in C[vo]. ll. 32 and 34.

18 ya ji vaṣaśato jivi apaśu udakavaya[a]
muhuta jivita ṣebh.[b] paśato udakavaya○

Cf. Dhammap., 113.

a. B, 13 has already made us familiar with the orthography *udaka*=*udaya*. *Śato* and *apaśu* represent side by side the two equivalents *o* and *u* for the termination *aṁ*, so often ascertained in this Ms. *Ji* and *ja* are spellings entirely equivalent; it can be ascertained by our *ji* being in the place of *ja* in the two verses which contain them.

b. This is the character which I read *bh*.

19 ya ja vaṣaśata jiv. apaśu dhamu utamu
m.huta jivita .e.hu paśatu dhamu utamu

Cf. Dhammap., 115.

20 ya ja vaṣaśata jatu[a] agi pariyara vane
..................sa pi telena divaratra atadrito

21 [[1]eka ji bhavitatmana muhuta]viva p.a?[b]
sameva puyana ṣebha yaji vaṣaśata hotu[c] ○

[*Foot-note*: [1] Fr. C XXIX.]

Cf. Dhammap., 107.

a. The ślока of six pâdas of the Pâli appears in our manuscript under the form of a regular double śloka; the third and fourth pâdas develop the idea contained in the first two. I dare not propose anything to fill up the gap of three syllables. The reading *jatu* of our Ms. suggests instead a correction for the Pâli text, which appears to me to be certain. *Jantum* has only been explained as =*jantu*, a nominative, by some unacceptable devices. It is *jātu* that should be read in the Pâli, and understood here. The vowel has been omitted by the copyist in *pariyara* which must be *pariyari* or *pariyare*. "He who, for a hundred years, continually keeps up the sacred fire in forest, day and night unwearied,........ ...with oil ...."

b. I take *muhutaviva*=*muhutameva*. For the last letter, the head of an "*a*" is still recognisable; the copyist had no doubt written *puae* with elision of the *y*=*j*.

c. *Sameva*=*sāyeva*. *Hotu*=*hutaṁ* shows to what extent (though small) *o* and *u* are made equivalent easily in the eye of our scribe.

22 [[1]ya keja yaṭha[a] va ho. va lok..........................

....ti ahivadana ujukateṣu ṣiho

[*Foot-note* : [1] Fr. C IV.]

Cf. Dhammap., 108.

a. *Keja* and *yaṭha*=*kiji* and *yiṭha*; the scribe cares little for the vowels.

23 ~~~~~~~~~~~~~~~~~~~~~~~~~~~~~~~~~~~~ga 17

24 [[2]śilamatu suyisacho[a]] dhamaṭho sadhujivano atmano karako sadhu[b] ta jano kurati[c] priu○

[*Foot-note* : [2] Fr.C IV completed by fr. C II.]

Cf. Dhammap., 217.

a. As parallel to *śilamatu*, scil. *śīlamantaṁ* I recall *vatamata*, C, 37. The reading *suyisacho* seems to be well established by the agreement of the two fragments IV and II. *Suyi*=*śuci* is warranted by several examples; *sacho* can only be=*sacaṁ*, *satyaṁ*, but then it must be admitted that the aspirate is faulty. I do not see any other alternative. The compound *śucisatya*, although it is rendered well in French with a unique literalness "(he) who speaks the pure truth," is not, however, a current expression. *Sādhujīvana* : "of good life."

b. The resemblance with the Pâli is here only general. *Kāraka* appears to me used *absolutely*, as in the commentary of the Dhammapada, pp. 150-151; in co-ordinating *kārakaṁ* and *sādhuṁ* I mean "who is active and conscientious himself," that is to say, who does with zeal and conscience whatever concerns him.

c. The hook at the foot of the *r* not being exactly closed, as would suit to explain the *u*, I do not dare to affirm that the copyist may have wished to write *kuruti*, that is to say, *kurute*, though to me it may be very probable.

25 [[1]ṣadhu śilena sabano yaśabhohasamapitu][a]
yena yeneva vayati[b] tena teneva puyita ○

[*Foot-note* : [1]Fr. C II, the top of the letters for the second pâda being completed by the main leaf.]

Cf. Dhammap., 303.

a. *Ṣadhu*=*śrāddhaḥ*. I find no trace of *o* in the *ś* of *yaśa*. *Bhoha* is certain as far as the consonants are concerned. But it almost seems that the *h* is accompanied down on the left by a small hook expressing the vowel *u*. Must the scribe have written *yaśabhohu* for *yaśubhoha*? Besides, I take *bhoha*=*bhoga*, through an intermediate form *bhoya*, just as we have *ṣeho*=*śreyaḥ* and as we shall in the next line meet with *dhamiho*=*dhamiyo*, for *dhammiko*.

b. *Vayati* might strictly be explained after the analogy of *abhivuya*, B, 30, 31 as=the Pâli *bhajati*. But it is more natural to think that it is=*vrajati*, and I should rather believe that *bhajati* of the Pâli, which it is very difficult to interpret, has sprung, by an inverse confusion, from an original *vajati*.

26 [[1]yo natimahetu na parasa hetu pavani kamani samaya]rea[a]
na ichia............ [[2]samidhi atmano so śilava] panitu[b] dhammiho sia

[*Foot-note* : [1] Fr. C II.
[2] Fr. C XXXI. These are nothing but a few traces; they do not appear to me sufficient for the purpose of restoring these few words with certainty.]

Cf. Dhammap., 84.

a. The construction of our text with an initial *ya* is more natural than that of the Pâli. *Pavani kamani samayarea*=*pāpāni kammāni samācareyya* in Pâli.

b. *Panitu*, that is to say, *paṇḍitaḥ* replaces *paññavā* of the Pâli. For *dhammiho* cf. the note on the previous line.

27 [[3] sañatu sukati yati drugati yati asañatu
ma sa viśpaśa[a]]...

[*Foot-note* : [3] Fr. C I.]

a. "The man who dominates his passions comes to a happy future; he who does not, to an unhappy future. Let not the former trust............................" I translate as if it were *viśraśe*; but this is a mere hypothesis.

28 [[1]savutu pratimukhasa idrieṣu ca pajaṣu
pramuni anu]...

[*Foot-note*: [1] Fr. C I.]

The first two pâdas are to be compared with Suttanip. 340 : *Saṁvutto pātimokkhasmiṁ indriyesu ca pañcasu*; we may also compare Dhammap., 375 : *pātimokhe ca saṁvaro*. As for *pramuni*, we have already met with it in A [1], 3. "By restraining oneself according to the precepts and in respect of the five senses, one obtains......................"

29 ....[[2] v.s.t.
śudhasa suyi]............................?sa samajakavata[a] O

[*Foot-note* : [2]Fr. C I.]

a. Besides *śudhasa* and *suyi*, that is to say, perhaps *suyikamasa* (=*śucikarma*), I cannot make anything out of these fragments, the concluding part of which suggests to me no reasonable explanation. I expect a more faithful memory than mine to discover the Pâli reflex of it.

30 [[3] dhamu cari sucarita] [[4] ???carita cari dhamaẏari suh.] śeti asmi loki parasa yi O

[*Foot-notes* : [3] Fr. C XIII.
[4] Fr. C V.]

Cf. Dhammap., 169.

31 [[1] ah][[2] o nako va sagami cavadhi vatita śara[a] ativaka ti] .... [[3] druśilo hi bah]o jano O

[*Foot-notes* : [1] Fr. C XIII.
[2] Fr. C V.
[3] Fr. C XXII.]

Cf. Dhammap., 320.

a. The termination *dhi*, for *taḥ*, in *cavadhi* = *cāpātaḥ* would again afford an instance of the change of *t* into *dh*, if a direct transition could be admitted from *te* to *dhe*, *dhi*, with the Māgadhism *te* for *to*. I have nothing more convincing to suggest; this, however, does not mean that the explanation satisfies me.

32 [[4]. sa acata[a] druśilia malua vavi lata vani[b] kuya su tadha].[[5] tmana yadha na viṣamu[c] ichati O]

[*Foot-notes* : [4] Fr. C V.
[5] Fr. C XXII.]

Cf. Dhammap., 162.

a. I know few cases in our Ms. where it would be tempting to seek for an anusvâra under-written, more than in the *ca* of *acata*, so much accentuated is the hook at the foot. But that would be imprudent; if one compares *dhi* of *cavadhi* in the foregoing line, and *ca* of *carita* in the line preceding that, one will, I think, share this impression and conclude that the scribe, while at work, readily amused himself with making manifest the minute details of certain characters.

b. We see that in this pâda our text deviates from the Pâli version, and simply says: "He whose malignity is extreme like (*ivāpi*) [that of] the mālukā creeper in the forest"; and, in fact, a passage of the Lalitavistara (p. 259, l. 2) characterises this plant by the epithet *asukhedā*, without any other explanation; for my part, as I am ignorant of what exactly the plant in question is, I should not hope to elucidate the reasons for this vexatious name; the verse on p. 207, l. 5 appears to indicate that it is a parasite plant and that it destroys the tree to which it attaches itself. The turn of expression in our recension seems to me more simple and original. Whatever it may be, given the Sanskrit form *mālu*, I suppose that *mālua* is = *mālukā* and that the Pâli *māluvā* is only another spelling for *māluā*, formed on the basis of the Pâli rule which does away with *hiatus*.

c. *Kuya* = *kuryāt*. *Na* = *naṁ*, *nanu*. *Viṣama* has a sense, "vicious, wicked", more vague and less expressive than the *diso* (= *dviṣ*, "enemy") of the Pâli.

33 ....[[1] yok.ḍ.[a] bh] ....
.... a raṭhapina asañatu

[*Foot-note:* [1] Fr. C v.]

Cf. Dhammap., 308.

a. All that we can see from the commencement of verse is that in *guḍa* the *g* has been hardened into *k*, as is so often.

34 ....[[2]ga 10]

[*Foot note:* [2] Fr. C XLI.]

35 ida ja mi keca ida ji karia ida kari........
.... vinamana abhimadati muca?? saśoa[a]

a. I have not discovered the Pâli reflex of this stanza. What remains of it would, I suppose, give in Sanskrit *idañ ca me kṛtyaṁ idañ ca kāryaṁ idaṁ k* .... *vindamāno 'bhimardati mṛtyu.. saśokaṁ*; which, with the reservation of the necessary complements, can go back to a general sense like "by properly understanding one's duty, one crushes death and the pains of it."

36 ?dha vaṣa kariṣamu[a] ?dha h.matagi ....

Cf. Dhammap., 286.

a. It is not quite possible to decide if *kariṣamu* is, on the analogy of the Pâli, a first person singular with an inaccurate orthography (cf. *phuṣamu*, B, 25), or if it regularly represents the first person plural.

37 ta putrapaśusamadha[a] ....

Cf. Dhammap., 287.

a. I have pointed out *à propos* l. 14 this particular orthography *samadha* for *samata* = *sammatta*, and cited analogies.

38 puve i kica parijaga [[1]??——kici kicakali adea[a]
tata diśa parika][[2]ma kicakari no ; kicakici ali
adea]

[*Foot-notes* : [1] Fr. C XXVII.
[2] Fr. C XXX.]

a. Although the gap is comparatively small, I have not been able to find out the exact sense of this stanza. The gap before *kici* should, beyond doubt, be completed by *no i* as in the fourth pâda, the two having, I think, been identical, and hence I conclude that the last one ought to be read *no i kici kica[k]ali adea* which is transcribed : *na ca kiñcit kṛtyakāle adeyaṁ*, and may mean : "and in the hour of duty he should not recoil from any sacrifice." But I do not know exactly how to complete *parijaga*, which must go back to the verb *pari* or *pratijāgarati*.

By applying *purve* to the time preceding the hour of sacrifice, we may, however, understand: "it is indispensable (for him) to be awake to his duty" (cf. stanza 35), and we might complete (the word) as *parijagarea* or *parijagaritva*. The third pâda has quite perplexed me. As for *kicakari* it must be a verb; we might assume that it is hidden in *diśa* which stands for *diśe*, and that *tata* = *tatra* has, as occasionally in this manuscript, the sense of "in this world"; but the rendering "let the dutiful man teach in this world the preparation" would morally involve *parikarma* into a usage which appears to me little probable, and I think that the true analysis fails me. Here is what at all events would, according to these provisional hypotheses, be the general sense of the stanza: "He must at first be thoroughly convinced of his duty; for in the moment of performing it he must not shrink from any sacrifice; let the dutiful man teach in this world the preparation for it; for in the moment of performing the duty he must not shrink from any sacrifice."

39 ya puvi karaniani [[3]pacha ṣakaru ichati[a]
atha dubakati[b] balu] [[1]suhatu parihayati]

[*Foot-notes*: [3] Fr. C xxvii.
[1] Fr. C xxx.]

a. I admit that *ṣakara* is for *saṅkara*, just as we have pointed out *ṣaga* for *saṅga* in B. 3, 27, and I take the word to denote the trouble and tumult of the outer life contrasted with the tranquil duties of religious life.

b. The true analysis of *dubakati* fails me, I am afraid; if we take *kati* = *gati*, *duba* would be left, of which I cannot make out anything; so I am led to hold that *dubakati* = *duṣprakṛti*; and on the strength of the use of *pakatattā* to mean "regular observer of his duties" (*Jātaka*, I, 236; S. B. E. xvii, 340 n.), I understand it to mean: "who does not observe the rule or the duty." I should add that the letter which I transcribe *ka* might very well be interpreted = *śp*. But what to make out of *dubaśpati*? In short I translate: "He who, having once loved his duties, loves the tumult of the world, the fool, forgetful of the rule, loses happiness."

40 akita kuki. [[2]ṣehu[a] pacha tavati drukita
kita nu sukita ṣeh].[[3]ya kitva nanutapa(?)ti]

[*Foot-notes*: [2] Fr. C XXVII.
[3] Fr. C XXX.]

Cf. Dhammap., 314.

a. *Kukṛtaṁ* for *duṣkṛtaṁ* gives no difficulty. I cannot, on account of the break, affirm if it is exactly *ṣehu* and not *ṣeho* that our copyist has written.

Below this line we have some slight, but certain, traces of at least two lines: the top of a first letter, and the bottom of three or four. There is, of course, absolutely nothing to draw out of it.

41 asava teṣa vaḍhati ara te asavacha[(a)] ....

....

Cf. Dhammap., 253.

a. To complete, *asavachaya*, as in Pâli. We see that our recension has a plural (construction) instead of singular. Anyhow this half-verse can only end after a previous description of "those men," and in fact the Pâli half-verse forms the end of a stanza; in our manuscript it begins a line; whence it follows that either it formed the end of a *śloka* of six pâdas, or the thought, collected into a single stanza in the Pâli, filled here two (of the pâdas) which completed themselves.

42 yeṣa tu susamaradha nica kayakata sma ....

....

43 satana sabrayanana taṣa?[a] ....

Cf. Dhammap., 293.

a. This is to believe that we had, as in the Pâli, a stanza of six pâdas and that the third and the fourth pâdas were at least very analogous to those of the Pâli. Yet, in the sixth, the two texts differ, and I cannot make out anything certain from our *taṣa*, perhaps a mistake for *teṣa*. It will be observed that the orthography *satana* is=*smṛtānāṁ*, side by side with *smati*.

C[vo]

1 ?.?.? ra athu? .... ???

....

2 yo vi varṣaśata jivi[a] so vi mucuparayano
na bhaje pari ....

a. As can be seen from its commencement, the verse belongs to the series which we have had above (C[ro], 17 fg.); this series is, as we have seen, represented in the Pâli recension; but there the present stanza has no exact counterpart. The beginning of the third pâda would appear to stand comparison with the commencement of Dhammap. 78; yet the identity is the more doubtful, as our fifth letter, though mutilated, well appears to have been, not *ra* of *paraka*, but *ri*. *Mucuparayana*: compare, for instance, Suttanip., 578 (678?). " Should one live a hundred years, one would remain vowed to death......... ".

3 parijinam ida ruvu roaniḍa [[1]prabhaguno[a]
bhensiti [(b)] p.ti] ....

[*Foot-note*: [1]Fr. C XXXII.]

Cf. Dhammap., 148.

a. ....

b. The compound which I read *ṅs* has exactly the appearance of the character to which I have already been induced to attribute this value (A[2], 6, note *c*; B, 34, note, *b*). It might be thought proper here to analyse it into *ts*, the *t* being added below the buckle of the *s*; but this explanation, perhaps acceptable here, would not do in other instances; the transcription *bheṁsiti* = *bhetsyati* (that is to say, *bhetsyate*) can, on the contrary, be justified by this tendency of nasalisation before the sibilant, of which Pâli and the Prâkrits offer more than one trace. I should only like to recall an example here, *viz.*, *bhiṁsana* = *bhīṣaṇa*. Anyhow our text has the future as against the present of the Pâli. In the Pâli verse I have introduced the certain correction *maraṇantaṁ*, long since urged by Childers.

4 ko nu h ?[a] .... [[1]lite sati an.kar.? prachiti[b] pra] ....

[*Foot-note* : [1] Fr. C XXXIII.]

Cf. Dhammap., 146.

a. The sheet, torn in this place, is not exactly readjusted in the glass-case. This commencement is warranted by the fragment which contains a portion of what follows.

b. If the reading is not conclusive, it is at least certain that our text had a variant here. *Pra*, which begins the last pâda, seems to indicate that the termination was alike in the two parts. In all probability, we should have here had an equivalent of *andhakārena onaddhā*. *An(dh)akar* fits well, and *prachita* = *prakshipta* equally; only the termination *ti* is astonishing; it is also sure that we had something else than the termination °*kāre* or *kāraṁ*; besides the metre, the traces that exist below the line after the letter r demonstrate it. I have not arrived at any convincing restoration.

5 yam eva paḍhama rati gabhirasati manavo avi ṭhi[a] ....

a. The transcription in Sansksit: *yam eva prathamāṁ rātriṁ gambhīrasmṛtir māṇavaḥ api sthi-* , appears to suggest itself; it gives no component parts of a construction permitting of a glimpse into the general sense.

6 yasa rativivasina ayu aparato sia
apodake[a] ....

a. The gap, which extends too much, again renders the understanding of the remnants impossible here. I transcribe: *yasya rātrivivāsena āyur aparataṁ syāt alpodake.* But I know no instance of the use of *aparata,* and *aparānta* would not, as far as I can see, give any sense. The bottom of the initial letter is perhaps not completely intact; it is perhaps *u* which the manuscript originally had. Even with *uparata* we hardly see what the subject can be: "whose life stops with the dawn."

7 ye hu dhayeyu[a] dahara ye ca majhima puruṣa
anupa ? ....sa nica maranato bhayo[b] ○

a. The final *y* is joined to the following *d* in a cursive connection forming a ring, which marks perhaps an intention to denote *u*; anyhow it is necessary. *Dhayeyu* is the potential of *dhayati,* "to suck."

b. Cf. Suttanip., 576: *evaṁ jātānaṁ maccānaṁ niccaṁ maraṇato bhayaṁ.* I do not hope to fill up the gap, which does not this time hinder the understanding of the uniform sense. "Suckling infants or mature men..................(on all) always (hangs) the dread of death."

8 ?dha phalana pakana nica patanato..........................
....ya ayu payeti panina[a] ○

Cf. Suttanip., 576, and Dhammap., 195.

a. Our verse seems to be made up by patching together, though quite incoherently, a half of each of these stanzas. The final *u* of *aya,* however necessary it may be, is still more doubtful than that of *dhayeyu* in the preceding line; somewhat of the same method appears briefly indicated.

9 yadha nadi pravatia racha vahati ?[a] ....

....tavi oharanaseva satii Ↄ

a. What we see more clearly here is that the verse is inspired by the same spirit as verse 18, chapter I of the Udānavarga: " Like the waters of a stream, the hours of man's life lapse day and night; gradually it runs to its end." I am not sure of the reading *racha* or *vacha*; anyhow I can only see in it a reflex of *vṛkṣa*, whether for *vracha* or for *rukkha*. *Pravatia* = *pravarteya*. Lastly, I take *ohārana*, not on the strength of any instances, for they fail me, but on the strength of the etymology and the evidence of the Abhidhānappadīpikā, in the sense of " suppression, end." " As a river beginning to flow, carries away the trees ..... towards its terminus."

10 yadhavidanivikoti yayedevaoduopati

apakabhotivo...

11 emam eva manuś..............................s(?).ti(?) pranayo

yaya avi?sati(?)rati(?) maranaseva satii

I regret not to be able to draw any continued sense from these two remnants of verse. The uncertainty weighing upon many readings gets complicated with the lacunae. Having nothing probable to suggest for the first two pâdas of the first stanza, nor for the second and third pâdas of the second, I prefer not to multiply conjectures, which the discovery of a Sanskrit or Pâli counterpart will, some day, render superfluous.

12 sati[a] eki na diśati pratu diṭho bahojano

pratu eki na diśati sati diṭha bahojano O

Cf. Jâtaka, IV, 127, st. 6 (Dasarathajâtaka).

a. I do not know how to explain our form *sati* or *sadi* = *sāyaṁ*; *sai* would do well; but this intercalary dental is, at least, highly exceptional. I do not, however, see how there can be any doubt on the equation.

13 tatra ko viśpaśi macu daharo dhitijivit.[a]
..........................?vi miyati nara nari ca ekada[b]○

a. *Tatra*, that is to say, "in this world." As *viśpaśi* requires a complement, I suppose it is necessary to read *dhitijivite*, of which in fact I believe I recognise the traces; and I take *dhitijivita*, that is to say, *dhṛtijīvitaṁ* somewhat in the sense which would require *jīvitadhṛti*, "the solidity, the duration of life." *Macu*=*martyaḥ*.

b. I consider *vi* to be the second syllable of *sarvi*=*sarve*, of which the first letter appears still sufficiently recognisable. Before it, either *manuśa* or some equivalent is dropped. Above the *ca* appears a sort of ring, like the *i* of the Devanâgari alphabet. I perceive neither the utility nor the possible signification of it. "What mortal, however young, could in this world rely on the duration of life? All (mankind), men or women, are destined to die one day."

14 ayirena vatai kayu paḍha.......................... [[1]ṣiti ruchu[a]]..........................viñana niratha ba kaḍigaru○

[*Foot-note*: [1] Fr. C XLI[VO].]

Cf. Dhammap., 41.

a. *Rucho*, Pâli *rukkho* "rough, rude," may very well take, in our text, the place of the Pâli *chuddho*, "vile, despicable." Our text appears also, in the compound *apetaviññāno*, to have replaced *apeta* by some synonym. We discover in fact a character besides, and none of the letter-heads standing apparent carry the vowel stroke *e*.

15 .... [[2]avathani a . . u ? ? ? ? ?[a]
..........................] [[3]ni śiṣani tani diṣṭani ka] rati[b]○

16 [[4]yanimani prabhaguni vichitani diśodiśa[c (b?)] kavotaka].[[5]aṭhini tani diṣṭani ka] rati ○

[*Foot-notes*: [2] Fr. C XIV.
[3] Fr. C XXII[VO].
[4] Fr. C XIV.
[5] Fr. C XXII[VO].]

Cf. Dhammap., 149.

a. I have brought together these two stanzas, a half-verse from each of which makes up a whole stanza in Pâli. This line, I am indeed of opinion, can be confidently restored: [*yanimani*] *avathani alapuni va sarade*; none of the traces that remain contradict this hypothesis.

b. I have no means to re-establish the first syllables of this line; the result is that the interpretation of what remains visible, *ni śiṣani*, remains uncertain. The last pâda of the two lines has *tani diṣṭani* as opposed to *tāni disvāna* of the Pâli. The reading does not seem to be contestable, although the *ṭ* affects a form which is purely conventional. It would seem rather derived from the dental *t*. The construction is therefore less normal, but not unacceptable in this form.

c. *Prabhaṁguni* (written in the same character as *prabhaguna* of the next line) implies a base *prabhaṅgu*, identical in meaning with *prabhaṅga*, which has given, in Pâli and in our dialect, *prabhaṅguna*. The verse that follows confirms this form. *Vichitani*=*vikshiptāni*.

17 [[1] imina putikaena aturena pabhaguna
nicaśuhavijinena jaradhamena s]..........
. . dha parama śodhi yokachemu anutara [a] ○

[*Foot-note*: [1] Fr. C xiv.]

. This verse may be compared with stanza 321 of the Theragāthā, which, though not identical, is analogous in sense and quite similar in structure, and to which more precisely corresponds our line 20 :

ajaraṁ jīramānena tappamānena nibbutiṁ
nimmissaṁ paramaṁ santiṁ yogakkhemam anuttaraṁ.

Certainly we have not in our manuscript the first person form *nimmissaṁ*; but as the third letter *dha* is certain, as an *m* (perhaps *me* ?) appears also certain immediately before, and as an *i* accompanied the preceding consonant, *nimadha* or *nimedha* would appear probable; it is assured by line 20; it will be rendered "make." I understand *nicaśuhavijinena=nityāśubhavicīrṇṇena*, "ever full of impurities." I translate therefore: "With this body, which is nothing but a rottenness, which is diseased, doomed to destruction, incessantly full of impurities, subject to decrepitude, ..., obtain perfect purity, the supreme bliss."

18 [[1]imina putikaena vidvarena..
[[2](nicaśuhavijinena)]..
..........dha parama śodhi yokachemu anutara ○

[*Foot-notes*: [1] Fr. C XIII.
[2] Fr. C XIV.]

19 [[3]imina putikaena viśravatena putina[b]
nica][[4]śuhavijinena jaradha]..
-[[5]medha parama śodhi yokachem.] anutara[a]

[*Foot-notes*: [3] Fr. C XXI.
[4] Fr. C I.
[5] Fr. C XL.]

a. These fragments enable us to recognise that the two stanzas were generally cast in the same formula as verse 17.

b. *Viśravatena, viśravantena,* from *vi-sru* "flowing, being decomposed." *Pūti*, adjective.

20 [[6]ayara] jiyamanena ḍajhamanena nivruti[a]
nimedha[b]] [[7]parama sodhi yokachemu anutara]

[*Foot-notes*: [6] Fr. C I.
[7] Fr. C XXVI.]

a. I refer back to the verse of the Theragāthā which I have cited with reference to line 17.

b. For *nimedha*, cf. l. 17. "With this [body] doomed to decrepitude, to suffering, obtain the undiminishing joy, the perfect purity, the supreme bliss."

21 [[1]jiyati hi rayaradha sucitra[a] adha śarira bi jara [uveti
na ta tu dharma ca ja][[2]ra (u)veti[b]] .... kaO

[*Foot-notes:* [1] Fr. C I.
[2] Fr. C XXVI.]

a. *Jīyati=jiryate.*

b. The *n* which begins the third pâda is of a somewhat peculiar form; I do not, however, see any other possible reading. I will say the same about the character which follows *dharma*, and which I transcribe as *ca*. Perhaps the verse-end would have explained the present tense here. I understand the verse thus:- "The royal chariot, inspite of all its splendour, comes to destruction; similarly destruction invades the body; but destruction never invades this Law ...."

22 [[3]muj. p.rat. muj][[4]u pachatu majhatu muju[a] bhavasa parako
sarvatra vi ....](na punu jatijaravuvehisi)[b]

[*Foot-notes:* [3] Fr. C I. For this beginning of line this fragment has preserved but few traces of heads of letters. I believe, however, that in the light of the Pâli and on the analogy of what follows, the letters, such as I have transcribed, may be restored with certainty.
[4] Fr. C II.]

Cf. Dhammap., 348.

a. The spelling *muju* corresponds not to the imperative *muñca* which the Pâli has, but to the present participle *muñcan*, which is so suitable to the construction.

b. I have enclosed the last pâda in parenthesis; the traces that remain of it, permit, in the light of the Pâli version, of an interpretation as I have given. But evidently I cannot vouch for the several details.

23 ....ga 25]

24 [[1]aroga parama labha satuṭhi parama dhana vaśpaśa[a] parama mitra] nivana paramo suha

[*Foot-note :* [1] Fr. C II.]

Cf. Dhammap., 204.

a. In *vaśpaśa* instead of *vi*°, we have a clear instance of negligence of vowel-notation. I believe that the word really contains two vowels and that it should be *viśpaśo*. I take *ārogya, santuṭṭhi* and *vissāsa* not as members of compound, but as nominatives, and I believe that the Pâli should have *ārogyaṁ* and *vissāso* exactly as it has *nibbānaṁ*.

25 ....[[2]saghara parama duha eta ñatva ya]dhabh.tu nivana paramo suha[a] O

[*Foot-note :* [2]Fr. C II.]

Cf. Dhammap., 203.

a. In the Pâli we must choose between *jighacchāparamā rogā* with *saṁkhāraparamā dukhā* and *saṁkhārā paramā dukhā* with *jighacchā paramo rogo*.

26 ....

........................matrasuha dhiro sabaśu vi . la suha[a] O

Cf. Dhammap., 290.

a. *Sabaśu=sampaśyan*, with the usual softening of the tenues into sonant after the nasal. The missing letter cannot be *pu* ; on the other hand, as *vi* and *la* appear certain, it is most probably *vu* which we must read, *vivula* for *vipula*.

27 .... u . eṣu anusua
(usu)eṣu manuśeṣu viharamu anusua O

Cf. Dhammap., 199.

28 suhai vata jivamu viraneṣu averana
[[1] veraneṣu ma]nuśeṣu viharamu averana O

[*Foot-note :* [1] Fr. C XXIV.]

Cf. Dhammap., 197.

a. *Suhai=sukhāya*, that is to say, "for happiness, in happiness." It quite seems that our copyist, who writes *verana* everywhere, may have had the impression of an adjective *verana* and not of *verina* derived from *verin, vairin,* which is reflected in *averino* of the Pâli. The locative *verinesu* of the Pâli is indeed difficult enough. I would readily incline to allow an adjective *averana* as the original reading ; perhaps it is not as improbable as it appears at first, if, to start with, the negative *averana* is taken as formed from a substantive *verana, vairaṇa,* which might be explained as=*vaira* ; the adjective *kiñcano* of the next verse would support this interpretation.

29 suhai .... jivamu kijaneṣu akijana[a]
kijaneṣu ma . u . . u . haramu akijana O

a. In interpreting Dhammap., 200, which partially corresponds to this verse and the next, Childers (*Dict.*, s. v.) hesitated on the translation of *kiñcana.* Was the word composed by means of the technical substantive *kiñcana* which comprises the triple category *rāga, dosa, moha* ? It seems that the *dedoublement* of the stanza in our text indicates that the two possible ideas floated alike in traditional thought and were afterwards detatched each into a particular strophe. Whatever it may be, the adjective *kiñcana* can, I think, be only explained, even as I have proposed to do in the case of *verano,* as derived from the negative *akiñcana*. In the present case, the necessity for this periphrasis appears to me quite striking.

30 suhai vata jivamu yeṣa mu nathi kajani[(a?)]
kijaneṣu manuśeṣu viharamu akijana

Cf. Dhammap., 200.

a. The form *mu*, *mo*=*naḥ* is known, for instance, in the language of the Mahâvastu. *Kajani* is a mistake of the copyist, for *kijana*.

31 na ta driḍha ban(d)hanam aha dhira ya asa daruva [babaka va[a]
saratacita manikunaleṣu[b] putreṣu dareṣu ya ya [aveha

Cf. Dhammap., 345.

a. I do not decide if the original reading was *āhu dhīra* or *āha dhīro*. The metre proves that the error of the copyist does not consist in a simple inversion *yaasa*, for *ayasa*, but, as the Pâli text indicates, in the omission of the second *ya*, *ya asa* for *ya ayasa*. The first word being an adjective, I take *daruva* =*dāruvaṁ*, for *dāruyaṁ*, *dārujaṁ* and not for *dāru* followed by *vā*. It is curious that in the next word *babaka* we find, inversely, the hardening of *j* into *k*.

b. The reading *saṁrattacittā* is certainly preferable to the Pâli *sārattarattā* which is tolerably obscure. *Kunala*, that is to say, *kuṇḍala*.

32 eta driḍha ban(d)hanam aha dhira oharina śiśila [drupamuchu[a]
eta bi chitvana parivrayati anavehino kamasuhu [prahai

Cf. Dhammap., 346.

a. I have already pointed out the substitution of *ś* for a *th* etymological ; the last letter might perhaps be strictly read *ju* instead of *chu*. Yet the transcription which I give is to me by far the most probable. The memory of words like *mokṣa* may have facilitated the mistake.

33 ye rakarata anuvatati[a] sotu saigata..........................
eta b. ch.tvana parivrayati anavehino kamasuha
[prahai

Cf. Dhammap., 347.

a. But for the Pâli text, I would not have hesitated to take it for *anuvartanti* instead of *anupatanti*. The second expression appears to me so little natural that I have to ask if *anupatanti* is not the result of an artificial restoration made on a text, oral or written, which had *anuvata(ṁ)ti*, like our own.

34 ahivadanaśilisa nica vridhavayarino[a]
catvari tasa vardhati ayo kirta[b] suha bala○

Cf. Dhammap., 109.

a. The scribe has made a confusion between *apacâyin* and *upacârin*. He ought to have written either *vriḍho-vayarino* or *vriḍhavayayino*. A comparison with Pâli turns the balance in favour of the second form.

b. It should be *kirti*, *kīrtti*.

35 d.l.bh.p.r.ṣ.?..........................
..........................yati viru ta kulu suhu modati[a]○

Cf. Dhammap., 193.

a. Mahâvastu, III, 109, 5, where this verse is repeated, has *vīra* like our Ms., which appears to me indeed preferable. On the other hand, the repetition agrees with the Pâli text and with the metre so as to condemn our *sukhaṁ modati*, which is nothing but a *lectio facilior* introduced through the unconstraint of our scribe or his predecessor, the meaning of which, however, is hardly satisfactory.

36 [[1]?????? ya narethina[a] v.].[[2] .u.
suha śichi]tasavasa kici teṣa na vijati[b]○

[*Foot-notes*: [1] Fr. C IX.
[2] Fr. C XVI.]

a. I take *narethina* = *naritthīnaṁ*, "of men and women."

b. Of course it should be understood in Pâli as *sukho sikkhitasaṁvāso.* The last pâda is less clear in sense than in form. I take it as equivalent to *te* (that is to say, the *sikkhitas*)) *akiñcanā bhonti*, and I render: ". . The association with learned men is a blessing; they have no stain."

37 [[3]suha darśana ariana sa][[4]vaso vi sada suho[a]
adaśanena] balana nicam eva suhi sia ○

[*Foot-notes*: [3] Fr. C IX.
[4] Fr. C XVI.]

Cf. Dhammap., 206.

a. The only variant of our stanza, noticeable from a comparison with the Pâli, is *savaso pi* for *sannivāso*; the sense is equivalent, and the addition *pi* marks the gradation, *darśana*, from accidental connection, in the corporation of life.

38 [[1].lasagatacariu drigham adhvana śoyiṣu[a]
dukha balehi] .vasu amitrehi va savrasi[b]○

[*Foot-note*: [1] Fr. C XVI.]

Cf. Dhammap., 207.

a. Here we have the plural instead of the singular of the Pâli. I take *śoyiṣu* as a common aorist which amounts to the sense of the present tense. The omission must naturally be supplied as *bala*°; it is °*carino* or °*carinu* that we expect to have. I do not see any way to do away with the hypothesis of a mistake by the copyist. It seems to me that the simplest correction would be to admit that the copyist has written *u* for *i*, the two characters differing only in the elongation, on the right of the vertical stroke, of the extremity of the lower hook; °*cari i* would be = *cūrī* (for *cārıṇo*) *ca*. In *sagata* the form of the *g* will be noticed; ....

b. *Savrasi* can only correspond exactly to *sabbadā* if we admit a double irregularity, a Mâgadhism and the substitution of *s* for *ś*, so as to get a form *sarvaśo*. To my mind it is much more probable that the scribe is mistaken and has read *savrasi* for *savradhi* (*sabbadhi* in Pâli), *s* and *dh* differing in this manuscript only in the direction of the lower hook.

39 ....[a] [[2] suhasavasa ñatihi va samakamo[b]
dh][[3]ira hi prañai] bhayeya panito dhorekaśila
[vatamata aria[c]

[*Foot-notes*: [2] Fr. C XXXVI.
[3] Fr. C XXXV.]

40 [[1] tadiśa sapuruṣa sumedha bhay ... [[2] nachatra-
[patha va cadrimu○
ra]dhe arovacamasa parikica uvahana[d]

[*Foot-notes*: [1] Fr. C XX.
[2] Fr. C XXXV.]

41 ....[[3] jahati kamana tada sa majati] [[4] s.h.
sarva ca suhu] ichia sarvakama paricai ○

[*Foot-notes*: [3] Fr. C XX.
[4] Fr. C XXXV.]

Cf. Dhammap., 207, 208.

a. We see that in these three lines the verses overlap one another. Inspite of the punctuation at the end of l. 38, the first two pâdas of l. 39 of this manuscript belong, like verse 207 of the Dhammapada, to the preceding stanza, which is thus made up of six pâdas. The metrical difference between the commencement of the line and the following does not leave any doubt in this respect. The comparison with Dhammap.,

208 agrees with the punctuation that follows *cadrimu*, so as to prove that with this word ends a new stanza in the middle of l. 40. What follows must have been a fresh śloka of six pâdas finishing with l. 41, and, moreover, our l. 40 has not the concluding punctuation at the end.

b. The traces preserved by Fr. XXXVI for the commencement warrant the reading *suhasavaso*.

c. Inspite of its resemblance with the Pâli version, our text deviates in a manner which is sensible enough : the verb *bhajati* repeated in the last pâda appears from the first ; it is here in the third person ; I cannot decide if *paṇḍito* is the subject or if it represents an accusative *paṇḍitam*, coordinated with others. The *hi* that follows *dhira* seems to be equivalent to *tasmā hi*, which by a singular exception precedes this strophe in the Pâli text. I do not doubt that our text had not a good tradition, and that the addition *tasmā hi* is not a minor extension of our simple particle, an extension that would quite explain the frequent use of this formula in other constructions. Our *dhoreka* is = Sanskrit *dhaureya*, with *k* for *y*, as we have already met with. I doubt very much if the Pâli *dhorayha* should veritably be = *dhauravâhya* (after Fausböll and Childers).

d. I regret not to have been able as yet to discover a counterpart of this stanza, so that the whole beginning remains quite obscure to me. It seems that the first pâdas ought to be transcribed in Sanskrit *ratha* (°*the*) *āropyacarmano pariṣkṛtyodvāhanaṁ* ; and supposing this transcription to be exact, we might draw out of it some sense like "having prepared the strap for the foot-board that helps to mount the car," but besides the fact that this would be quite confusing I cannot imagine, given what follows, how the beginning was joined to the end of the stanza. I think that it is necessary to complete the commencement as *yada*. I take *kamana* either for *kāmāni* or for a genitive performing the function of the accusative, as is to be met with so often in the style of the Mahâvastu. Admitting then that *majati* = Sanskrit *majjati* and that *s.h.* represent *suha*, *sukhaṁ*, I get this meaning : "when one suppresses the desires, one plunges into happiness : let a man wish for happiness and let him cast off all desires."

42 [[1] nena yo atmano] ....
.................................?? so duha na parimucati[a]O

[*Foot-note:* [1] Fr. C xix.]

a. "He (whose description is lost with the first pâdas) is not freed from sorrow." This is what I can compare with, and what is more analogous to, Dhammap., 189:—
na .... *sabbadukkhā pamuccati.*

43 jaya v.ra [[2] prasahati[a] dukhu śayati parayitu uvaśatu sohu śa]yati[b] hitva jayaparayaaO

[*Foot-note:* [2] Fr. C xix.]

Cf. Dhammap., 201.

a. The *h* of *prasahati* is very clear. I do not see how this could be anything else than a gross mistake of the scribe.

b. We see that our text has *śayati* or *śeti* without any differentiation.

44 anica vata [[3] saghara upadavayadhamino upaji ti nirujhati] teṣa uvaśamo suho[a]

[*Foot-note:* [3] Fr. C xix.]

a. That is to say, *anityā vata saṁskārā utpādavyaya-dharmiṇaḥ utpadya te nirudhyante teṣām upaśamaḥ sukhaḥ.* "The saṁskâras are impermanent, subject to production and destruction; scarcely are they produced when they disappear: their suppression is a blessing." *Upaji* for *upaja*, like *ji* for *ca.*

Fragments of C.

To preserve analogy, I mark by the sign $_{ro}$ (recto) the fragments of dark colour which must be connected with that face of leaf C which I have denoted in the same way, and by ^{vo} (verso) the fragments of brighter colour which belong to the opposite side.

I^{ro}. fits below fr II^{ro}. See C^{ro}, ll. 27-29.

1 sañatu sukati yati drugati yati asañatu
ma sa viṣpaśa ...
2 savutu-pratimukhasa idrieṣu ya pajaṣu
pramuni anu ...
3 ... ... v.s.t
śudhasa suyi ...

I^{vo}. fits above fr. II^{vo}. Cf. C^{vo}, ll. 19-22.

1 ... śuhavijinena jaradha ...
2 .yara jiyamanena ḍajhamanena nivruti
nimedha? ...
3 jiyati hi rayaradha sucitra adha śarira bi jara uveti
na ta tu-dharma-ca ja ...
4 (muj. p. rat. muj) ...

II^{ro}. fits below fr. IV^{ro}. Cf. C^{ro}, ll. 24-26.

1 ... u . . . o ...
2 ṣadhu śilena sabano (yaśabho)hasamapitu ...
3 yo natmahetu na parasa hetu pavani kamani
[samaya-

II^{vo}. fits below fr. I^{vo}. Cf. C^{vo}, ll. 22-25.

1 ....u pachatu majhatu muju bhavasa parako sarvatra vi...

2 ....ga 25

3 aroga parama laḅha satuṭhi parama dhana vaśpaśa parama mitra...

4 ....saghara parama duha eta ñatva ya...

III^{ro}. Line-end.

1 ....avaja ida vidva samucari[a] O

2 ....pruvina savasañoyanachaya O

a. The fragment clearly has *mu*, although the use of *samuccarati* be very rare, and that of samācarati, on the contrary, frequent. It may be transcribed: *āvadya(ṁ) idaṁ vidvān samuccaret.*

b. It may be transcribed: *pūrveṇa sarvasaṁyojana-kshaya(ṁ).*

IV^{ro}. fits above the fr. II^{ro} and with the commencement of ll. 22-24.

1 ya keja yaṭha va ho. va lok...

2 ....

3 śilamatu s.yis.ch...

V^{ro}. The top fits on the right with fr. XIII^{ro}. Cf. ll. 30-33 of C^{ro}.

1 ....carita cari dhamayari suh...

2 (aho) nako va sagami cavadhi vatita śara ativaka ti...

3 . sa acata druśilia malua vavi lata vani
kuya su tadha ......
4 ...... yok.ḍ.bh ......

VI^{ro}. fits with C^{ro}, 1.

...... yamaloka ji ......

VII^{ro}. belongs to ll. 4-7 of C^{ro}, and fits with the last line of fr. XI.

1 ...... ?ne
abhi.o ......
2 ...... ga 15
3 ...... hasasahasani sagami manuṣa jini
eka ji ......
4 . ... sa bi ya gaśana anathapa[a] ......

a. ——Or *anartha*°; the foot of the character has disappeared.

VIII^{ro}. belongs to line 12 of C^{ro}.

. samase sahasena yo yaea śatina ca
neva ......

IX^{ro}. fits below line 10.

1 ...... gadha ......
2 masamasi sahasina yo yaea ......

IX^{vo}. forms the commencement of lines C^{vo}, 36, 37, and fits on its left with fr. XV^{vo}.

1 ...... ya narethina v ......
2 suhu darśana ariana sav ......

X^{ro}.

śudhasa hisadaśi gu śudhasa posarudra[a] ....

a. We have already met with *gu=khalu* (B, 21); I suppose that it is the same here, and I propose to transcribe *śuddhasya hiṁsādarśī khalu*; but the fragment is too short to permit of any attempt at interpretation until the Sanskrit or Pâli redaction of it be met with elsewhere.

XI^{ro}. agrees with fr. VII^{ro}.

1 .... padasahita
e ....
2 śata bhaṣe anathapadasahita

XII^{ro}.

1 jini ....
2 . kavayapada ....

XIII^{ro}. fits on the right with the top of fr. V.

dhamu cari sucarita ....
ah? ....

XIII^{vo}. fits below fr. XIV^{vo} and begins line C^{vo}, 18.

imina putikaena vidvarena ....

XIV^{vo}. fits below line C^{vo}, 14. Cf. ll. 15 fg.

1 . avathani a.u ....
2 yanimani prabhaguni vichitani diśodiśa
kavotaka ....

3 imina putikaena aturena pabhaguna nicaśuhavijinena jaradhamena s ......

4 ......

(nicaśuhavijinena) ......

XVvo.

1 ...... bhayo emu jatasamaca ......

2 ...... ya emu ne(?)rayamuca ......

XVIvo. fits with Cvo, ll. 36-38.

1 ...... u. suha śichita ......

2 ...... (sa)vaso vi sada suho adaśanena ......

3 .Jasagatacariu drigham adhvana śoyiṣu dukha balehi ......

XVIIvo.

...... satohiṣasabhi pravera(ya) ......

XVIIIvo. Line-end.

1 ...... ti so gachu na nivatati ○

2 ...... va maṅsana ki teṣa ukumulana″ ○

a. The transcription of these few remnants does not, at least with regard to the second line, afford any complete sense: *sa gacchan na nivartati*: "he never turns back from his course"; *māṁsānām kin teṣām okaunmūlanaṁ*. *Māṁsa* should be the part of a compound referring to *teṣāṁ*. If the form only were taken into account, one would think at once of a form *ulkū-unmūlana*; but this is a form of speech which is very little likely and I believe rather in the transcription which I have suggested: "The destruction of their abode . . .".

XIX^{vo}. agrees with lines 42-44 fg.

1 ....nena yo atmano..................
2 sahati dukhu śayati parayitu
uvaśatu so hu ś ....
3 ....saghara upadavayadhamino
upaji ti nirujhati ....

XX^{vo}. fits after fr. xxxv^{vo}, ll. 39-41.

1 ....?u.s.v.s..................
..........diśa sapuruṣa sumedha bhay ....
..................jahati kamana tada sa majati ....

XXI^{vo}. fits below fr. xiii^{vo}. Cf. ll. 19-20.

iminaputikaena viśravatena putina nicaś ....

XXII^{ro}. fits with line C^{ro}, 31, on the left of fr. v^{ro}.

1 ....? druśilo hi bah..................
2 ....tmana yadha na viṣamu ichati

XXII^{vo}. fits with fr. C xiv^{vo}; cf. ll. 15-16.

1 .... ni śishani tani diṣṭani ka ....
2 .... aṭhini tani diṣṭani ka ....

XXIII^{vo}. Line-end.

.... lapabhavabanana O

XXIV^{vo}. fits within line C^{vo}, 28.

.... veraneṣu ma ....

XXV^{vo}.

1 .... radhamena savaśu ni ....
2 .... ? ? ? ....

XXVI^{ro}. fits below line 19. Cf. ll. 20-21.

1 .... ????? ....
2 .... parama śodhi yokachemu anutara
3 .... ra uveti ....

XXVII^{ro}. fits on the left with fr. xxx^{ro}, and finds place in ll. C^{ro}, 38-40.

1 .... ?? .... kici kicakali adea tata diśa parika ....
2 pacha ṣakaru ichati atha dubakati balu ....
3 ṣehu pacha tavati drukita kita nu sukita ṣeh

XXVIII^{ro}.

.... yati unaḍana pra ....

XXIX^{ro}. Commencement of line C^{ro}, 21.

eka ji bhavitatmana muhut. .. ..

XXX^{ro}. fits after fr. XXVII^{ro}. Cf. ll. 38-40.

1 . . . ma kicakaṛi no i kica kiciali adca
2 ... . suhatu parihayati
3 ya kitva nanutapa(?)ti

XXXI. fits with the fragments of letters preserved by line 26, in :

samidhi atmano so śilava .. .

XXXII^{vo}. fits with C^{vo}, 3.

.. . prabhaguno bhensiti p . ti.......... ....

XXXIII^{vo}. fits with C^{vo}, 4.

. lite sati an.kar.? prachiti pra.

XXXIV^{ro}.

. . . . .suruga... . ...

XXXV^{vo}. fits on the left with lines 39-41, and on the right with fr. XXXVI and XX.

1 .... .ira hi prañai
2 .... nachatrapatha va cadrimu O ra
3 s.h. sarva ca suhu .

XXXVI^vo. fits with the preceding.

s.h.s.v.s. ñatihi va samakamo ....
dh . . . . .

XXXVII^ro.

1 . . ..j . . . t.s..
2 chirena ....

XXXVIII^vo.

.... rasa ṣaga

XXXIX^vo.

ka parama. ok. ....
ruha paricai ..

XL^vo. Remnant of line 19; only the top of the letters is preserved.

medha paramaśodhi yokachem ....

XLI^ro. belongs to C^ro, l. 34.

.. .... ga 10

XLI^vo. fits with C^vo, 14.

.. .. șiti ruchu ....

XLII^ro. fits with C^ro, 15.

.... ea śatena ca ....

M. SENART'S POSTSCRIPT.

I am happy to be able now to rectify the transcription which I was at first induced to suggest for the verse of the manuscript "Dutreuil de Rhins" that forms line 38 of C^ro^. I had reasons to present my interpretations only as a provisional hypothesis. The discovery which I have made, in a recent reading, of a very analogous Pâli counterpart, though not wholly identical, has put me in a position to improve it sensibly.

I do not see any reason to change the material reading of the characters, but rather the divisions of the words, and I transcribe now:

pure i kica parijaga—–kici kicakali adea
ta tadiśa parikamakicakari no i kica kicinli adea

The Pâli verse is found in the Samuddavâṇijajâtaka (Fausböll, IV, 166 fg.). This is the history of a thousand families of carpenters who, harassed by pressing creditors, expatriated themselves on a boat constructed by their own hands. The wind drove them into the open sea towards a fortunate isle where they settled down only to live in abundance. The company was divided into two, and each obeyed its chief; one of the chiefs was prudent and the other was swayed by greediness; the latter manufactured rum and through intoxication lost the condition which the deities of the isle had put on the sojourn of the new comers. The deities became inclined to avenge themselves by raising up a flood of the ocean that would sweep away the entire island. Warned by a compassionate deva, the wise carpenters prepared a vessel on which they escaped in the moment of danger, the others preferring to believe in the delusive promises of another deva; they perished victims to their idle optimism.

A moral in three stanzas is put into the mouth of the Buddha (*abhisambuddhagâthâ*), urging on the necessity of foresight. The third one is construed in the text of M. Fausböll as follows:

Anāgatam̐ paṭikayirātha kiccam̐
mâ mam̐ kiccam̐ kiccakāle vyadhesi
tam̐ tādisam̐ paṭikatakiccakārim̐
na tam̐ kiccam̐ kiccakāle vyadheti

"It is necessary to anticipate future emergency, so that in the hour of need it may not lead us to suffering; he who acts thus, who does what should be done to prevent the occasion, him, in the hour of need, it does not lead to suffering."

I would prefer to have in the second pâda *mā naṁ* or *mā taṁ*; but strictly, by supplying *iti* at the end, the first person is left open to interpretation. *Vyadheti* is, I believe, = *vyathayati*, although the scholiast may seemingly write *vyādhesi*, which the metre does not support and which he seems to take as a denominative from *vyādhi*.

Whatever it may be, the direct relation of this strophe with that of our Kharoṣṭhī Ms. is not less apparent than the differences which distinguish it. From a comparison it follows that it must be understood, by restoring the anusvâras which the manuscript does not note, as follows :

pure (h)i kica(ṁ) parijaga—ma ta(ṁ) kica(ṁ) kicakali adea
ta(ṁ) tadiśa(ṁ) parikamakicakari(ṁ) no (h)i kica(ṁ) kica(k)ali adea

The difficulties are not avoided though the general sense is certain. There is first of all the gap of four syllables : for the first two I can only provisionally maintain the conjecture by virtue of which I have proposed to complete *parijagarea*; *parijaga* being perfectly clear, I do not see how a literal correspondence with *paṭikaroti* of the Pâli could be admitted. The next two syllables would be *ma naṁ* or *ma taṁ*.

In the third pâda *parikama*, *parikarma* is on the whole little removed from *pratikṛta*; but the substantive cannot exactly fill the function of the participle. If *kṛtya* were not wholly employed in all the strophes in the sense of "want", *parikarmakṛtya* would very well be rendered : "what has to be done by way of preparation." Inspite of the difficulties which the particular application of *kṛtya* in *kicakale* seems to present against this interpretation, I do not yet see anything else to suggest.

If we pass from the *i*, certainly wrong, of *kici* for *kica* to the second and the fourth pâdas, there still remains a stumbling block in *adea*. To judge it by the Pâli, it would be *vadhea* = *vyathayeya*. A similar deformation is too abnormal to be easily admitted, but the explanation which I have attempted = *adeyaṁ* failing necessarily, I have nothing satisfactory to suggest; *ādeyya*, from *ādīyati*, could be explained, in the sense of "to take, to domineer, to rule", only by forcing the ordinary meaning in a troublesome way.

II

The Kharoṣṭhī Manuscript of the Dhammapada

With improved readings and readjustments

[1. Magavaga]

The heading here, as in other chapters, is our own, and is not to be found in the Kharoṣṭhī manuscript. But the title chosen suggests itself from the burden of the verses themselves. The chapter, as may be judged from its colophon "ga 30" (I. A³, 5) consists of 30 stanzas, of which 17 (*i.e.*, 10-26) are missing from the manuscript in hand. With the exception of the first three which are to be traced in the Saṁyutta-nikāya, all the stanzas are to be found in the Pāli Dhammapada, distributed in two chapters, *viz.*, the Magga and the Pakiṇṇaka, verses 4-9 being in the Pakiṇṇakavagga and 27-30 in the Magga. The total number of verses may itself be regarded as a proof of the combination of two groups of verses of the Pāli recension under one chapter of the Prakrit. The Maggavagga which just precedes the Pakiṇṇakavagga in the Pāli recension, contains 17 stanzas and the Pakiṇṇaka 16. Rockhill's translation of the Tibetan version of the Udānavarga shows that the verses under notice are distributed in the latest known Sanskrit recension in two chapters, the Mārga and the Smṛiti, of which the former contains 20 stanzas, and the latter 28. The Chinese recension, *Fa-kheu-king*, has two chapters, which are named and juxtaposed in the same way as in Pāli. But, as a matter of fact, the similarity between the two recensions is only in name, the stanzas being entirely different though the chapters bear the same title.

1 (u)[1]juo namo so magu abhaya namu sa diśa
radho akuyano namu dhamatrakehi sahato O

(A⁴, 1)*

2 hiri tasa avaramu smati sa parivarana
dhamahu saradhi bromi samediṭhipurejavu O

(A⁴, 2)

3 yasa etadiśa yana gehiparvaitasa va
sa vi etina yanena nivanaseva satie O

(A⁴, 3)

Cf. Saṁyutta, ed. Feer, I. p. 33† :—

Ujuko nāma so maggo abhayā nāma sā disā
Ratho akujano[2] nāma dhammacakkehi saṁyuto,
Hirī tassa apālambo saty-assa[3] parivāranaṁ
Dhammâhaṁ sārathiṁ brūmi sammādiṭṭhipurejavaṁ.
Yassa etādisaṁ yānaṁ itthiyā purisassa vā
Sa ve etena yānena nibbānass'eva santiko.

—which Mrs. Rhys Davids (" *Kindred Sayings*," p. 45) renders:

" Straight is the name that Road is called, and Free
From Fear the Quarter whither thou art bound.
Thy chariot is the Silent Runner named,
With wheels of Righteous effort fitted well.
Conscience the Leaning Board ; the Drapery
Is Heedfulness ; the driver is the Norm,
I say, and Right Views, they that run before.
And be it woman, be it man for whom
Such chariot doth wait, by that same car
Into Nibbāna's presence shall they come."

Notes.—The Prakrit verses (1-3), as M. Senart points out, are closely bound up in thought, as they complete together a sort of allegory founded on the imagery which likens Buddhist teaching to a *yāna* or 'vehicle'. The Pāli

* The reference is to M. Senart's arrangement.
† An asterisk indicates M. Senart's identification.
[1] Supplied by us.
[2] The Singhalese edition reads *akūjano*, and this reading is adopted in the commentary.
[3] The variant is *sat'assa*.

parallels of these verses are to be found in the Saṁyutta as belonging to a group of four stanzas, named *Accharā* ('the nymphs') from the catchword of its first verse which is left out in our text, and which reads:

Accharāgaṇa-saṅghuṭṭhaṁ, pisācagaṇasevitaṁ
Vanan-taṁ mohanaṁ nāma, kathaṁ yātrā bhavissatîti ?

The imagery developed in these verses serves to throw the Buddhist idea of the silent spiritual progress of man along the path of Righteousness into clear relief, by contrast with the popular aspiration to attain rebirth in the heaven where Indra, king of the gods, visits the enchanting Nandana-grove in a rattling chariot, surrounded by 'troops of nymphs' making the chariot and the paradise resonant with their music and melody[1], and attended by a 'guard of fiendish warriors'[2]; and *à priori* with the popular admiration of luxurious life of princes on earth,[3] who frequent in the same way the royal pleasure grove, escorted by troops of women and bands of ferocious soldiers[4]; in other words, with a life of pomp and pleasure.

The central idea of these verses, divested of poetic imagery and spiritual contrast, *i.e.*, in its more primitive natural

---

[1] The first of the *Accharā*-group, quoted above, expressly mentions the pleasaunce as the place which is resounded with the song and music of the nymphs. The idea that the chariot was made similarly resonant can be supplied from the second verse, where the description of the Buddhist Path compared to 'a chariot rattling noiselessly on' (*ratho a-kūjano*) implies by contrast the idea of a chariot of just the opposite character.

[2] Buddhaghosa takes *pisācagaṇa* in the first *Accharā*-verse to be in apposition with *accharāgaṇa* : "*tam eva accharāgaṇaṁ pisācagaṇaṁ*," *i.e.*, "the troops of nymphs are but the troops of fiends." The commentator can rightly suggest this in respect of a god who is surrounded only by the troops of nymphs, and his interpretation fits well, no doubt, into the context which he has supplied, though from what source of authority nobody knows. The *Accharā*-verses, taken together, seem to have reference rather to Indra's visit to the celestial pleasaunce or paradise than that of an ordinary devaputta, "accosted as their lord by nymphs with song and music." The grammatical form of the expression *pisācagaṇa*, 'troops of male fiends,' prevents taking it as appositional with *accharāgaṇa*, 'troops of female nymphs,' unless it be supposed that the former alludes to the female body-guards, dressed and armed like men.

[3] The text of the *Accharā*-verses, as the commentator rightly suggests, contrasts the life of the gods in the heaven of the Thirty-three with the *summum bonum* of the Buddhists. But the mythological conceptions of heaven and hell being anthropomorphic, the imagery of the verses can be interpreted also as implying a contrast with the sensuous and luxurious life of princes on earth.

[4] Cf. the description of royal visit to the Buddha in the Dīgha, I., p. 49 Sec. 9; Sumaṅgala-vilāsinī, I., pp. 148-9; and Laṅkāvatāra-Sūtra, Fasc. I., p. 2.

psychological form, can be traced in a few verses of the Suttanipāta e.g. 1106, 1107, 1109 and 1111, containing Buddha's replies to the questions of the Brāhman youth Udaya. The questions and replies together constitute a poem known as *Udayamāṇavapucchā* belonging to the Pārāyaṇa-group, which as a separate entity constituted one of the oldest known materials of the Pāli canon.[1] In fact, our verses may be justly regarded as a later recast of the idea of the Pārāyaṇa discourse, and the link in the transformation is preserved in a few technical expressions which, though not exactly identical in both, have at least a striking likeness proving their kinship *e.g. nivāraṇaṁ* (of the Suttanipāta) and *parivarana* (of our Prakrit); *dhammatakkapurejava* and *dhamatrakehi sahato, samedithipurejavu*; *satassa* and *smatisa*; *nibbānam iti vuccati* and *nivanasera satie*; and here it may be noted with profit that the Suttanipāta verses themselves presuppose similar Indian ideas, such as those which can be traced in the *Kaṭhopanishad* (I. 3, 3-9):

"Ātmānaṁ rathinaṁ viddhi, sarīraṁ rathaṁ eva tu
Buddhiṁ tu sārathiṁ viddhi, manaḥ pragraham eva ca.
Indriyāṇi hayān āhur viṣayāṁsteṣu gocarān,
Ātmêndriyamanoyuktaṁ bhoktêtyâhur maṇīṣiṇaḥ.
Yastvavijñānavān bhavatyayuktena manasā sadā
Tasyêndriyāṇyavaśyāni duṣṭâśvā iva sāratheḥ.
Yastu vijñānavān bhavati yuktena manasā sadā
Tasyêndriyāṇi vaśyāni sadaśvā iva sāratheḥ."

Compare also *Manu* (II. 88):—

"Indriyāṇāṁ vicaratāṁ viṣayeṣvapahāriṣu
Saṁyame yatnamâtiṣṭhedvidvānyantêva vājinām."

Verse 1.—(U)juo=*ujuko*. The initial *u* stands for the Sk. *ṛ* exactly as in Pāli. The guttural *k* is elided between *u* and *o*. The word is a derivative of *uju*, Sk. *ṛju*, 'straight.' **Namo**=Pāli *nāmo*, Sk. *nāma* (from *nāman*), 'by name,' 'called,'—the same as *namu* which occurs twice in this verse. The shortening of *nā* into *na* is due to a special feature of the dialect of our text which completely does away with all long vowels. M. Senart is not fully certain about the reading *o* in the syllable *mo* of *namo*. The balance of probability lies with the form *namu*, but the change of *u* into *o* in this exceptional form may have been

[1] Fausböll's Preface to the Suttanipāta, pp. iv-v; Buddhist India, p. 188.

due to euphony, as it is preceded and followed by words ending in *o* sounds. This is not to say, however, that a strong case is thus made out for the form *namo* in preference to *namu*, in view of the uncertainty of the reading. **So**—the same as in Pāli. **Magu**=Pāli *maggo*, Sk. *mārgaḥ*, road. Here is an instance of a nom. sing. form where a masculine stem ending in *a* is declined with the termination *u*, instead of *o* as in *ujuo* and *so*. For *u* instead of *o*, cf. *avaramu* (verse 2). We meet with a regular form *mago* in v. 29 below. *Magu* is therefore to be regarded as optional. Both the forms *magu* and *mago* stand nearer to Sanskrit (*mārgaḥ*) than the more primitive forms where Māgadhism holds a greater sway and where the masculine and neuter stems ending in *a* are declined alike in the nominative singular, *e.g.*, '*sukhe dukkhe jīvasattame*' (Dīgha I. p. 56: extract from the Buddhist version of the doctrine of Pakudhakaccāyana, an elder contemporary of the Buddha), and "*n'atthi attakāre, n'atthi parakāre n'atthi purisakāre, n'atthi balaṁ, n'atthi viriyaṁ, n'atthi purisa-thāmo, n'atthi purisa-parakkamo*" (Dīgha I. p. 53: extract from the Buddhist version of the doctrine of Gosāla, the Ājīvika teacher), of which the Jaina parallel reads: "*n'atthi uṭṭhāṇe i vā kamme i vā bale i vā vīriye i vā purisakkārapparakkame i vā*" (Uvāsagadasāo, Lec. VI., § 166). In our text such masculine and neuter stems are distinguished in declension, though not so distinctly as in Pāli, the masculine form mostly terminating in *o* and the neuter, as we shall see later on, in *u*. The underlying moral of the sentence *ujuo namo so magu* ('straight by name is the road') is a familiar Indian idea which is expressed more clearly in the later Buddhist songs. Cf. *uju re uju chāḍi mā lehu re vaṅka, i.e.*, "leaving what is straight and straight indeed, O thou shouldst not take to what is crooked" (*Bauddha-Gān o Dohā*, No. 32, p. 49). **Abhaya**=Pāli and Sk. *abhayā*, an instance of the feminine *ā*-declension in the nominative singular. For the shortening of the final vowel, see *Namo* above. **Namu**—see *Namo* above. **Sa**=Pāli and Sk. *sā*; for the final vowel, cf. *abhaya*. **Diśa** (feminine)=Pāli *disā*, Sk. *diśā*. The *ś* makes the word more akin to Sanskrit than to Pāli, and supplies a bond of kinship of the dialect of our text with those of the Shahbazgarhi and Mansehra recensions of Asoka's Rock Edicts [cf. *Priyadraśisa* (Shah. I), *Priyadraśine* (Man. I).] **Radho**=Pāli *ratho*, Sk. *rathaḥ*, chariot,—an instance of *th* changed into *dh*, and of the regular form of the masc. nom. singular in *o*.

Akuyano = Pāli *a-kujano* according to the Saṁyutta reading; consequently, the Sk. would be *a-kujanaḥ*, and the meaning, as suggested by M. Senart, would be 'the resort of honest people' and the explanation, 'where the wicked are none.' This interpretation of *akuyano* and the Pāli reading *akujano* on which it is based, are open to dispute for the obvious reason that the meaning suggested and applied to the chariot is hardly in keeping with the appositional adjectives *ujuo* and *abhaya*, 'straight' and 'free from fear', as applied to the road and to the direction. The very expression *ratho akujano*, 'the chariot where the wicked are not,' is quite unprecedented in Indian literature, not to say, unidiomatic. The meaning which fits into the context, is 'that which is free from creaking' *i.e.*, 'runs noiselessly on,'—*akūjano*, "the silent Runner." In fact, the reading in the Singhalese edition of the Saṁyutta is *akūjano*, and the same reading is followed in the commentary, which explains the word as follows :— "*na kūjati na viravati tasmā akūjano ti*". In the language of our text the form *akuyano* can also be allowed in the sense of Pāli *akuyāno*, *i.e.*, 'not a bad vehicle', but such a word has not been met with in Pāli phraseology. **Dhamatrakehi** = Pāli *dhammacakkehi* (according to Saṁyutta) and Sk. *dharmacakraiḥ*. M. Senart has suggested with strong reasons on his side that the correct reading in Prakrit can only be *dhamatrakehi* or *dhamadrakehi*, the first of which may be interpreted as *dhammatakkehi* in Pāli and *dharmatarkaiḥ* in Sanskrit. He cites the evidence of the Suttanipāta verse 1101, which speaks of *aññāvimokha* as *dhammatakkapurejava*, a form which is nearer the expression *samedathipurejava* in the next verse of our text. Considering that the Suttanipāta verse is found in the Pārāyana-group of poems, which as a separate entity formed one of the oldest materials of the Pāli canon (*Buddhist India*, p. 188), it is, as suggested by M. Senart, quite probable that the reading *tarka* is older than the reading *cakra*, which, to quote his own words, "being more ingenious and piquant could, once established, no more have been displaced." It must be readily conceded that the Prakrit form *dhamatrakehi* clearly preserves the memory of the Pāli expression *dhammatakka*, Sk. *dharmatarka*, although to complete the idea of the analogy of the Buddhist "Path" with the 'chariot rolling noiselessly on,' the substitution of *cakra*, 'wheel' for *tarka*, 'reasoning' was natural and inevitable. Even granting that there is no mistake on the part of the scribe or in the reading, the Prakrit form must be taken in the sense of 'wheels.' The change of *tarka* into *traka* is accountable by the principle of *Metathesis*. Cf. *drumedhino* for *durmedhasaḥ* (Apramadavaga, v. 8); *pravatatho* for *parvatasthaḥ* (*ibid* v. 10); *drugha* for *durgāt* (*ibid*, v. 23); *druracha drunivarana* for *dūrakṣyam* (*dur-rakṣyam*) *durṇivāraṇaṁ* (Citavaga, v. 5); *drugati* for *durgatiḥ* (Dhamaṭhavaga, v. 4), *drugatio* (Bhikhuvaga, v. 1); *drigham* for *dīrgham* (Suhavaga, v. 38). This kind of change is familiar to the student of Asoka's Rock Edicts, of which the Shahbazgarhi and Mansehra recensions have so close a kinship, in respect of phonology and orthography, with the dialect of our text—a feature which goes to prove the common geographical location of the two dialects (cf. *dhrama* for *dharma*, *draśi* for *darśī* Shah. I., Mans. I; *savra* for *sarva* S. M. II; *pruva* for *pūrva* S. M. V., Girnar V; *grabha* for *garbha*, S. M. VI; *kramantara* for *karmāntara*, S. M. VI; *krataviye* for *kartavya* M. XI. The instrumental plural termination *ehi* is a common feature of all Prakritic languages and alike of their ancient prototypes the Pāli and Ardhamāgadhī. **Sahato** = Pāli *saṁhato* according to M. Senart, but it seems that *saṁhito*, *sahito* ('joined', 'linked') would be the proper Pāli equivalent. The Saṁyutta variant of the word—*saṁyuto* ('connected', 'fitted with') attests the correctness of the above suggestion. The Upanishad passage singled out above as the basis of the Buddhist verses contains the expression *yuktena*, conveying the idea 'linked with', and the phrase *yuktena manasā*, *i.e.*, 'with mind linked to' is an older psychological counterpart of the Pāli *dhammacakkehi saṁyuto*, 'fitted with the wheels of Righteousness', and of the Prakrit *dhammacakkehi sahato*, 'rounded off with (the wheels of) reasoned discussions on the Norm', the phrases breathing the Buddhist intellectual bias and moral sentiments.

Verse 2.—**Hiri** = Pāli, *hirī*, Sk. *hrī*, an instance of *Epenthesis*, meaning, according to the commentator, *hiri-ottappaṁ*, modesty, conscientiousness. **Tasa** = Pāli *tassa*, Sk. *tasya*. **Avaramu** = Pāli, *apālambo*. This is the only instance, as noticed by M. Senart, where *r* is substituted for *l*. As for *m* = *mb*, compare *udumaresu* = *udumbareṣu* in B, 40. The word means, according to Senart, 'skid.' The meaning which agrees with the commentary is 'leaning-board' (*Kindred Sayings*, p. 45: yodhānam apatanatthāya dārumayam ālambanakam, a wooden structure protecting the soldiers from falling down). This is also an instance of sandhi *ava+aramu*, corresponding to Pāli *apa+ālambo.* Note also the change of *p* into *v*. **Smatisa**=*smati+asa*= Pāli *saty-assa*, or *sattassa*, or *satassa* (*sati+assa*). The Prakrit form is more akin to Sanskrit *smṛti*, a Buddhist technical term which means 'mindfulnesss.' *Parivarana*= Pāli, *parivaraṇaṁ*, which M. Senart renders 'the roof'; but Mrs. Rhys Davids, following the commentary translates it 'the drapery.' The absence of the cerebral nasal *ṇ* is a peculiarity of the language of our text. The word, as has been pointed out above, is a later counterpart of *nivāranaṁ* (*Suttanipāta* v. 1106) or 'prevention.' The sense is that mindfulness (*smati*) is like a drapery (*parivarana*) preventing the influx of impurities from outside. **Dhamahu**=Pāli *dhammāhaṁ*, another instance of sandhi—*dhamu+ahu* corresponding to Pāli *dhammaṁ+ahaṁ*. The scarcity of double consonants is a characteristic feature of the text. It is to be noted that final *aṁ* of Pāli and Sk. is represented in our Prakrit, generally by *u* as here, or by *o* as elsewhere, and occasionally by *a* as in *parivarana*. **Saradhi**= Pāli *sārathiṁ*, charioteer, driver. For *dh*=*th*, see *radho* (verse 1). **Bromi**=Pāli *brūmi*, I say. The Prakrit form is nearer to Sk. *bravīmi*; the shortening of *ava* into *o* is common in the Pāli and all Prakritic languages, but neither the Prakrit *bromi* nor the Pāli *brūmi* may be said to square with this rule unless it be supposed that the vowels *o* and *i* are assimilated into *o* or *u*. **Samedithipurejavu**=Pāli *sammādiṭṭhipurejavaṁ*, a compound, meaning 'the right views which like horses run ahead.' The form *same* stands closer to the Sanskrit *samyak* phonetically than to Pāli *sammā*.

Verse 3.—**Yasa**=Pāli *yassa*, Sk. *yasya*. **Etadiśa**=Pāli *etādisaṁ*, Sk. *etādṛśaṁ*, like this, such. The Prakrit has followed the Pāli in dispensing with *ṛ*, but unlike Pāli it retains *ś* and in this respect stands closer to Sanskrit. For *a*=*aṁ*, see *parivarana* v. 2. The significance of the word 'such,' as implied in the Dhammapada verse 323, is "such a vehicle whereby a person can reach the untraversed region (*agataṁ disaṁ*), *i.e.*, Nirvāṇa. **Yana**=Pāli and Sk. *yānaṁ*, vehicle. For the final *a*, see *etadiśa* above. The conception of the Path as a vehicle is a later imagery, later than *ayana* or *magga* of the older Buddhist discourses, both denoting 'path.' Cf. *Ekāyano ayaṁ maggo* (*Satipaṭṭhānasutta*, *Majjh.*). This imagery was consummated in the subsequent growth of the conceptions of

Mahāyāna' and 'Hīnayāna,' distinguished as two prominent phases of the Buddhist faith, perhaps on the lines, in a sense, of the Vedic and post-Vedic distinction between *Devayāna* and *Pitṛyāna*, with this difference that the word *yāna* in the older texts does not imply the idea of conveyance but of the path along which the soul proceeds, after death, to its destined end. **Gehiparvaitasa va**=Pāli *gihino pabbajitassa vā*. The genitive termination has been dropped in *gehi metri causa*. Here is an instance where Pāli *i* is represented by *e*. The opposite process, *i.e.*, the change of Pāli *e* into Prakrit *i* is noticeable in *etina* below, which stands for Pāli *etena*; that is to say, *i* and *e* are interchangeable. *Parvaitasa*=Pāli *pabbajitassa*, Sk. *pravrajitasya*. The *rva* is a metathesis for the Sk. *vra*, probably on account of a false analogy with forms like *sarva*. *Va*=Pāli and Sk. *vā*. The whole expression means 'of the householder or of the recluse.' The Pāli verse has the variant *itthiyā purisassa vā*, *i.e.*, 'of women or of men.' The Pāli idea seems to be older, as pointing to a time when Buddhism was considered fundamentally a religion of the Bhikkhus, while the Prakrit seems to belong to a time when the Buddhist community, as distinguished from a mere Bhikkhusaṁgha, having been formed, provision had to be made both for the householder and the Bhikkhu in one religious scheme, as was done by Asoka (See *Bhabra Edict*). **Sa**=Pāli *so*, Sk. *saḥ*. **Vi**=Pāli *ve*, Sk. *vai*, 'indeed.' The Sanskrit diphthongs *ai* and *au* are absent in our Prakrit. The *a-i* in *parvaitasa* is not to be regarded as a diphthong. As a matter of fact, M. Senart has noted a *parvahita* in the St. Petersburg fragments, the intervening *h* preventing hiatus like the *y* of the Ardhamāgadhī orthography. For the *i* in *vi*=*e* of Pāli, compare *etina*=*etena* following (in the verse). **Yanena**=Pāli and Sk. *yānena*, instr. of *yana*. **Nivanaseva**=*nivanasa*+*eva*, an instance of sandhi corresponding to Pāli *nibbānasseva*=*nibbānassa*+*eva*. **Satie**=Pāli and Sk. *santike*, near. Note the elision of *k* between *i* and *e*. The occurrence of an alternative form *satii* (B. 32) is no more than an instance of the interchange of *i* and *e* in the Prakrit itself.

4 supraudhu praujhati[1] imi gotamaṣavaka
yeṣa diva ya rati ca nica budhakata smati ○

(A[4], 4)

---

[1] The Kharoṣṭhī Ms. reads *praujati*.

Cf. Dhammapada, 296† (Pakiṇṇakavagga, v. 7) :—

Suppabuddhaṁ pabujjhanti sadā Gotamasāvakā
Yesaṁ divā ca ratto ca niccaṁ Buddhagatā sati.

Cf. Udānavarga[1], ch. xv. ("smṛti"), 12 :—

"The disciple of Gautama is always well awake, day and night reflecting on the Buddha."

5 supraudhu praujhati imi gotamaṣavaka
yeṣa diva ya rati ca nica dhamakata smati ○

(A⁴, 5)

Cf. Dhammapada, 297† (Pakiṇṇakavagga, v. 8) :—

'Suppabuddhaṁ pabujjhanti sadā Gotamasāvakā
Yesaṁ divā ca ratto ca niccaṁ Dhammagatā sati.

Cf. Udānavarga, ch. xv. ("smṛti"), 13 :—

"The disciple of Gautama is always well awake, day and night reflecting on the law."

6 [s]upraudhu praujhati imi gotamaṣavaka
yeṣa diva ya rati ca nica saghakata smati ○

(A⁴, 6)

Cf. Dhammapada, 298† (Pakiṇṇakavagga, v. 9) :—

Suppabuddhaṁ pabujjhanti sadā Gotamasāvakā
Yesaṁ divā ca ratto ca niccaṁ Saṁghagatā sati.

Cf. Udānavarga, ch. xv. ("smṛti"), 14 :—

"The disciple of Gautama is always well awake, day and night reflecting on the church."

---

1 Rockhill's translstion of the Tibetan version of the Udānavarga.

7 [sup]raudḥu praujhati imi gotamaṣavaka
yeṣa diva ya rati ca nica kayakata smati O
(A⁴, 7)

Cf. Dhammapada, 299† (Pakiṇṇakav., v. 10) :—

Suppabuddhaṁ pabujjhanti sadā Gotamasāvakā
Yesaṁ divā ca ratto ca niccaṁ kāyagatā sati.

Cf. Udānavarga, ch. xv. ("smṛti"), 18 :—

"The disciple of Gautama is always well awake, day and night reflecting on what appertains to the body."

8 supraudhu praujhati imi gotamaṣavaka
yeṣa diva ya rati ca ahiṅsai rato mano O
(A⁴, 8)

Cf. Dhammapada, 300† (Pakiṇṇakav., v. 11) :—

Suppabuddhaṁ pabujjhanti sadā Gotamasāvakā
Yesaṁ divā ca ratto ca ahiṁsāya rato mano.

Cf. Udānavarga, ch. xv. ("smṛti"), 21 :—

"The disciple of Gautama is always well awake, day and night delighting in kindness of heart."

9 supraudhu p[r]aujhati[1] imi gotamaṣavaka
yeṣa diva ya rati ca bhamanai rato mano O
(A⁴, 9)

Cf. Dhammapada, 301† (Pakiṇṇakav., v. 12) :—

Suppabuddhaṁ pabujjhanti sadā Gotamasāvakā
Yesaṁ divā ca ratto ca bhāvanāya rato mano.

---

[1] The Kharoṣṭhī Ms. reads *praujati*, which is evidently an error of the scribe.

Cf. Udānavarga, ch. xv. ("smṛti"), 22:—

"The disciple of Gautama is always well awake, day and night delighting in meditation."

Notes.—The verses (4-9) correspond in wording and sequence to the six verses (7-12) in the 'Miscellaneous' group of the Pāli Dhammapada. The Udānavarga which presupposes an older Sanskrit recension, contains all these verses in its Smṛti-group, the sequence being broken after the third verse, as well as after the fourth, by the intervention of some additional verses which seem to have been composed at some later date on similar lines. The total number of Udāna verses cast into the same mould are 17. There are three verses (9-11) in the same chapter of the Udānavarga, preceding the 'Suprabuddha' series, which, though not regular counterparts, are analogous in thought to the first three of our series, as will appear from Rockhill's translation quoted below:—

"They who day and night are reflecting on the Buddha, and who go to the Buddha for a refuge, these men have the profits of mankind."

"They who day and night are reflecting on the law (dharma), and who go to the law for a refuge, these men have the profits of mankind."

"They who day and night are reflecting on the church (sangha), and who go to the church for a refuge, these men have the profits of mankind."

The 'Supraudhu' verses which are primarily intended to eulogise the disciples of Gotama, cannot be found in any other canonical text than the Dhammapada, a negative evidence, which has some bearing on the age of the Dhammapada. We have discussed in our "Asoka's Dhamma" (*loc. cit.*) how the eulogium of the Three Refuges came to occupy a prominent place in the Buddhist faith and how the older conception of the Three *Refuges* (*tisaraṇas*) in the Dhammādāsa (Dīgha, II. p. 93) changed into the later poetical ideas of the Three *Jewels* (*tiratanas*) in the Ratanasutta (Suttanipāta and Khuddakapāṭha). We have further shown that this change of idea took place in no less than a century. The ruling idea of the 'Supraudhu' verses which seems to have been a supergrowth of the *tisaraṇa* or *tiratana* idea, must be relegated to a time when the sāvakas became the mainstay of the Buddhist faith. And judging from the optimistic tone of the verses, it seems that these were the compositions of a time of active Buddhist propaganda when Buddha's disciples deserved to be praised as 'truly awakened' only by carrying their master's behest expressed in the words "ārabbhatha nikkhamatha yuñjatha Buddhasāsane"[1] (start, come out and flock to Buddha's standard) and "Ko attho supitena vo"[2] (what's the use sleeping?). The Pāli Dhammapada contains the minimum number of 'Supraudhu' verses and the Udānavarga the maximum. Our text, the Prakrit Dhammapada, contains all the 'Supraudhu' verses of the Pāli text, and as 17 verses (10-26) of Magavaga are missing from the Kharoṣṭhī Ms., it is difficult to say how many of them belonged to the 'Supraudhu' group. But we have other instances where the number of verses of a particular group, *e.g.*, the 'Sahassa' group, varies in different recensions, the minimum generally being in the Pali and the maximum in the Udānavarga,—the Prakrit and the older Sanskrit being 2nd and 3rd in order. It is, therefore, reasonable to think that of the verses missing in the Kharoṣṭhī Ms., some at least must have belonged to the 'Supraudhu' group,—in other words, that the Prakrit verses outnumbered the Pāli. One may look upon this multiplication of verses as a result of a most mechanical attempt to swell the number of verses without any new articulation. But to us it has a two-fold significa-tion:—*first*, that it brings out certain ideas which are implicit in the central theme, and *secondly*, that it sets forth a chronology of thought as well as of literature.

Verse 4.—**Supraudhu** = Pāli, *suppabuddhaṁ*, accusative adverb. The word is cognate adverbial object to the verb *praujhati*, the idea being 'they awake with a good awakening.' The conjunct consonant *pr* is not to be found in Pāli and Ardhamāgadhī and seems to be a special feature of the dialect of our text as well as of the Shahbazgarhi and Manschra recensions of Asoka's Rock Edicts. In Pāli *r* combines with a preceding labial *b* in such exceptional cases as *Brahmā*, *Brāhmaṇa*, *Brahmadatta*, and with dentals *t* and *d* in a few words like *yatra*, *tatra*, *bhadra* and *indriya*. The Prakrit has kept to the Sanskrit so far as *pr* is concerned. The omission of *b* between *a* and *u* can be explained by an intermediate change of the labial *b* into the semivowel *v*, which latter merged

[1] See references under 'Apramadavaga,' v. 15.
[2] Suttanipāta, v. 331.

into *u*, the two sounds *vu* and *u* being very much similar. The simplification of *ddh* into *dh* is one of the many instances which exemplify the tendency of the dialect of our text to do away with double consonants. The final *u*=*aṁ* (cf. *purejavu*, v. 2). **Praujhati**=Pāli *pabujjhanti*, Sk. *prabudhyante*, 'they awake.' The Prakrit and Pāli forms are in the Parasmaipada, while the Sanskrit is in the Ātmanepada. For the omission of *b* between *a* and *u*, cf. *supraudhu*. The *jh* seems to have been simplified from *jjh* which corresponds to Sk. *dhy*. The *ti* which is a plural termination corresponding to *nti*, is an instance of phonetic decay. **Imi**=Pāli and Sk. *ime*. For the change of *e* into Prakrit *i* see *etina* (v 3). This reading is, according to M. Senart, much better than the Pāli *sadā*. But we cannot agree with him as *imi* is quite unintelligible here, the verse being detached from the context. We think that a general term like *sadā* is better. **Gotamaṣavaka**=Pāli *Gotamasāvakā*, Sk. °*śrāvakāḥ*. This is an instance of genitive compound. The *ṣ* seems to stand midway between Sk. *śr* and Pāli *s*. The final *ā* of the plural is shortened, as all long vowels are, in our text. **Yeṣa**=Pāli *yesaṁ*, Sk. yeṣāṁ. The Prakrit stands closer to Sanskrit so far as the *ṣ* is concerned. For the final *a* standing for Pāli *aṁ*, see *yana* (v. 3.). **Diva**=Pāli and Sanskrit *divā*. **Ya**=*ca*. Cf. *ayara*=*ācāra* (B. 19). **Rati**=Pāli *ratti*, Sk. *rātri*. The idiomatic form ought to have been *ratto*. The form *rati* (nom. sing. instead of locative) is perhaps an instance of false analogy with *diva* considered as nom. sing. **Ca**—We have an optional form *ya* above. **Nica**=Pāli *niccaṁ*, Sk. *nityaṁ*. For *tya*>*cca*>*ca* cf. *dhya*>*jjha*>*jha* in *praujhati* above. **Budhakata**=Pāli *Buddhagatā*, 'turned towards the Buddha'. The Prakrit *ka* is here equal to Pāli *ga*. The word is a compound. **Smati**—See verse 2.

Verse 5.—**Dhamakata**=Pāli *dhammagatā*, 'turned towards the Dhamma'.

Verse 6.—*Saghakata*=Pāli *saṅghagatā*, 'turned towards the Saṁgha'. The *gha* corresponding to *ṅgha* is perhaps an instance of phonetic decay.

Verse 7.—**Ahiṁsai**=Pāli *ahiṁsāya*, Sk. *ahiṁsāyaṁ*. The final *i* replacing the *yaṁ* is an instance of phonetic decay. **Rato**=Pāli *rato*, Sk. *rataḥ*, 'delighting in'. **Mano**=Pāli *mano*, Sk. *manas*.

Verse 8.—Bhamanai = Pāli *bhāvanāya*, Sk. *bhāvanāy ṁ*, 'in meditation'. For the change of *v* into *m* cf. Pāli *nāvaṁ* = Prakrit *nama* (B, 35).

27[1] savi saghara anica ti yada prañaya paśati
tada nivinati dukh(a[2]) [eṣo magu viśodhia][3] O[4]
(A[3], 1)

Cf. Dhammapada, 277† (Maggav., 5), and
Theragāthā, p. 69 :—

Sabbe saṁkhārā aniccā 'ti yadā paññāya passati
Atha nibbindati dukkhe, esa maggo visuddhiyā.

Cf. Udānavarga, XII. ("The Way"), 5 :—

"'All created things are impermanent'; when one has seen this through knowledge, he is no longer afflicted by pain: this is the way to perfect purity."

28 savi saghara dukha ti yada prañae gradhati
tada nivinati dukha eṣo magu viśodhia O
(A[3], 2)

Cf. Dhammapada, 278† (Maggav., 6) :—

Sabbe saṁkhārā dukkhā 'ti yadā paññāya passati
Atha nibbindati dukkhe, esa maggo visuddhiyā.

Cf. Udānavarga, XII. ("The Way"), 6 :—

"'All created things are grief'; when one has seen this through knowledge, he is no more afflicted by pain: this is the way to perfect purity."

---

[1] M. Senart's Fragment A[+] ends with our verse 9, and Fr. A[3] commences with our 27, that is to say, verses 10-26 are missing from the Kharoṣṭhī Ms.

[2] Supplied by us.

[3] M. Senart refers to two small fragments where he finds traces of the clause *eṣo magu vi[śodhia]* which completes the verse.

[4] Supplied by us.

29 sarvi dhama anatma ti yada paśati caśhuma tada nivinati dukha eṣo mago viśodhia ○

(A³, 3)

Cf. Dhammap., 279† (Maggav., 7) :—

Sabbe dhammā anattā 'ti yadā paññāya passati
Atha nibbindati dukkhe. esa maggo visuddhiyā.

Cf. Udānav., XII. (" The Way"), 7 :—

" 'All created things are empty (çunyata)'; when one has seen this through knowledge, he is no more afflicted by pain: this is the way to perfect purity."

Notes.—Here is another group of verses, three in number, which inculcate the religious significance and necessity of viewing 'all created things', in the light of the Buddhist doctrine of impermanence, suffering, and non-identity, as constituting the path to Purity *i.e.*, Nirvāṇa. These verses cannot be traced in the older portions of the Nikāyas, though the views of life which they embody can be ascribed to the Buddha himself.

It is evident from Buddha's exhortation to his son Rāhula[1] that he wanted to impress upon his son and to others, who were in a similar stage of ignorance and inexperience, the necessity of constantly being mindful of the three supreme truths or facts of common experience viz., impermanence, suffering and unsubstantiality. Not that he was indulging in a pessimistic vein, but that he was, viewing fact as fact, trying to incite and inspire the thoughtless and indolent to be active and energetic for the attainment of that tranquil and serene state of consciousness which is possible to attain through the effort of human will in this very life. There can be no mistake about this cardinal motive of Buddha's admonition, and he was consistent to the end, as may be judged from his last utterance: "*Handa dāni bhikkhave āmantayāmi vo: vayadhammā saṅkhārā appamādena sampādetha.*"[2] (Now I charge you, O bhikkhus: subject to decay are created things, be energetic in the performance of duties). A growing

---

[1] The *Mahā-Rāhulovāda* and the *Culla-Rāhulovāda* suttas of the Majjhima Nikāya.

[2] Dīgha II, p. 157.

change in Buddha's doctrine of *Appamāda* is perceptible in the later moralizing tendency and pensive mood of his disciples and followers, and it is no wonder that the death of so great a man like him served to heighten the feeling of impermanence and excite a pessimistic mood, which held a permanent sway over the Buddhist mind till at last the spirit of the doctrine was lost sight of, and that which had been to Buddha a means to an end, turned out in the hands of his followers to be almost an end in itself. Thus Sakka, king of the gods, was made to sing perhaps long before the Dhammapada verses were composed :—

"Aniccā vata saṅkhārā uppādavayadhammino,
Uppajjitvā nirujjhanti, tesaṁ vūpasamo sukho 'ti."[1]

The result was that the Buddhists of subsequent ages came to regard the truths as formulas for mystic repetition and as mantras for counting beads.

Verse 27.—The second line may be restored, with the help of vv. 27-28 as follows:—*tada nivinati dukh(a eṣo mago visodhia* ○). **Savi** = Pāli *sabbe*, Sk. *sarve*. The correct reading appears in v. 29. In other instances also we meet with *rv* instead of simply *v*. See, for instance, M. Senart's fragments B VI : [*sa*]*rvakeleśa*, and B XIV : *sarva*. M. Senart, however, has nothing to say regarding this difference. If the reading *savi* be correct we have to regard it as an optional form of *sarvi* which makes a nearer approach to Sk. *sarve*, the final *i* affording another instance of the interchange of *e* and *i*. **Saghara** = Pāli *saṅkhārā*, Sk. *saṁskārāḥ*, created things. Here it may be supposed to stand for 'organisms' or 'bodies with their different organs of sense and of action.' The substitution of the sonant *gh* for the surd *kh* with the guttural nasal *ṅ* is an instance of *Compensation*. **Anica** = Pāli *aniccā*, Sk. *anityāḥ*, impermanent. Cf. *nica*, v. 4. *Anicati* = *anica* + *iti*, an instance of vowel sandhi. **Yada** = Pāli and Sk. *yadā*. **Prañaya** = Pāli *paññāya*, Sk. *prajñayā*, with clear cognition. The optional forms are *prañae* (v. 38), *prañai* (I. A³, 9). **Paśati** = Pāli *passati*, Sk. *paśyati*. The *ś* makes the Prakrit form closer to Sanskrit. **Tada** = Pāli and Sk. *tadā*, correlative of *yada*. **Nivinati** = Pāli *nibbindati*, Sk. *nirvindati* or -*te*. The Sk. forms mean 'gains,' which is not applicable to the sense here. The Pāli and Prakrit bear

[1] Digha, II., p. 157.

resemblance to Sanskrit only in form; but in idea they seem to be connected with Sk. *nirveda*, Pāli *nibbeda*, 'sense of indifference in regard to pain, arising out of a true knowledge of the real character of existence.' This meaning is suggested by Buddhaghosa, and is also borne out by the Tibetan version. M. Senart quotes Childers who interprets it: "only does he conceive disgust for [existence which is nothing but] pain." For the omission of *r* compare *sari* above; *n* for *nd* is a phonetic decay. **Dukh(a)** stands for Pāli *dukkhe*. The Prakrit seems to be an accusative singular corresponding to Pāli *dukkhaṁ*, in which case the verb *nivinati* must mean 'rightly understands'. As regards the Pāli *dukkhe*, we might take it as an acc. plural, though a locative singular construction would have been more idiomatic.

Verse 28.—**Dukhati**=*dukha*+*iti*, another instance of vowel sandhi. Cf. *anatma ti* (v. 29). **Prañae**=*prañaya* of v. 27, the final *e* standing for *ya*. **Gradhati**=Sk. *granthati* (according to M. Senart), to be explained on the analogy of *saṅkhāra*=*saghara* (v. 27). *Gradhati* stands for Pāli *passati*, sees. It may be necessary to inquire if the Prakrit word has anything to do with Pāli *gādhati* (Udāna, p. 9), 'dives into,' 'penetrates.' *Gradhati*=*granthati* according to M. Senart, means, as he understands, 'deduces, reasons, concludes.' There is no such word as *granthati* in Sanskrit, the proper form being *grathnāti*, if we are to derive it from the root *grath* 'to link, to weave.' M. Senart's suggestion is ingenious enough, and would have commended itself to our ready acceptance if the form could be settled from the philological stand-point. The equation of *gradhati* with *granthati* would be quite on the lines of the change of *saṅkhāra* into *saghara* (vv. 27, 28), *i.e.*, the change of the first aspirate conjoined with the nasal of the group into the second aspirate. But the equation is not permissible in the present case by the meaning of the word. *Gradhati* is apparently used in the same sense as *paśati* of the preceding verse. Accordingly, it must be equated with a Pāli or a Sanskrit word of which the derivative meaning would be 'to see.' Such a Pāli word we can think of is *gādhati* (Sk. *gāhate*) 'to dive,' hence 'to penetrate, to realise.' Cf. the Pāli *Udāna*, I, p. 9: "*Yattha āpo ca pathavī tejo vāyo na gādhati.*" The difficulty is to account for the *gra* in place of *gā*. This may be explained by a process of *False Analogy* with the Sanskrit form *gṛhṇāti* from $\sqrt{grah}$, 'to receive,' the familiar notion of the *grāhya-grāhaka* relation of senses and objects being presupposed. A phrase "*yattha paññā na gādhati*" occurs in a Jātaka verse (Fausböll, III. p. 508 f.), and *gādhati* is explained in the commentary as meaning "*gādhaṁ patiṭṭhaṁ na labhati*" *i.e.*, "(where wisdom) gains no footing."

Verse 29.—**Sarvi** = Pāli *sabbe*, Sk. *sarve*. The Prakrit form almost coincides with the Sanskrit, the *i* replacing the *e*, a feature which is very common in the Prakrit of our text. **Anatmati** = Pāli *anattāti* (*anattā* + *iti*) Sk. *anātmēti* (*anātmā* + *iti*). This is another instance of vowel sandhi, similar to *dukhati* in v. 28, and *anicati* in v. 27. The Prakrit form keeps closer to Sanskrit. Such instances as these may, we think, have been the results of the process of Sanskritization of an older Buddhist dialect. No Buddhist conception has been so much misunderstood by critics, both ancient and modern, as that of *anātmā*, which literally means 'no-soul.' The negative form of the word *ātmā* or *ātman* does not imply the negation of all the idea of a percepient. It implies indeed the negation of the older Upanishadic theory of the soul as an unchangeable substratum of all changes and mental functions as well as of the naive animistic notion of an in-dwelling spirit capable of going out and coming into the body at its sweet will, a notion which is prevalent among all ancient peoples. The Buddhist theory of 'no-soul' replaced these older ideas by a psychological theory of the mind as a stream of consciousness. The verse under notice does not seem so much concerned to bring out the philosophical idea of 'no-soul' as to accentuate the necessity of renunciation. **Cachuma** = Pāli *cakkhumā*, Sk. *cakṣuṣmān*, 'he who has eyes to see.' In this instance the Prakrit keeps closer to Pāli. For the change of *kkh* into *ch*, compare *rachati* for *rakkhati* (I. A[3], 14), and *avechiti* for *avekkhati* (I. A[3], 16). We also meet with a reading *cakhuma* in the next verse. The change is from *kṣ* through assimilation into *kkh*, which is first palatalised into *cch*, and is then reduced to *ch* for facility of pronunciation. *Ma* for Sk. *mān* is an instance which shows that the Prakrit like Pāli has done away with the final consonant, so that the equation would be *ma* = *mā*, but since our Prakrit has no long vowel, the *ā* is shortened into *a*. The interest of the reading *paśati cachuma* instead of *prañaya paśati* as in verse 27, and *prañae gradhati* as in verse 28, lies in the fact that it makes manifest the underlying metaphor of wisdom regarded as an eye or mode of perception, the *prajñā* being considered as the *prajñā-cakṣu*.

30 magana aṭhagio śeṭho sacana cauri pada
viraku śeṭho dhamana praṅabhutana cakhuma O

(A³, 4)

Cf. Dhammap., 273† (Maggav. v. 1.) :—

Maggān' aṭṭhaṅgiko seṭṭho saccānaṁ caturo padā,
virāgo seṭṭho dhammānaṁ dipadānañ ca cakkhumā.

Cf. Udānavarga, ch. XII. ("The Way"), v. 4 :—

"Among truths the four truths (are the best); the eightfold way is the best of ways; the best of bipeds is he who sees; the greatest of virtues (dharma), passionlessness."

....ga 30

(A³, 5)

Notes.—This verse, as will appear from the first quotation above, occurs at the beginning of the Pāli Maggavagga. In our text it is placed after the "*anatma*" verse, *i.e.*, v. 29, while in the Udānavarga it precedes the "*anica*" verse, *i.e.*, v. 27, and in the Pāli it is placed before three verses preceding the "*anica*" verse The verse under notice cannot be traced in any other extant canonical work, though the underlying idea is a familiar one. The praise of the Path which is the theme of our verse serves to wind up the teaching of this chapter.

Magana=Pāli *maggānaṁ*, genitive of the Prakrit *mago* or *magu*. The genitive is in the sense of the locative; *of the Paths*=*among the Paths*. The significance of the genitive plural of the word *mago* or *magu* is that it makes explicit the contrast of the Buddhist Path with those followed by others, a contrast which is tacitly implied in many genuine utterances of the Buddha. Compare, for instance, the expression "*Ekāyano ayaṁ bhikkhave maggo*"—"This, O bhikkhus, is the only Path" (*Mahāsatipaṭṭhāna-suttanta*, Dīgha II). **Aṭhagio**=Pāli *aṭṭhaṅgiko*, Sk. *aṣṭāṅgikaḥ*, an instance of sandhi and compound (*aṭha*+*agio*), meaning that which has eight parts, 'the eightfold.' *Aṭha* is simplified from Sk. *aṣṭa* through the intermediate Pāli *aṭṭha*. *Agio*=Pāli *aṅgiko*, Sk. *āṅgikaḥ*. It has already been noted that *ṅ* of Pāli and Sk. is dropped in our Prakrit in instances where it is conjoined with a surd of the same consonantal group, and the surd itself changes into the corresponding sonant (*e.g.*, *paga* for Pāli *paṅka* I. A[1], 5; *saghara* for *saṅkhāra*, v. 27; *sagapa* for *saṅkappa* I. A[3], 9). But here we have an instance where the nasal of the guttural group is conjoined with the sonant *g*. The nasal is dropped but the sonant remains unchanged. Cf. *sagamu* for *saṅgāmo* (I. C[ro], 6). The *k* is dropped between *i* and *o* here. For the omission of *k* between *i* and *e*, cf. *satie* (v. 3), between *i* and *i* cf. *satii* (I. B, 32), between *u* and *o* cf. *ujuo* (v. 1). But it is not dropped after *a*, as in *akuyana* (v. 1), *savaka* (vv. 4-9). *Aṭṭhaṅgiko* or 'the eightfold' is a Buddhist technical term denoting the Buddhist Path which leads to *Nirvāṇa* conceived in its negative aspect as the complete cessation of suffering, a generic name for all painful experiences of mankind. The significance of the term 'Eightfold' is that the Path is expounded as consisting of eight parts or categories, the right views, the right resolve, and so forth. This path is counted as one of the Four Truths, *viz.*, the fourth, concerning the way. **Śeṭho**=Pāli *seṭṭho*, Sk. *śreṣṭhaḥ*. For the simplification of *ṭha* from Pāli *ṭṭha*, cf. *aṭhagio* above. **Sacana**=Pāli *saccānaṁ*, Sk. *satyānāṁ*, genitive plural. For *c* see *anica* (v. 27). **Cauri** corresponds to the Pāli reading *caturo*. It strictly equates with Pāli *cattāri*, Sk. *catvāri*. M. Senart rightly points out that *cattāri* or *catvāri* is in the Buddhist dialects readily used for the masculine. He further suggests that though *cauri* appears to be the direct reflex of *catvāri*, it may better be connected with *caturo*, the change of *o* into *i* being only mechanical. Indeed *cauri* is the result of a mixing up of the two forms—masculine and neuter—*caturo* and *cattāri*, *catvāri*. See M. Senart's Notes (p. 12). **Pada** corresponds to the Pāli reading *padā*. The corresponding form in Sanskrit would be *padāni* (neuter pl.). But the question is whether *caturo padā* cannot be regarded as the Pāli counterpart of the Sanskrit '*catvāraḥ pādāḥ*,' 'four portions or divisions,' taking *pādāḥ* in the sense of *mātrāḥ*. For the conception of the 'four pādas' cf. the Māṇḍūkya Upanishad: *So'yamātmā catuṣpāt: prathamaḥ pādaḥ, dvitīyaḥ pādaḥ*, etc. The masculine form of the Pāli will be well accounted for, if we trace it to the Upanishadic conception of 'four divisions.' The Prakrit *pada*, considered without the neuter numeral *cauri*, leaves us in the dark as to the gender it denotes, for it may stand alike for *pāda* and *padāni*. In the case of *cauri* we have presupposed with M. Senart the intervention of an intermediate form *caturo*. A similar confusion of two forms—masculine and neuter, *padā*, pl. (Pāli), *pādāḥ* (Sk.), and *padāni* (Pāli and Sk.)—can be said to hold good in the case of the Prakrit *pada*, which appears to have retained a masculine form in an undetectable way. It seems that the history of *pāda* was forgotten in Pāli and the word came to be confounded with *pada*. A glaring instance of such confusion is furnished by the Buddhist expression *cattāri dhammapadāni* (in the sense of *dhammapādā*), explained also as the four *divisions* of the Norm, that is to say, explained in the light of the old Upanishadic classification of 'four pādas,' though in the garb of *pada*. As a matter of fact, there is no difference in sense between *pāda* (masc.) and *pada* (neut.), though there is much in respect of grammar. *Saccānaṁ caturo padā* is another way of saying *cattāri ariyasaccāni*, the familiar expression for the Four Noble Truths. **Viraku** = Pāli *virāgo*, Sk. *virāgaḥ*, 'dispassionateness.' For the change of the sonant *g* into the corresponding surd *k*, generally after *a*, cf. *Budhakata* for *Buddhagatā* (v. 4.), and for the final *u* for *o*, cf. *magu* (v. 1). **Pranabhutana** would equate with Pāli *pāṇabhūtānaṁ*, an instance of *samāsa*. The meaning is—'of living beings.' The Pāli reading is *dipadānaṁ* ('of the bipeds'), a narrower comparison which is implied also in the Udānavarga. The form *pāṇabhūta* equated with *pranabhuta* actually occurs in Pāli. Cf. the expression: "*ye keci pāṇabhūt' atthi*" (Suttanipāta, v. 146). The Prakrit *pranabhutana* and the Pāli *pāṇabhūtānaṁ* seem to have been the result of a confusion of Sanskrit *bhṛta* with *bhūta*. Having regard to the fact that the older Upanishadic expression *prāṇabhṛt* denotes a living being (cf. *prāṇabhṛtsu*, Ait. Āraṇyaka II. 3. 2. 2), this theory of confusion would seem sufficient to explain the Pāli or the Prakrit form as corresponding literally to Sanskrit *prāṇībhūtānāṁ* or *prāṇabhṛtānāṁ*, the former of which, however, would not be free from objection on one ground or another. The Sanskrit genitive plural of *prāṇabhṛt* is *prāṇabhṛtāṁ*. The form *prāṇabhṛtānāṁ* will be justified if it is corroborated by the actual use of a stem *prāṇabhṛta* in Sanskrit literature. The proper Pāli form would have been *pāṇabhatānaṁ* and the corresponding Prakrit *pranabhatana*. Cf. Pāli *bhato* equating with Sk. *bhṛta* in the Nikāya expression "*bhato nesaṁ bharissāmi*" (Dīgha III. p. 189). **Cakhuma** keeps closer to Pāli *cakkhumā* than *cachuma* of the preceding verse. Indeed this reading is a typical illustration bearing out our hypothesis of the derivation of many Prakrit words of this text through some intermediate Pāli forms.

Ga 30—M. Senart takes *ga* to stand for *gadha* (*gāthā*), thereby interpreting it to imply that the group or chapter contains 30 stanzas. But unfortunately he has not made use of this numbering to systematise the verses according to chapters as has been attempted in the present edition. This has been the cause of a very serious drawback in his otherwise valuable work, and we shall see more of it when we deal with the next group of verses.

[2. Apramadavaga]

The group of verses under this head, all deal with '*apramada*', and this is the justification of the title we have chosen for it. The group consists of 25 stanzas, as may be judged from the number mentioned in the colophon "ga 25" (I. A[1], 8). In the Pāli recension the '*Appamāda*' group has 12 verses, and forms the second chapter of the book. The Udānavarga verses grouped under 'Apramāda' (wrongly rendered "Purity" by Rockhill) number 35 and form the 4th chapter. These three recensions of the Dhammapada have many 'Appamāda' verses in common. The title in the Chinese *Fa-Kheu-pi-u* (see sec. x., Beal's translation) is the same as in Pāli, but the chapter has hardly any verse in common with the latter. The Pāli 'Appamāda' verses can not be traced in any other canonical text, but there are some in the Prakrit text and the Udānavarga which can be traced. It will be noticed how M. Senart has laboured under a disadvantage in trying to number serially whole verses on a leaf, regardless of their central theme and of the number indicated in the colophon marking the close of a chapter.

1 utiṭhe[1] na pramajea dhamu sucarita cari
dhamacari suhu śeati asmi loki parasa yi ○

(A[3], 6)

Cf. Dhammap., 168† (Lokavagga, v. 2) :—

Uttiṭṭhe nappamajjeyya dhammaṁ sucaritaṁ care
Dhammacārī sukhaṁ seti asmiṁ loke paramhi ca.

---

[1] The reading in M. Senart's edition is *utitha*, but he says that the omission of the final *e* may be due to the negligence of the scribe and not to any dialectic peculiarity.

Notes.—This verse which marks the beginning, according to our arrangement, of the second chapter of the Prakrit text seems rightly included in the 'Apramada' group; the occurrence of it in the 'Loka' group of the Pāli text is hardly justifiable, as its relevancy to the general reflections on the world is very slight. The Pāli arrangement of verses, as noticed before, is generally loose, the compiler having in many cases made an injudicious selection of verses for a group, for he seems to have been careless of the distinctive tone of a paricular verse justifying its inclusion in a particular group. For instance, in the present verse, though a greater stress is laid on *Appamāda* than on *Loka*, the verse seems to have been included in the 'Loka' group simply because it happens to contain a word about *Loka*. The compiler might as well have put it in the 'Appamāda' group, but so far as the device is mechanical, he is consistent. On the other hand, though the Prakrit text has quite consistently grouped together all the verses of which the main theme is *apramada*, it has a serious drawback in that it does not put in the beginning, as has been done in the Pāli text and the Udānavarga, the most important verse *e.g.*, "apramadu amatapada" etc. (v. 6 *infra*), which brings out the essence of the teaching of the 'Apramada' discourse as a whole.

Utiṭhe=Pāli *uttiṭṭhe*, Sk. *uttiṣṭhet* (Optative), 'one should rise up.' The word reminds one of the exhortation in the Pāli *Uṭṭhānasutta*:—'*Uṭṭhahatha nisīdatha ko attho supitena vo*' (Suttanipāta, Bk. II. No. 10[1]). **Na pramajea**=Pāli *nappamajjeyya*, 'one should not relax,' an optative form keeping close to the Pāli. *Pramajea*, as opposed to *utiṭhe*, implies primarily an idea of sleep or dozing or a morbid state of body and mind as experienced by a person dead drunk, and secondarily, as here, that of a state of inactivity, indolence, thoughtlessness, moral cowardice or a want of will, energy and religious enthusiasm to strive for the best within human reach.

---

[1] Cf. (i) *Therag.*, v. 411:—

"Uṭṭhāhi nisīda Kātiyāna mā niddābahulo ahu jāgarassu,
mā tam alasaṁ pamattabandhu kūṭen' eva jinātu maccurājā."

(ii) *Kaṭhopanishad*, I. 3.14:—

"Uttiṣṭhata jāgrata prāpya varān nibodhata ||
Kṣurasya dhārā niśitā duratyayā durgaṁ pathastat kavayo vadanti ||"

(iii) *Taittirīya Āraṇyaka*, I. 27. 2:—

"Uttiṣṭhata mā svapta agnim icchadhvam Bhāratāḥ."

Dhamu sucarita cari, which corresponds to the Pāli *dhammaṁ sucaritaṁ care*, reminds us at once of the Taittirīya command '*dharmaṁ cara*' (*i.e.*, 'fulfil the law'—moral but not discordant with the cosmic). This expression, when coupled with *na pramajea*, reminds us of another Taittirīya command '*dharmān na pramaditavyam*', *i.e.*, 'one should not swerve from the principle' (see Taittirīya Up., I. 11. 1). In *sucarita cari* we have another instance of a Buddhist expression where a past participle *sucarita* is used as a cognate adverb (cf. *supraudhu pravjhati*, Magava., v. 4 ff.). For **dhamacari** compare a variant *dhamayari* in I. c^ro, 30—another evidence of the interchange of *c* and *y*. As to **śeati** M. Senart thinks that it rests "not on the usual form *śeti*, but on the form *śayati*, *aya* being written *e*". But it would have been, perhaps, more correct to say that it is a compromise between *śeti* and *śayati*, evincing a tendency to incline to the latter form. That the normal use is *śeti* is clear from I. c^ro, 30. The word *śeati* is significant as showing how the Buddhist verse dwells upon the idea of sleeping; here it means the enjoyment of a blissful rest, *i.e.*, *Nirvāṇa*. **Asmi**=Pāli *asmiṁ*, Sk. *asmin*. In the Prakrit of our text *sm*, unlike the Pāli, is nowhere changed into *mhi*. **Parasa**= Pāli *parassa*, a form with a genitive termination but used in a locative sense (cf. *sagaraudasa* for *saṁkūrakūṭasmiṁ*, I. c^ro, 3). **Yi**=Pāli *ca*, the usual form being *ya* (see Magava. vv. 4 f.). The *i* of *yi* is, perhaps, due to a desire to maintain a rhythm with the *i* of the previous word *asmi*.

2 uṭhanena apramadena sañamena damena ca
divu karoti medhavi ya jara nabhimardati ○

(A³, 7)

Cf. Dhammap., v. 25 † (Appamādav. v. 5):—

Uṭṭhānena appamādena saññamena damena ca
Dīpaṁ kayirātha medhāvī yaṁ ogho nâbhikīrati.

Cf. Udānav., ch. IV. ("Purity"), v. 5:—

The wise man through earnestness, virtue, and purity makes himself an island which no flood can submerge."

6

Notes.—The Prakrit verse exactly corresponds to the Pāli, so far as its first line is concerned. In the second line we have, in *karoti*, a present singular form in place of the Pāli optative plural *kayirātha*, and in *medhavi* a nom. sing. form in place of the Pāli plural *medhāvī*. The Udānavarga reading, so far as it may be judged from Rockhill's translation, is similar to the Prakrit. The verse-end with the reading **jara nabhimardati**, of which the Pāli would be *jarā nâbhimaddati*, 'decay does not crush', is peculiar to our text, while the Dhammapada and the Udānavarga agree in having a different reading. As it is, the Pāli expression *ogho nâbhikīrati* appears more appropriate than the Prakrit *jara nabhimardati* in a simile where the imagery of an island is present. But virtually there is no difference, for it is really a *jarā-ogha*, 'the flood of decay', that is meant here, as is evident from the testimony of Therag., v. 412:—

> "Sayathâpi mahâsamuddavego evaṁ jâtijarâtivattate taṁ,
> So karohi sudîpam attano tvaṁ, na hi tâṇaṁ tava vijjateva aññaṁ."

The sense of *ogha* in the Pāli reading is too indefinite, the Prakrit makes it explicit by *jara*, and *abhimardati* is as aptly used with *jara* as *abhikirati* is with *ogho*. M. Senart's suggestions (I. A³, 7) seem rather laboured and far-fetched.

3 uṭhanamato smatimato suyikamasa niśamacarino
sañatasa hi dhamajivino apramatasa yaśidha vaḍhati O

(A³, 8)

Cf. Dhammap., v. 24 † (Appamādav., v. 4) :—

> Uṭṭhānavato satimato sucikammassa nisammakārino
> Saññatassa ca dhammajīvino appamattassa yaso 'bhivaḍdhati.

Cf. Udānav., ch. IV. ("Purity"), v. 6 :—

> 'Tis the earnest that become far-famed by their diligence, reflection, the purity of their lives, their judgment, their perfect observance (of the commandments), by their whole life which is according to the law."

Notes.—This verse is in tone the same as vv. 1-2, and corresponds in form to the Pāli except for **hi** in place of *ca* after *sañatasa* and **yaśidha vaḍhati** in place of *yaso'bhi°*. There is nothing more to notice than the change of *c* into *y* in **suyikamasa**, the change of *k* into *c* in **niśamacarino**, and a vowel sandhi in **yaśidha** (*yaśa+idha*). The expression *niśamacarino* might also be equated with Pāli *nisammacārino* which is a synonym, in a narrower sense, of *dhammacārino*.

4 uṭhanaalasa[1] anuṭhahato yoi bali alasieuvito
saṅsanasagapamanosmatima[2] prañai maga alasu
na vinati O

(A,[3] 9)

Cf. Dhammap., v. 280 † (Maggav., v. 8) :—

Uṭṭhānakālamhi anuṭṭhahāno yuvā balī ālasiyam upeto
Saṁsannasaṅkappamano kusīto paññāya maggaṁ alaso
na vindati.

Cf. Udānav., ch. XXXI. ("The Mind"), v. 32 :—

"He who remains seated when it is time to rise, who, though strong and young, sits slothfully at home, who is always careless in his thoughts, will not find the road to wisdom."

Notes.—This verse which sets forth the evil effect of indolence and thoughtlessness, exactly corresponds in form as well as in tone to the Pāli except for the word **smatima** in place of *kusīto*, 'indolent.' M. Senart rightly points out that the expression *smatima* is inexplicable, unless it be supposed that it is *asmatima*, the initial vowel being elided through a *sandhi* with the previous word. In this verse, as in many others, one cannot fail to notice the Buddhist method of defining a term by juxtaposing a host of synonyms differing from each other in slight shades of meaning, the total effect being the intensification of the main idea. **Uṭhana-alasa anuṭhahato**=Pāli *utthānakālamhi anutthahāno*, "he who remains seated when it is time to rise" (Udānavarga), a

---

[1] The Ms. reads *uthane alasa*. The alteration has been made above according to M. Senart's suggestion.

[2] *Smatima* is joined to the preceding word because of sandhi.

negative expression followed by a positive synonym in the second foot. We fully agree with M. Senart that in *uṭhanaalasa* we have another form with a genitive termination for the locative (cf. *parasa* in v. 1.). **Yoi** stands, according to M. Senart, for *yo ayaṁ*. He thinks that "this reading is assuredly preferable to *yuvā*." But in both the Dhammapada and the Udānavarga we have *yuvā*, and we need not necessarily suppose that *yoi*=*yo ayaṁ*, since *yoi* may alike be equated with *yuvā*, *i* being a change from *vā*, perhaps through an intermediate *ya*. **Saṅsanasagapamano** = Pāli *saṁsannasaṅkappamano*, 'having an irresolute mind,' 'in a state of indecision.' In a few instances the nasal *ṅ* is retained before *s* as in *ahiṅsai* (=*ahiṁsāya*), Magavaga, v. 8, and *bheṅsiti* (=*bhetsyati*), Jaravaga, v. 5. As for the change of *ṅk* into *g* (*sagapa*=*saṅkappa*), see notes on *aṭhagio* in Magavaga., v. 30, and *saghara*, op. cit., v. 27.

5 na tavata dhamadharo yavata baho bhaṣati
yo tu apa bi ṣutvana dhamu kaena phaṣai ○
sa ho dhamadharo bhoti yo dhamu na pramajati ○

(A[3], 10, 11)

Cf. Dhammap., v. 259 † (Dhammaṭṭhav., v. 4):—

Na tāvatā dhammadharo yāvatā bahu bhāsati
Yo ca appaṁ pi sutvāna dhammaṁ kāyena passati
Sa ve dhammadharo hoti yo dhammaṁ na-ppamajjati.

Notes.—The expressions of the Prakrit verse are similar to those of its Pāli counterpart except for **tu** in place of *ca* and **ho**(=*kho*) in place of *ve*. The verse undervalues 'much learning' without any original vision or perception of truth. In the Pāli Dhammapada we have two other verses, vv. 18-19, where this Buddhist view of learning is inculcated more emphatically and with a direct reference to the established method of Vedic study: cf. "*Bahumpi ce sahitaṁ bhāsamāno*" etc. A man who can recite many hymns (*saṁhitā*) but does not act according to the injunctions laid down therein, is compared to a cowherd who counts the cattle of others without being able to claim them as his own. In course of time when Buddha's doctrine and discipline were rehearsed and put together, or when the Buddhist texts were compiled, the old evil crept into the Buddhist system. The lack of insight and originality of conception have been the bane of all Sanskritic studies. The Buddhist judgments on two contrasted types are well worth consideration : (1) a *Dhammadhara* without an original vision, and (2) a *Kāyasakkhī* who has a direct perception of truth. **Dhamadharo** = Pāli *dhammadharo*, a custodian of the Buddhist faith. In a passage of the Mahāparinibbānasuttanta a *Dhammadhara, i.e.*, a custodian or rehearser of the Sutta Piṭaka in later nomenclature, has been distinguished from a *Vinayadhara* or a *mātikadhara*, the terms being replaced in later phraseology by *Vinaya Piṭaka* and *Abhidhamma Piṭaka.* **Dhamu kaena phaṣai** would strictly equate with a Pāli *dhammaṁ kāyena phussati*, 'touches the law with his mind.' Nevertheless the Prakrit reading **phaṣai** is as good as the Pāli *passati*, 'sees.' Here we have a description of a *kāyasakkhī* (see Aṅguttara, I. p. 118, Majjhima, I. p. 478).

6 apramada amatapada pramadu mucuno pada
apramata na miyati ye pramata yadha mutu O[1]
(A[3], 12)

Cf. Dhammap., v. 21 † (Appamādav., v. 1) = Fausboll's Jātaka, v. p. 99 = Dīpavaṁsa p. 46 :—

Appamādo amatapadaṁ pamādo maccuno padaṁ
Appamattā na mīyanti ye pamattā yathā matā.

Cf. Udānav., ch. IV. ("Purity"), v. 1 :—

"The pure man knows not death ; he who is impure dwells with death ; he who is pure will not die ; he who is impure dies repeatedly."

7 eta viśeṣadha ñatva apramadasa panito
apramadi pramodia ariana goyari rato O
(A[3], 13)

Cf. Dhammap., v. 22 † (Appamādav., v. 2) :—

Etaṁ visesato ñatvā appamādamhi paṇḍito
Appamāde pamodanti ariyānaṁ gocare ratā.

---

[1] The circle is supplied by us.

Cf. Udānav., ch. IV. ("Purity"), v. 2:—

"The wise who knows this difference delight in modesty and purity; their pleasure is that of the elect."

Notes.—The teaching of the whole chapter is put in a nut-shell in verse 6 and, as a matter of fact, this verse is put at the head of the chapter in other recensions than the Prakrit. The moral inculcated reminds one of Shakespeare's famous pronouncement that 'cowards die many times before their death', while 'the valiant die but once.'

Verse 6.—**Yadha mutu** (singular) would strictly equate with a Pāli *yathā mato*, Sk. *yathā mṛtaḥ*, 'like one dead.' The Prakrit reading seems more emphatic than the Pāli.

Verse 7.—**Viśeṣadha** improves the Pāli reading *visesato*, meaning 'particularly' (cf. *visesena* of the commentary). M. Senart takes *viśeṣadha* as 'formed by the suffix *dhā*, which may in this case very well supply the suffix *taḥ* of the Pāli'. To us, however, it seems that *viśeṣadha* = Pāli *visesattaṁ*, Sk. *viśeṣatvaṁ*, 'difference.' **Apramadasa** = Pāli *appamādamhi*. Here is another form with a genitive termination for the locative singular, cf. *parasa*, Magav., v. 27.

8 pramada anuyujati bala drumedhino jana
apramada tu medhavi dhana śeṭhi va rachati ○

(A[3], 14)

Cf. Dhammap., v. 26 † (Appamādav., v. 6) = Saṁyutta, I. p. 25 = Therag., v. 883:—

'Pamādaṁ anuyuñjanti bālā dummedhino janā
Appamādañ ca medhāvī dhanaṁ seṭṭhaṁ va rakkhati.

Cf. Udānav., ch. IV. ("Purity"), v. 10:—

"The (mind of the) fool who is given up to carelessness is perverted; the wise man must be careful, as is the head of a caravan watching his treasures."

Notes.—There is nothing more in this verse to explain than the simile **dhana śeṭhi va rachati,** which, according to M. Senart, should be equated with a Pāli *dhanaṁ seṭṭhī va rakkhati* (*i.e.,* like a banker watching his treasures). To M. Senart the reading *śeṭhi* appears to be decidedly better than the Pāli *seṭṭhaṁ,* which gives only "a vague and colourless epithet." While we cannot dispute his interpretation of *śeṭhi* as a banker, "the head of a caravan" (Udānavarga), it seems that the expression *dhanaṁ seṭṭhaṁ va* is not at all colourless as he thinks, the idea being 'as a man keeps watch over a precious possession' *e.g.,* over the seven jewels, as the commentary suggests, or over a 'Kohinoor,' for instance.

9 apramatu pramateṣu suteṣu bahojagaru
avalaśa va bhadraśu hitva yati sumedhasu O[1]

(A[3], 15)

Cf. Dhammap., v. 29 † (Appamādav., v. 9) :—

Appamatto pamattesu suttesu bahujāgaro
Abalassaṁ va sīghasso hitvā yāti sumedhaso.

Notes.—This verse closely resembles in form its Pāli parallel except for the reading **bhadraśu** (=*bhadrasso*) in place of *sīghasso.* The expression *bhadraśu* is less satisfactory as an antithesis of **avalaśa** (=*abalassaṁ*) than *sīghasso.* The term *bhadraśu* denotes a well-trained horse, cf. *asso bhadro kasāmiva,* Dhammapada, v. 143. The simile in the second line is that of a race in which a fast horse leaves behind a weak one. The teaching of the present verse is somewhat different from the moral of the story of the Hare and the Tortoise, in Æsop's Fables, which is that the slow but steady win the race. **Avalaś** =Pāli *abalassaṁ,* a vowel saudhi (*avala*+*aśa*). M. Senart singles this out as the only instance where *v* has been substituted for *b.* **Bhadraśu**=Pāli *bhadrasso,* a sandhi (*bhadra*+*aśu*). **Sumedhasu**=Pāli *sumedhaso,* a compound meaning 'having a good brain-power,' which is a synonym of *medhavi* in the preceding verse.

---

[1] The circle is supplied by us.

10 pramada apramadena yada nudati panitu
praňaprasada aruyu aśoka śoino jana
pravataṭho va bhumaṭha dhiru bala avechiti O[1]

(A[3], 16)

Cf. Dhammap., v. 28 † (Appamādav., v. 8)
= Vinaya I, p. 5 = Milinda, p. 387 :—

Pamādam appamādena yadā nudati paṇḍito
Paññāpāsādam āruyha asoko sokinim pajam
Pabbataṭṭho va bhummaṭṭhe dhīro bāle avekkhati.

Cf. Udānav., ch. IV. ("Purity"), v. 4 :—

"When the wise men through earnestness have overcome heedlessness, then, steadfast through wisdom, they ascend to above the abode of the gods, and, free from sorrow and pain, they look down as from the summit of a mountain at the fools on the face of the earth."

Notes.—The teaching of this is in spirit the same as that of the previous verse with this difference that the similes are changed. The first simile is that of a royal personage looking down from the balcony of a palace at the multitude, who walk along the street. **Aruyu** = Pāli *āruyha*. For the reading, see M. Senart's Notes. We might just notice that the *u* of *yu* (= *hya*) is due, perhaps, to the loss of the aspirate resulting partly from the interchanged positions of *h* and *y* in Pāli. Since the Prakrit form appears to be possible more from *yh* than from *hy*, it is necessary to point out that it presupposes a Pāli original. **Bhumaṭha** and **bala** have singular accusative endings.

11 apra[madena makabha[2] devana samidh(i) gat]u
apramada praśajhati pramadu garahitu sada O[3]

(A[3], 17 and A[2], 1 completing together the entire verse)

Cf. Dhammap., v. 30 † (Appamādav., v. 10) :—

Appamādena Maghavā devānam seṭṭhatam gato
Appamādam pasamsanti pamādo garahito sadā.

---

[1] The circle is supplied by us.
[2] In M. Senart's edition *madena makabha* are linked together (see. I. A[2], 1).
[3] The circle is supplied by us.

Notes.—In M. Senart's adjustment of the plates of the Kharoṣṭhī Ms., line A², 1, with the reading ". . *madenamakabha devanasamidh(i) gat.*", appears as a remnant of a verse of which he was able to trace no parallel. The discovery of the connexion of A², 1 with A³, 17 is a momentous event in the compilation of the present edition. We need not point out at length the errors to which the French scholar was led on account of this oversight on his part. **Makabha**=Pāli *Maghavā*. The aspiration of *b* compensates for the change of *gh* into *k* through an intermediate *g*. **Samidhi**=Pāli *samidhiṁ*, which may be substituted as a synonym for the Pāli *seṭṭhataṁ*, cf. *samiddhiṁ att·no*, Dhp. v. 84. *Praśajhati*=Pāli *pasaṁsanti*, Sk. *praśaṁsanti*. M. Senart assures us of the correctness of his reading. But we should have expected a reading like *praśaṅsati*, remembering that in our text the *ṁ* is changed into *ṅ* before *s*.

12 (hi)[1]na dhama na sev(e)[2]a pramadena na savasi
michadiṭhi na roy(e)[3]a na sia lokavaḍhano O[4]

(A², 2)

Cf. Dhammap., v. 167 † (Lokav., v. 1) :—

Hīnaṁ dhammaṁ na seveyya pamādena na saṁvase
Micchādiṭṭhi na seveyya na siyā lokavaddhano.

Notes.—In this verse, which is exactly similar in expression to its Pāli counterpart except for **royea** (=*roceyya*) in place of *seveyya*, we have an exhortation not to have anything to do with sensuality, thoughtlessness, wrong views and popularity.

13 yo tu puvi pramajati pacha su na pramajati
so ita loku ohaseti abha muto va suriu O

(A², 3)

Cf. Dhammap., v. 172 † (Lokav., v. 6)
=Majjhima, II. p. 105=Therag., v. 871 :—

Yo ca pubbe pamajjitvā pacchā so na-ppamajjati
So'maṁ lokaṁ pabhāseti abbhā mutto va candimā.

1, 2, 3, 4 Supplied by us, some in accordance with M. Senart's suggestions.

Cf. Udānav, ch.. XVI. ("Miscellaneous"), v. 5 :—

"He who formerly was heedless and who afterwards has become careful, like the moon free from clouds, he brightens up the whole world."

Notes.—In this verse we can perceive a change of tone, as we have in it a message of hope for those who have so far been thoughtless, like an Aṅgulimāla, and cannot aspire to live a better life on account of their sinful disposition. The teaching of the simile in the second line is that sin is but a passing shadow of the mind which darkens man's spiritual prospects. **Pramajati**=Pāli *pamajjati*. A right reading would, according to M. Senart, have been *pramajeti* or *pramajiti*=*pramajitva*. As for *ita*=*etaṁ*, see M. Senart's Notes. **Suriu**=Pāli *sūriyo*, an instance of *Epenthesis* (*riu*=*ryaḥ*). It seems that in the language of our text an aspirate after *y* is vocalized and changed into *u* ; cf. *aruyu* (v. 10). The Prakrit reading is a stronger expression than the Pāli *candimā*.

14 [1] arahadha nikhamadha yujatha budhaśaśane
dhunatha macuno sena nalagara ba kuñaru ○
(A², 4)

Cf. Theragāthā †, vv. 256, 1147
=Saṁyutta, I. pp. 156-7 :—

Ārabbhatha nikkhamatha yuñjatha buddhasāsane
Dhunātha maccuno senaṁ naḷāgāraṁ va kuñjaro.

Cf. Divyâvadāna, pp. 68, 138 :—

Ārabhadhvaṁ niṣkramata yujyadhvaṁ buddhaśāsane
Dhunīta mṛtyunaḥ sainyaṁ naḍāgāram iva kuñjaraḥ.

Cf. Udānavarga, ch. IV. ("Purity"), v. 34 :—

"Arise, commence a new life, turn towards the doctrine of the Buddha ; trample down the hosts of the lord of death as an elephant does a house of mud."

---

[1] This verse together with verses 15 and 16 is to be considered as a blended whole. In the Theragāthā, the Saṁyutta and the Divyâvadāna, the counterpart of the Prakrit verse 15 is absent and those of vv. 14 and 16 only are found grouped together, while in the Dīghanikāya vv. 15 and 16 constitute a whole, v. 14 being absent.

Notes.—Now comes the awe-inspiring command or the charge, as if in a lion's roar, from a great conquerer like Buddha the Sākyan hero. The command and its tone are indeed worthy of such a master who achieved self-conquest through a valorous will not to cease to strive, whether 'the sky be rent asunder or the earth leave her fixed station' (*nabhaṁ phaleyya, paṭhaviṁ caleyya*). It will be noticed that the Udānavarga verse has a different simile, and the expression is weaker than the Prakrit or its Pāli counterpart. **Dhunatha**=Pāli *dhunātha* =*dhunīta* (Divyâvadāna), "trample down." The expression is metaphorical, implying the idea of distending cotton. **Macuno sena**=Pāli *maccuno senaṁ*="the hosts of the lord of death" (Udānavarga). Here, death is but another epithet of the tempter Māra, whose fighting units are mentioned in the *Padhānasutta* (Suttanipāta, No. 28), vv. 436-39.

15 apramata smatimata suśila bhotu bhichavi
susamahitasagapa sacita anurachadha ○

(A², 5)

Cf. Dīgha, II. p. 120[1] :—

Appamattā satimanto susīlā hotha bhikkhavo
Susamāhitsaṅkappā sacittaṁ anurakkhatha.

Cf. Udānav., ch. IV. ("Purity"), v. 33 :—

"The Bhixu who is truly moral and who delights in earnestness brings thus all his thoughts well under control, and his mind is in safety."

Notes.—This verse sets forth the first requisites of self-conquest which are that the Bhikkhus intent on defeating the hosts of Māra must be of an undaunted spirit and well-behaved, having a well concentrated will and a well controlled mind. **Bhotu**=Pāli *hotu*, Sk. *bhavatu*, a singular verb used with a plural nominative.

---

[1] M. Senart cites as a parallel the Dhammapada verse 327.

16 yo imasa[1] dhamavinau apramatu vihaṣiti
prahai jatisaṅsara dukhusata[2] kariṣa(t)i ○[3]

(A², 6)

Cf. Dīgha, II. p. 121=Saṁyutta I. p. 157 =Therag., v. 257 :—

Yo imasmiṁ dhammavinaye appamatto vihessati
Pahāya jāti-saṁsāraṁ dukkhass' antaṁ karissati.

Cf. Divyâvadāna, p. 68 :—

Yo hyasmin dharmavinaye apramattaś cariṣyati
Prahāya jātisaṁsāraṁ duhkhasyântaṁ kariṣyati.

Cf. Udānav., ch. IV. ("Purity"), v. 35 :—

"Whoever has lived according to this law of discipline, in gentleness and purity, will, having cast off transmigration, put an end to his misery."

Notes.—Now comes the persuasion as an argument in support of the heroic command in the preceding two verses. For comments on this verse the reader is referred to M. Senart's Notes. We have just to add that **imasa** (=Pāli *imasmiṁ*) is another instance where a genitive termination has been used for the locative.

17 ta yu vadami bhadrañu yavatetha samakata
apramadarata bhodha sadhami supravediti ○

(A², 7)

Notes.—The Pāli counterpart of this verse cannot be traced. It is the result of a new combination of three set expressions, which are :—

(1) *Taṁ vo vadāmi bhaddaṁ vo yāvant'ettha samāgatā* (Dhp. v. 337 ; Jat. III, p. 387. l. 21)—for the 1st line ;
(2) *appamādaratā hotha* (Dhp. v. 327)—for the 3rd foot ;
(3) *saddhamme suppavedite* (Itivuttaka, p. 78)—for the 4th foot.

---

[1] In M. Senart's reading *sa* is connected with *dhama*.
[2] The correct reading, according to M. Senart, would be *dukhasata*.
[3] The circle is supplied by us.

For the explanation of the Prakrit forms, the reader is referred to M. Senart's Notes.

18 pramada parivajetva[1] apramadarata sada
bhavetha kuśala dhama yokachemasa prataa.

Notes—The Pāli counterpart of this verse cannot be traced. The Suttanipāta verse 425 contains the expression *yogakkhemassa pattiyā* which corresponds to the Prakrit verse-end. As a matter of fact, a Jātaka verse (Fausböll, I. pp. 275, 278) supplies us with an almost exact Pāli parallel to the 2nd line by the reading—*Bhāreti kusalaṁ dhammaṁ yogakkhemassa pattiyā*. **Prataa**=Pāli *pattiyā*. The Prakrit form rests on a Sanskrit rather than a Pāli word.

19 . . . prata suhino[2] apramadaviha . .

....

(A[1], 1)

Cf. Udānav., ch. VI. ("Morality"), v. 20 :—

"This is the road that leads to happiness ; he who has entered on this road of perfect purity[3] will by keeping to it cast off the bonds of Māra."

Notes.—The Pāli parallel of the above verse cannot be traced. Rockhill's translation of the Tibetan version of the Udānavarga verse, cited above, is also so tentative that it is difficult to establish a complete identification. There is, moreover, no certainty that the second line of the Prakrit is identical with that of the Udānavarga verse. It is unmistakably true that the verse under notice is modelled on a gāthā of which the counterpart is supplied by the Dhammapada, v. 57 and the Udānavarga, v. 19, ch. VI, which are quoted below :—

Tesaṁ sampannasīlānaṁ appamādavihārinaṁ
Sammadaññāvimuttānaṁ Māro maggaṁ na vindati.

---

[1] The Ms. reads *parivajeti* : the alteration has been made according to M. Senart's suggestion.

[2] M. Senart reads *prata* and *suhino* as one word. We, however, think it better to separate them in the light of our restoration.

[3] Rockhill's rendering of *apramada*.

"They therefore who leave in thoughtfulness, who are perfectly purified by their moral conduct and who are emancipated by the perfectness of their knowledge, will not meet with the road of Māra."

The first foot might be completed, in the light of the expression *te khemapattā sukhino* (of the Pāli verse in Majjhima, III. p. 187), as *te chema aprata suhino,* and the second, in the light of the Dhammapada verse cited above, as *apramadaviharino.* As regards the third and fourth feet, we are at a loss to decide whether these are similar to those of the Dhammapada verse 57, or of the Udānavarga verse 20, or of the Majjhima verse or of a different one. In this state of uncertainty we can at the most hazard this fourfold restoration :—

(1) in the light of the Dhammapada verse 57 :—

samadañavimutana maro magu na vinati ○

(2) in the light of the Udānavarga verse 20 (ch. vi) :—

apramata viharata jahati m rabanana ○

(3) in the light of the Majjhima verse

("Sabbaverabhayâtītā sabbadukkhaṁ upaccaguṁ") :—

savavirabhayatita savraduha uva·ai ○

(4) in the light of the Apramada v. 25 (*i.e.,* Senart's A[1], 7) :—

apramata viharata pranoti paramu sukhu ○

Adopting the last alternative, the verse might be restored thus :—

(te chema)prata suhino apramadaviha(rino)
apramata viharata pranoti paramu sukhu ○

Chemaprata suhino=Pāli *khemapattā sukhino,* 'those who are happy after having attained to the state of security, *i.e.,* Nirvāṇa'. *Chema* is a shorter form of *yokachema* =Pāli *yogakkhema,* a synonym of *Nibbāna.* This is the same in meaning as *paramu sukhu.*

20 apramadi pramodia ma gami ratisabhamu
apramato hi jhayatu viśeṣa adhikachati ○

(A[1], 2)

21 apramadi pramodia ma gami ratisabhamu
apramato hi jhayatu chaya dukhasa pramuni O
(A[1]; 3)

Cf. Dhammap., v. 27 † (Appamādav., v. 7) =Majjhima, II. p. 105=Saṁyutta I. p. 25 =Therag., v. 884 :—

Mā pamādam anuyuñjetha mā kāmaratisanthavaṁ
Appamatto hi jhāyanto pappoti vipulaṁ[1] sukhaṁ.

Cf. Udānav., ch. IV. ("Purity"), v. 8 :—

"Have nothing to do with false doctrines, have nothing to do with the heedless; he who delights not in false theories shall not continue (in) the world".

Cf. *Ibid*, ch. IV., v. 11 :—

"He who is not given up to carelessness, who finds no delight in pleasures, whose mind is always attentive, will put an end to sorrow".

Notes.—The exact counterpart of the Prakrit verses connot be traced in the Pāli canon, and the parallel cited above is an extract from the verses ascribed in the Majjhima Nikāya and the Theragāthā to Aṅgulimāla Thera. The Pāli verse occurs also in Saṁyutta I. We cannot but think that the Prakrit verses were manipulated later on one single model which is no other than the Pāli verse. The variations are not inexplicable. The verses are in essence the same, and there are numerous instances where new verses are manipulated by adjustment of certain set expressions. The parallel cited from the Udānavarga is similar to v. 21.

Verse 20.—**Apramadi pramodia**=Pāli *appamāde pamodeyya*, 'one should delight in earnestness', which is a positive expression for the Pāli *mā pamādaṁ anuyuñjetha*, 'have nothing to do with thoughtless indolence'. For the change of *eyya* into *ia*, see M. Senart's Notes. **Ma gami ratisabhamu** is a better expression, according to M. Senart, than the Pāli

[1] Variant, *paramaṁ*.

mā kāmaratisanthavaṁ, 'one should not delight in associating with sensual joys". He takes *gami* as an aorist singular form of √gam (to go), and **sabhamu**=Sk. *saṁbhramaṁ*, the whole expression implying "do not proceed to care for sense-delight". We fail to find any "gross" mistake in the Pāli expression, as opined by M. Senart, except that it is somewhat elliptical, or how *saṁbhramaṁ* could give a better meaning than *saṁstavaṁ* or "companionship". Who knows that the reading *sabhamu* for the Pāli *santharaṁ* is not a gross mistake of the scribe, or that *gami* is not a phonetic change from *kāma*, the final *i* being accounted for as due to a desire to maintain rhythm with *rati* following. We quite appreciate that *ma gami rati*, in the sense in which M. Senart takes it, improves the Pāli reading. But it is rather desirable to leave open the question raised by him as to the chronology of the two expressions. **Viśeṣa adhikachati**=Pāli *visesaṁ adhigacchati*, (see Fausböll's Jātaka, I. p. 435). This is a mode of expression which is substituted for *pappoti vipulaṁ* (or, *paramaṁ*) *sukhaṁ*. *Viśeṣa* means an extraordinary achievement which is *Nibbāna*.

Verse 21.—**Chaya dukhasa pramuni**=Pāli *khayaṁ dukkhassa pāpuṇe* (Itivuttaka, pp. 30, 87), Sk. *kṣayaṁ duḥkhasya prāpnuyāt*. *Chaya dukhasa*, 'the destruction of suffering,' is a negative expression for *parama sukha*.

22 (apramada)[1]rata bhodha khano yu ma uvacai
khanatita (h)i śoyati niraeṣu samapi(ta)[2] O[3]

Notes.—Here is just another instance of a new verse constructed out of some stereotyped Pāli materials with a different setting. The materials are :—

(1) *appamādaratā hotha* (Dhp. v. 327)—for the first foot of the Prakrit. Cf. v. 17 above.

(2) *khaṇo ve mā upaccagā* | *Khaṇātītā hi socanti nirayamhi samappitā* ‖ (Dhp. v. 315 ; Therag. v. 403)—for the rest of the verse.

---

[1], [2], [3] Supplied by us.

This expression constitutes the refrain of two distinct verses (cf. Suttanipāta v. 333 and Theragāthā, v. 1005).

For **uvacai**=Pāli *upaccagā*, we have nothing more to add to M. Senart's notes than that the process of the change of *ga* into *i* is through *ja* changed into *ya*, i.e., *ga=ja =ya=i*.

23 apramadarata bhodha sadhami supravedite
drugha udhvaradha atmana pagasana va
kuñ(aru)[1] O[2]
(A [1], 5)

Cf. Dhammap., v. 327 † (Nāgav. v. 8) :—

Appamādaratā hotha, sacittam anurakkhatha
Duggā uddharath' attānaṁ paṅke sanno[3] va kuñjaro.

Cf. Udānav., ch. IV. ("Purity"), v. 26 :—

"The Bhixu who delights in purity and who looks with dread on impurity will pull himself from out the evil way as the elephant pulls himself from out of the mire."

Notes.—The form and the spirit of the above verse are analogous to those of v. 22. In this case the new Pāli materials are :—

(1) *saddhamme suppavedite*,—for the second foot,—"in the good norm well explained," "under the well propounded system," which is the same in meaning as *dhammapade sudesite* (see reference under Pusav., v. 12); but compare Itivuttaka, p. 78, where we have the expression *saddhamme suppavedatha* ;

(2) *duggā uddharath' attānaṁ paṅke sanno va kuñjaro*, —for the second line,—"pull yourselves from out the evil away as an elephant pulls himself from out of the mire"; the simile forms a refrain of the Udānavarga verse, cited above, which is a later parallel of the Dhammapada verse 39.

For the forms **drugha udhvaradha**, we have nothing more to add to M. Senart's notes than that the aspiration of the sonant in *drugha* is due perhaps to the loss of *āt* in Sk. *durgāt*. The word seems to have reference to 'mud-forts'.

---

[1], [2] Supplied by us. [3] Variant : *satto*.

24 nai kalu pramadasa aprati asavachaye
pramata[1] duhu amoti siha ba muyamatia ○
(A[1], 6)

Cf. Udānav., ch. IV. ("Purity"), v. 12 :—

"He who has put an end to sorrow, and is not given to carelessness in this world, can no more be hurt by the careless than can the lion by the antelope."

Cf. Fausböll's Jātaka, I. p. 389 :—

Na vissase avissatthe vissatthe pi na vissase
Vissāsā bhayam anveti sīhaṁ va migamātukā.

Notes.—This verse of which the parallel is cited from the Udānavarga is the result of a new combination of certain set Buddhist expressions in Pāli which are as follows :—

(1) *nāyaṁ kālo pamādassa*, for the first foot;

(2) *appatte āsavakkhaye* (cf. the verse-end *appatto āsavakkhayaṁ*, Dhammap., v. 272)—for the second foot.

(3) *pamattā dukkhaṁ papponti sīhā va migamātukā* (*i.e.*, the indolent experience pain like the lions beguiled by the gazelles), or *pamādā dukkham anveti sīhaṁ va migamātukā* (*i.e.*, from indolence pain follows a man as it follows the lion beguiled by the gazelle)—for the second line.

Pramata=Pāli *pamattā*. A reading *pramada* (=Pāli *pramādā*, ablative) would make the second line of our text a close parallel to the Pāli, provided that *amoti* could be equated with *anveti* of the Pāli verse. Thus, we have a choice between *amoti*=(*p*)*apponti*, as suggested by M. Senart, and *amoti*=*anveti*. The change of *p* into *m* through an intermediate *b* is the easiest possible, but we have to consider that in the following verse we have *pranoti* as a Prakrit counterpart of *papponti*. We have, therefore, to enquire if the change of *nve* (*anveti*) into *mo* (*amoti*) is possible. There are several instances where *nve* is changed into *ve* (cf. *aveti*=Pāli *anveti* Sahasavaga, vv. 6-11). There are also instances where *v*

[1] A reading *pramada* might also be adopted at the risk of the supposition that the reading *pramata* is due to the scribe.

is changed into *m* (cf. *namu*=Pāli *nāvaṁ*, Bhikhuv., v. 25). This would give us *ameti* or *amiti* for *anveti*. If we accept this reading we cannot but have to dispute M. Senart's *amoti*. **Siha ba muyamatia** would correspond to Pāli *sihā* (or *sīhaṁ*) *va migamātukā*. M. Senart imagines that the simile refers to a story where the lion killed himself by his negligence in fancying to have to deal with a gazelle instead of some formidable enemy. The Jātaka story is that the trouble of the lion was due to his going to be intimate with the she-deer in disregard of any danger. *Muya*=Sk. *mṛga*=Pāli, *muga*, *maga*, *miga*; and *matia*=Sk. *mātṛkāya* (abl.), Pāli *mātukā(ya)*.

25 nai pramadasamayu aprati asavachayi

apramato hi jhayatu[1] pranoti paramu sukhu · O

(A[1], 7)

....ga 25

(A[1], 8)

Notes.—This verse of which no exact counterpart can be traced in the Piṭakas also results from a combination of three set expressions transformed into Prakrit, so that the first foot **nai pramadasamayu**=Pāli *nāyaṁ pamādasamayo*, the second is the same as in verse 25, except for *chayi* in place of *chaye*; the second line=Pāli *appamatto hi jhāyanto pappoti paramaṁ sukhaṁ* (see Majjh. II. p. 105, Therag. v. 884; Dhp., v. 27). Reading through the Prakrit verses 20-27, one is apt to feel as though one original verse as represented by Dhp. 27 were expanded to enclose within its two lines many verses constructed out of set expressions, and this may account for the absence of their parallels in the existing Pāli canon. The exhortation of all these verses is in tone the same as that of verses 14 and 15, with this difference that while Nos. 14 and 15 purport to be commands, verses 20-27, no less than Nos. 16-19, bring out the reasons in support thereof. **Pranoti**=Pāli *pappoti*, Sk. *prāpnoti*. It is to be specially noted that the Prakrit form is an immediate change from Sanskrit.

The chapter contains 25 stanzas, hence **ga 25**.

---

[1] The Ms. reads *jayatu*, which we regard as a mistake of the scribe.

[3. Citavaga]

M. Senart's transcript of a few small, broken and detached fragments shows clear traces, among others, of five stanzas, all belonging to the Citta-group as known to us through the Pāli Dhammapada. These stanzas are no more than the Prakrit parallels of the Pāli verses 37, 34, 38, 39 and 33. Five verses of the Citta-group are cited in the extant commentary on the Telapatta Jātaka (No. 96), and these are the same as the Pāli verses, 35, 36, 37, 38 and 33. That the existing group of the 'Mind'-verses stood in the original Kharoṣṭhī Ms. immediately after the *Apramada*, is apparent from the position of the fragments themselves (see M. Senart's "Fragments of A"). But, in the absence of the colophon which is missing from the existing Ms., it is impossible to say exactly how many verses were contained in the third chapter of the Prakrit text. So far as we can conjecture, this particular chapter contained no less than 11 verses in all, and probably a little more than that. The Citta-group, representing as it does the third chapter of the Pāli Dhammapada, has altogether 11 verses, and the same group in the Udānavarga forms its 31st chapter and contains 64 stanzas, or more accurately, 63, leaving out of account the verse 45 which is a mere repitition of verse 44. Of the existing 5 Prakrit verses of the Cita-group only two, *viz.*, 2 and 5, are to be found in the Udānavarga in which the number of Mind-verses could so much swell up partly from the incorporation of verses occurring in different chapters of the Pāli text. The Chinese *Fa-Kheu-King* also has a whole section on "the Mind", containing 12 verses, of which only 2 or 3 are similar to the Pāli. Like the Pāli and Prakrit texts, the *Citta*-group stands next to the *Appamāda* in the Fa-Kheu-King, while, strangely enough, it is placed in the Udānavarga immediately before the *Bhikkhu*. The significance of the arrangement of chapters has been discussed in the Introduction. It only remains here to point out that the Citta-group teaches nothing that is absolutely Buddhistic in its main conception, for the Upanishads, both pre-Buddhistic[1] and post-Buddhistic[2], abound in self-same or similar ascetic reflections on the nature of the mind. Indeed the *Cita*-verses teach that the necessity of the strenuous effort of the will to attain the supreme good, so much dwelt upon in the *Apramada*-verses, arises from the flighty, unstable and pleasure-seeking dispositions of the mind itself.

---

[1] *E.g.*, Chāndogya Up., VII. 5.
[2] *E.g.*, Maitri Up., Maitrāyaṇī Up., Mahôpa., etc.

1 [d]ur.(?)ga. e..

....

(Frag. A I)

Cf. Dhammap., 37 † (Cittavagga, v. 5) :—

Dūraṅgamaṁ ekacaraṁ asarīraṁ guhāsayaṁ
Ye cittaṁ saññamessanti mokkhanti Mārabandhanā.

2 vario va thale chi..

....

(Frag. A I)

Cf. Dhammap. 34 † (Cittav., v. 2) :—

Vārijo va thale khitto okamokato ubbhato
Pariphandat' idaṁ cittaṁ Māradheyyaṁ pahātave.

Cf. Udānav., ch. XXXI. ("The Mind"), v. 2 :—

"To escape from the abode of Māra one is filled with trembling, like a fish taken from its watery abode, and thrown on dry land".

3 anuvaṭhitacitasa..

....

(Frag. A I)

Cf. Dhammap. 38 † (Cittav., v. 6) :—

Anavaṭṭhitacittassa saddhammaṁ avijānato
Pariplavapasādassa paññā na paripūrati.

4 anuvaṣutacita..

....

(Frag. A I)

Cf. Dhammap., 39 † (Cittav., v. 7) :—

Anavassutacittassa ananvâhatacetaso
Puññapāpapahīnassa n' atthi jāgarato bhayaṁ.

5 ....la cita druracha drunivarana
u..

(Frag. A VIII)

Cf. Dhammap., 33 † (Cittav., 1) :—

Phandanaṁ capalaṁ cittaṁ dūrakkhaṁ dunnivārayaṁ
Ujuṁ karoti medhāvī usukāro va tejanaṁ.

Cf. Udānav., XXXI. ("The Mind"), v. 8 :—

"......... the mind being uncertain, changeable, flighty, and hard to control, he must straighten it by application as the fletcher straightens (his arrows) with fire".

Notes.—The difficulty as to the interpretation of the above verses arises chiefly from their incompleteness. One has to depend a good deal on conjecture in reconstructing the Prakrit verses from a few expressions or catchwords which now survive. The task would no doubt have been simple enough if it could be supposed that differences between the Prakrit and Pāli verses were mere phonetic. But these differences, real or imagined, cannot be shelved as such and are, therefore, not immaterial, since instances are not rare where the verses in the two texts agree on the whole, and yet there appear in them a few words, phrases or clauses, which greatly modify their sense. In the present case, however, no other assumption would avail us than that of complete identity or correspondence. Accordingly, the *Citta*-verses might be reconstructed and read as follows :—

1 dur(a)ga(ma) e(kacara[1] aśarira[2] guhaśaya[3]
ye[4] cita sañameṣati[5] mochati[6] marabanana[7] ○)

---

[1] Cf. eka in Cro, 6, 9, 10 ; *cara* in B, 36. [2] Cf. *śarira* in Cvo, 21.
[3] This word is nowhere to be found in the Kharoṣṭhī Ms. [4] Cf. *ye* in Cvo, 7, 33.
[5] Also *sañamiṣati* ; cf. *sañamu* in B, 9 ; [6] Cf. *rachati* for the Pāli *rakkhati* in A*, 14. [7] Cf. *banana* in Frag. C. XXIIIvo ; also *bandhana* ; cf. *dridha bandhana* in Cvo, 31, 32 ; and *muto bandhana* in B, 52.

2 vario va thale chi(tu[1] okamokato[2] ubhato[3]
pariphanatida[4] cita mucudhea[5] pahatae[6] O)

3 anuvaṭhitacitasa (sadharma[7] avijanatu[8]
paripalaaprasadasa[9] praña[10] na paripurati[11] O)

4 anuvaṣutacita(sa anavahatacetaso[12]
puñapavapahinasa[13] nathi[14] jagarato[15] bhayo[16] O)

5 (phanana[17] . capa[18])la cita druracha drunivarana
u(ju karoti[19] medhavi[20] usukaro[21] va teyana[22] O)

Verse 1.—Duragama = Pāli and Sk. *dūraṅgamaṁ*, an instance of compound, meaning 'far-going', 'that which travels far'. The question whether the correct Prakrit reading would be *duragama* or *durugama* must be left open. The same holds true of the reading of the final syllable *ma* or *mu*. For *mu* cf. *ratisabhamu* in A[1], 2. In support of the vowel *a* before *g* in *duragama* we might cite here a parallel instance, namely *aṭhagio* (Magav. v. 30) which equates with Pāli *aṭṭhaṅgiko*. In this latter Prakrit word the vowel *a* appears unchanged, in M. Senart's reading, before *g*. The Buddhist commentator's explanation of the word *duraṅgama* is :—"*cittassa hi makkaṭasuttamattakampi puratthimādi-disābhāgena gamanaṁ nāma n'atthi; dūre santampi pana ārammaṇaṁ sampaṭicchatīti duraṅgamaṁ nāma jātaṁ.*" That is, "even during 'monkey-sleep'[23] (dreaming state), mind has no exit in the east and other directions[24]; even remaining at a distance, it entertains the object, hence arises the predicate *far-going*". This

---

[1] Also *chito*. [2] Cf. *maranato*, Cvo, 7; also *okamokadha*. [3] Cf. *anudhato* for the Pāli *anuddhato* in B, 11. [4] Cf. *nivinati* for the Pāli *nibbindati* in A[3], 1-3. [5] Also *Maradhea*. [6] No such infinitive form is met with in the Kharoṣṭhī Ms. [7] Cf. *sadharma* in B, 22, 23. [8] Cf. *vivaśatu* for Pāli *vipassato* in B, 12. [9] Also *pariplava*; cf. *keleśa* for Pāli *kilesa* and Sk. *kleśa* in B, 46; cf. *prasadasa* in Cro, 11-13. [10] Cf. *prañaya*, *prañae*, *prañai* in A[3], 1, 2, 9. [11] The verbal form occurs nowhere in the Kharoṣṭhī Ms. [12] Cf. *aveti* for the Pāli *anveti* in Cro, 11-16; cf. *sumedhasu* in A[3], 15. [13] Cf. *puñe*, *pave* in B, 3; cf. (*hi*)*na* in A[2], 2. [14] Cf. *nathi* in B, 16, 38. [15] See f. n. 23. [16] Cf. *maranato bhayo* in Cvo, 7. [17] For *phanana* cf. *pariphanati* (f.n. 11 above). [18] Also *cavala*; cf. *cavadhi* for the Pāli *cāpato* in Cro, 31. [19] Cf. *kariṣati* in A[2], 6; *kuruti* for the Pāli *kurute* in Cro, 24. [20] Cf. *medhavi* in A[3], 14. [21] Cf. *anakara* in Frag. C. XXXIIIvo. [22] Cf. *kuyana* for *kujana* in A[4], 1.

[23] Cf. the Milinda expression *kapi-niddā* (Milinda-pañho, p. 299). The Milinda theory of dream has been fully discussed by Mr. Shwe Zan Aung in his Introductory Essay to the *Compendium of Buddhist Philosophy*, P. T. S. pp. 48 f.

[24] Cf. Bṛihad Āraṇyaka Up., IV. 3. 10, where Yājñavalkya says :—"*Na tatra ratvā na rathayogā na panthāno bhavanti. Atha rathān rathayogān pathaḥ sṛjate.*"

explanation derives its authority from the time-honoured oral traditions of the Theras, and one can safely regard it as a sound statement of the Buddhist psychological position which would demur a mere philological interpretation of *dūraṅgama,* a word which in its literal sense signifies a belief in the existence of a mind or spirit (German *Geist*) capable of going far away and returning at its sweet will to the body. According to the Buddhist notion, the mind is *dūraṅgama* in the sense that it can think of a distant object, just as a person in India can think of St. Paul's cathedral in the city of London. The expression requires a further word of explanation. It is indeed just one of the many instances where the Buddhists read their own meaning into a current expression, which would yield a contrary sense if a literal interpretation were adhered to. As we shall see in the case of *ekacara* and other predicates of *cita,* the expressions were manipulated by the Buddhists on the basis of Upanishadic phraseology. It seems certain that the predicate *duraṅgama* has preserved reminiscences of primitive animistic notions of soul or spirit[1] which are not without their influence upon the Upanishadic theories of waking, dream and sleep.[2] Cf. the Upanishad expressions *āsīne dūre vrajati*" (Kaṭha., II. 20); "*mano dūrataraṁ yāti*" (Mahopa., III. 18).

Ekacara = Pāli and Sk., *ekacaraṁ,* compound, meaning 'that which moves about alone'. According to the interpretation of the Dhammapada commentary, this predicate implies the Buddhist belief in the unity of mental life. To quote its own words, "seven or eight *cittas* are so strung together that they are not capable of arising at the same thought-moment. When a consciousness arises, it arises as a unit, and this having ceased to be, others arise one at a time"[3]. One must admit that this Buddhist explanation of *ekacaraṁ* closely follows on the lines of

---

[1] Prof. Rhys Davids notes (*Buddhist India,* p. 252): "Certain forms of disease were supposed to be due to the fact that the soul had escaped out of the body; and charms are recorded for bringing it back" (Atharva-Veda, V. 29·5; VI. 53·2; VII. 67. Cf. Aitareya Āraṇyaka, III. 2. 4. 7). Two older notions cited by Yājñavalkya are:

(1) "Tadete ślokā bhavanti:
Svapnena śārīram abhiprahatyâsuptaḥ suptān abhicākaśīti.
Śukram ādāya punareti sthānaṁ hiraṇmayaḥ puruṣa ekahaṃsaḥ;
(Bṛihad Ār. Up; IV. 3. 11).

(2) "Tannāyataṁ bodhayed ityâhuḥ, durbhisajyaṁ hâsmai bhanati yamêṣa na pratipadyate. (Bṛihad Ār. Up; IV. 3. 11).

[2] Cf. Bṛihad Ār. Up. IV. 3. 19; Chāndogya, VIII. 12. 3.

[3] "Sattaṭṭhacittāni pana ekato kaṇṇikabaddhāni ekakkhaṇe uppajjituṁ samatthāni nāma n'atthi. Uppattikāle ek'ekam eva cittaṁ uppajjati, tasmiṁ niruddhe pana ek'ekam eva uppajjatîti ekacaraṁ nāma jātaṁ".

Pratardana's theory of the unity of mental life[1]. But the predicate *ekacara* seems to have been based rather upon Yājñavalkya's expressions, all applied to soul, *e.g.*, "*asaṅgo na hi sajjate*" (Bṛihad Ār. Up. IV. 2. 4); "*ekahaṁsaḥ*" (*ibid*, IV. 3. 11-12); "*svapne ratvā caritvā*" (*ibid*, IV. 3. 15-16). **Aśarira** = Pāli *asarīraṁ*, a compound, meaning 'that which is without a body', 'incorporeal'. Mind has no bodily form nor has any such colour-distinction as yellow and the like[2]. Such is the commentator's interpretation. The predicate reminds us at once of Yājñavalkya's sxpressions "*aśīryo na hi śīryate*" (Bṛihad Ār. Up., IV. 2. 4).[3] **Guhaśaya** = Pāli *guhāsayaṁ*, Sk. *guhāśayam*, a compound, meaning 'that which lies in a cave', 'a cave-dweller'. The Dhammapada-Commentary says, "the cave is that which is built up of the four great elements. It is depending on the heart that the mind comes into play, hence its predicate 'a cave-dweller' ".[4] The Buddhist predicate of *citta* reminds us at once of the Upanishadic notions of the soul, e.g. "*nihitó guhāyām*" (Kaṭha, II. 20), 'that which dwells in the cavity of the heart'[5]; cf. Muṇḍaka, III. 1. 5. **Cita** = Pāli and Sk. *cittaṁ*, mind.

It is clear from the foregoing discussion of the historical significance of the expressions *duragama* and the rest, how close the resemblance is between the Buddhiṣt conception of mind and the Upanishadic conception of soul :—(1) *citta* is *dūraṅgama* in the sense that it can think of an object from a great distance; and soul remaining stationary can travel far ('*āsīno dūre vrajati*", Kaṭha, II. 20); (2) *citta* is *ekacara* in the sense that all mental operations take place one at a time, as a unit with regard to time; and soul as a lonely bird roams about alone during dream ("*ekahaṁsaḥ .... svapne ... caritrā .... bhavatyasaṅgo*", Bṛihad Ār., IV. 3. 12-16); and all the senses being unified perform their functions, the operations taking place one at a time ("*ekabhūyaṁ vai prāṇā bhūtvā ekaikaṁ sarvāṇyevaitāni prajñāpayanti*" Kauṣītaki, III. 2); (3) *citta* is *asarīra*

[1] Kauṣītaki Up., III. 2: "ekabhūyaṁ vai prāṇā bhūtvā ekaikaṁ sarvāṇyêvaitāni prajñāpayanti".

[2] "Cittasa sarīrasaṇṭhānaṁ vā nīlâdippakāro vaṇṇabhedo vā n' atthîti asarīraṁ nāma jātaṁ".

[3] This is a very common idea in the Upanishads.

[4] "Guhā nāma catumahābhūtaguhā idaṁ ca hadayarūpaṁ nissāya vattatîti guhāsayaṁ nāma jātaṁ".

[5] Cf. Bṛihad Ār. Up., IV. 3. 7; V. 6; Chāndogya, VIII. 3. 3; Taittirīya, I. 6. 1.

in the sense that it is incorporeal; and soul is *aśīryo na hi śīryate* (Bṛihad Ār., IV. 2. 4); (4) *citta* is *guhāsaya* in the sense that it comes into play depending on the heart as its physical basis; and soul is said to dwell in the cavity of the heart (*'nihito guhāyām'*); cf. the later Buddhist expression *'hadayavatthu'*. **Marabanana** or **Marabandhana** = Pāli *Mārabandhanā*, Sk. *Mā·abandhanāt*, 'from the bonds of Māra'. But it seems better not to introduce the word *mara* which nowhere occurs in the extant Kharoṣṭhī Ms. As an alternative we might accept a reading *bhavabanana*, answering to Pāli *bhavabandhanā*, on the strength of a fragmentary expression, *lapabhavabanana* (I. Fr. c. XXIII^{vo}., p. 92).

Verse 2.—**Vario** = Pāli *vārijo*, Sk. *vārijaḥ*, fish. The elision of *j* between *i* and *o* presupposes an intermediate change of *j* into the semi-vowel *y*. Such an elision as this is a common characteristic of all Prakritic languages (see Vararuci's rule II. 2: *k, g, c, j, t, d, p, y, vāṁ prāyo lopaḥ*). The simile of the fish jumping when thrown on land after having been taken out of its watery home, is a familar and very striking imagery serving to call up a vivid picture of the innate strife of the mind to get off from the domain of death. **Okamokao** = Pāli *okamokato*, 'from the watery home'. According to the Dhammapada-Commentary, the expression resolves itself into two separate words, *oka-m-okato*, the former standing for 'water' (*udakaṁ*), and the latter for 'home' (*ālayo*, cf. *"okaṁ pahāya aniketasārī"*). **Mucudhea** = Pāli *Maccudheyyaṁ*, which is the same in meaning as *Māradheyyaṁ*, 'the kingdom of Death' (see Dhammapada, vv. 34 and 86). **Pahatae** = Pāli *pahātave*, 'in order to avoid', a survival of the Vedic infinitive. It seems that *v* in such cases was pronounced close to *y* and has here glided into the full vowel sound of the succeeding *e*.

Verse 3.—**Anuvaṭhitacitasa** = Pāli *anavaṭṭhitacittassa*, Sk. *anavasthitacittasya*, an instance of compound, meaning 'of one whose mind is unsteady'. M. Senart says that the *u* of *anu* is perfectly certain, as much in this word as in *anuvaṣuta* of the next verse, and that the scribe has, perhaps, been drawn into this blunder by the thought of *anuvathita* = *anupasthita*, which floated in his mind. **Avijanatu** = Pāli *avijānato*, 'of one who does not know'. For the reading see foot-note 8, p. 143.

Verse 4.—**Anuvaṣutacitasa** = Pāli *anavassutacittassa*, an instance of compound, meaning 'of one of undissipated thought'. We prefer *anavaṣutacitasa*, as the reading *anuvaṣuta* cannot be defended on the same ground as *anuvaṭhita*, and it is not unlikely that the scribe wrote *anuvaṣuta* on false analogy with *anuvaṭhita*. **Anavahatacetaso** = Pāli *ananvāhatacetaso*, an instance of compound, meaning 'of one with unperplexed mind'. For *v* standing for Pāli *nv*, cf. *areti* equating with Pāli *anveti* (I. c^ro^, 11-16). **Punapava** = Pāli *puññapāpa*, Sk. *puṇya-pāpa*, '(of one who is devoid of) merit and demerit'. This expression strikes the keynote of Indian religions of which the good lies beyond both merit and demerit, a transcendental state of mind which none but an Indian *yogi* can experience.

Verse 5.—**Phanana** = Pāli *phandanaṁ*, Sk. *spandanam*, 'trembling, vibrating, or precipitating towards sensuous objects', as the Dhammapada-Commentary puts it. Here the expression 'trembling or vibrating' is used rather figuratively, its primary sense being associated with the pulsation of life (cf. *prāṇaṁ prāṇantaṁ*, life pulsating, Kauṣītaki, III. 2), an idea, perhaps derived originally from the palpitation of heart. The idea *phandana* was deepened later into a more scientific Buddhist theory of apperception (*javana*). **Capala** = Pāli and Sk *capalaṁ*, 'unsteady'. Like *phanana*, the expression *capala* is to be taken in a figurative sense. The genesis of this idea of the unsteady nature of mind can be traced to electrical phenomena, such as the flash of lightning. Cf. the Mahôpanishad verses (IV. 99-100):

Na hi cañcalatāhīnaṁ manaḥ kvacana dṛśyate,
Cañcalatvaṁ manodharmo vahnerdharmo yathoṣṇatā
Eṣā hi cañcalāspandaśaktiścittatvasaṁsthitā
Tāṁ viddhi mānasīṁ śaktiṁ jagadāḍambarâtmikām.

Druracha = Pāli *dūrakkhaṁ*, Sk. *dūrakṣyaṁ* (*dur* + *rakṣyam*), a compound, meaning 'that which is difficult to guard'. **Drunivarana** = Pāli *dunnivāraṇaṁ*, Sk. *durnivāraṇaṁ*, a compound, meaning 'that which is difficult to resist'. It affords another instance of the change of *dur* into *dru*. Cf. *dhamatrakehi* and notes, pp. 102-3; *pravataṭho*, p. 128; and *drugha*, p. 137.

[4. Puṣavaga]

The distinctive characteristic of the verses of this group lies in the simile of the flower which occurs in each of them. The Pāli parallels of them are rightly designated 'the verses of the flower-group', *Pupphavagga*, in the Pāli Dhammapada chap. IV. The Pāli Flower-verses number 16. The number of the Prakrit verses, as may be judged from the colophon "ga 15" (I. c^ro^, 5), is 15. Only four out of 15 verses have survived in the Kharoṣṭhī Ms. The 12th section of the Chinese *Fa-kheu-king* corresponds to the Pāli *Pupphavagga*, and, as in the Pāli and Prakrit texts, it is placed immediately after the *Cittavagga*; and the section contains altogether 17 verses. In the Udānavarga the Flower-group forms the 18th chapter and contains 27 verses, or more accurately, 26, leaving out of account the verse 20 which is a mere repitition of 18. As in other instances, the Udānavarga collates the Flower-verses from the different chapters of the Pāli text. But exception must be taken to vv. 283-284 which have a very remote connection with the Flower-verses. The group is of little importance but for the simile of flower which seems to bring home the distinction between a good and a bad man in a very interesting and familiar way.

12[1] .... [yamaloka ji][2] ita[3] sadevaka
ko dhamapada sud.śita kuśalo[4] puṣaviva
payeṣiti O[5]
(C^ro^, 1)

13 budhu pradha................ṣiti yamaloka ji eta sadevaka
budhu dhamapada sudeśita kuśalo puṣaviva
payeṣiti O
(C^ro^, 2)

---

[1] Verses 1-11 are missing from the Kharoṣṭhī Ms.
[2] Frag. C. vi^ro^ (p. 88).
[3] *Ita* which is a variant of *eta* of the next verse.
[4] M. Senart reads *kuśala*, which according to the grammar of our dialect, would be either an accusative singular form or a nominative plural; but the sense required here is that of the nom. sing. The mistake is perhaps due to the scribe.
[5] This is supplied by us.

Cf. Dhammap., vv. 44-45 † (Pupphavagga, vv. 1-2) :—

Ko imaṁ paṭhaviṁ vijessati[1] Yamalokañ ca imaṁ sadevakaṁ,
Ko dhammapadaṁ sudesitaṁ kusalo puppham iva pacessati[2] ?
Sekho paṭhaviṁ vijessati Yamalokañ ca imaṁ sadevakaṁ,
Sekho dhammapadaṁ sudesitaṁ kusalo puppham iva pacessati ?

Cf. Fa-kheu-pi-u, sec. XII. ("Flowers"), p. 89[3] :—

"Who is able to select (conquer ?) the earth (i.e., the place of his abode), to escape Yama, and lay hold of heaven ? Who (is able) to repeat the verses of the Law as one who selects choice (excellent) flowers ?

The enlightened (one) selects the earth, avoids Yama, seizes heaven, illustriously repeats the verses of the Law, is able to cull the flowers of virtue".

Cf. Udānav., ch. XVIII. ("The Flower"), vv. 1-2 :—

"Who is there that can overcome the world of the gods, of the lord of death (Yama) and of men, who knows how to expose the most delightful law, as one would flowers ?

It is the disciple (sekhas) who can overcome the world of the gods, of the lord of death and of men, who knows how to expose the most delightful law, as one would flowers."

Notes.—The Prakrit verses might be restored in the light of the Pāli *gāthās* and those in the Fa-kheu-pi-u and the Udānavarga as follows :—

ko pradhavi vijeṣiti[4] yamaloka ji eta sadevaka
ko dhamapada sudeśita kuśalo puṣaviva payeṣiti O
budhu pradhavi vijeṣiti yamaloka ji eta sadevaka
budhu dhamapada sudeśita kuśalo puṣaviva payeṣiti O

---

[1] Some Ms. reads *vicessati* ; the Comy. adopts *vijessati*.

[2] Fausböll reads *iva-ppacessati* ; the Commentary adopts *vacessate* as well as *vicessati*.

[3] Beal's translation.

[4] Also *vijiṣiti viceṣiti, viciṣiti*.

Verse 12.—**Pradhavi**=Pāli *paṭhaviṁ*, Ardha Māgadhī *puḍhaviṁ*, Sk. *pṛthivīm*, 'the earth', *i.e.*, 'the world of men'. For the change of *pṛ* to *pr*, cf. *nivruti*, Jarav., v. 23. We also meet with the form *puḍhavi* in Jarav., v. 17. **Vijeṣiti**=Pāli *vijessati* or *vicessati*, translated "*superabit*", (Fausböll) *i.e.*, 'will overcome'; "can overcome" (Udānavarga); "is able to select (conquer ?)" (Fa-Kheu-pi-u). It is clear that the Udānavarga adopts a form similar to the Pāli *vijessati*, and the Fa-kheu-pi-u another similar to the Pāli *vicessati*. The Dhammapada-Comy. explains *vijessati* in the same sense as *vicessati* : *vijessati*=*vijinissati*, *vijānissati*, *paṭivijjhissati*, *sacchikarissati*, 'will fully know, cognise, apprehend, realise' =*vicessati*=*vicinissati*, *upaparikkhissati*, 'will discriminate, investigate'. According to this interpretation, *vijessati* seems=Sk. *vijñāsyati*. The other interpretation accepted by the Tibetan translator of the Udānavarga and by the modern translators of the Dhammapada, *viz.*, *vijessati*= "*superabit*", "will conquer", "will overcome" seems more acceptable. **Yamaloka**=Pāli *Yamalokaṁ*, "the realm of Death"=four nether worlds (*catubbidhaṁ apāyalokaṁ*, Dhammapada-Comy.). **Eta**=Pāli *etaṁ*. M. Senart says that this reading is more appropriate than the Pāli *imaṁ*, and we have nothing to say against it. **Sadevaka**=Pāli *sadevakaṁ*, 'together with the world of the gods". **Dhamapada**=Pāli *dhammapadaṁ*, Sk. *dharmapadam*, translated by Fausböll "versus legis"; by Beal "the verses of the law"; by Rockhill "the law"; and by Max Müller "the path of virtue"="the norm or the path of virtue categorised as the 37 constituent parts of enlightenment or beatitude (*sattatiṁsa-bodhipakkhika-dhamma-saṅkhātaṁ*, Dhammapada-Comy.). That the term implies the idea of the path or the norm, virtue, purity, or any other synonym of Nirvāṇa is evident from the Suttanipāta, v. 88 (Cundasutta, v. 6) : *yo dhammapade sudesite magge jīvati* (see also the Paramatthajotikā, Vol. II. Pt. I. p. 164). There are again passages where the term in a plural form is applied to such moral topics as *anabhijjhā*, *aryāpāda*, etc. To discriminate the path of virtue according to this interpretation is to distinguish between a good and a bad doctrine, *i.e.*, to understand the excellence of the Buddhist doctrine as contrasted with those of others. The other interpretation, that *dhammapada*="Law-verses", seems more suitable for a text like the Dhammapada. To select or collect the beautifully expressed law-verses like a skilful wreath-maker collecting the choice flowers and making them into wreaths is to discriminate carefully the more exquisite and elegant stanzas from others which are comparatively prosaic and to collate and arrange them according to metre, theme and logical sequence of thought, as has been done in the several recensions of the Dhammapada. An interesting account of the compilation of the Dhammapada is given in the preface to the Fa-kheu-king. **Kuśalo pusaviva payeṣiti** is the same in meaning as the Pāli *kusalo puppham iva pacessati*, "like a skilful (wreath-maker) collecting the (choice) flowers". An Indian explanation of this expression is well brought out in Rockhill's translation of the Tibetan version which reads: "Like unto a clever wreath-maker, who, having taken flowers from a garden, has manufactured them into beautiful wreaths and has then given them away, is he who, having gathered a quantity of precepts from out the Śāstras and formed them into a pleasing collection, does teach them to others". This goes to show that the Dhammapada is not a mere mechanical compilation of select stanzas, but judging it as a whole, it is to be considered a highly artistic product, a poetic creation which, like a most skilfully woven wreath, has made the lofty message of Buddhism appeal alike to the intellect and the emotion of so many Asiatic nations. The analogy, as applied by the Dhammapada-Commentary, brings home how intelligently the entire Buddhist system of faith was built up with its 37 parts interwoven into a harmonious whole to the exclusion of materials, rejected after a careful sifting.

Verse 13.—**Budhu** = Pāli *Buddho*, "the enlightened one" (Fa-Kheu-pi-u). The Pāli reading is *sekho*, a 'Learner', "the disciple" (Udānavarga). 'Sekho' is a Buddhist technical term applied to persons filling up the seven ranks of disciples below the Arahants who have reached the summit of moral perfection and spirituality. It is not clear how far the Prakrit *budhu* is influenced by the Mahāyāna conception of Buddha's personality, though the substitution of this term for the Pāli *sekho* is a significant fact. But *budhu* may also be taken simply in the sense of an Arahat. The two questions raised in v. 12 are answered in the verse under notice.

14 yadha saga(ra)[1]uḍasa ujhitasa mahapathi
padumu tatra jaea suyigan(d)[2]ha manoramu ○

(C^ro, 3)

15 (emu)[3] saghadhadhamac[4]andhah(u)[5]te prudhija[ne
abhi(r)[6]o][7](a)[8]ti prañai samesabudhaṣavaka ○[9]

(C^ro, 4)

[. . . . . ga 15][10]

(C^ro, 5)

Cf. Dhammap., vs. 58-59 † (Pupphav., 15-16):—

Yathā saṁkāradhānasmiṁ[11] ujjhitasmiṁ mahāpathe
Padumaṁ tattha jāyetha sucigandhaṁ manoramaṁ ;
Evaṁ saṁkārabhūtesu andhabhūte puthujjane
Atirocati paññāya sammāsambuddhasāvako.

Cf. Fa-kheu-pi-u, sec. XII. (" Flowers "), p. 91 :—

" As a ditch in the field, close beside the highway, will produce the lily in its midst, and spread far and wide its delightful perfume, so in the midst of life and death (that is, the phenomenal world), beside the way of false speculation (universal inquiry), the wise man diffuses his glad sentiments in becoming a disciple of Buddha ".

Cf. Udānav., ch. XVIII. ("The Flower"), vv. 9-10 :—

" As on piles of filth and in dirty water grows, unaffected by them, the *padma*, pure, sweet-smelling and lovely, so the disciple of the perfect Buddha shines by his wisdom among other men, who are blind and (like) a heap of filth ".

Notes.—These two verses complete together the likeness of a saintly Bhikkhu of humble birth to a lovely lotus in a heap of filth. In all the older recensions of the

---

[1] Restored according to M. Senart's suggestion.
[2] M. Senart's restoration. [3] Supplied by us. For the word cf. Frag. C. XV^vo., p. 90. [4] M. Senart reads °*dhamaa*, which we have slightly altered for symmetry. [5] Supplied by us; M. Senart suggests *h(o)te*.
[6] Supplied by us. [7] Frag. C. VII^ro, 1 (p. 88). [8],[9] Supplied by us.
[10] Frag. C. VII^ro, 2 (p. 88). [11] Some Ms. reads *saṅkāra*° and °*ṭṭhānasmiṁ*.

Dhammapada these are put at the end of the Pupphavagga; the Pāli counterparts of them can be traced in no other canonical text than the Dhammapada. They serve to throw into clear relief the contrast between the life of the multitude who are blind to the brighter side of human nature and steeped in the filth of worldliness, and that of a Buddhist saint who, though born among the common mortals, outshines them by their wisdom, like unto a lotus or lily, sweet-scented and lovely, growing among the heaps of refuse and filth beside a high road. They seem to indicate the lofty aim of Buddhism, which opened the door of salvation, many centuries before the advent of Christianity and Vaiṣṇavism, to the persons of humble birth and of poor circumstances,—a feature which can be traced back to the Sāmaññaphala Sutta (Dīgha. I. p. 61).

Verse 14.—**Sagaraudasa** = Pāli *saṅkārakūṭasmiṁ*, which is the same in meaning as *saṁkāradhānasmiṁ* or *saṁkāratthānasmiṁ* (cf. *saṅkāra-puñja*, Therag., v. 578) =' on piles of filth and in dirty water" (Udānavarga); "in a ditch in the field" (Fa-kheu-pi-u). **Ujhitasa** = Pāli *ujjhitasmiṁ*, Sk. *ujjhite=chaḍḍite*, "thrown away" (Dhammapada-Comy.). Here are two instances where the Genitive case-ending has stood for the Locative.

Verse 15.—**Saghadhadhamae**—this is substituted for the Pāli *saṁkārabhūtesu* (see the Dhammapada-Comy., which speaks of a disciple of Buddha as *saṁkāra-bhūtesu pi puthujjanesu jāto*, 'born among average men who are no better than filthy heaps'). As to the Prakrit reading, M. Senart says that the form *saghadhadhamaa* appears to him certain, though the last letter might be *e* or *i*. Nevertheless, "the word remains difficult", he says, and suggests that the only way of avoiding the difficulty with regard to the first part of the word, would be "by admitting that the scribe has, through mistake, written *saghadha* for *sagara=saṅkāra*." There is, no doubt, something wrong somewhere, but not probably where M. Senart locates it. **Dhamaa** or **dhamae** is not certainly=*dharme*, as he supposes. Some consonant like *k* appears to have been elided between the two final vowels. *Saghadhadhamaa* is perhaps=Pāli *saṅkhatadhammakā* or *saṅkhatadhammāse* (see Jātaka IV. p. 266) and *saghadhadhamae*=Pāli *saṅkhatadhammake*. In these two equations, an objection can be raised as to the possibility of the change of *t* to *dh*, seeing that *dh* in the Prakrit text mostly represents the

20

Pāli and Sk. *th*. But there are instances where *dh* represents *t* also. Cf. *viśeṣadh* (I. A[3], 13) for Pāli *visesato*; °*ṣaghadhio* (I. B, 37) for *saṅgātigo*; *kusidhu* (I. C[ro], 17) for *kusīto*; *cavadhi* (I. C[ro], 31) for *cāpato*; *samadha* (I. C[ro], 37) for *samata, sammatta*. If the reading *saghadhadhamaa* be accepted, it may be taken to refer to *budhaṣavaka*, 'the Buddha's disciples who explain well the law'. The reading *saghadhadhamae=saṅkhatadhammake*, "in the midst of life and death" (Fa-kheu-pi-u), would mean a phenomenal existence characterised by growth, persistence and decay. **Prudhijane**=Pāli *puthujjane*, 'average men', a Buddhist technical term that denotes persons below the rank of a *gotrabhū*, and distinguished as good (*kalyāṇa*) and most common. **Prudhi**=Sk. *pṛthak*, 'other than (the instructed)' or *pṛthu*, 'stupid' (*sthūla*). For the change of *pṛ* to *pr(u)*, cf. *pradhavi*, vv. 12-13; and for that of *ak* to *i*, cf. *same=samyak*, and note that *e* and *i* are interchangeable in the dialect of our text. **Abhiroati**= *abhirocanti*. M. Senart holds that it may very well be used=*atirocati* (Pāli), but that cannot be, since the nom. in the Prakrit text is in the plural.

The chapter contains 15 stanzas.

[5. Sahasavaga]

The naming of the chapter is, as before, ours. The exaltation of 'the one' out of 'a thousand' forms the burden of the following group of 17 verses, and it is only in a few stanzas that the number 'hundred' is substituted for 'thousand'. The 'Number'-group in the Pāli Dhammapada (chap. VIII.) and the Chinese Fa-kheu-king, (sec. XVI.), contains 16 stanzas. The whole of a Sahasravarga containing 24 gāthās is quoted in the Mahāvastu (III, pp. 434-36), as "*dharmapadeṣu sahasravargaḥ*", thereby undoubtedly presupposing an older Sanskrit recension, older, we mean, than the Udānavarga, and Sanskrit in the sense that it was the outcome of an earlier attempt at sanskritisation. The corresponding group in the Udānavarga (chap. XXIV.) has 34 verses. As to the number as well as the arrangement of the verses, these recensions differ, though they betray a common purpose in that they emphasize a particular fact, practice or principle by singling it out of a hundred or a thousand. And the practices or principles thus emphasized are all Buddhistic, sharply contrasted with those of the Brahmanic faith. The increase of numbers in the later recensions is lue to a most mechanical multiplication of the stanzas conveying the same sense. Having regard to the fact that the Number-verses cannot be traced in any other canonical text in the form in which they occur in the Dhammapada, a doubt is apt to arise if they were composed in the time of the Buddha. Even supposing that these were composed then, we have reason to believe that their number was far less than what it is in the several recensions of the Dhammapada. This hypothesis is borne out by the fact that we find one or two verses in the Manu Saṁhitā and the Jaina text which in their present forms are far later than the oldest portions of the Buddhist Nikāyas. Seeing that the Number-verses are mostly intended to contrast the Buddhist practices and principles with the Brāhmanic rituals, sacrifices, hymn-chanting and poetic composition, their origin cannot be dated farther back than the sophistic period immediately preceding the advent of Buddhism, during which several schools of Wanderers appear to have broken away from the ancient tradition and condemned the Brāhmanic system of learning and religious rites and dogmas with a vehemence perhaps unparalleled in the history of human culture. These revolutionary ideas gathering strength with the progress of time assumed at last a more rational, systematic and compromising shape in the teaching of Gotama Buddha, another revolutionary, perhaps the most powerful of all because of his synthetic genius. The Muṇḍaka and Gotamaka condemnation of the Brāhman priests with their elaborate system of sacrifice and *mantras*,[1] and the Keśakambala declaration of the unfounded character of the sacrifices[2] found a saner expression in the Buddha's utterances setting forth the sacrifices as less valued in comparison with the more dignified practices of religion. Thus we read in the Kūṭadanta-sutta (Dīgha I. pp. 143 f. ; Dial. B, II. pp. 180-3) : "The sacrifice performed with ghee, oil, butter, milk, honey and sugar only is better than that at which living creatures are slaughtered. Better than this mode of sacrifice is charity, especially that which is extended to holy and upright men. Better still is the putting up of monasteries. But better than this is certainly the observance of moral precepts. And the best of all sacrifices is the four-fold meditation".[3] One can justly point out this prose discourse as the historical basis of the Number-verses which, in their ultimate analysis, present but a universal idiom, e.g., one in a hundred, one in a thousand, or one in a million.

---

[1] See the Muṇḍaka and Kaṭha Upaniṣads.

[2] Dīgha I. p. 55.

[3] This is a mere summary of Buddha's views. Cf. Śankara's views in the *Viveka-cūḍāmaṇi*, V. 2.

1 yo (sa)[1][hasa sahasani sagami manuṣa jini
eka ji][2] (jini)[3] atmana sȯ ho sagamu utamu ○

(C^{ro}, 6)

Cf. Dhammap., v. 103 † (Sahassavagga, v. 4) :—

Yo sahassaṁ sahassena saṅgāme mānuse jine
Ekañ ca jeyya-m-attānaṁ sa ve saṅgāmajuttamo.

Cf. Mahāvastu, Sahasravarga, v. 3 :—

Yo śatāni sahasrāṇāṁ saṁgrāme manujā jaye
Yo caikaṁ jaye ātmānaṁ sa vai saṁgrāmajit varaḥ.

Cf. Udānav., ch. XXIII. ("Self"), v. 3 :—

"He who conquers a thousand times a thousand men in battle, a greater conqueror than he is he who conquers himself."

Notes.—As appears from Rockhill's translation, the reading of the Udānavarga verse is similar to the Pāli. The Prakrit verse differs from the Pāli by these two words—*sahasani* (=Pāli *sahassāni*), and *jini* (=Pāli *jine*). The difference could be minimised, if *sahasani* could have been interpreted, as M. Senart suggests, as an inversion for the Pāli *sahassena*. But this cannot very well be done as we find that the verse in the Mahāvastu contains the word *śatāni* which is the same in form as the Prakrit *sahasani*. A comparative study of these four recensions makes it clear that the Pāli form is the oldest, and that the Prakrit is older than the earlier Sanskrit. The teaching inculcated in the verse is that the greatest enemy of man is after all his own self and accordingly every effort must be made to conquer self. This lofty idea of self-conquest is illustrated in the Buddhist literature by a graphic poetic description

---

[1] Supplied by us.

[2] Frag. C. VIIro, 3.

[3] Frag. C. XIIro, 1,—not adjusted by M. Senart.

of the inner struggle of the ascetic Siddhattha with Māra[1], and no less by that of Buddha's disciples[2]. An earlier form of the conception of self-conquest, bereft of the later Buddhist imagery of a heroic fight with the lower nature of man is to be found in the teaching of the Mundakas[3], and a Jaina parallel of it is embodied in a dialogue of the Uttarâdhyayana Sūtra[4]. The truth of the teaching of the Buddhist verse under notice was confirmed by two powerful Buddhist kings, king Asoka of India and king Duṭṭhagāmani of Ceylon, both of whom came to feel remorse and intense agony of heart at the recollection of their experiences on battle-fields[5]. In the teaching of Asoka the idea of conquest by the *dhamma* took the place of the principle of self-conquest : "*mu(kha)mute dhammavijaye*". The idea of self-conquest which shaped itself in the teaching of the Śramans proper, came to be recognised by the Buddhist teachers and kings as a distinct principle of action, and that in a form of conquest of hatred by love[6], claimed in the Rājovāda Jātaka[7], a marked advance on the 'tit for tat' principle. In this respect Buddhism can claim as much superiority to the juristic faith of the Brāhmans[8] as Christianity to the Mosaic doctrine of the Israels.

Sahasani=Pāli *sahassāni*, Sk. *sahasrāṇi*. If this be not an inversion for the Pāli instrumental singular form *sahassena*, it must be interpreted as referring to *manuṣa*, like *śatāni* in the Mahāvastu verse. **Ho**=Pāli *kho*, an expletive denoting assertion. **Sagamu utamu**=Pāli *saṅgāmajuttamo*. M. Senart considers the Pāli reading as the result of a confusion of writing. But there is no confusion here at all. It is simply *saṅgāmaji*+*uttama*, a compound, which by the Pāli rule of sandhi has beaome *saṅgāmajuttamo*. Cf. *saṁgrāmajit* of the Mahāvastu.

---

[1] Padhāna Sutta, Suttanipāta, No. 28=Lalitavistara, chap. XVIII.; Mahāvastu ; Mārasaṁyutta, Saṁyutta Nikāya, I. Cf. Lalitavistara, chap. XXI. and Buddhacarita, Bks. XIII-XIV.

[2] Bhikkhuṇī-Saṁyutta, Saṁyutta Nikāya, I.

[3] Muṇḍaka Up., II. 2. 3-4.

[4] Uttarâdhyayana, IX. 20-22.

[5] Asoka's Rock Edict, XIII ; Mahāvaṁsa, XXV. 108.

[6] Dhammapada, v. 5.

[7] Rājovāda-jātaka, No. 24, where the *akkodhena jine kodhaṁ* principle is contrasted with the *daḷhena daḷhaṁ khepanaṁ*.

[8] The Sanskrit Epics condemn only "wrath without any provocation" (*vinā vairaṁ rudratā*).

2 saḥa[sa bi ya gaśana[1] anathapa][2][dasahita e][3][ka vayapada][4] ṣebha[5] ya ṣutva uvaśamati O[6]

(C^ro, 7)

Cf. Dhammap., v. 100 † (Sahassav., v. 1):—

Sahassam api ce vācā anatthapadasaṁhitā
Ekaṁ atthapadaṁ seyyo yaṁ sutvā upasammati.

Cf. Fa-kheu-pi-u, sec. XVI. ("The Thousands"), p. 104. :—

"To repeat a thousand words without understanding, what profit is there in this? But to understand one truth, and hearing it to act accordingly, this is to find deliverance."

Cf. Mahāvastu Sahasravarga, v. 1 :—

Sahasram api vācānāṁ anarthapadasaṁhitā
Ekā arthavatī śreyā yāṁ śrutvā upaśāmyati.

3 .... [śata bhaṣe anathapadasahita][7] e...ṣ.hu ya ṣutva uvaśamati O[8]

(C^ro, 8)

Cf. Dhammap., v. 102 † (Sahassav., v. 3) :—

Yo ca gāthā sataṁ bhāse anatthapadasaṁhitā
Ekaṁ dhammapadaṁ seyyo yaṁ sutvā upasammati.

Cf. Udānav., ch. XXIV. ("Numbers"), v. 2 :—

"It is better to speak one word of the law which brings one nigh unto peace, than to recite a hundred gāthās which are not of the law".

---

[1] A very doubtful word. [2] Frag. C. VII^ro, 4. [3] Frag. C. XI^ro, 1.
[4] Frag. C. XII^ro, 2,—not adjusted by M. Senart.
[5] That the second letter is *bh*, though written in a peculiar hand in the Ms., has been verified by M. Senart. The variants are *ṣehu*, *ṣeho* occurring in the succeeding verses.
[6] The circle is supplied by us. [7] Fr. C. XI^ro, 2.
[8] The circle is supplied by us.

The Prakrit verse can be easily restored :—

(yo ja gadhaśata) bhaṣe anathapadasahita
e(ka dhamapada) ṣ(e)hu ya ṣutva uvaśamati ○

4 (saha)[1]sa bi ya gadhana anathapadasahita
eka gadhapada ṣeho ya ṣutva uvaśamati[2] ○

(Cro, 9)

Cf. Dhammap., v. 101 † (Sahassav., v. 2) :—

Sahassam api ce gāthā anatthapadasaṁhitā
Ekaṁ gāthāpadaṁ seyyo yaṁ sutvā upasammati.

Cf. Mahāvastu Sahasravarga, v. 2 :—

Sahasram api gāthānāṁ anarthapadasaṁhitā
Ekā arthavatī śreyā yāṁ śrutvā upaśāmyati.

5 (yo)[3] ja gadhaśata[4] bhaṣe anathapadasahita
eka gadhapada ṣeho ya ṣutva uvaśamati ○

(Cro, 10)

Cf. Verse 3 above. The verse can be easily rendered in Pāli :

Yo ca gāthā sataṁ bhāse anatthapadasaṁhitā
Ekaṁ gāthāpadaṁ seyyo yaṁ sutvā upasammati.

Cf. Jātaka IV. p. 175 :—

Aṭṭha te bhāsitā gāthā, sabbā honti sahassiyo,
Patigaṇha mahābrahme, sādh'etaṁ tava bhāsitaṁ.
Na me attho sahassehi satehi nahutehi vā,
Pacchimaṁ bhāsato gāthaṁ kāme me na rato mano.

Cf. Fa-kheu-pi-u, sec. XVI. ("The Thousands"), p. 104 :—

"Although a man can repeat a thousand stanzas (sections), but understand not the meaning of the lines he repeats, this is not equal to the repetition of one sentence well understood, which is able when heard to control thought."

---

1 Supplied by us.
2 M. Senart reads *uvasamati*.
3 Supplied by us. Also *ya* ; Sec. v. 12 *infra*.
4 Partly completed by Frag. C. IXro, 1.

Cf. Fa-kheu-pi-u, sec. XVI. ("The Thousands"), p. 104 :—

"A man may be able to repeat many books, but if he cannot explain them, what profit is there in this? But to explain one sentence of the Law, and to walk accordingly, this is the way to find supreme wisdom".

Cf. Udanav., ch. XXIV. ("Numbers"), v. 2 :—

"It is better to speak one word of the law which brings one nigh unto peace, than to recite a hundred gāthās which are not of the law".

Notes.—These four verses (2-5) are very much alike, differing only, in the words of M. Senart, in some differentiation of detail. All of them teach that one Dhammapada *gāthā*, full of poetry and meaning, is far better and valuable than so many hundreds, thousands or millions (as the Jātaka puts it) of the Vedic hymns regarded as dealing with useless subjects, *i.e.*, setting forth, in the language of the Dhammapada-Comy., the descriptions of the sky, the mountains, the forest and the like, which do not throw light on the path to salvation (*ākāsavaṇṇanā-pabbatavaṇṇanā-vanavaṇṇanādīni pakāsakehi aniyyānadīpakehi anatthakehi padehi saṁhitāyā va bahukā honti*). History, however, goes to prove that the Buddhists themselves, especially the Mahāyānists, were not immune from the same kind of adverse criticism not only from the modern critics[1], but at the hands of their brethren, the advocates of the Sahajiyā doctrine[2].

Verse 2.—**Eka vayapada** would correspond to a Pāli *ekaṁ vācapadaṁ*. **Ṣebha**=Pāli *seyyo*, Sk. *ś eyas*. The *bh* may be accounted for as due to the influence of the final *s* or *ḥ* which is dropped in both Pāli and Prakrit. Similarly the *ṣ* may be said to have been due to the desire to compensate for the lost sound *r* in *śr*.

---

[1] See Dr. R. L. Mitra's observations in the introduction to his edition of the Aṣṭasāhasrikā Prajñāpāramitā (Bibl. Indica series).

[2] Bauddha Gān-o-Dohā, p. 88.

6 [masamasi sahasina yo yaea][1] śatena ca
neva[2] budhi prasadasa kala aveti ṣoḍaśa O

(C^{ro}, 11)

7 [(ma)[3]samase sahasena yo yaea śatina ca
neva][4] (dhami)[5] prasa(da)[6]sa kala aveti ṣoḍaśa O

(C^{ro}, 12)

8 masamase sahasina yo yaea śatena ca
neva saghi prasadasa kala aveti ṣoḍaśa O

(C^{ro}, 13)

Cf. Fa-kheu-pi-u, sec. XVI. ("The Thousands"), p. 105 :—

"Although a man for a hundred years worship and sacrifice to the spirit of Fire, his merit is not equal to that of the man who for a moment pays reverence to the three Holy Ones ; the happiness consequent on one such act of homage excels that resulting from all those hundred years".

Cf. Mahāvastu, Sahasravarga, vv. 4-6 :—

Yo jayeta sahasrāṇāṁ māse māse śataṁ śataṁ
Na so Buddhe prasādasya kalām arghati ṣoḍaśīṁ.
Yo jayeta sahasrāṇāṁ māse māse śataṁ śataṁ
Na so dharme prasādasya kalāṁ arghati ṣoḍasīṁ.
Yo jayeta sahasrāṇāṁ māse māse śataṁ śataṁ
Na so saṁghe prasādasya kalām arghati ṣoḍasīm.

Cf. Udānav., ch. XXIV. ("Numbers"), vv. 26-28 :—

"He who for a hundred years makes a thousand sacrifices each month, is not worth the sixteenth part of him who has faith in the Buddha".

[N.B. For vv. 27-28, substitute "in the holy law" and "in the church" respectively, in place of "in the Buddha" of v. 26.]

---

[1] Frag. C. IX^{ro}, 2. [2] M. Senart reads *nevi*. We read *neva* for the sake of consistency with the next verses. [3] Supplied by us.
[4] Frag. C. VIII^{ro}. [5] Supplied by us ; also *dhama*, as M. Senart suggests ; in which case it must be joined to the next word.
[6] Supplied by us.

9 masamasi sahasena yo yaea śatena ca
neva saghasadhameṣu kala aveti ṣoḍaśa ○

(C^ro, 14)

Cf. the last half of the Dhammap., v. 70 † (Bālav., v. 11) = Mahāvastu, Sahasravarga, v. 14 :—

....

Na so saṁkhatadhammānaṁ kalam agghati soḷasim.

Cf. Mahāvastu, Sahasravarga, v. 8 :—

Yo jayeta sahasrāṇāṁ māse māse śataṁ śataṁ
Na so svākhyātadharmāṇāṁ kalām arghati ṣoḍaśīṁ.

Cf. Udānav., ch. XXIV. ("Numbers"), v. 33 :—

"He who for a hundred years makes a thousand sacrifices each month, is not worth the sixteenth part of him who explains well the holy law".

10 masamase sahasena yo yae[a śatena ca][1]
(neva sabanaśil)[2]eṣu kala aveti ṣoḍaśa ○

(C^ro, 15)

Cf. Mahāvastu, Sahasravarga, v. 7 :—

Yo jayeta sahasrāṇāṁ māse māse śataṁ śataṁ
So va saṃpannaśīlānāṁ kalāṁ nârghati ṣoḍaśīṁ.

11 masamase sahasena yo yaea śatena ca
ekapananuabisa kala naveti ṣoḍaśa ○

(C^ro, 16)

Cf. Fa-kheu-pi-u, sec. VII. ("Metta"), p. 17 :—

"If a man lives a hundred years, and engages the whole of his time and attention in religious offerings to the gods, sacrificing elephants, and horses, and other things, all this is not equal to one act of pure love in saving life."

---

[1] Frag. C XLIII^ro.
[2] Supplied by us. For *b* = Pāli *mp*, cf. °*nuabisa* of the next verse, and *sabano* (= Pāli *sampanno*), Panitavaga, v. 2 (I. C^ro, 25, p. 63).

Cf. Udānav., ch. XXIV. ("Numbers"), vv. 29-31 :—

"He who for a hundred years makes a thousand sacrifices each month, is not worth the sixteenth part of him who is merciful to sentient creatures" (varied in vv. 30, 31 by 'animated creatures' and 'beings' respectively).

Cf. Manu, V. 53 :—

varṣe varṣe 'śvamedhena yo yajeta śataṁ samāḥ
māṁsāni ca na khadedyastayoḥ puṇyaphalaṁ samam.

Notes.—It is a strange fact that the parallel of none of these verses (6-11) is to be found in the Dhammapada or in any other canonical text. We must admit that the basic idea out of which they had grown, is embodied in a prose discourse, the Kūṭadanta-sutta of the Dīghanikāya. A comparison of the Prakrit verses with their parallels in the Fa-kheu-pi-u and other recensions of the Dhammapada makes it clear how easy it was for the Buddhists to multiply the number of this class of stanzas by merely changing a certain word or expression. It is also clear that the chief motive of these verses is to extol the principles of practical Buddhism, which are of far greater worth than the hundreds and thousands of sacrifices performed each month by the Brāhman householders. The Buddhist principles emphasized herein are just three, *viz.*, (1) faith in the Three Jewels, (2) observance of the moral precepts, and (3) compassion for the living beings.

Verses 6-8.—**Masamasi, masamase**=Pāli and Sk. *māse māse*, 'each month'. In colloquial Bengali the idiom *māse māse* means quite the same thing, and *māsāmāsi*, which equates with the Prakrit form *masamasi*, means 'extending over a month'. In these verses there are numerous instances where *i* and *e* are interchanged **Sahasina śatena, sahasena śatina**=Pāli *sahassena satena*, which is as idiomatic as *sahasrāṇāṁ śataṁ śataṁ* of the Mahāvastu verses. **Yaea**=Pāli *yajeyya*, Sk. *yajeta* ; *y* and *j* being inverted in *jayeta* of the Mahāvastu verses quoted above. **Neva** (written *neri* in v. 6)=Pāli or Sk. *nāpi*, as M. Senart points out. The reading *na vi* or *na ve* would be the correct from ; *neva* may be regarded as an inversion for *na ve*. But *ne va* taken as=Pāli *n'eva* or Sk. *naiva* would free us from the risk of such conjectures as *neva*=*nāpi*. **Aveti**=Pāli *anveti* or *appoti* = Sk. *āpnoti*, 'attains', *i.e.*, 'deserves' (*agghati* or *arghati*). We trust that it was not by mistake that the scribe wrote *aveti* for *aghati*.

Verses 9-11.—**Saghasadhameṣu** = Pāli *saṅkhatadhammesu*, 'among those who have well understood the Norm'. Cf. the explanation given in the Dhammapada-Commentary, v. 70:—"Saṅkhatadhammā vuccanti *ñātadhammā, tulitadhammā*." The meaning of the word was changed when it came to be Sanskritised as *svākhyāta-dharmāṇāṁ*, 'of those who have well *explained* the law'. For the reading see M. Senart's notes (pp. 59-60). **Sabanaśileṣu** would be in Pāli *sampannasīlesu*, 'among those who have fully observed the rules of morality'. The adoption of the locative form for the genitive (cf. *sampannaśīlānāṁ* of the Mahāvastu verse quoted above) is a peculiarity noticeable in the Prakrit verses 9-10. For the opposite process cf. *parasa* (Apramadavaga, v. 1), p. 121; *uṭhanaalasa* (ibid, v. 4), p. 123; *apramadasa* (ibid, v. 17), p. 126; *imasa* (ibid, v. 16), p. 132; *saga audasa* (Puṣavaga, v. 14), p. 152. **Ekapananuabisa** would correspond to a Pāli *ekapāṇānukampissa*, Sk. *ekaprāṇānukampinaḥ*, 'of one who is compassionate towards a single living creature'.

12 ya ja vaṣaśata jivi kusidhu hinaviyava
muhutu[1] jivita ṣebha virya arahato dridha ○

(C^{ro}, 17)

Cf. Dhammap., v. 112 † (Sahassav., v. 13):—

Yo ca vassasataṁ jīve kusīto hīnaviriyo
Ekâhaṁ jīvitaṁ seyyo viriyam[2] ārabhato daḷhaṁ.

Cf. Mahāvastu, Sahasravarga, v. 19:—

Yo ca varṣaśataṁ jīve kuśīdo hīnavīryavān
Ekâhaṁ jīvitaṁ śreyo vīryam ārambhato dṛḍhaṁ.

Cf. Udānav., ch. XXIV. ("Numbers"), v. 4:—

"He who lives a hundred years in laziness and slothfulness, a life of one single day is better if one exerts oneself to zealous application."

---

[1] Verses 13 and 14 have *muhuta*.
[2] Another reading, *vīryaṁ*, with ī metri causa.

13 ya ji vaṣaśato jivi apaśu udakavaya
muhuta jivita ṣebha[1] paśato udakavaya O

(C^ro, 18)

Cf. Dhammap., v. 113 † (Sahassav., v. 14) :—

Yo ca vassasataṁ jīve apassam udayavyayaṁ[2]
Ekâhaṁ jīvitaṁ seyyo passato udayavyayaṁ.

Cf. Mahāvastu, Sahasravarga, v. 23 :—

Yo ca varṣaśataṁ jīve apaśyam udayavyayaṁ
Ekâhaṁ jīvitaṁ śreyo paśyato udayavyayaṁ.

Cf. Udānav.. ch. xxiv. (" Numbers "), v. 6 :—

" He who lives a hundred years without perceiving birth and dissolution, a life of one single day is better if one perceives birth and dissolution ".

14 ya ja vaṣaśata jiv(i)[3] apaśu dhamu utamu
m(u)[4]huta jivita [ṣ][5]e(b)hu paśatu dhamu utamu O[6]

(C^ro, 19)

Cf. Dhammap., v. 115 † (Sahassav., v. 16) :—

Yo ca vassasataṁ jīve apassaṁ dhammam uttamaṁ
Ekâhaṁ jīvitaṁ seyyo passato dhammam uttamaṁ.

Cf. Mahāvastu, Sahasravarga, v. 23 :—

Yo ca varṣaśataṁ jīve apaśyaṁ dharmam uttamam
Ekâhaṁ jīvitaṁ śreyo paśyato dharmam uttamam.

---

[1] The next verse has *ṣebhu*, and v. 17 *ṣiho*.
[2] Variant, *udayabbayaṁ*. [3], [4] Supplied by us.
[5] Frag. C. xxxviii^ro, 1,—not adjusted by M. Senart. The Frag. bears traces of the previous word *jivita*. [6] The circle is supplied by us.

Cf. Udānav., ch. xxiv. ("Numbers"), v. 10 :—

"He who lives a hundred years without knowing the ideal knowledge that is hard (to arrive at), life of one single day is better if one knows the ideal knowledge that is hard (to arrive at)".

15 ya ja vaṣaśata jatu agi pariyar(e)[1] vane
[chirena][2] sapitelena[3] divaratra atadrito

16 [eka ji bhavitatmana muhuta][4]viva p(u)[5] a(e)[6]
sameva puyana ṣebha ya ji[7] vaṣaśata hotu ○

(Cro 20-21)

Cf. Dhammap., v. 107 † (Sahassav., v. 8) :—

Yo ca vassasataṁ jantu aggiṁ paricare vane
Ekañ ca bhāvitattānaṁ muhuttam api pūjaye—
Sā yeva pūjanā seyyo yañ ce vassasataṁ hutaṁ.

Cf. Mahāvastu, Sahasravarga, vv. 15-16 :—

Yo ca varṣaśataṁ jīve agniparicaraṁ caret
Patrâhāro chavāvāsī karonto vividhaṁ tapaṁ
Yo caikaṁ bhāvitâtmānaṁ muhūrtam api pūjayet
Sā ekapūjanā śreyo na ca varṣaśataṁ hutaṁ.

Cf. Udānav., ch. xxiv. ("Numbers"), v. 17 :—

"If a man live for a hundred years in a forest, wholly relying on fire (Agni), and if he but for one single moment pays homage to a man who meditates on the self, this homage is greater than sacrifices for a hundred years."

---

[1] M. Senart reads *pariyara*, but suggests that it should be *pariyare* or *pariyari*. [2] Frag. C. xxxviiro, 2,—not adjusted by M. Senart.
[3] M. Senart puts it separately as *sa pi telena*. [4] Frag. C. xxixro.
[5], [6] Supplied by us, according to M Senart's suggestion.
[7] M. Senart combines the two words into *yaji*.

17 [ya keja yaṭha va ho(tu)[1] va lok(e)[2]][3]
(savachara[4] yaea puñapekho[5]
sarva vi ta na [6]caubhakame)[7]ti
ahivadana ujukateṣu ṣiho O[8]

(C^{ro}, 22)

Cf. Dhammap., v. 108 † (Sahassav., v. 9) :—

Yaṁ kiñci yiṭṭhaṁ ca hutañ ca loke
Saṁvaçcharaṁ yajetha puññapekho
Sabbaṁ pi taṁ na catubhāgam eti,—
Abhivādanā ujjugatesu seyyo.

Cf. Fa-kheu-pi-u, sec. XVI. ("The Thousands"), p. 108 :—

"To sacrifice to spirits in order to find peace (merit), or, after this life expecting reward, his happiness is not one quarter of that man's who pays homage to the good".

Cf. Mahāvastu, Sahasravarga, v. 17 :—

Yat kiṁcid iṣṭaṁ ca hutaṁ ca loke
Saṁvatsaraṁ yajați puṇyaprekṣo,
Sarvaṁ pi taṁ na caturbhāgam eti
Abhivādanaṁ ujjugateṣu śreyaṁ.

Cf. Udānav., ch. XXIV. ("Numbers"), v. 34 :—

"No matter what sacrifice a man may offer in this world to acquire merit, it is not worth the quarter of doing homage to one who has a quieted and upright mind."

ga 17

(C^{ro}, 23)

Notes.—The verses (12-17) are a blended whole and constitute a series which, as distinguished from the preceding one, teaches that the spiritual efforts, the philosophic insight and

[1] Supplied by us; cf. *hotu* of the preceding verse. [2] Also *loki*.
[3] Frag. C. I^{vro}, 1. [4] Cf. *savatu* = Pāli *saṁvuto* (C^{ro}, 28), p. 64.
[5] Also *puñavekhu* or *puñavechu*. [6] Also *catubhagameti*.
[7] Supplied by us. [8] The circle is supplied by us.

the higher form of Buddhist worship are of far superior worth than the fire-worship and sacrifices of the *Vānaprastha* hermits. The Buddhist's is a simple moral under-estimation which must be carefully distinguished historically:

(1) from the Muṇḍaka's bold condemnation—

> Iṣṭāpūrtam manyamānā variṣṭhaṁ nânyacchreyo vedayante pramūḍhāḥ ।
> Nākasya pṛṣṭhe te sukṛte 'nubhūtvêmam lokam hīnataraṁ vāviśanti.[1] ॥

and (2) from the Keśakambala's philosophical denial—

> N'atthi yiṭṭhaṁ, n'atthi hutaṁ, n'atthi sukaṭa-dukkaṭānaṁ kammānaṁ phalaṁ vipāko[2].

But comparing the Muṇḍaka views and those of the Buddhists a little more closely, we must admit that these are in spirit the same, the latter having a milder form of expression than the former.

Verse 12.—**Hinaviyava**=Sk. *hīnavīry.vān* (Mahāvastu verse), which is the same in meaning as the Pāli *hīnaviriyo*. **Ṣebha**=*ṣebha* (v. 14), *ṣiho* (v. 17)=Pāli *seyyo*, Sk. *śreyaḥ*. These are instances where *ṣ* equates with Sk. *śr*. **Arahato**=Pāli *ārabhato*, Sk. *ārambhataḥ*. These forms go to prove that *i* and *e*, and *bh* and *h* are interchangeable in the dialect of our Prakrit text.

Verse 13.—**Udakavaya**=Pāli *udayavyayaṁ* or *udayabbayaṁ*, Sk. *udayavyayaṁ*, 'growth and loss'. The change of *y* to *k* appears to be along the lines of the change of *j* to *k*; cf. *babaka*=Sk. *pabbaja*, Suhavaga, v. 8 (I. c^vo^, 31, p. 80.)

Verses 15-16.—**Chirena sapitelena divaratra atadrito** =Pāli *khīreṇa sappi-telena divārattaṁ atandito*. This line is to be found neither in the Pāli *gāthā* nor in the Udānavarga verse. The Mahāvastu verse substitutes for it: *patrâhāro chavāvāsī karonto vividhaṁ tapaṁ*. **Muhutaviva** would correspond to a Pāli *muhuttamiva*: a vowel sandhi (*muhuta* + *iva*). **Sameva**=Pāli *sā yeva*: a vowel sandhi (*sa* + *eva*). The reading *sameva* is a change from *saveva*. The Mahāvastu reads *sā eka°*.

---

[1] Muṇḍaka Up. I. 2. 10.
[2] Dīgha, I. p. 55.

Verse 17.—Yaṭha = Pāli *yiṭṭhaṁ*, Sk. *iṣṭaṁ*. The root in the Prakrit word has not, like the Sk., undergone any transformation.

Ga 17 marks the end of the chapter and means, as before, that the chapter contains 17 stanzas.

[6. Panitavaga or Dhamaṭhavaga]

This group, of which the name is suggested by the word *dhamaṭha* occurring in v. 1 or by *panita* in v. 3, *infra*, consists of ten stanzas, as may be ascertained from the colophon, "ga 10" (I. cro, 34). Verse 3 of the Prakrit group has a parallel in one of the verses of the Paṇḍitavagga of the Pāli Dhammapada (ch. VI.), and some of the rest of the same group in other chapters of the Pāli.[1] The Dhammaṭṭhavagga of the Pāli Dhammapada (ch. XIX.) contains 17 stanzas, of which none is to be found in the Prakrit group. The corresponding chapter in the Fa-kheu-pi-u (sec. XXVII.) also contains 17 stanzas which agree generally with the Pāli. Chapter XI. of the Udānavarga has 16 stanzas, of which four are similar to those in the Pāli group. The *Pa ita* or *Dhamaṭha* group is comparatively of little importance; it teaches whom we are to regard as virtuous and what should be his conduct.

1 [silamatu suyisacho][2] dhamaṭho sadhujivano
atmano karako sadhu ta jano kurati[3] priu ○

(Cro, 24)

Cf. Dhammap., v. 217 † (Piyavagga, v. 9):—

Sīladassanasampannaṁ dhammaṭṭhaṁ saccavādinaṁ
Attano kamma kubbānaṁ taṁ jano kurute piyaṁ.

Cf. Udānav., ch. V. ("Agreeable Things"), v. 25:—

"He who observes the law, who is perfectly virtuous, modest, speaking the truth, doing what he ought to do, delights the rest of mankind."

---

[1] Dhammapada, chap. VI. (Paṇḍitavagga)—14 stanzas
Fa-kheu-pi-u, sec. XIV. ("The wise man")—17 „
Udānavarga, chap. VI. ("Morality")—20 „

[2] Frag. C. IVro, 3, completed by fr. C. IIro, 1.

[3] M. Senart dares not change it into *kuruti*, though he thinks such a reading is very probable.

Notes.—The expressions in the Prakrit verse are somewhat different from those in its Pāli and Sanskrit parallels. The verse embodies some fundamental principles of *Dharma*, enumerated differently in Indian literature. The principles referred to in it are—*śila* (morality), *suyi* (purity), *sacha* (truthfulness), *sadhujivana* (innocent life) and *atmano karana* (dutifulness); cf. Asoka's Pillar Inscription, II: *apāsinave bahukayāne, dayā, dāne, sache, sochaye*; also Rock Edict XIII: *savabhūtānaṁ achatiṁ, sayamaṁ, samacheraṁ, mādavaṁ*, etc.; Śaṅkhasaṁhitā, I. 5: *kṣamā, satya, dama, śauca*; Jātaka verse (Fausböll, II. p. 280): *saccaṁ, dhammo, dhiti, cāgo*; Rāmāyaṇa, V. I. 193 (Bombay edition): *dhṛti, dṛṣṭi, mati, dākṣya*; Chāndogya, III. 17. 4: *tapa, dāna, ārjava, ahiṁsā* and *satyavacana*; Manu enumerates ten principles: *dhṛti, kṣamā, dama, asteya, śaucaṁ, indriya-nigraha, dhī, vidyā, satyaṁ, akrodha* (VI. 92). Similar principles are enumerated under ten numerical heads in the Saṅgīti Suttanta (Dīgha, IV.), and throughout the Aṅguttara Nikāya. The Jaina texts also are not wanting in this kind of enumeration.

Śilamatu would correspond to a Pāli *sīlavanto*, almost the same in meaning as *sīladassanasampanno* of the Pāli text. This is not an accusative singular form as M. Senart supposes it to be. **Suyisacho**—'he who is pure and truthful', a compound with a peculiar grammatical construction. Instead of *suyi* (purity) the Pāli verse has *dassana* (insight). The Prakrit reading *śilamatu suyisacho* etc., (as nominative singular) appears to be better than the Pāli accusative singular. **Atmano karako** would strictly equate with a Pāli *attano kārako*, 'he who does his own duty'. The expression is elliptical, some word being understood between *atmano* and *karako*. **Ta jano kurati priu**= Pāli *taṁ jano kurute piyaṁ*, 'him people hold dear'. Rockhill's translation "he...... delights the rest of mankind", or the Tibetan version itself, seems open to dispute.

2 [ṣadhu śilena sabano yaśabhohasamapitu |[1]
yena yeneva vayati tena teneva puyita O

(C^{ro}, 25)

Cf. Dhammap., v. 303 † (Pakiṇṇakavagga, v. 14):—

"Saddho sīlena sampanno yasobhogasamappito
Yaṁ yaṁ padesaṁ bhajati tattha tatth' eva pūjito.

---

[1] Frag. C. II^{ro}, 2.

Notes.—*Ṣadhu*=Pāli *saddho*, 'the faithful', the initial sibilant ṣ distinguishes this word from *sadhu* answering to *sādhu*. This is not the first instance in our Prakrit where ṣ equates with Sk. *śr*; cf. *ṣavaka* (Sk. *śrāvakāḥ*), Puṣav. v. 15 (p. 152); *ṣebha*, *ṣebhu*, *ṣehu*, *ṣeho*, *ṣiho* (Sk. *śreyaḥ*), Sahasavaga (pp. 158-167); *ṣutra* (Sk. *śrutrā*) ibid, vv. 2, 3 fg. (p. 156). **Sabano**=Pāli *sampanno*. For *b*=*mp* see *anuabisa* (Sahasav. v. 11). For **bhoha**=**bhoga**, see M. Senart's notes (p. 63). **Vayati** would straightway equate with Pāli *vajati*, Sk. *vrajati* 'walks', 'travels', 'passes'; cf. *sabbattha ve sappurisā vajanti* (Dhammap., v. 83). M. Senart says: "*Vayati* might strictly be explained after the analogy of *abhivuya* (=Pāli *abhibhūya*), B. 80, 31 as=the Pāli *bhajati*. But it is more natural to think that it is=*vrajati*, and I should rather believe that *bhajati* of the Pāli, which it is very difficult to interpret, has sprung, by an inverse confusion, from an original *vajati*". We, on our part, think that the expression *yaṁ yaṁ padesaṁ bhajati* (*i.e.*, 'whatever regions he adopts or lives in') is quite different from *yena yena vayati i.e.*, 'by or through whatever (land) he passes'. The former conveys the idea of settlement in a place, the latter that of the journey of a missionary. Indeed, the latter expression is quite natural to a Buddhist missionary from India, compiling a text of the Dhammapada, adapting the language of the original verses to the local dialect of the Gandharan region extending as far as Khotan.

3 [yo natimahetu na parasa hetu pavani kamani
samaya][1]rea
na ichia (adhamena)[2] [samidhi atmano so śilava][3]
panitu dhammiho[4] sia O[5]

(C^{ro}, 26)

Cf. Dhammap., v. 84 † (Paṇḍitav., v. 9):—

Na attahetu na parassa hetu na puttam icche
na dhanaṁ na raṭṭhaṁ
N' iccheyy' adhammena samiddhim attano
sa sīlavā paññavā dhammiko siyā.

---

[1] Frag. C. II^{ro}, 3. [2] Supplied by us. [3] Frag. C. XXXI^{ro}.
[4] The reading *dhammiho* is probably due to the error of the scribe.
[5] The circle is supplied by us.

Notes.—Natimahetu na parasa hetu=Pāli *na attahetu na parassa hetu*, 'neither on personal grounds nor for others' sake'. The form *natima* is an instance of sandhi and of *Epenthesis* (cf. Pāli *ātuma*=*ātma*). The Prakrit reading **pavaṇi kamaṇi samayarea** would equate with a Pāli *pāpāni kammāni samācareyya*; it brings out the underlying idea of the verse more clearly than the Pāli *na puttam icche* etc. There is reason to believe that by the two expressions, *atimahetu* and *parasa hetu*, are meant the four *agatis* or principles of iniquity, *viz.*, *chanda* (personal consideration), *dosa* (hatred), *bhaya* (fear) and *moha* (delusion). Cf. Jāt. V. p. 147 :—

Na paṇḍitā attasukhassa hetu
Pāpāni kammāni samācaranti
Dukkhena phuṭṭha khalitâpi santā
Chandā ca dosā na jahanti dhammaṁ.

4 [sañatu sukati yati drugati yati asañatu
ma sa viśpaśa][1] [avaja ida vidva samu cari[2]O][3]

(C[ro], 27)

For the last pāda, cf. Jāt. IV. p. 172 :—

Pathavyā sāliyavakaṁ gavassaṁ dāsaporisaṁ
Datvā vā nâlam ekassa, iti vidvā samañ care.

The Pāli counterpart would be :—

Saññato sugatiṁ yāti duggatiṁ yāti asaññato
Mā so vissāsa-m-avajjo idaṁ vidvā samaṁ care.

Notes.—We are unable to trace any Pāli or Sanskrit counterpart of this verse, though it is certain that the teaching of it is very familiar to a student of Buddhism and that it strikes the keynote of Indian religions. **Drugati**=Pāli *duggatiṁ*. For the form *drugati*=Sk. *durgatiṁ*, cf. *druracha*, Citavaga, v. 5, *supra*. **Ma**=Pāli and Sk. *mā*. The particle is used here without the verb expressed. This usage is not uncommon in Pāli. See Childers : *mā h'evaṁ bhante*, not so, lord ; *alaṁ bhikkhave mā bhaṇḍanaṁ*,

[1] Frag. C. I[ro], 1. [2] M. Senart reads *samucari*.
[3] Frag. C. III[ro], 1. not adjusted by M. Senart.

enough priests, no quarrelling. Cf. also Jāt. V., p. 99, v. 306 :—*madā pamādo jāyetha, pamādā jāyate khayo* | *khayā padosā jāyanti, mā mado Bharatūsabha* ‖ where *mā mado*, as the scholiast explains, is=*mā pamajja*, *mā pamādi*. **Avaja**=Pāli *āvajjo* Sk. *āvadyaḥ*, low, bad, inferior. Childers says *āvaditabbo ti āvajjo*, according to a Pāli Tīkā. **Ida**=Pāli *idaṁ*. **Vidva**=Pāli *vidvā*. It cannot, on the strength of the Jātaka parallel, equate with Sk. *vidvān*, as M. Senart has suggested. **Samu cari**=Pāli *samaṁ care*, 'one should lead a life of spiritual calm'. M. Senart, suggests a reading *samuccaret* (Sk.), which would be meaningless in this context.

5 [savutu pratimukhasa idrieṣu ca pajaṣu
pramuni anu][1][pruvina savasañoyanachaya O][2]

C^ro, 28)

For the first half cf. Suttanipāta, v. 340 †
(Rāhulasutta, v. 6) :—

Saṁvuto pātimokkhasmiṁ indriesu ca pañcasu
(Sati kāyagatā tyatthu nibbidābahulo bhava.)

For the last half cf. the last two pādas of the Jātaka verses on pp. 275, 278 (Jāt. I) :—

Pāpuṇe anupubbena sabbasaṁyojanakkhayaṁ.

Notes.—We have not as yet been able to trace to a certainty any Pāli or Sanskrit parallel to the above verse. The combination of the half-verses belonging to two different stanzas is an innovation in the Prakrit text.

Pratimukhasa is an instance of the genitive for the locative. See notes on *sabanaśileṣu*, p. 164. **Pajasu**=Pāli *pañcasu*, 'in regard to five'. The change of *ñc* to the sonant of the palatal group is characteristic of the dialect of the Prakrit text; cf. *sagapa*=*saṅkappa*, Apramadav., v. 4, v. 15, pp. 123, 131, *sagara*=*saṅkhārā*, Puṣav v. 14, p. 152; *saghara*=*saṅkhārā*, Magav., vv. 27, 28, p. 111; *anuabisa*=*anukampinaḥ*, Sahassav., v. 11, p. 162. But cf. *duhusata*=*dukkhass' antaṁ*, Apramadav., v. 16, p. 132; *yavatetha*=*yāvant'ettha* (ibid v. 17), p. 132;

---

[1] Frag. C. I^ro, 2. [2] Frag. C. III^ro, 2,--not adjusted by M. Senart.

jhāyatu=jhāyanto (ibid, vv. 20, 21), pp. 134, 135. **Anupruvina**=Pāli *anupubbena*, 'by degrees', 'gradually'. For *pru=pur*, *cf. drugati* in v. 4 *supra*. This word indicates that Buddhism, like Brāhmanism, provided for a graduated system of religious training: *adhisīlasikkhā*, *adhicitta-sikkhā* and *adhipaññāsikkhā*. The subject is discussed at length in the Gaṇaka-Moggallāna Sutta (Majjhima, III., No. 107).

6 [śudhasa hi sada phagu[1] śudhasaposadhu[2] sada][3]
[śudhasa suyi][4](kamasa sa)[5]da[6] samajate[7] vata ○

(C[ro], 29)

Cf. Vatthûpama Sutta, Majjhima, I. p. 39 :—

Suddhassa ve sadā phaggu, suddhass'uposatho sadā,
Suddhassa sūcikammassa sadā sampajjate vataṁ.

—which is translated by the Bhikkhu Sīlācāra :—

" Upon the pure smiles constant May,
The pure keep endless holy day ;
The pure, by actions pure confest,
Their every offering is blest ".

Notes.—The Pāli parallel to the above verse belongs to a group of stanzas in which the Buddha deprecates the washing of sin in the sacred waters, *e.g.*, of the Bāhukā, the Adhikakkā, the Gayā (or Phaggu), the Sundarikā, the Sarassatī, the Payāga and the Bāhumatī, as well as the Brāhmanic method of sabbath-keeping. The verse teaches that a man is really purified by his pure actions and that by doing pure deeds he keeps the sabbath. Such a protest as this against the Brāhmanic faith is not peculiar to the Buddhist, as it can be traced, though in a less pronounced form, in the Muṇḍaka, the Kaṭha and other Upanishads, which may be supposed to embody the views of the Muṇḍasāvakas, the Gotamakas and other Bhikkhu

---

[1] M. Senart has *śigu*.
[2] M. Senart has *posarudra*; the half-verse is completed, according to his reading, by *v s.t.* (cf. Frag. C. I[ro], 3).
[3] Frag. C. X[ro],——not adjusted by M. Senart.
[4] Frag. C. I[ro], 3.
[5] Supplied by us.
[6] M. Senart reads *sa*.
[7] M. Senart reads *samajakuvata*.

orders referred to in the Aṅguttara Nikāya (see Buddhist India, p. 145: Dial. B., Vol. II. Pt. I, pp. 220-222). The reading of the fragments in M. Senart's edition is, so far as this verse is concerned, hardly satisfactory. **Hi**—'indeed', 'surely'—may very well be substituted for the Pāli *ve*. **Śudhasaposadhu** = Pāli *suddhass' uposatha*, an instance of vowel sandhi (*śudhasa* + *uposadhu*). For the *m* of **samajate** see notes on *anuabisa* (Sahasav., v. 11. p. 164).

7 [dhamu cari sucarita][1] [(na ta du)[2]carita cari
dhamayari suh(a)[3]][4] śeti asmi loki parasa yi O
(Cro, 30)

Cf. Dhammap., v. 169 † (Lokav., v. 3):—

Dhammaṁ care sucaritaṁ na taṁ duccaritaṁ care,
Dhammacārī sukhaṁ seti asmiṁ loke paramhi ca.

Cf. Udānav., ch. xxx. ("Happiness"), v. 5:—

"Perform carefully the precepts of the law; abstain from all evil deeds: he who keeps the law finds happiness in this world and in the other.

Notes.—With this verse compare v. 1 of the Apramadavaga, p. 119. **Dhamu cari sucarita** = Pāli *dhammaṁ care sucaritaṁ*. For this exhortation cf. the Taittirīya command "*yānyasmākaṁ sucaritāni tāni tvyopasyā*". **Śeti** has a variant *śeati* in Apramadav., v. I.

8 [aho][5][nako va sagami cavadhi vatita śara
ativaka ti][6](tikhisa)[7] [druśilo hi bah][8]o jano O
(Cro, 31)

Cf. Dhammap., v. 320 † (Nāgav., v. 1):—

Ahaṁ nāgo va saṅgāme cāpato patitaṁ saraṁ
Ativākyaṁ titikkhissaṁ dussīlo hi bahujjano.

---

[1] Frag. C. XIIIro, 1. [2] Supplied by us. [3] Supplied by us.
[4] Frag. C. vro, 1. [5] Frag. C. XIIIro, 2. [6] Frag. C. vro, 2.
[7] Supplied by us,—a tentative suggestion, such future forms being nowhere met with in the Prakrit text. [8] Frag. C. XXIIro, 1.

Cf. Fa-kheu-pi-u, sec. XXXI. ("The Elephant"), p. 171 :—

"I am like the fighting elephant, without any fear of the middle arrow (the arrow wounding the middle part). By sincerity and truth I escape the unprincipled man (lawless man)".

Cf. Udānav., ch. XXIX. ("Day and Night"), v. 21 :—

"As the elephant in battle (is patient though) pierced by the arrows shot from the bows, so likewise be patient under the unkind words of the crowd".

The original Sanskrit of the Tibetan version, of which the above is an English rendering, is as follows (Yugavarga, ch. XXIX) :—

Ahaṁ nāga iva saṁgr[āme]...[pa]titaṁ śaraṁ
Ativākyaṁ titikṣāmi duḥṣilo hi mahājanaḥ.

Cf. Manu, VI. 47 :—

Ativādāmstitikṣeta nâvamanyeta kañcana
Na cêmaṁ deham āśṛtya vairaṁ kurvīta kenacit.

Cf. Āyāraṁga Sutta, II. 16. vv. 2-3 :—

Tudaṁti vāyāhi abhiddavaṁ narā
Sarehi saṁgāmagayaṁ va kuṁjaraṁ
....
....
Titikkhae naṇi aduṭṭhacetasa.

Notes—The Prakrit verse and its Pāli, Ardhamāgadhī and Sanskrit parallels, explaining one another, presuppose a common origin that leads us in the last resort to a popular Indian maxim. All these teach men to patiently bear up with the unkind words of the multitude, by the simile of an elephant in battle, pierced by the arrows, remaining yet patient. **Cavadhi**=Pāli *cāpato*, Sk. *cāpataḥ*. We have nothing more to add to M. Senart's comment on this word than that the form with the final vowel *i* is partly due to an attempt to maintain rhythm with the preceding word with the same ending, *sagami*. **Vatita**=Pāli and

Sk. *patitaṁ*. The change of the *p* to *v* seems to have been effected through an intermediate change of *p* to *b*. **Ativaka**=Pāli and Sk. *ativākyaṁ*=*ativādām* (Manu). The form *vaka* presupposes an intermediate change of *kya* to *kka* through assimilation. **Druśilo**=Pāli *dussīlo*, Sk. *duḥśīlaḥ*. The derivation is through a false analogy with forms like *drugati*, v. 4, *supra*.

9 [(ya)[1]sa acata druśilia malua va vitata[2] vani
kuya su tadha][3] (a)[4][tmana yadha na viṣamu
ichati ○][5]

(C^ro, 32)

Cf. Dhammap., v. 162 † (Attav., v. 6) :—

Yassa accanta dussilyaṁ māluvā sālam iv'otataṁ
Karoti so tath'attānaṁ yathā taṁ icchati diso.

Cf. Udānav., ch. xi. ("The Śramana"), v. 10 :—

"He who, breaking all his vows, (is held) as is a Śāla tree by a creeper, brings himself to that state to which his enemy would like to bring him".

Notes.—**Druśilia**=Pāli *dussilyaṁ*, Sk. *dauḥśīlyaṁ*, 'malignity', 'iniquity'. The form is an instance of false analogy, cf. *druśilo*, v. 8, *supra*. **Malua va vitata vani**=Pāli *māluvā va otata vane*. The simile is less expressive or pointed than the Pāli *māluvā sālam iv'otataṁ*, but the Prakrit *vani* may be taken to stand for *śalavani*. Here the imagery is that of a *śāla* forest overgrown by the intertwining and fast growing *Māluvā* creeper. M. Senart's reading *malua vavi lata vani* gives the simple notion of the creeper rapidly growing in a forest, cf. *taṇhā vaḍḍhati māluvā viya* (Dhammap., v. 334). **Kuya**=Pāli *kareyya*, Sk. *kuryāt*. **Viṣamu**=Pāli *visamo*, Sk. *viṣamaḥ*, which may very well be used as a synonym of the Pāli *diso*, 'an enemy'.

---

[1] Supplied by us. [2] M. Senart reads *vavi lata*. [3] Frag. C. v^ro, 3.
[4] Supplied by us. [5] Frag. C. xxiii^ro, 2.

10 .... [yok.ḍ. bh][1]........

....a raṭhapina asañatu ○[2]

(C^{ro}, 33)

....[ga 10][3]

(C^{ro}, 34)

Cf. Dhammap., v. 308 † (Nirayavagga, v. 3) =Itivuttaka, p. 43 :—

Seyyo ayoguḷo bhutto tatto aggisikhûpamo
Yañ ce bhuñjeyya dussīlo raṭṭhapiṇḍaṁ asaññato.

Cf. Udānav., ch. IX. ("Deeds"), v. 2 :—

" Better it would be that a man should eat a lump of flaming iron than that one who is unrestrained and who has broken his vows should live on the charity of the land".

Notes.—The Prakrit verse might be restored, in the light of the Pāli verse and its parallel in the Udānavarga, as follows :—

ṣeho ayokuḍo bhu*to tatu[4] agiśikhupamu
ya ye bhujiya druśila raṭhapina asañato.

Ayokuḍo=Pāli *ayoguḷo*, 'a (red-hot) ball of iron'. We think the allusion is to a horrible form of punishment where the criminal was killed by a red-hot iron-ball thrust into his mouth. **Bhujiya**........**raṭhapina**=Pāli *bhuñjeyya* ....*raṭṭhapiṇḍaṁ*, 'that (a wicked mendicant) should live the charity of the land'; cf. *saddhā-deyyāni bhojanāni bhuñjitvā*, Dīgha, 1. pp. 5-12.

The chapter contains 10 stanzas.

---

[1] Frag. C. v^{ro}, 4. [2] The circle is supplied by us. [3] Frag. C. XLI^{ro}.
[4] For the second *t* cf. *aprate* (Pāli *appatte*, Sk. *aprāpte*), Apramadav., vv. 24, 25. pp. 138, 139.

[7. Balavaga]

It is as difficult to suggest definitely a title for the present group as it was for the preceding one. But it appears that the group dilates chiefly upon the ways of the fool. It is, moreover, quite relevant that, after having dwelt upon the conduct of the wise in the foregoing chapter, some idea should be given of a fool and his manners. Whatever its appropriate name, the group as we have it in the extant Kharoṣ.hī Ms., is not complete; only 8 stanzas are preserved. The Bālavagga of the Pāli Dhammapada (ch. 5) consists of 16 stanzas, while the corresponding group in the Fa-kheu-king (sec. XIII.) contains 21. This group forms the 13th chapter of the Udānavarga and has 16 verses.

1 ida ja mi keca ida ji karia ida kari..........................
..................vinamana abhimadati muca??[1] saśoa O[2]

(C^{ro}, 35)

Cf. Mahābhārata, XII. 175. 20 :—

Idaṁ kṛtaṁ idaṁ kāryaṁ idaṁ anyat kṛtâkṛtaṁ
Evamīhâsukhâsaktaṁ kṛtânta kurute vaśe.

Notes.—No parallel of this verse have we been able to trace either in Pāli or in Sanskrit. M. Senart thinks that what remains of it would give in Sanskrit :—

Idañ ca me kṛtyaṁ idañ ca kāryaṁ idaṁ k..................
..................vindamāno, bhimardati mṛtyu. . saśokaṁ.

We have nothing to say against this sanskritization except that M. Senart has completely lost sight of the spirit of the Prakrit stanza. It teaches that death overpowers the fool

---

[1] We ha e tentatively interpreted it as *mucu*. But M. Senart's *muca*, followed by two doubtful letters, tempts us at the same time to a reading *muca(ti) (na) sa śoa*=Pali *muñcati na sa sokā* ; for a similar construction cf. *so duha na parimucati* (I. C^{ro}, 42). This would, however, leave *abhimadati* unconstrued.

[2] The circle is supplied by us..

who overestimates his own undertakings. This contention is borne out by the word **vinamana**, which, as we take it, is an accusative singular form = Pāli *vindamānaṁ*. In determining the real purpose of the verse we have to fall upon other verses of the group, most of which are meant to bring out the thought and conduct of a fool. We might restore it, in the light of its Sanskrit parallel from the Mahābhārata, as follows :

ida ja mi keca ida ji karia ida kari(miti)
(suhu) vinamana abhimadati mucu (balu) saśoa ○

If this restoration be correct, it is clear that the teaching of this verse is in spirit the same as that of—

(1) Dhammap., verse 74 :—

" Mam' eva kataṁ maññantu gihī pabbajitā ubho
Mam' evâtivasā assu kiccâkiccesu kismici,
Iti bālassa saṅkappo, icchā māno ca vaḍḍhati. "

and (2) Udānav., verse 4, ch. XIII. :—

" Let both priests and laymen, whosoever they may be, imagine that it is I (who have done it); in whatever is to be done or not done, let them be subject to me ; such is the mind of the fool, and his desires greatly increase ".

The reflections such as those embodied in the above verse, may be supposed to have been the outcome of moralising upon the tragic end of persons like Devadatta, who was so very anxious to make his influence strongly felt among others.

2 ?dha,vaṣa kariṣamu ?dha h.matagi

(C^ro, 36)

Cf. Dhammap., v. 286 † (Maggav., v. 14) :—

Idha vassaṁ vasissāmi idha hemantagimhisu
Iti bālo vicinteti antarāyaṁ na bujjhati.

Cf. Udānav., ch. I. ("Impermanency"), v. 38 :—

"'This (abode) will do for winter and (this) for summer'; thus ponders the rapidly decaying fool who has not seen the danger".

Notes.—The Prakrit verse might be restored, in the light of the Pāli gāthā and its parallel in the Udānavarga, as follows :—

idha vaṣa kariṣamu idha hematagiṣmisu[1]
iti balu viciteti ataraya na bujhati ○

We have reason to think that there is an allusion in this verse to the frivolous life of the rich who spent their time in the company of women, four months in the rainy abode, four months in the winter and four months in the summer—as described in the Vinaya Mahāvagga (Vin. I. p. 15). The sentiments displayed in the verse are very natural to the recluses who were the avowed champions of morality and self-control.

Vaṣa kariṣamu—the same in meaning as the Pāli *vassaṁ vasissāmi*. The Prakrit expression is a later idiom, associated with the idea of the Buddhist Lent ("*catumāsaṁ vassaṁ vasissāmi*"—Dhammapada-Comy.).

3 ta putrapaśusamadha ....

[sutu ga][2]..........

(C^ro^, 37)

Cf. Dhammap., v. 287 † (Maggav., v. 15) :—

Taṁ puttapasusammattaṁ byāsattamanasaṁ naraṁ
Suttaṁ gāmaṁ mahogho va Maccu ādāya gacchati.

---

[1] Also, *himatagimisu*.
[2] Frag. C. XXXIV^ro^,—not adjusted by M. Senart. He reads *suruga*.

Cf. Fa-kheu-pi-u, sec. XXVIII. ("The Way"), p. 157 :—

"Men concern themselves about the matters of wife and child; they perceive not the inevitable law of disease (and death), and the end of life which quickly comes as a bursting torrent (sweeping all before it) in a moment".

Cf. Mahābhārata, XII. 175. 18 :—

Taṁ putrapaśusampannaṁ vyāsaktamānasaṁ naraṁ
Suptaṁ vyāghro mṛgam iva mṛtyur ādāya gacchati.

Notes.—The Prakrit verse might be restored as follows :—

ta putrapaśusamadha (biasatamanasa[1] naru[2])
sutu ga(mu mahoho va mucu adaya gachati ○)

In the foregoing two verses the term 'fool' is applied to the Bhikkhus and princes who are ambitious for lordship over others, and to the rich who lead a frivolous life, while in the present verse a case is made out against the householders in general who are unable to pursue the higher aspirations of human life on account of their excessive attachment to their wife, children and wealth. Cf. "*Dukkho gharavāso, abbhokāso pabbajjā*", painful is household life, free is the life of renunciation. Thus a sharp distinction is drawn between the two modes of human life, and the contrast is beautifully brought out in the Dhaniya Sutta (Suttanipāta, No. 2). In the Prakrit verse, however, only the miserable life of the householder is dwelt upon, as also in the Dhammapada verse 62 :—

'Puttā m'atthi dhanaṁ m'atthi' iti bālo vihaññati.

Samadha = Pāli *sammattaṁ*, 'maddened'. The change of *tt* into *dh* presupposes an intermediate change of *tt* to *th*. See Puṣavaga, v. 15, notes on *sagadha* (p. 154). **Sutu gamu mahoho va** = Pāli *suttaṁ gāmaṁ mahogho va*, 'like a great flood (sweeping away) a sleeping village'. The simile is perhaps the outcome of a knowledge of the torrential river-floods to which the people of the Punjab and Bengal are a victim.

---

[1] Also, *viasatamanaso*.

[2] Also, *naro*.

4 puve i kica parijaga [(ma ta)[1] kici[2] kicakali adea ta tadiśa[3] parika][4][makicakari no i kica kica(k)ali adea][6]O[7]

(Cro, 38 ; see also p. 96)

Cf. Samuddavāṇijajātaka, No. 466 † (Fausböll's Jātaka, IV. p. 166) :—

Anāgataṁ paṭikayirātha kiccaṁ, mā maṁ kiccaṁ
kiccakāle vyadhesi,
Taṁ tādisaṁ paṭikatakiccakāriṁ, na taṁ kiccaṁ
kiccakāle vyadheti.

Notes.—This verse, as also the next, condemns procrastination and urges immediate action—one of the salient features of early Buddhism. **Puve i** = Pāli *pubbe hi*, 'beforehand'; this meaning is otherwise expressed in Pāli by *anāgataṁ paṭikayirātha*, explained in the Jataka-Comy. as *puretaraṁ kareyya*. **Parikamakicakari** = Pāli *paṭikatakiccakārī*, 'one doing his duty beforehand' (*paṭigacch'eva kattabbakiccakārī*, Jātaka-Comy.).

5 ya puvi karaniani [pacha ṣakaru[8] ichati atha dubakati balu][9] [suhatu parihayati][10] O[11]

(Cro, 39)

Cf. Therag. vv. 225, 261 :—

Yo pubbe karaṇīyāni pacchā so kātum icchati
Sukhā so dhaṁsate ṭhānā pacchā ca-m-anutappati.

---

[1] Supplied by us following M. Senart's reconstruction on p. 96.
[2] M. Senart understands it as *kica* after the Pāli parallel (see his *Postscript* on p. 96).
[3] M. Senart at first read *tata diśa* (see p. 67).
[4] Frag. C. xxviiro, 1.
[5] This reading is adopted after the Pāli parallel, and M. Senart understands it as such. The original reading in his edition is *kicakici ali*.
[6] Frag. C. xxxro, 1.
[7] The circle is supplied by us.
[8] Could it not be read *ṣakatu* ?
[9] Frag. C. xxviiro, 2.
[10] Frag. C. xxxro, 2.
[11] The circle is supplied by us.

Cf. Fausböll's Jātaka, I. p. 319, v. 70:—

Yo pubbe karaṇīyāni pacchā so kātum icchati
Veraṇakaṭṭhabhañjo va sa pacchā-m-anutappati.

Notes.—The Prakrit verse may be read in Pāli:—

Yo pubbe karaṇiyāni pacchā sakkātum icchati
Atha duppakati bālo sukhato parihāyati.

Ṣakaru or **ṣakatu ichati** = Pāli *sakkātuṁ* (*i.e., sat-kātuṁ*) *icchati*, 'wishes to get (them) well done'. We think the same meaning might be made out of M. Senart's interpretation, which is *ṣakaru = saṅkara(ṁ)*. **Dubakati** = Pāli *duppakati*, Sk. *duṣprakṛti*, 'ill-natured'. For the expression **suhatu parihayati** cf. *so sukhā na vihāyati* (Therag. v. 232).

6 akita kuki(ta)[1] [ṣehu pacha tavati drukita
kita nu sukita ṣeh][2](u)[3] [ya kitva nanutapati[4]][5] O[6]

(C^ro, 40)

Cf. Dhammap., v. 314 † (Nirayav., v. 9) = Saṁyutta, I. p. 49:—

Akataṁ dukkataṁ seyyo pacchā tapati dukkataṁ
Katañ ca sukataṁ seyyo yaṁ katvā nânutappati.

Cf. Udānav., XXIX., v. 53 ("B 41" in Prof. Pischel's edition):—

Akṛtaṁ kukṛtāc chreya(ḥ) paścāt tapati duṣkṛtam
Śocate duṣkṛtaṁ kṛtvā śocate durgatiṁ gataḥ.

Notes.—**Drukita** = Pāli *dukkataṁ*, Sk. *duṣkṛtaṁ*, an instance of false analogy, cf. *druśila*, Panitav., vv. 8, 9, *ante*. This kind of phonetic change is due evidently to Iranian influence.

---

1 Supplied by us. 2 Frag. C. XXVIII^ro, 3. 3 Supplied by us.
4 M. Senart entertains doubt about the letter *pa*, and he puts a query after it (see p. 69).
5 Frag. C. XXX^ro, 3. 6 The circle is supplied by us.

7 asava teṣa vaḍhati ara te asavacha............................

....

(C^ro, 41)

Cf. Dhammap., v. 253 † (Malavagga, v. 19) :—

Paravejjânupassissa niccaṁ ujjhānasaññino
Āsavā tassa vaḍḍhanti ārā so āsavakkhayā.

Notes.—We have nothing to say against M. Senart's observations except that we need not suppose that a *śloka* of six pādas, or the thought, was collected into a single stanza in the Pāli text. We have another instance where the pādas of the Pāli *gāthā* are inverted in the Prakrit (see *Jaravaga*, v. 16, *infra*). However, in the absence of the remains of the middle line, if there was any, and for want of a parallel of three-lined stanza in any other work, one would be justified in restoring the Prakrit verse, in the light of the Dhammap., v. 253, as follows :—

asava teṣa vaḍhati ara te asavacha(ya)
(paravejanupasina[1] nica ujhanasañina ○)

8 yeṣa tu susamaradha nica kayakata sma............

....

satana sabrayanana taṣa ?............................

(C^ro, 42-43)

Cf. Dhammap., v. 293 † (Pakiṇṇakav. v. 4) =Therag. v. 636 :—

Yesañ ca susamâraddhā niccaṁ kāyagatā sati
Akiccan te na sevanti kicce sātaccakārino
Satānaṁ sampajānānaṁ atthaṁ gacchanti āsavā.

Cf. Udānav., XXXI. ("The Mind"), v. 56 (?) :—

"He whose attentive mind delights in the truth and adheres to the (four) truths, he always walks in the way with his body, he is safe in speech and in mind, and, casting off sorrow, he will experience no more suffering".

---

[1] Also, *paravejanubasina.*

Notes.—This verse with which the chapter, as it survives in the Kharoṣṭhī Ms., is broken off, emphasizes the necessity for constant meditation on the transitoriness of the body. Thus it introduces us to the teaching of the Jaravaga, but in the absence of a complete and unimpaired Ms. it cannot be said with certainty whether the Jaravaga formed a sequel to the present chapter. The Prakrit verse might be restored, in the light of its Pāli counterpart, as follows :—

yeṣa tu susamaradha nica kayakata sma(ti)
(akica te na sevati kici satacakarino)
satana sabrayanana taṣa (gachati parichaya ○)[1]

Taṣa=Pāli *tasiṇā* (*taṇhā*), Sk. *tṛṣā* (*tṛṣṇā*), thirst, desire. The Prakrit form keeps closer to Sanskrit. M. Senart considers it to be a mistake for *teṣa*.

The colophon indicating the total number of verses contained in this chapter is missing, and we cannot say if there were more verses after this.

[8. Jaravaga]

A few chapters appear to be missing from the extant Kharoṣṭhī Ms. between the *Bala* and *Jara* groups. The *Jara* group, as may be judged from the colophon "ga 25" (I. c^{vo}, 23), contained 25 stanzas of which 2 are missing (vv. 1-2). The same group forms the 11th chapter of the Pāli Dhammapada and consists only of 11 verses, of which 4 are contained in our *Jaravaga*. The Prakrit group contains 2 verses which are to be found in chaps. III. (*Citta*) and XXIV. (*Taṇhā*) of the Pāli text. The remaining verses are collected from various canonical sources, such as the Saṁyutta Nikāya, the Sutta-nipāta, the Thera-Therīgāthā and the Jātaka. The first chapter of the Fa-kheu-king, which deals with 'Impermanence', contains 21 verses, of which two occur in the Prakrit Jaravaga and one in the Pāli chapter. Section XIX. of the Chinese recension bears the title *Jarāvagga* and contains 14 verses, of which one (v. 1) is to be found in both the Pāli and Prakrit chapters. The Udānavarga has no separate chapter on 'Old Age', but treats of 'Impermanence'

[1] It will be noticed that the 6th foot of the Prakrit verse differs from that of the Pāli; the restoration has been suggested on the basis of the Dhammapada-Comy., where *atthaṁ*=*parikkhayaṁ*.

and 'Old Age' in its first chapter, which contains 41 verses. The Udānavarga and the Prakrit text have many verses in common. Of the Udāna verses 13 are to be found in the Pāli text, four in the Jarā group and the rest in other groups. Fausböll has in his excellent edition of the Dhammapada noticed a few ślokas in the Manu-saṁhitā, the Mahābhārata and the Rāmāyaṇa, containing ascetic reflections on 'Impermanence', similar to those in the Dhammapada vv. 148 and 150.

3[1] ?. ?. ?re[2] athu ?..? ??

....

(C^{vo}, 1)

Cf. Saṁyutta, V., p. 217 :—

Dhītaṁ jammī jare atthu dubbaṇṇakaraṇī jare
Tāva manoramaṁ vimbaṁ jarāya abhimadditaṁ.

Cf. Fa-kheu-pi-u, sec. 1. ("Impermanency"), p. 43 :—

"Old age brings with it loss of all bodily attraction".

Cf. Udānav., ch. I. ("Impermanency"), v. 30 :—

"Thou art foolish and despicable, and dost not that which is right; for that body (rūpa) in which thou delightest will be the cause of thy ruin".

Notes.—M. Senart was able to read only *ra athu* of the first line. In his text the sign "?" indicates that there are faint traces of characters, and the bold dots mean that so many letters are completely missing. None but those who have ever seriously attempted the identification of a verse, so hopelessly mutilated as the one under discussion, can realise how difficult a task it is to find out a parallel in Pāli or in Buddhist Sanskrit. It was indeed by accident that we after repeated searches chanced upon two verses in the Saṁyutta,

---

1 There are 23 verses surviving altogether in this chapter and they occur without break, but the colophon records the total number as 25; consequently, two verses are missing towards the beginning.

2 M. Senart reads *ra* with the preceding query (standing for a doubtful character) put apart. We read the word in the light of the Pāli parallel, *jare*.

corresponding to this verse and the next one. Supposing that the Prakrit verse is on the whole similar to the Pāli, it might be reconstructed as follows :—

(dhitu jami ja)re athu (druvanakarani[1] jare
tava manoramu viba[2] jaraya[3] abhimardita[4] ○)

4 **yo vi varṣaśata jivi so vi mucuparayano**
na kiji[5] pari..

(C^{vo}, 2)

Cf. Saṁyutta, V., p. 217 :—

yo pi vassasataṁ jīve so pi maccuparāyaṇo
na kiñci parivajjeti sabbam evâbhimaddati.

Cf. Udānav., ch. I. ("Impermanency"), v. 31 :—

"One may live a hundred years, yet he is subject to the lord of death; one may reach old age, or else he is carried off by disease".[6]

Notes.—The Prakrit verse might, perhaps, be reconstructed as follows :—

yo vi varṣaśata jivi so vi mucuparayano
na kiji parivajeti[7] sarvam evabhimardati ○

Mucuparayano = Pāli *maccuparāyaṇo*, Sk. *mṛtyu-parāyaṇaḥ*, 'subject to death'. In many instances Pāli words seem to obey the grammatical rules governing the changes of *n* into *ṇ*, while the Prakrit of our text, as appears

[1] Also, *druvranakarani*.

[2] The form is to be taken tentatively. We may as well read *vima* on an approximate likeness with *gamira* = Pāli *gambhira* (I. B. 6, p. 27).

[3] Also *jarae*; cf. *prañaya prañae* (Magavaga, vv. 27, 28, p. 111).

[4] Cf. *jara nabhimardati* (Apramadavaga, v. 2, p. 121).

[5] M. Senart reads *bhaje*, which is evidently incorrect. We read *ki* for *bh*, consistently with the Pāli counterpart. The appearance of the character is much like the peculiar stroke of *bh*, which M. Senart has taken so much pains to establish in other instances, (see I. A^{2}, 1, note, pp 5-6). The stroke over the *ja* justifies the reading *ji* instead of *je*.

[6] The second half of Rockhill's translation seems open to dispute.

[7] Cf. *parivajetva* (Apramadav., v. 18, p. 133).

from M. Senart's readings, is characterised by the absence of the cerebral nasal. **Kiji**=Pāli *kiñci*, Sk. *kiñcit*. M. Senart reads *bhaje*, which gives no meaning. We have an alternative form of *kiji* in *kici* (Suhavaga, v. 13, *infra*) which stands closer to Pāli *kiñci*.

5 parijinamida[1] ruvu roaniḍa [prabhaguno
bheṁsiti p.ti][2] ....

(C^vo^, 3)

Cf. Dhammap., v. 148 † (Jarāv., v. 3) :—

Parijiṇṇam idaṁ rūpaṁ roganiḍḍaṁ pabhaṅguṇaṁ
Bhijjati pūtisandeho maraṇantaṁ hi jīvitaṁ.

Cf. Fa-kheu-pi-u, sec. XIX. ("Old Age"), p. 118 :—

"When old, then its beauty fades away; in sickness, what paleness and leanness—the skin wrinkled, the flesh withered, death and life both conjoined".

Cf. Udānav., ch. I. ("Impermanency"), v. 35 :—

"The end of life is death, this body bent down by age, this receptacle of disease, is rapidly wasting away; this mass of corruption will soon be destroyed".

Notes.—The Prakrit verse, supposing that it is on the whole similar to the Pāli, as the portion which survives indicates, might be completed and read as follows :—

parijinamida ruvu roaniḍa prabhaguno
bheṁsiti puti(saneho[3] maranata hi jivitu[4] O)

—This verse cannot be traced in any other canonical texts, though reflections similar to those contained in it are met with throughout the texts of the Sutta Piṭaka.

---

[1] M. Senart reads *parijinam ida*.
[2] Frag. C. XXXIIvo, M. Senart reads *prabhaguno*.
[3] For *n*=Pāli *nd*, cf. *nivinati* (Magav., vv. 27-29, pp. 111-112).
[4] Also, *jivita*.

Fausböll has drawn his readers' attention to similar reflections in the Manu, VI. 77, the Rāmāyaṇa, II. 105. V. 14, and the Mahābhārata, XI. vv. 48, 207 and XII. v. 829. One will look in vain through the older Dharmasūtras for such pessimistic reflections on the destructive side of nature. The Manu and Viṣṇu codes in their present form are recasts of a time when a Stoic mode of life was so firmly established among the asceties and recluses as to find its way into the naive positivism of the juristic thinkers. We need not be surprised to come across these reflections in the Hindu Epics, which mainly uphold and idealise the systems of the Smṛitis, because the epic kernels which survive in the shape of ballads in the canonical Jātaka Book and the Upâkhyānas of the Mahābhārata bristle with them. As will be shown below, some of the important *Jara*-verses of the Prakrit text are to be found in the Dasaratha Jātaka, a Buddhist version of the older Rāma-story which, like the version in the Mahābhārata, was primarily intended to exhort people to keep up their spirits in the midst of trials and bereavements, considering that these are inevitable experiences of mankind.

Parijinamida = Pāli *parijiṇṇam idaṁ*, an instance of vowel-sandhi (*parijina* + *ida*), the intervening *m* having developed to prevent *hiatus*. *Parijina* or 'wasted' is virtually the same in meaning as *jarā-śoka-samāviṣṭaṁ* ('permeated with decay and sorrow') of Manu VI. 77. It will be noticed that the Prakrit form stands close to the Pāli, but the latter fulfils the grammatical rules about the changes of *n* into *ṇ*, which the Prakrit does not. **Roaniḍa** = Pāli *roganiḍḍaṁ*, a compound, meaning 'the abode of diseases' (*rogānaṁ nivesanaṭṭhānaṁ*, Dhammapada-Comy; cf. Manu, VI. 77: *rogāyatanaṁ*). It is clear from this that the Buddhist commentator is inclined to identify *niḍḍa* with *nīḍa* or *nīḍya*, 'nest'. *Roa* is an alternative form of *roka* (see Suhavaga, v. 2, *infra*). **Prabhaguna** = Pāli *pabhaṅguṇaṁ* or *pabhaṅguraṁ*, Sk. *prabhaṅguraṁ*, a compound, meaning 'that which is frail or fragile'; cf. *āturaṁ* in Manu, VI. 77, and Dhammapada, v. 147. The final letter *na* instead of *ra* makes the word deviate from Sanskrit and keep closer to the Pāli. For **bheṅsiti**, see M. Senart's notes (pp. 70-71). **Putisaneho** = Pāli *pūtisandeho*, a compound, meaning 'the body which is stinking' (*pūtiko samāno tadeva deho*, Dhammapada-Comy.; cf. *arūkāyaṁ*, Dhammapada, v. 147, *pūtikāyaṁ*, Comy.; *rajasvalaṁ*, Manu, VI. 77).

Maranata hi jivitu=Pāli *maraṇantaṁ hi jīvitaṁ*, Sk. *maraṇântaṁ hi jīvitaṁ* (cf. Divyâvadāna, p. 100; Mahāvastu, III. p. 183; Rāmāyaṇa, II. 105. v. 14; Udānavarga, I. v. 22; Fa-kheu-king, I. p. 41; Vasubandhu's Gāthāsaṅgraha, v. 23). This corresponds to the expressions *n'atthi dhuvaṁ ṭhiti* (Dhammap., v. 147), *anityaṁ* (Manu, VI, 77), and *jātā jātā marantídha evaṁdhammā hi pāṇino* (Therag., v. 553). Note how this idea of life ending with death is expanded in a verse incorporated in the Rāmāyaṇa, II. 105, st. 16 and the Divyâvadāna, p. 100 :—

Sarve kṣayântā nicayāḥ patanântās samucchrayāḥ
Saṁyoga-viprayogântā maraṇântaṁ ca jīvitam.

Life and death are one of the three pairs of constant and opposed phenomena whereby Makkhali Gosāla, the third great leader of the Ājīvikas, characterised the organic world, the two remaining pairs being those of gain and loss, and pleasure and pain (*lābhaṁ, alābhaṁ, suhaṁ, dukhaṁ, jīveyaṁ, maraṇaṁ*)[1]. The Buddha conceived of eight principles (*aṭṭha loka-dhammā*), divisible into four pairs: *lābho, alābho, yaso, ayaso, nindā, pasaṁsā, sukhaṁ, dukkhaṁ*, to which was afterwards added another pair *viz., jīvitaṁ, maraṇaṁ*, as can be seen from the Theragāthā, vv. 664-670. All these come under Pakudha Kaccāyana's two principles, *sukhe, dukhe* (Dīgha, I. p. 56).

6 ko nu h ?.............................[lite sati
an.kar.? prachiti pra][1]..............................

(C[vo], 4)

Cf. Dhammap., v. 146 † (Jarāvagga, v. 1)=Jāt. V. p. 11, ll. 25-26 (Kumbhajātaka, No. 512).

Ko nu hāso kim ānando niccaṁ pajjalite sati,
Andhakārena onaddhā padīpaṁ na gavessatha.

Cf. Fa-kheu-pi-u, sec. XIX. ("Old Age"), p. 117 :—

"What (room for) mirth, what (room for) laughter, remembering the everlasting burning (or fire). Surely this dark and dreary (world) is not fit for one to seek security and rest in".

---

[1] Dr. Barua's paper on the Ājīvikas, Jour. of the Dept. of Letters, Calcutta University, 1920, Vol. II., p. 25.

Cf. Mahāvastu, III., p. 376 :—

Kā nu krīḍā kā nu rati evaṁ prajvalite sadā
Andhakārasmiṁ prakṣiptā pradīpaṁ na gaveṣatha.
Ko nu harṣo ko nu ānando evam prajvalite sadā
Andhakārasmiṁ prakṣiptā ālokaṁ na prakāśaya.

Cf. Udānav., ch. I. ("Impermanency"), v. 4 :—

"To one who is being burnt, what joy can there be, what subject of rejoicing? Ye who dwell in the midst of darkness, why seek ye not a light?"

Notes.—The Prakrit verse might be completed and read as follows :—

ko nu h(aso kimanano[1] nica praja)lite sati
anakarasmi[2] prachiti[3] pra(dipa na gaveṣatha[4] O)

—This verse cannot be traced in any canonical text other than the Dhammapada. The Prakrit text substitutes *prachiti* in the 2nd line for Pāli *onaddhā*. The reading of the Udānavarga seems to have been analogous to that of the Pāli text. The exhortation of this verse is no more than a poetical summary of the teaching of such Fire-sermons as (1) the Ādittapariyāya-sutta (Vinaya Mahāvagga, pp. 66-67) on the basis of which the Gokulikas, or better, the Kukkulikas are said to have formulated a doctrine of 'universal pessimism' (Kathāvatthu, I. 7, with Comy., and Preface to the "Points of Controversy"), and (2) the Aggikkhandhûpama-sutta which, according to the Ceylonese chronicles (see Mahāvaṁsa, XII. 34), Asoka's Indo-Bactrian missionary, Dhammarakkhita had made the principal text of his sermon to the people of Aparanta. The Prakrit verse seems to be older than the two verses in the Mahāvastu which appear to have been quoted from an older Sanskrit recension of the Dhammapada.

---

[1] Cf. *nivinati* (Magav. vv. 27-29, pp. 111-112).
[2] Following the Mahāvastu. Also, *anakarena* or *andhakarena* ; cf. *bandhana* in I. B. 52.
[3] The reading *prachiti* is permissible, if it is a case of locative absolute.
[4] Cf. *bhavetha*, I. A[2], 8. Also, *gaviṣadhu* ; cf. *bhodha*, in I. A[2], 7.

Prajalite sati = Pāli *pajjalite sati*, locative absolute, meaning 'while the world is burning (with passions and other painful mental qualities)'. The Mahāvastu reads *prajvalite sadā*. **Anakarena prachiti** would strictly correspond to a Pāli *andhakārerna pakkhilte*, an expression which is the same in meaning as *andhakārena onaddhā*. It seems that *andhakāre pakkhittā* is more grammatical than *andhakārena*; cf. *rattikhittā* (Dhammap., v. 304) = *andhakāre khittā* (Comy.); *andhakārasmiṁ prakṣiptā* (Mahāvastu).

7 yameva[1] paḍhama rati gabhi vasati[2] manavo
aviṭhi[3] ....[ti so gachu na nivatati O][4]

(C^vo, 5)

Cf. Ayogharajātaka, No. 510 (Fausböll, IV. p. 494) :—

Yam ekarattiṁ paṭhamaṁ gabbhe vasati mānavo
Abbh' uṭṭhito va sayati sa gacchaṁ na nivattati.

Cf. Udānav., ch. I. ("Impermanency"), v. 6 :—

"One who has heretofore been subject to the misery of birth from the womb may go to the highest place and come no more back again (into the word)."

Notes.—The Prakrit verse might be completed and read as follows :—

yameva (*or*, eka) paḍhama rati gabhi vasati manavo
aviṭhi(to va saya)ti so gachu na nivatati O

Yameva = Pāli *yam evaṁ*, a vowel-sandhi (*ya* + *eva*); cf. *parijinamida*, v. 5 *supra*. The expression *yam eva paḍhama rati* = Pāli *yam eva paṭhamaṁ rattiṁ*, 'the

---

[1] M. Senart's *yam eva* have been joined together here on account of sandhi.

[2] M. Senart reads *gabhirasati*, which is hardly correct; *gabhirasati* would be = Pāli *gambhirassati*, which gives no sense. But, we have in Prakrit *gamira* for *gambhira*, cf. I. B. 6 (p. 27).

[3] M. Senart reads *avi ṭhi*, put apart.

[4] Frag. C. XVIII^vo, 1,—not adjusted by M. Senart.

very first night', is somewhat different from the Pāli *yam ekarattim paṭhamam*, 'the one night when for the first time', but the Prakrit reading gives a better sense. According to the commentary, the appropriateness of the word *ratti* lies in the fact that men are generally conceived in the mother's womb at night, though, as a matter of fact, *ratti* includes both day and night. **Aviṭhito** = Pāli *abbh'uṭṭhito*, a vowel-sandhi (*avi* + *uṭhito*), *avi* standing for Pāli *abhi*. For *v*=*bh*, cf. *abhivuyu* (=*abhibhūya*), I. B. 30, 31 (p. 38). The Comy. suggests *abbho* + *uṭṭhito*, and explains *abbho* as meaning a piece of cloud, which, however, seems a mere etymological conjecture. *Abbh'uṭṭhito* may simply be equated with Sk. *abhyutthitaḥ*. Accordingly, *abbhuṭṭhito va sayati* may be rendered 'he lies down as if being upborne'. According to the Comy., the general sense of the verse is: "Just as a piece of cloud having arisen, comes into existence, moves about being chased by the wind, in the same way a man since his first conception in the womb undergoes successive stages of gestation and development in such a manner that he cannot retrace the steps that have already been undergone". The developmental stages of man mentioned in the Comy., *manda*, *khiḍḍā*, etc., remind one of Gosāla's eight stages, *mandabhūmi*, *khiḍḍābhūmi*, etc. (see Sumaṅgala-vilāsinī, I. p. 163).

8 yasa rativivasina ayu apataro[1] sia
apodake [va mansana ki teṣa nu[2] kumalaka[3] O][4]

(C[vo], 6)

Cf. Mūgapakkhajātaka (No. 538, illustrated by a carving on the railing of the Bharaut Stūpa), Fausböll, VI. p. 26 :—

Yassa ratyā vivasane āyum appataram siyā
Appodake va macchānam kin nu komārakam tahim.

---

[1] M. Senart reads *aparato*, which gives no sense unless it be supposed that *rato* is a change by *Metathesis* from *taro* or that the reading is *kato*. The Pāli parallel being °*taram*, it is clear that the Prakrit *aparato* cannot but be due to a mistake of the scribe, who has inverted the reading.

[2] M. Senart reads simply *u*.

[3] M. Senart reads *ukumulana*; our reading is tentative.

[4] Frag. C. XVIII[vo], 2,—not adjusted by M. Senart.

Cf. Fa-kheu-pi-u, sec I. ("Impermanency"), p. 40:—

"Every day and night takes from the little space given to each one born; there is the gradual decay of a few years and all is gone, as the waters of a pool are cut off (or exhausted)".

Cf. Udānav., ch. I. ("Impermanency"), v. 34:—

"Man is like a fish in a shallow pool of water; day and night this life is passing away; what subject of rejoicing is there in so brief a thing?"

Cf. Mahābhārata, XII., 175, 11, 12:—

Rātryāṁ rātryām vyatītāyām āyur alpataraṁ yadā
Tadaiva vandhyaṁ divasam iti vindyād vicakṣaṇaḥ
Gādhodake matsya iva sukhaṁ vindeta kas tadā
Anavāpteṣu kāmeṣu mṛtyur abhyeti mānavam.

Notes.—Rativivasina = Pāli *rattivivāsena*, Sk. *rātrivivāsena* (if M. Senart's reading is correct). In order to equate with the Pāli *ratyā vivasane*, the Prakrit reading must be either *rativivasani* or *rativivasane*. **Apataro** = Pāli *appataraṁ*, 'less', 'lesser'. M. Senart's reading *aparato* conveys no sense. **Maṅsana** = Pāli *macchānaṁ*, Sk. *matsyānām*, 'of fishes'. For *ṅs* = *tsy*, cf. *bheṅsiti* (Sk. *bhetsyate*), Jaravaga, v. 5 (p. 189), and M. Senart's notes under C^vo, 3 (pp. 70-71). **Teṣa** = Pāli *tesaṁ*, Sk. *teṣām*, and is closer to Sanskrit on account of the *ṣ*. The correlative of *yasa* is *tasa*, but here *teṣa* appears to refer to the fishes. The Pāli reading is *tahiṁ*, a locative form of *taṁ*, meaning 'there', 'in that'; cf. the Udānav. expression "there, in so brief a thing". **Kumalaka** or **komalaka** or **komaraka** = Pāli *komārakaṁ*, Sk. *kaumāryam* = *taruṇabhāvo*, (Jātaka-Comy.) 'youth', 'young age'. With regard to his reading *ukumulana*, M. Senart suggests that it might be equated with Sk. *oka-unmūlanaṁ*, "the destruction of their abode". He also points out that if the form only were taken into account, one would think at once of a form *ulkā-unmūlana*, which, he says, is a form of speech, very little likely. Neither *oka-unmūlana* nor *ulkāunmūlana* can fit well with the meaning of the clause *ki teṣa* etc. Rockhill's translation of the Tibetan version of the Udānavarga, which is at best tentative, connects the idea of mirth with this clause—"What subject of rejoicing is there in so brief a thing?" The idea of rejoicing can very well be associated with *komārakaṁ*. Supposing that the reading *ukumulana* is on the whole correct and that it has reference to fishes, it might be slightly altered into *ukumujana* and equated with a Pāli *okā ummujjanaṁ*, 'jumping out of water' (cf. Suppārakajātaka No. 463, Fausböll, IV. p. 139; *macchā .... udake ummujjanimujjaṁ karonti*).

9 ye vudha[1] ye yu[2] dahara ye ca majhima poruṣa
anupa ?.............................[lapaka va banana][3] O

(C^{vo}, 7)

For the first half, cf. Vessantarajātaka, No. 547 (Fausböll, VI. p. 572), first line of verse 642 :—

Ye ca vuddhā ye ca daharā ye ca majjhimaporisā
Mam eva upajīveyyuṁ, tatiy' etaṁ varaṁ vara.

and Dasarathajātaka, No. 461 (Fausböll, IV. p. 127) :—

Daharā ca hi vuddhā ca ye bālā ye ca paṇḍitā
Aḍḍhā c'eva daliddā ca sabbe maccuparāyanā.

Cf. Ayogharajātaka, No. 510 (Fausböll, IV. p. 495) :—

Dumapphalān' eva patanti mānavā
Daharā ca vuddhā ca sarīrabhedā
Nariyo narā majjhimaporisā ca.

---

[1], [2] M. Senart reads *hu dhayeyu*, of which the first letter is written in such a way as to easily warrant a reading *vu*. In adjusting the reading of the first pāda we have the advantage of the Pāli parallels, which M. Senart could not discover.

[3] Frag. C. XXIII^{vo},—not adjusted by M. Senart, who reads *lapabhavabanana*. We have reason to change his *pabha* into *paka* from a comparison with *kije* which he read incorrectly as *bhaje* (see v. 4 *supra*). For the last quarter-verse M. Senart has *sa nica maranato bhayo* O (see C^{vo}, 7, p. 72), but a careful examination of the shape and position of the fragment makes it clear that it fits into the main plate only when it is pushed a little below and thrust into the next line, *i.e.*, C^{vo}, 8—an arrangement which is established beyond doubt by the fact that there is an exact Pāli counterpart to the Prakrit verse thus adjusted (*q. v.* under v. 10 *infra* p. 198). Accordingly, the aforesaid quarter-verse has been shifted to the line-end of v. 10, and the gap thus caused is filled by Frag C. XXIII^{vo} with sufficient reason on our side.

Cf. Udānav., ch. I. ("Impermanency"), v. 10 :—

"Some are old, and some are young, some are grown up; by degrees they all do disappear, like ripe fruit falling".

Notes.—Almost the whole of the second line of the above verse is missing from the extant Kharoṣṭhī Ms.. A detached fragment, marked XXIIIvo, contains the line-end of a certain verse belonging to Plate Cvo. This fragment with the line-end—*lapabh vabanana* O—needs adjustment, but we know of no verse of the plate under notice into which it may fit. M. Senart, too, has no suggestions to offer. Let us suppose for argument's sake that his reading is correct and see if any meaning can be made out of it. It admits of a two-fold construction : either (1) *lapa bhavabanana* = Pāli *lapa bhava-bandhanaṁ*, 'cut off the ties of existence', or (2) *la pabhavabanana* = Pāli—some word ending with *lā* or *ṛā* plus *pabhava-bandhanā*, 'the ties spring from'. But these interpretations afford us no clue to the adjustment of the fragment. Two assumptions are possible: either (1) that it contains the line-end of one of the first two *Jara*-verses which are missing, a verse similar, perhaps, in thought to the following stanza (Jātaka, VI. p. 27) :—

Tattha kā nandi kā khiḍḍā kā rati kā dhanesanā,
Kiṁ me puttehi dārehi, rāja mutto'smi bandhanā;

or (2) that it contains the line-end of the verse under discussion, in which latter case M. Senart's reading must be slightly altered as (*pha*)*lapaka va banana* or (*ta*)*lapaka va banana*. The reading *phalapaka va banana* (= Pāli *phalapakkaṁ va bandhanā*) is suggested by the final words of the Udānavarga verse: "like ripe fruit falling", and *t lapaka va banana* by the final words of a verse in the Pāli Udāna (I. 1. 10): *tālapakkaṁ va bandhanā*. This simile of a ripe fruit or palm falling from the bunch is quite in keeping with our verse. Accordingly, the Prakrit stanza might be completed and read as follows :—

ye vudha ye yu dahara ye ca majhima poruṣa
anu(patati sarvi te ta)la paka va banana O

—which will read in Pāli :—

Ye vuddhā ye ca daharā ye ca majjhimaporisā
Anupatanti sabbe te tālapakkaṁ va bandhanā.

Yu is nothing but *ya* (=*ca*). It is obvious that *ya* has been influenced by *vu* of *vudha* as a result of the natural tendency to read two sets of three syllabus alike, viz. *ye vu dha* and *ye yu da.*

10 (ya)[1]dha phalana pakana nica patanato [bhayo emu jatasa maca][2]sa nica maranato bhayo O[3]

(C^{vo}, 8)

Cf. Sallasutta (Suttanipāta, No. 34, Majjhima Nikāya), v. 576, Dasarathajātaka, No. 461 (Fausböll, IV. p. 127), and Mūgapakkhajātaka, No. 536 (Fausböll, VI. p. 28):—

Phalānam iva pakkānaṁ niccaṁ patanato bhayaṁ
Evaṁ jātānaṁ maccānaṁ niccaṁ maraṇato bhayaṁ.

Cf. Udānav., ch. I. ("Impermanency"), v. 11:—

"As the ripe fruit is always filled with the dread of falling, so likewise he who has been born is filled with the fear of death".

Cf. Rāmāyaṇa, II. 105. v. 17:—

Yathā phalānāṁ pakvānāṁ nânyatra patanād bhayaṁ
Evaṁ narasya jātasya nânyatra maraṇād bhayaṁ.

Notes.—The simile and main idea of this verse is tacitly implied in that of the foregoing one. Its intrinsic value and historical significance lies indeed in the fact that it stands in form midway between the verse in the Dasarathajātaka and that in the Rāmāyaṇa. As in the Sanskrit epic, the Prakrit verse begins with *yadha*= Pāli and Sk. *yathā*, while the simile is indicated in Pāli by the particle *iva*, put after *phalānaṁ*. In both the epic and the Prakrit

---

[1] Supplied by us.
[2] Frag. C. xv^{vo}, 1,—not adjusted by M. Senart.
[3] This line-end is connected by M. Senart with the preceding verse. He reads instead—*ya ayu payeti panina* O—as the line-end of this verse, but we have transferred it to the line-end of the next verse on the strength of a closefitting Pāli parallel (*q. v.* p. 199).

text we have a genitive singular form, *jāta—jata*, while in Pāli the form is that of a genitive plural. The occurrence of identical and similar reflections in the Dasarathajātaka and the Rāmāyaṇa goes to prove that the narrative of the Sanskrit epic was woven out of an older Rāma-story, which is preserved in ballad forms in the aforementioned Jātaka, the Mahābhārata, and in the first canto of the Rāmāyaṇa itself. Although the epic narrative has far outgrown its original and completely changed its moral, one may notice that the original story with its morals still lurks within its four corners.

Emu = Pāli and Sk. *evaṁ*. The change of *v* into *m* is a peculiarity of the Prakrit of our text, but the form *eva* is not rare (see v. 14 *infra*).

11 ....[ra

emu jara ya mucu][1] ya ayu payeti panina O[2]

(Cvo, 8)

Cf. Dhammap., v. 135 (Daṇḍavagga, v. 7) :—

" Yathā daṇḍena gopālo gāvo pāceti gocaraṁ
Evaṁ jarā ca maccu ca āyu pācenti[3] pāṇinaṁ".

Cf. Fa-kheu-pi-u, sec. I. ("Impermanency"), p. 39 :—

" As a man with his staff in his hand goes along tending and pasturing the cattle, so are old age and death, they also watch over the life that perishes."

Cf. Udānav., ch. I. (" Impermanency"), v. 17 :—

" As a cowherd with his staff gathers his cattle into the stable, so disease and old age bring mankind to the lord of death ".

---

[1] Frag. C. xvvo 2,—not adjusted by M. Senart. He reads the fragment as follows :—

....ya
emu ne(?)rayamuca..

[2] This line-end was connected by M. Senart with our v. 10 (see p. 198, f. n. 3).

[3] A Burmese Ms. reads *pāceti*.

Notes.—Almost the whole of the first line of the above verse is missing from the extant Kharoṣṭhī Ms., and the remnant —*ya ayu payeti panina* O—has been misplaced by M. Senart, who tags it to the end of the preceding verse. As has been established, M. Senart's C^vo^, 8 is not, as he says, a patchwork of two half-verses, but of two separate, though fragmentary, verses which have been wrongly adjusted, not by the scribe but by himself. However, our adjustment of the fragments has gone a long way to enable us to complete the verse as follows :—

yadha danena[1] gopalo gavo payeti goyara
emu jara ya mucu ya ayu payeti panina O

—This stanza cannot be traced in any other canonical text than the Dhammapada. The simile calls up a vivid picture of a cowherd driving the cattle of a village to the common pasture, and strikingly brings home to an agricultural people like the Indo-Aryans the idea of the manner in which death drives all beings to their destiny.

Payeti = Pāli *pāceti*, an instance of causative.

12 yadha nadi pravatia racha vahati ?..............................
....[2]

(C^vo^, 9)

Cf. Mūgapakkhajātaka, No. 536 (Fausböll, VI. p. 26) :—

Yathā vārivaho pūro gaccharh nûpavattati
Evam âyu manussānaṁ gacchaṁ nûpavattati.
Yathā vārivaho pūro vahe rukkh'ūpakūlaje
Evaṁ jarāya maraṇena vuyhante vata pāṇino.

Cf. Fa-kheu-pi-u, sec I. ("Impermanency"), p. 39 :—

"As the waters of a river ever hasten on and flow away, and once gone, never return, such is the life of man. That which is gone knows not any return".

---

[1] Cf. *dana* (=Pāli *daṇḍaṁ*, I. B. 39, p. 42) ; *manikunaleṣu* (=Pāli *maṇikuṇḍalesu*), Suhavaga, v. 8, *infra* (C^vo^, 31).

[2] For the line-end here M. Senart has—*tavi oharanaseva satii* O—which, however, fits better with v. 13. The Udānavarga has a verse (ch. I. v. 18) of which the final words correspond to *oharanaseva satii* : "As the waters of a brook, so flow on by day and night the hours of man's life ; it draws nearer and nearer to its end".

Cf. Udānav., ch. I. ("Impermanency"), v. 15 :—

"As a river that is always running swiftly by and never returns are the days of man's life—they depart and come back no more".

Notes.—The whole of the second line of the above verse is missing from the extant Kharoṣṭhī Ms. in spite of M. Senart reading, as a line-end, *tavi oharanaseva satii* ○—which fits better with the line-end of the following verse. The Prakrit verse might, however, be completed in one of the following two ways :—

[1] yadha nadi pravatia racha vahati (upakulaja
emu jaraya maranena vuhati vata panino ○)

[2] yadha nadi pravatia racha vahati (na nivatati
emam ayu manuṣana gachu na upavatati ○)

Pravatia = Pāli *pavattitvā*, Sk. *pravartya*, 'beginning to flow', a gerund. The form is closer to Sanskrit. **Racha** = Pāli *rukkhaṁ*, Sk. *vṛkṣaṁ* (cf. *rucha*, Asoka's Rock-Edict II, Mansehra version). M. Senart says : "I am not sure of the reading *racha* or *vacha*; anyhow I can only see in it a reflex of *vṛkṣa*, whether for *vracha* or for *rukkha*." For the form *vracha*, cf. *vrachā* in Asoka's Rock-Edict, II, Girnar version. If it is *vacha*, cf. Pāli *mālāvacchaṁ*, Suttavibhaṅga, I. p. 179.

13 yadha vi dani vitati[1] ya ye deva oduopati[2]
apaka bhoti [3]vitavi oharanaseva satii ○[4]

(C^vo, 10)

---

[1] M. Senart reads *vikoti* according to the script, but this does not give any sense. He joins the words together as *yadhavidanivikoti*.

[2] In M. Senart's edition the words are run together and read *yayedevaoduopati*.

[3] He reads, and the Ms. clearly has, *vo°* which, again, seems to have been influenced by the *o* of the preceding word *bhoti*. The final *i* is due to the influence of the preceding syllables. The words are run together in M. Senart's edition and read *apakabhotivo*............

[4] He connects the line-end *tavi oharanaseva satii* with v. 12 (see C^vo, 9, p. 73). Our adjustment is warranted by the sense of the verse as well as by the mutilated shape of the line-end.

14 emam eva manuś(eṣu)[1] (avi)[2]dha[3](va)ti[4] pranayo
ya ya avi(śi)[5]sati rati[6] maranaseva satii (O)

(C[ro], 11)

Cf. Mūgapakkhajātaka, No. 538 (Fausböll, VI. p. 26):—

Yathā pi tante vitate yaṁ yaṁ dev'ūpavīyati
Appakaṁ hoti vetabbaṁ evaṁ maccāna jīvitaṁ.

Notes.—The Pāli verse seems to have been expanded later into two Prakrit stanzas, which are bound up together in thought and serve to illustrate the course of human life by the imagery of weaving. The sense is: when the loom is spread out, no sooner are the threads spun out than what remains to be spun grows less and less;—a striking illustration of how the hours of man's life ceaselessly pass away. The imagery reminds us of the ancient myth where the Goddess of Fate is represented as a woman engaged in spinning the thread of man's life. The Prakrit verse 13 differs from the Pāli by its closing words *oharanaseva satii* (which would equate with Pāli *oharaṇass'eva santike*). **Dani vitati** = Pāli *tante vitate*, Sk. *taṁtre vitate*,—(loc. absolute, 'the loom being spread out'). **Oduopati**, if the reading be correct, would strictly correspond to Sk. *udvapati*, used impersonally, meaning 'casts out or is cast out'. The reading, as M. Senart is also of opinion, is very doubtful. **Oharana** = Sk. *avaharaṇa*, better *apaharaṇa*, a synonym of *marana* in v. 14. Verse 14 expanding the idea of the Pāli clause *evaṁ maccāna jīvitaṁ*, would read in Pāli:—

Evam eva manussesu abhidhāvanti pāṇayo
Yaṁ yaṁ āvisissati rati maraṇass'eva santike.

---

[1] Supplied by us. [2] Supplied by us, following the sense of the previous verse, though tentatively.

[3], [4] We have changed M. Senart's *s* into *dh*, as these two letters have often been confounded in the Kharoṣṭhī Ms.: cf. *masuru* for *madhuru* = Pāli *madhuraṁ* I. B. 11 (pp. 28-29); see also M. Senart's °*dhiti* for °*siti* (= Pāli °*smiti*), v. 16 *infra*. After M. Senart's *s* there is a gap, quite sufficient for one letter, which we have tentatively filled by a reading *va*. This gives us *avidhavati*, meaning 'they run the course of life' (quite in keeping with the simile of the thread being spun out).

[5] Filled by us on the strength of clear traces of the upper part of an *ś* in the fac-simile. We have taken *aviśisati* as the future, 3rd pers. sing. of Sk. *ā* + √*viś*, 'to enter', hence 'to approach, occupy'.

[6] M. Senart entertains doubt as to the correctness of his reading here as well as in the previous words.

15 sati[1] eki na diśati pratu diṭho[2] bahojano
pratu eki na diśati sati diṭha bahojano O

(C^vo, 12)

Cf. Dasarathajātaka, No. 461 † (Fausböll, IV. p. 127), and •Mūgapakkhajātaka, No. 538 (*ibid*, p. 28) :—

Sāyam eke na dissanti pāto diṭṭhā bahujjanā,
Pāto eke na dissanti sāyaṁ diṭṭhā bahujjanā.

Cf. Udānav., ch. I. ("Impermanency"), v. 7 :—

"One sees many men in the forenoon, some of whom one will not see in the afternoon; one sees many men in the afternoon, some of whom one will not see in the (next) forenoon".

Sati stands for *sai* (=Pāli and Sk. *sāyaṁ*, cf. *nai*= *nāyaṁ*, Apramadav., vv. 24-25). The *t* has intervened through False Analogy with *diśati*. For the first *o* in **bahojano**, see *poruṣa* (v. 9. *supra*)=Pāli *porisā* (also *purisā*). The Prakrit *o* can also be explained as having been lengthened from *u* to make up for the loss of a *j* in the Pāli *jj* following.

16 tatra ko viśpaśi macu daharositi[3] jivit.
.... ?vi miyati nara nari ca ekada O

(C^vo, 13)

Cf. Mūgapakkhajātaka, No. 538 (Fausböll, VI. p. 26) :—

Daharâpi hi mīyanti narā ca atha nāriyo,
Tattha ko vissase poso daharo 'mhîti jīvite.

---

[1] M. Senart says that *sai* would do well.

[2] *Diṭho* has a variant *diṭha* in the second line.

[3] M. Senart reads *dhiti*, which is clearly a mistake for °*siti* (°*smīti*). In Kharoṣṭhī the letters *dh* and *s*, being very much alike, have produced many a confusion of reading and writing, cf. *masuru* for *madhuraṁ* (I. B, 11, pp. 28-29).

Notes.—It is clear from the above citation that the lines of the Pāli verse are inverted in the Prakrit. The first line of the Prakrit verse has *macu* (= Pāli *macco*, 'the mortal') for *poso* of the Pāli. Instead of Pāli *narā ca atha nāriyo*, the Prākrit verse reads *nara nari ca ekada*, which appears to be an improvement on the Pāli reading without altering the sense. The Prakrit verse might be completed thus :—

tatra ko viśpaṣi macu daharositi jivit(e
dahara hi) vi miyati nara nari ca ekada ○

Viśpaśi = Pāli *vissase*, Sk. *viśvaset*, an optative, 'one should trust.' **Siti** = Pāli *(a)mhīti*, Pāli and Sk. *(a)smīti*, a vowel-sandhi (*daharo + asmi + iti*). The mistaken reading *dhiti* has led M. Senart to equate it with Sk. *dhṛti* (see footnotes under *avidhavati*, v. 14 *supra*).

17 ayirena vatai kayu paḍha........[ṣiti
ruchu][1]........viñana niratha ba kaḍigaru ○

(C^vo, 14)

Cf. Dhammap., v. 41† (Cittavagga, v. 9) :—

Aciraṁ vat' ayaṁ kāyo paṭhaviṁ adhisessati
Chuddho apetaviññāṇo niratthaṁ va kaliṅgaraṁ.

Cf. Udānav., ch. I. ("Impermanency"), v. 36 :—

"Alas! this body will soon lie on the earth unnoticed, empty, senseless, thrown away in a cemetery like a billet of wood".

Cf. Manu, IV. 241 :—

Mṛtaṁ śarīram utsṛjya kāṣṭhaloṣṭrasamaṁ kṣitau
Vimukhā bāndhavā yānti dharmas tam anugacchati.

Notes.—The Prakrit verse or its Pāli counterpart which is one of the most important and exquisite in the whole collection, cannot be traced in any other canonical text than the Dhammapada. It appears to have expanded the idea of the first line of Manu, IV. 241, which also occurs

[1] Frag. C. XLIvo.

in the Mahābhārata. It seems, moreover, to be a later poetical summary of the Vijaya Sutta (Suttanipāta, No. 11), vv 8-9, and Sumedhā's psalms (Therīgāthā, vv. 468-469), containing ascetic reflections on the loathsomeness and transitoriness of the body. The interest of the Vijaya verses and Sumedhā's psalms lies in the fact that these show richer combination of the Dhammapada verse and the Manu śloka :—

Yadā ca so mato seti uddhumāto vinīlako,
Apaviddho susānasmiṁ anapekhā honti ñātayo.
Khādanti naṁ supāṇā ca sigālā ca vakā kimī,
Kākā gijjhā ca khādanti ye ca aññe santi pāṇayo.
(Vijaya Sutta)

Nibbuyhati susānaṁ aciraṁ kāyo apetaviññāṇo
Chuṭṭho[1] kaliṅgaraṁ[2] viya jigucchamānehi ñātīhi.
Chaḍḍūna[3] naṁ susāne parabhattaṁ nhāyanti jigucchantā
Niyakā mātāpitaro kiṁ pana sādhāraṇā janatā.
(Therīgāthā)

—We are far from saying that the Buddhists were borrowers from the Mānavas or vice versa. The truth is that both the Buddhists and the Mānavas, no less than the poets of the Mahābhārata, had drawn upon a common source, which goes back at last to the people at large: we mean that the higher reflections contained in the verses under notice sprang originally from a cruder popular wisdom, crystallized in the shape of maxims which are preserved and used by the community in more forms than one. The language of these maxims in their popular forms is generally Prakrit, the term denoting no more than the current speech of a locality or community. Sumedhā's verses preserve a few remnants of Prakrit forms, e.g., *chuṭṭho* for *chuddho*; *kaḷikaraṁ, kaliṅkaraṁ* for *kaliṅgaraṁ*; *chaḍḍūna, chaṭhuna, chaṭhana, chaṭṭhana* for *chaḍḍita*; *niyakā*, a Prakrit survival in Pāli. The reflections in the Vijaya Sutta and Sumedhā's verses are only a poetic version of the teaching of the *kāyānupassanā* or *kāyagatasati* section of the prose Satipaṭṭhāna Sutta (Majjhima, I) or Mahāsatipaṭṭhāna Suttanta (Dīgha, II); see also the Up., Prapāṭhaka I.

[1] *Chuṭṭha* may also be taken in the sense of *chaḍḍita*, 'thrown off', considering that Sumedha's expressions are almost the same as those in the Manu śloka : *Chuṭṭho kaliṅgaraṁ viya=utsṛjya kāṣṭhaloṣṭrasamaṁ.* Cf. Bengali, *chuṭā, choḍā. choṅḍā.* Prof. Pischel notes a variant *cuddho.*

[2] Variants—*kaḷikaraṁ kaliṅkaraṁ.*

[3] Variants—*chaṭhuna, chaṭhana, chaṭṭhana.*

The Prakrit verse might be completed thus:—

ayirena vatai kayu paḍha(vi adhiśe)ṣiti
ruchu [1] (apeta)viñana niratha va kaḍigaru ○

The Dhammapada groups the Pāli counterpart of this verse under the Cittavagga, but it has little bearing on the main theme of the chapter. The mere occurrence of the word *viññāṇa* or of the idea that a corpse lies senseless or devoid of consciousness, does not surely entitle it to a place in the Cittavagga. The Prakrit text and the Udānavarga have rightly grouped it among the *Jara* verses.

Ayirena = Pāli and Sk. *acirena*, an adverb with instrumental termination, meaning 'without delay', 'very soon'. The Pāli form *aciraṁ* is a counterpart of Sk. *acirāt* which has an ablative termination. **Vatai** = Pāli *vatāyaṁ*, a vowel-sandhi (*vata* + *ai*); for *ai* = *ayaṁ*, cf. *nai* = *nāyaṁ*, (Apramadav., vv. 24, 25, pp. 138, 139). **Paḍhavi** = Pāli *paṭhaviṁ*, Ardhamāgadhī, *puḍhaviṁ*, Sk. *pṛthivyām*. The form of the Prakrit text stands mid-way between the Pāli and the Ardha Māgadhī. **Adhiśeṣiti** = Pāli *adhisessati*, 'will lie (on the earth)', can be compared with *mato seti susānasmiṁ*, 'the deceased lies down in the cemetery'; the expressions give an idea of exposure of dead bodies. We must understand by the word *adhisessati* or *seti* not that a man casts off his body, like the brute creation in general, to lie on the earth (which is rather an exception than a rule),[2] but that after his death his body is thrown away by his kinsmen or friends (ñātayo or bāndhāva)[3] in a *śmaśāna* where it undergoes the natural process of decomposition[4] or is eaten up by the worms and carnivorous birds and beasts[5]. **Ruchu** is according to M. Senart = Pāli *rukkho* (Sk. *rukṣmaḥ*), 'rough, rude', which may very well take the place of the Pāli *chuddho*, 'vile, despicable'. But we cannot fully agree with the French savant, for the Prakrit *ruchu* is a weaker expression than the Pāli *chuddho* which does not surely mean 'vile, despicable' as he supposes.

---

[1] Also *apeta* or *aveta*. For *aveta*, cf. *uveti*, v. 24 *infra*

[2] In cases of deaths by accident, e.g., of persons dying by ship-wreck, or in a desert or out of the way place. The Apaṇṇaka Jātaka (No. 1) preserves the account of a perilous journey of caravans over a vast sandy desert where hundreds of Indian merchants lay dead or killed, their dead bodies or remains being left undisposed of. Cf. a similar account of the fate of the *pesunaka corā* in the Vedabbha Jātaka (No. 48).

[3] See Manu, IV. 241, and Sumedhā's psalms cited *supra*.

[4], [5] See Vijaya Sutta, vv. 8-9; Satipaṭṭhāna Sutta (Majjhima, I. pp. 58 fg.).

His rendering of the Pāli word, no less than the commentators' paraphrase, is tentative and ultimately untenable. *Chuddho=apaviddho*, 'despised' (Dhammapada-Comy.); *chuddha=chaḍḍita*, 'forsaken', 'cast-off' (Jātaka-Comy. Fausböll, V. p 303). The former interpretation is based upon a canonical text like the Vijaya Sutta, v. 8, —*apaviddho susānasmiṁ*—and the latter on Sumedhā's psalm (Therīgāthā, v. 469)—*chaḍḍūna naṁ susāne.* These canonical passages do not bear out these interpretations. In the Vijaya Sutta the meaning of *chuddho* is expressed by these three words; *uddhumāto, vinīlako* and *apaviddho*,—'bloated, discoloured and despised'. Both the words *chuṭṭho* and *chaḍḍūna* occur in Sumedhā's psalms (Therīgāthā, vv. 468-469), and the former word might have been taken in the sense of 'useless' (*chuṭṭho kaliṅgaraṁ viya=niratthaṁ va kaliṅgaraṁ*), if it had not referred to *kāyo.* We think that the Pāli *chuddho* is=the Sk. *kṣubdhaḥ*, 'agitated'. This word indicates the successive stages of decomposition undergone by a dead body in a cemetery (cf. Vijaya Sutta, v. 8; Satipaṭṭhāna· Sutta, Majjhima, I. p. 58). Such a condition was very useful to the development of the science of anatomy in India, as natural decomposition in 'charnel fields' served well the purpose of scientific dissection. **Aveta-**(or **apeta-**) **viñana**=Pāli *apetaviññāṇaṁ*, lit. 'from which consciousness has departed', 'devoid of consciousness', 'senseless'. M. Senart observes that the Prakrit text appears to have replaced *apeta* by some synonym but does not suggest what it might be. Kullūkabhaṭṭa,, the commentator of the Manu Saṁhitā connects the idea of *acetana*, 'senseless' with a log of wood (*kāṣṭhaloṣṭravad acetanam*). **Kaḍigaru**=Pāli *kaliṅgaraṁ* (variant, *kaḷikaraṁ*), 'a log or billet of wood'=*katthakhaṇḍa* (Dhammapada-Comy.)= *kāṣṭhaloṣṭra* (Manu śloka). The Prakrit is, on the whole, more correct than *kaliṅgaraṁ*, and it stands closer to the Pāli variant *kaḷikara*, even if the forms *kali*, *kaḷi* and *kaḍi* may all be said to have been derived from the Sk. *kāṣṭha* : cf. Bengali *kaḍi, kāṭhi, kāṭh*. According to the Dhammapada-Comy., the comparison is with the useless parts of a tree left off in the wood, and this explanation is borne out by a Manu śloka (v. 69), the first line of which contains the expression *araṇye kāṣṭhavat tyaktvā*, 'casting away like a piece of wood in the forest'. The word *kaḍigaru* or *kaliṅgaraṁ* may also mean a log of wood, lying useless in a *śmaśāna*, partly burnt or wholly unburnt, if not in the sense that it is not brought back home for consumption.

18 .... [avathani a..u ? ? ? ? ?
............][1][ni śiṣani tani diṣṭani ka][2] rati O
(C vo, 15)

19 [yanimani prabhaguni vichitani diśodiśa
kavotaka][3](ni)[4] [aṭhini tani diṣṭani ka][5] rati O
(C vo, 16)

Cf. Dhammap., v. 149 † (Jarāvagga, v. 4) :—

Yān' imāni apatthāni[6] alāpūn' eva sārade
Kāpotakāni aṭṭhīni tāni disvāna kā rati.

Cf. Fa-kheu-pi-u, sec. xix. ("Old Age"), p. 120 :—

"When old, like autumn leaves, decayed and without covering, life ebbed out and dissolution at hand, little good repentance then!"[7]

Cf. Udānav., ch. I. ("Impermanency"), v. 5 :—

"Those pigeon-coloured bones are thrown away and scattered in every direction; what pleasure is there in looking at them".

Cf. Vasubandhu's Gāthāsaṅgraha, v. 21 (Rockhill's Udānavarga, Appendix) :—

"They (the bodies) are thrown away and scattered in every direction, like those pigeon-coloured bones; what pleasure, then, is there in looking at them".

Fausböll identifies the Prakrit verses with the following in the Divyâvadāna, p. 561 :—

Yānimāny apaviddhāni vikṣiptāni diśo daśa
Kapotavarṇāny asthīni tāni dṛṣṭveha kā ratiḥ.
Imāni yāny upasthānāni alâbur iva śārade (?)[8]
Śaṅkhavarṇāni śīrṣāṇi tāni dṛṣṭvêha kā ratiḥ.

---

[1] Frag. C xiv vo, 1. [2] Frag. C. xxii vo, 1. [3] Frag. C. xiv vo, 2.
[4] Supplied by us, in place of the dot of omission (see I. C vo, 16, p. 74).
[5] Frag. C. xxii vo, 2. [6] Variant, *avatthāni*.
[7] Beal's rendering seems far from correct.
[8] The Ms. used by Cowell and Neil reads *serabhe*, which is meaningless. The mistake is perhaps due to the scribe.

Notes.—The two Prakrit verses appear to have grown out of one verse incorporated in the Pāli Dhammapada and the Udānavarga, and are, on the whole, similar to two verses quoted in the Divyâvadāna, probably from an older Sanskrit recension of the Dhammapada resembling that from which a whole chapter is quoted in the Mahāvastu, III. pp. 434 foll. The Prakrit verses stand, as the resemblance of certain words go to prove, nearer in point of date to the Pāli gāthā. Verse 18 might be restored as follows :—

(yanimani) avathani a(lap)u(ni va sarade[1]
saghavarna[2])ni śiṣani tani diṣṭani ka rati O

It is somewhat difficult to say whether it is a charnel-field or a crematorium, of which the Pāli gāthā and the Prakrit verses depict the scene. The expressions *saghavarnani śiṣani* (*i.e.*, 'the skulls looking white like conch-shells') and *kavotakani aṭhini* (*i.e.*, 'the pigeon-coloured bones') can as well be associated with a burning scene[3] as with the picture of a charnel-field. But scanning the verses closely, one can discover that these form an appropriate sequel to v. 17 and complete the description of the fate of a dead body thrown away in a charnel-field. Verse 17 does not proceed farther than the description of a dead body undergoing the process of decomposition and lying in the cemetery like a log of wood, and it leaves to verses 18 and 19 to describe what befalls the bodily remains after decomposition and consumption by the worms, birds and beasts, *viz.*, the skeleton and the bones. As a matter of fact, these two verses, no less than verse 17, are based upon the Kāyânupassanā section of the Satipaṭṭhāna or Mahāsatipaṭṭhāna Discourse, which actually contains the distinctive expressions, e.g., *disā-vidisā vikkhittāni, aṭṭhikāni setāni* (corresponding to *kāpotakāni* of the Pāli, and *k votakani* of the Prakrit verse) *saṅkhavaṇṇūpanibhāni* (Majjhima, I. p. 58). For such asectic reflections in Indian literature, it is important to bear in mind the following references, which are interesting :—

1. Maitrāyaṇī Up. I. 3=Vijaya Sutta, vv. 2-7=Satipaṭṭhāna Sutta, secs. 6-7.

---

[1] With regard to the restoration of the first line we have followed the suggestion of M. Senart (*q. v.* p. 75). But instead of *alapu* one may read *alavu*.

[2] Also, °*vranani*.

[3] Ajitakesakambala says, "āsandipañcamā purisā matam ādāya gacchanti, yâva āḷāhanā padâni paññāpenti, kāpotakâni aṭṭhīni bhavanti, bhassantâhutiyo" (Dīgha, I. p. 55). "Kāpotakānīti kapotaka-vaṇṇāni, pārāpatapakkha-vaṇṇāni" (Sumaṅgala Vilāsinī, I. p. 166). The story of Cūḷakāla and Mahākala in the Dhammapada-Comy. gives a detailed account of the possible changes of a dead body during cremation.

2. Prakrit verse 17=Dhammapada, v. 41=Vijaya Sutta, vv. 8-9=Therīgāthā, vv. 468-469=Satipaṭṭhāna Sutta, the first portion of sec. 8.
3. Prakrit verses 18-19=Divyâvadāna, p. 56=Satipaṭṭhāna Sutta, the latter portion of sec. 8.

Sec. 8 of the Satipaṭṭhāna Discourse, especially its latter portion, clearly indicates the importance of 'charnel-fields' in the history of the science of Anatomy in India, particularly in relation to Osteology (see Hoernle's *Studies in Indian Medicine*, Pt. I), long before the time when dissection became a desideratum.

Avathani=Pāli *apatthāni* (variant, *avatthāni*), Buddhist Sk. *upasthānāni* (Divyâvadāna)=*chaḍḍitāni*, 'thrown off' (Dhammapada-Comy.)="thrown away" (Udānavarga). It is difficult to understand how this meaning could be derived from *avathani*, unless we suppose that it is the neuter plural of *avatha*=Pāli *apatthaṁ* or *avatthaṁ*, 'dislocated', 'displaced'. When applied to *alapuni* ('pumpkins'), *avathani*=*vippakiṇṇāni*, 'scattered, at sixes and sevens' (Dhammapada-Comy.). **Alapuni va sarade**=Pāli *alāpūn'eva sārade*, Buddhist Sk. *alābur iva śārade*, 'like pumpkins during autumn'; 'scattered like pumpkins, exposed to heat and wind during autumn' (Dhammapada-Comy. : *sāradakāle vātātapahatāni tattha vippakiṇṇa-alāpūni viya*). **Diṣṭani** would strictly correspond to Pāli *diṭṭhāni*, Sk. *dṛṣṭāni*, 'seen'. M. Senart says that the construction is "less normal, but not unacceptable in this form". This may be an idiom. But if *tani diṣṭani ka rati* be not regarded as an idiomatic construction and *diṣṭani* not taken as a past participle qualifying *tani*, we can explain the form as *diṣṭana*, a Gerund corresponding to *disvāna* of the Pāli verse, the final *i* being accounted for as having developed out of rhythm with the preceding *tani*. The Buddhist Sanskrit form in the Divyâvadāna is also a Gerund, *dṛṣṭvā*. The Prakrit form keeps closer to the Pāli in having a suffix similar to the Pāli *tvāna*. **Prabhaguni**, 'fragile'. We have a singular form of the word in v. 5, *supra*. The word in this plural form cannot be equated with Sk. *prabhaṅgura*. M. Senart rightly suggests that it implies a base *prabhagu*, identical in meaning with *prabhaṅga*. **Diśodiśa**=Pāli and Ardha Māgadhī, *diso disaṁ*, 'in various directions', 'on all sides'. The Divyâvadāna verse reads *diśo daśa*, 'the ten cardinal points'.

20 [imina putikaena aturena pabhaguna
nicaśuhavijinena jaradhamena s][1](avaso)[2]
(nime)[3]dha parama śodhi yokachemu anutara ○
(C^{vo}, 17)

21 [imina putikaena vidvarena (pabhaguna)[4]][5]
[(nicaśuhavijinena)][6] (jaradhamena savaso)[7]
(nime)[8]dha parama śodhi yokachemu anutara ○
(C^{vo}, 18)

22 [imina putikaena viśravatena putina
nica][9][śuhavijinena jaradha][10](mena savaso)[11]
(ni)[12][medha parama śodhi yokachem(u)[13]] [14]
anutara ○[15]
(C^{vo}, 19)

Cf. Saṁyutta, I. p. 131 § 5 :—

Iminā pūtikāyena bhindanena pabhaṅgunā

....

Cf. Therag. v. 32† :—

....

Nimmissaṁ paramaṁ santiṁ yogakkhemam anuttaraṁ.

Cf. Fa-kheu-pi-u, sec I. ("Impermanency"), p. 43 :—

"What use is this body when it lies rotting beside the flowings of the Ganges? It is but the prison-house of disease, and of the pains of old age and death. To delight in

---

[1] Frag. C. XIV^{vo}, 3. [2], [3] Supplied by us. [4] Supplied by us.
[5] Frag. C. XIII^{vo}. [6] Frag. C. XIV^{vo}, 4. [7], [8] Supplied by us.
[9] Frag. C. XXI^{vo}. [10] Frag. C. I^{vo}, 1. [11], [12] Supplied by us.
[13] The *u* is supplied by us.
[14] Frag. C. XL^{vo}, and Frag. C. XXVI^{vo}, 1; the latter preserves, as is suggested by five queries (p. 92), so many faint traces of the bottom of the characters, of which the upper portion is in tact in the former.
[15] The circle is supplied by us.

pleasure, and to be greedy after self-indulgence, is but to increase the load of sin, forgetting the great change that must come, and the inconstancy of human life."

Cf. Udānav., ch. I. ("Impermanency"), v. 37 :—

"Continually afflicted by disease, always emitting some impurity, this body, undermined by age and death, what is the use of it."

Notes.—These three verses, which are quite peculiar to the Prakrit text, are bound up together in thought as completing the ascetic reflections in v. 5, *supra*. The Pāli parallel of the first line of v. 21, (and *à posteriori* of vv. 20, 22) is in the Saṁyutta verse cited above, and that of the third line of each of the three verses occurs in the Theragāthā, v. 32, and one need not be surprised if the parallel of the middle line, which is common to all the verses, be found out in some other Pāli verse, not yet discovered. The linking together of three lines, that is, of three separate ideas, into one verse, appears to be a novelty, serving to give altogether a new idea, though the combination seems somewhat incongruous. At any rate, they betray quite a mechanical growth, however much a commentator may try to make out some grand meaning by his ingenuity. We are confident that the process of such co-ordination is earlier in the Buddhist literature, and that in all probability the number of verses was originally less than three, and perhaps not more than one. As may be conjectured from the Saṁyutta verse and that in the Udānavarga, the original verse consisted of two lines, and ended with the question "what is the use of it?" or "*kā rati*" as in v. 19, *supra*, or with such reflections as we find in the second line of the Saṁyutta verse: *aṭṭiyāmi hariyāmi kāmataṇhā samūhatā*. However, taking the verses as they are, they seem to admit of a two-fold interpretation: either (1) that there is a break at the end of the second line, the construction lacking in some expression to complete the Stoic rune like that which might be translated "what do you gain (by)"; or (2) that these verses mark a turning-point in the general trend of thought, in that they draw the hearer's attention away from the vain moralising on the transitoriness of the body to the real purpose to which the body should be employed. The second interpretation leads us to understand the underlying idea of these verses as follows: 'Taking for granted that the body is such and such, the question henceforth arises, what use we should make of it. Is it not proper to create for each of us an unsurpassed state of safety even with the help of such a body ?' This is quite in keeping with the spirit of Buddhism, which as a heroic faith sought to shake off the cowardly ponderings over the loathsomeness of decaying body.

Verse 20.—Putikaena = Pāli *pūtikāyena*, 'with this body emitting impurity'; cf. *putisaueho* in v. 5, *supra*. **Aturena** = Pāli and Sk. *āturena*, which is identical in meaning with *roaniḍa* in v. 5, and *āturaṁ* in Dhammap., v. 147. **Nicaśuhavijinena** corresponds, according to M. Senart, to Sk. *nityāśubha-vicīrṇṇena*, 'permeated with impurities'. The expression is not to be met with in Pāli. **Jaradhamena savaso** = Pāli *jarādhammena saṁvāso*, 'association with what is conditioned to decay'; cf. "continually afflicted by disease" (Udānavarga). **Nimedha**, if the *dha* be regarded as a clerical error for *sa*, as is sometimes the case in the Ms. (see footnotes under *avidhavati*. Jarav., v. 14, p. 202), would give place to a form *nimesa*, which would tally well with the Pāli first-person form *nimmissaṁ* of the Theragāthā verse. If it be not such a mistake, then *dha* must be equated with the Pāli suffix *tha*, and *nimedha* classed with such second-person forms as *arahadha*, *nikhamadha*, *bhodha*, *udhvaradha*, etc. (pp. 130-137). **Parama śodhi** = Pāli *paramaṁ suddhiṁ*, Sk. *paramaṁ śuddhim* (or *śauddhim*), 'the highest purity', which is the same in meaning as *viśodhi* (Magav., vv. 27-29), a synonym of Nirvāṇa. The Theragāthā reads *santi*, 'tranquillity', 'peace', another synonym of Nirvāṇa.

Verse 21.—Vidvarena is a curious Prakrit form, conveying the same sense as the Pāli *bhindanena*, 'by (that which is) brittle'; cf. *bhedanadhamme kalevare*, Therīgāthā, v. 380; *parijina* in v. 5, *supra*. Some of the Pāli Mss. of the Saṁyutta read *bhindarena* (instead of *bhindanena*), a variant which has a justification from cases like *pabbaṅgura* —*pabbhaṅguna*. The Prakrit *vidvarena* sounds closer to *bhindarena*.

Verse 22.—Viśravatena putina = Pāli *vissavantena pūtinā*, 'with impurity flowing off', from the root √*sru* (to flow).

23 [(a)[1]yara jiyamanena ḍajhamanena nivruti
nimedha][2] [parama śodhi yokachemu anutara][3] (○)[4]
(C[vo], 20)

Cf. Therag., v. 32 † :—

Ajaraṁ jīramānena tappamānena nibbutiṁ
Nimmissaṁ paramaṁ santiṁ yogakkhemam anuttaraṁ.

Notes.—This verse, which is peculiar to the Prakrit text, clearly sets forth the moral of the foregoing three verses. The Theragāthā ascribes the authorship of the Pāli parallel to Suppiya Thera.

Ayara = Pāli *ajaraṁ*, 'the undecaying', a synonym of Nirvāṇa. **Jiyamanena** = Pāli *jīramānena*, 'by a person in a state of decaying'; cf. *khaṇe khaṇe jarāya abhibhuyyamānattā jīramānena* (Paramatthadīpanī). **Ḍajhamanena** = Pāli *ḍayhamānena*, a synonym of *tappamānena*, 'by a person in a state of burning'. **Nivruti** = Pāli *nibbutiṁ*, Sk. *nirvṛtiṁ*, a synonym of Nirvāṇa. Here the change is either from *rv* into *vr* as in Pāli (cf. *athra* of the Manserah Edicts), or from *vṛ* into *vr*.

24 [jiyati hi rayaradha sucitra adha śarira bi jara
uveti
sata tu[5] dharma na[6] ja][7][ra (u)veti][8] [sato hiva[9]
sabhi praveraya][10]ti[11] ○
(C[vo], 21)

---

[1] The *a* is supplied by us. [2] Frag. C. Ivo, 2.
[3] Frag. C. xxvivo, 2. [4] The circle is supplied by us.
[5], [6] M. Senart reads *na ta tu*, but doubts the *na* (p. 77). He also doubts the character which follows *dharma*, and which he tentatively reads *ca*. Our restoration is based on the Pāli parallel which M. Senart has unfortunately missed. [7] Frag. C. Ivo, 3. [8] Frag. C. xxvivo, 3.
[9] M. Senart has *hiṣa*, which gives no meaning. Our reading, however, is tentative. See notes (p. 215).
[10] Frag. C. xviivo, not adjusted by M. Senart, who reads .... *satohiṣasabhi pravera(ya)*.........................
[11] M. Senart reads *ka*. The letter is somewhat mutilated. In Kharoṣṭhī, *ti*, if written hurriedly, may very well appear like *ka*.

Cf. Dhammap., v. 151 (Jarāvagga, v. 6); Saṁyutta, I. p. 71; Jātaka, V. pp. 483, 494 :—

Jīranti ve rājarathā sucittā atho sarīraṁ pi jaraṁ upeti
Satañ ca dhammo na jaraṁ upeti santo have sabbhi pavedayanti.

Cf. Fa-kheu-pi-u, sec. XIX. ("Old Age"), p. 118 :—

"And when the body dies, and the spirit flees, as when a royal personage rejects a (broken) chariot, so do the flesh and bones lie scattered and dispersed. What reliance, then, can one place on the body?"

Cf. Udānav., ch. I. ("Impermanency"), v. 29 :—

"Even the brilliant chariot of the king is destroyed, the body also draws nigh to old age; but the best of men, who teaches others this best of all good laws, shall not know old age."

Notes.—This verse forms a fitting sequel to the foregoing one, as we reach in it a point where it is the turn of the compiler to say if there is anything within human experience which does not decay in the midst of decaying things. The reply given is in the affirmative, dilating upon the popular comparison of the body or material form to a chariot or royal chariot (cf. Kaṭha. I. 3, 3, quoted *ante*, p. 100, and Dhp. v. 171 : *imaṁ lokaṁ rājarathūpamaṁ*). The only thing that does not approach decay is **sata dharma** = Pāli *sataṁ dhammaṁ*, which is but a synonym of Nirvāṇa (Jātaka, V. p. 484). **Sato hiva sabhi praverayati** means the same thing as Pāli *santo have sabbhi pavedayanti*, 'the persons who have attained the tranquil state, discuss with the wise'. For *santo*, cf. Bengali *sādhu-santa*. *Hiṣa* of M. Senart is unintelligible unless it is taken, tentatively, as a mistake for *hiva* standing, with inverted vowels, in place of the Pāli *have*, that is to say, *hiva* from *havi* (by Metathesis) = Pāli *have*. For the second *r* of *praverayati* (= Pāli *pavedayanti*), cf. Sk. *aṣṭādaśa* = Pāli *aṭṭharasa*. This is the only instance of the equation of *r* with *d* in the extant Kharoṣṭhī Ms.

25 [muj. p. rat. muj][1][u pachatu majhatu muju bhavasa parako sarvatra vi............]^2 (na punu jatijaravuvehisi)[3] (O)[4]

(C[vo], 22)

[.................................ga 25][5]

Cf. Dhammap., v. 348 † (Taṇhāvagga, v. 15) :—

Muñca pure muñca pacchato majjhe muñca bhavassa pāragū,
Sabbattha vimuttamānaso na punañ[6] jātijaraṁ upehisi.

Cf. Bhaddasālajātaka, No. 465 (Fausböll, IV. p. 156) :—

Agge ca chetvā majjhe ca pacchā mūlaṁ vichindatha
Evaṁ me chijjamānassa na dukkhaṁ maraṇaṁ siyā.

Cf. Udānavarga (Prof. Pischel's 'Turfan-Recensionen des Dhammapada'), Yugavarga, ch. XXIX. v. 66 (B 57) :—

Muñca purato muñca paścato madhye muñca bhavasya pāragaḥ
Sarvatra vimuktamānaso na punar jātijaraṁ upeṣyasi.

Cf. Udānav., ch. XXIX. ("Day and Night"), v. 59 :—

"Having cast off what is before, having cast off what is behind, having cast off what is in the middle, one goes to the other shore of existence ; when the mind is free from everything, one will not be subject to birth and death."

Notes.—This Prakrit verse, with the exhortation not to proceed again towards birth and decay and with the suggestion about the means thereto, comes rightly at the end of the chapter. Having regard to the means, the Pāli parallel

---

[1] Frag. C. Ivo, 4.
[2] Frag. C. IIvo, 1.
[3] We have followed M. Senart's restoration.
[4] The circle is supplied by us.
[5] Frag. C. IIvo, 2.
[6] Variant, *puna*.

is entitled to a place in the Taṇhāvagga. But it is quite out of place in the chapter, entitled (in Rockhill's translation of the Udānavarga) "Day and Night", corresponding to the Yamakavagga of the Pāli text. It is out of place there because no verse in which the negative and positive phases of a single idea are not contrasted deserves a place among the "Twin-verses". The Prakrit verse might be restored, in the light of the Pāli gāthā and the English translation of the verse in the Udānavarga, as follows :—

muj(u) p(u)ratu muju pachatu majhatu muju bhavasa parako
sarvatra vi'mutamanaso) (na punu jatijaravuvehisi O)

Muju would strictly correspond to Pāli *muñcaṁ* (pres. part.), 'having cast off' (Udānavarga). In the Pāli verse we have an imperative form of $\sqrt{muc}$. **Puratu** = Pāli *purato*, Sk. *purataḥ*, 'what is before' (*purato*, Udānavarga). In the Pāli verse we have the locative form *pure*. **Pachatu** = Pāli *pacchato*, Sk. *paścato*, 'what is behind' (Udānavarga). **Majhatu** = Pāli *majjhato*, 'what is in the middle' (Udānavarga). The Pāli *majjhe* has a locative termination. The Pāli counterparts of *puratu*, *pachatu* and *majhatu* are explained in the Dhammapada-Comy. thus : *Muñca pure'ti atītesu khandhesu ālayaṁ nikantiṁ ajjhesanaṁ patthanaṁ pariyogāhaṁ parāmāsaṁ taṇhaṁ. Muñca pacchato'ti anāgatesu pi khandhesu ālayādīni muñca. Majjhe'ti paccuppannesu* :—(*i.e.*, 'Free yourself from the thirst for, the dealing with, the diving into, the solicitation for, the seeking after, the dwelling upon, the past, the future and the present aggregates'). The exhortation of the above verse is expressed in another form in the Bhaddekaratta Discourse (Majjhima, Suttas 131-134) :

Atītaṁ nânvagameyya, nappaṭikaṅkhe anāgataṁ,
Yad atītaṁ pahīnan taṁ, appattañ ca anāgataṁ,
Paccuppannañ ca yo dhammaṁ tattha tattha vipassati.

Thera Mahākaccāyana's interpretation of the Discourse (Majjhima, Sutta No. 133) which is the historical basis, as we take it, of the Sabbatthivāda doctrine, is this : *Kathaṁ ... atītaṁ nânvagameti? Iti me cakkhuṁ ahosi atītaṁ addhānaṁ iti rūpā ti na tattha hoti chandarāgapaṭibaddhaṁ hoti viññānaṁ*—(*i.e.*, "How is it that a person does not pursue the past? 'Such was my eye in the past, of this kind', to such a thought his mind is not attached with a passionate longing.") So also with regard to the remaining senses, all collectively termed *khandhā* in the Dhammapada Comy.; and the same explanation holds true of the future and the present.

The chapter contains 25 stanzas.

[9. Suhavaga]

The following 20 stanzas expressive of the optimistic outlook of the Buddhist recluse life constitute a group, similar to and partly identical with the Sukhavagga of the Pāli text (ch. XV.), where the total number of verse is 12. Sec. XXIII. of the Fa-kheu-king, corresponding to the Pāli Sukhavagga, contains 14 verses, and the same group in the Udānavarga (ch. XXX.) contains altogether 53 verses. Although the colophon indicating the total number of verses in the Prakrit group is missing from the existing Kharoṣṭhī Ms., it may be judged from the general trend of thought that the group ended with the 20th stanza. The juxtaposition of the *Jara* and *Suha* groups is a remarkable feature of the Prakrit text, and it serves to bring out prominently, by a contrast of two modes of reflection on two aspects of human life, the bright prospect that lay before the religious life of the Buddhist Bhikkhus.

1 [aroga parama labha satuṭhi parama dhana
viśpaśa[1] parama mitra][2] nivana paramo suha (○)[3]

(C^vo^, 24)

2 (jiga)[4][cha[5] parama (r)ok(a)][6] [saghara parama duha
eta ñatva ya][7]dhabh(u)[8]tu nivana paramo suha ○

(C^vo^, 25)

---

[1] M. Senart tentatively reads *vaśpaśa*, which is no doubt a mistake of the scribe. See his notes on the word (p. 78).

[2] Frag. C. II^vo^, 3.

[3] The circle is supplied by us.

[4] Supplied by us in the light of the Pāli *jigacchā*.

[5] M. Senart reads *ka*.

[6] Frag. C. XXXIX^vo^, 1,—not adjusted by M. Senart; *r* and *a*, put within brackets, are supplied by us.

[7] Frag. C. II^vo^, 4.

[8] Supplied by us.

Cf. Dhammap., vv. 204, 203† (Sukhav. vv. 8, 7) :—

Ārogya paramā lābhā, santuṭṭhī paramaṁ dhanaṁ
Vissāsa paramā ñāti, nibbānaṁ paramaṁ sukhaṁ.
Jigacchā paramā rogā, saṁkhārā paramā dukhā,
Etaṁ ñatvā yathābhūtaṁ nibbānaṁ paramaṁ sukhaṁ.

Cf. Udānav., ch. XXVI. ("Nirvāṇa"), vv. 6-7 :—

"Absence of disease is the best of possessions, contentedness the best of riches, a true friend the best of friends, nirvāṇa the greatest happiness."

"All compound things (saṅskara) are the greatest of pains, hunger the worst of diseases; if one has found this out, he has found the highest nirvāṇa."

Notes.—These two verses form an excellent pair serving to throw by contrast the two aspects of human life into clear relief. After lingering so long upon decay and impermanence, it is, indeed, a great relief to read two verses which contain a message of hope. In the midst of decay and decrepitude there is a state of health, contentment and bliss which abides. The logical succession of thought is kept up better in the order in which the verses occur in Prakrit and Sanskrit.

Aroga parama labha=Pāli *ārogya paramā lābhā*, 'health is a great gain'. Health is a medical term, used figuratively in the Buddhist phraseology to denote negatively a state of the absence of hunger or appetition. That health is a great blessing of life is a common-sense view, the natural desire of mankind, as, perhaps, of all forms of life being to live in valour, vigour and energy (*śaurye, vīrye, balasi*). The Buddhist teaching serves only to widen the idea of health, which is a state of well-being of the body as well as of the mind. A healthy mind is that which is free from sense-appetite. **Satuṭhi parama dhana**=Pāli *santuṭṭhi paramaṁ dhanaṁ*, 'contentment is a great possession'. Contentment is a positive nomenclature for *aroga*, as wealth is that for gain.

3 ....[suhaparicai][1]..
............matrasuha dhiro sabaśu vi(vu)[2]la suha ○

(C^vo, 26)

[1] Frag. C. XXXIX^vo, 2,—not adjusted by M. Senart, who reads *ruha*°.
[2] Supplied according to M. Senart's suggestion.

Cf. Dhammap. v. 290 † (Pakiṇṇakav., v. 1) :—

Mattāsukhapariccāgā passe ce vipulaṁ sukhaṁ
Caje mattāsukhaṁ dhiro sampassaṁ vipulaṁ sukhaṁ.

Cf. Udānav., ch. xxx. (" Happiness "), v. 32 :—

" If the stedfast man seeks for great happiness, and would give up little happiness, let him cast away the little happiness and look well to the great one. "

Notes.—The probable restoration of the Prakrit verse would be :—

(matra)suhaparicai (paśe[1] yi vivula suha ·
caji[2]) matrasuha dhiro sabaśu vi(vu)la suha ○

—Two words are important : **matra**=Pāli *mattā*, Sk. *mātrā*, 'a smaller measure', and **vivula**=Pāli and Sk. *vipulaṁ*, 'a larger measure'. °**paricai**=Pāli °*pariccāgā*. Cf. *uvacai* (I. B. 3, p. 25)=Pāli *upaccagā*. The verse teaches that when a man has a choice between two measures of happiness, he ought to strive for the larger one. The principle inculcated is not Utilitarian, *i.e.*, the greatest happiness of the greatest number. The happiness aimed at is an individual experience. In the Devadaha Sutta (Majjhima, No. 101) Buddha refutes the Jaina theory of the quantification of pleasure and pain. In his opinion one cannot say this quantity of pain (*ettakaṁ dukkhaṁ*) is due to self, and that to not-self. Here the idea of quantity implies no more than intensity of feeling.

4 .... u . eṣu anusua
(usu)eṣu manuśeṣu viharamu anusua ○

(C^{vo}, 27)

Cf. Dhammap., v. 199 † (Sukhav., v. 3) :—

Susukhaṁ vata jīvāma ussukesu anussukā
Ussukesu manussesu viharāma anussukā.

---

[1] From a comparison with the form *bhaṣe* (Sahasav. vv. 3, 5, pp. 158, 159).
[2] Cf. the form *cari*, Apramadav. v. 1, p. 119 ; Panitav., v. 7, p. 175. There are many other instances of such Optative forms ending in *i*.

Cf. Fa-kheu-pi-u, sec. XXIII. (" Rest and Repose "), p. 137 :—

" My life is now at rest, sorrowless in the midst of sorrow; all men have sorrow, but I have none."

Cf. Udānav., ch. xxx. (" Happiness "), v. 44 :—

" Ah ! let us live exceedingly happy, living without greed among men who are greedy, without greed in the midst of the greedy. "

The probable restoration of the Prakrit verse would be :—

(suhai vata jivamu) u(su)eṣu anusua
(usu)eṣu manuśeṣu viharamu anusua ○

5 suhai vata jivamu viraneṣu averana
[veraneṣu ma][1]nuśeṣu viharamu averana ○

(C^{vo}, 28)

Cf. Dhammap., v, 197 † (Sukhav., v. 1) :—

Susukhaṁ vata jīvāma verinesu averino,
Verinesu manussesu viharāma averino.

Cf. Fa-kheu-pi-u, sec. XXIII. ("Rest and Repose"), p. 137 :—

" My life is now at rest, with no anger amongst those who are angry (or those who hate). Men indeed on all sides feel anger, but my life (conduct) is free from anger."

Cf. Udānav., ch. xxx. (" Happiness"), v. 48 :—

" Ah ! let us live exceedingly happy, living without hatred amidst men who hate, without hatred among haters. "

6 suhai (vata)[2] jivamu kijaneṣu akijana
kijaneṣu ma(n)[3]u(śeṣ)[4]u (vi)[5]haramu akijana ○

(C^{vo}, 29)

---

[1] Frag. C. XXIVvo.

[2], [3], [4], [5] Supplied by us.

This would give in Pāli :—

Susukhaṁ vata jīvāma kiñcanesu akiñcanā,
Kiñcanesu manussesu viharāma akiñcanā.

7 suhai vata jivamu yeṣa mu nathi kijana[1]
kijaneṣu manuśeṣu viharamu akijana (○)[2]

(C^{vo}, 30)

Cf. Dhammap., v. 200 † (Sukhav., v. 4) = Fausböll, Jātaka VI. p. 55 :—

Susukhaṁ vata jīvāma yesaṁ no n'atthi kiñcanaṁ
Pītibhakkhā bhavissāma devā ābhassarā yathā.

Cf. Fa-kheu-pi-u, sec. XXIII. ("Rest and Repose"), p. 137:—

"My life is now at rest, in perfect peace, without any personal aim, feeding on (unearthly) joys, like the bright gods above (Abhâsvaras)."

Cf. Udānav. (Pischel), ch. XXX. (Sukhavarga), vv. 49-50 :—

Susukhaṁ bata jīvāmo yeṣāṁ no nāsti kiñcanam
Prītibhakṣā bhaviṣyāmo devā hy ābhasvarā yathā.
[Susu]khaṁ bata jīvāmo yeṣāṁ no nāsti kiñcanam
Prītibhakṣā bhaviṣyāmo satkāyenopaniḥśṛtā(ḥ).

[Rockhill's translation, ch. XXX. ("Happiness") vv. 50-51 :—

"Ah ! let us live exceedingly happy; though there be nothing to call our own, we shall feed on happiness like the shining gods."

"Ah ! let us live exceedingly happy, relying on nothing perishable ; and though there be nothing to call our own, we shall feed on happiness."]

---

[1] The Ms. has *kajani*, which M. Senart points out as a mistake of the copyist, for *kijana*. See p. 80.
[2] The circle is supplied by us.

Cf. Fausböll's Jātaka, VI. pp. 54-55 :—

Susukhaṁ vata jīvāma yesaṁ no n'atthi kiñcanaṁ,
Raṭṭhe vilumpamānamhi na me kiñci ajīratha.
Susukhaṁ vata jīvāma yesaṁ no n'atthi kiñcanaṁ,
Mithilāyaṁ ḍayhamānāya na me kiñci aḍayhatha.

Cf. Udānav., ch. xxx. (" Happiness "), v. 49 :—

" Ah ! let us live exceedingly happy; though Mithila burns, nothing of mine does burn, for I have nothing."

Cf. Mahābhārata, XII. 219. 50 :—

Susukhaṁ bata jīvāmo yeṣāṁ no nāsti kiñcanam
Mithilāyām dahyamānāyām na no dahyati kiñcanam.[1]

Notes.—These four verses (4-7), all characterised by a highly optimistic tone, constitute a sub-group and clearly depict the bright prospect that lay before the Indian religion of renunciation, especially in its Buddhist form. There is a general agreement in the reading of other recensions, while the Prakrit verses differ by substituting certain expressions which modify the sense. But it goes without saying that the Prakrit stanzas have considerably deteriorated the lofty tone of their Pāli and Sanskrit parallels.

From a comparative study of this sub-group in its several recensions we are led to think that the Dhammapada verses betray a process of later manipulation on a common model, and that this model is no other than the verse which occurs in a story common to the Mahābhārata and the Mahājanaka Jātaka (Fausböll, No. 539), designated on the railing of the Bharhut Stūpa as the story of " Janako rājā Sivali devī". Indeed, both the Mahābhārata and the Jātaka Book go to prove that the teaching of the verses under notice was formulated for the first time in history by a king of Videha, of which Mithilā was the capital. All the stories that are preserved, in Indian literature, of Videhan kings, such as those of Makhādeva, Nimi and the Janakas, bring home one fact, namely, that the personal examples of these princes gave a great impetus to the ideal of renunciation. The Jātaka literature, which will ever be read as the largest collection of the older specimens of Indian ballads and folktales, is found to associate such

---

[1] Cf. Mahāvastu, III. p. 453. 1 :—
Mithilāyāṁ dahyamānāyaṁ nāsya dahyati kiñcana.

examples with the kings of Mithilā and Benares. The city of Mithilā is set on fire, but it does not affect the mind of its ex-king, who lives exceedingly happy, having no earthly possession to claim as his own. The sentiments displayed are quite in accord with the national spirit of the Hindus in whose life, from the dawn of intellect, the spiritual motive predominates, throwing all material interests in the shade.[1] Now, so far as the Dhammapada verses are concerned, they are intended to contrast the life of the householder, who is so unhappy with his riches and relations, with that of the Bhikkhu who is so very happy and contented, although possession he has none. These set forth the remote object of recluse life which is to impress on the householders that the true source of happiness is neither material prosperity nor earthly power but renunciation and contentment. They also imply a criticism of ascetic rigorism tending to the opposite extreme of civil life, and teach that the right method of stimulating religious fervour among people at large lies not in appearing more miserable in austerity than they do in their worldliness, but in bringing home to them the sharp contrast that exists between the two pursuits, one leading to material advantage and the other to Nirvāṇa (*aññā hi lābhūpanisā, aññā nibbānagāminī*, Dhammapada, v. 75).

Verse 4.—**Suhai** would be in Pāli *sukhāya*, 'for the sake of happiness', a dative singular form of *suha*. The Pāli reading *susukhaṁ*, 'happily', seems better than the Prakrit which implies that happiness is the end of recluse life. The adverb *susukhaṁ* signifies, on the other hand, that the religious life is lived for its own sake, while happiness follows as a matter of course. **Usueṣu anusua**=Pāli *ussukesu anussukā*, Sk. *utsukeṣu anutsukāḥ*, 'without anxiety among those who are anxious'. Rockhill translates the Tibetan rendering of *utsukeṣu* as "among men who are greedy," and Beal translates the Chinese rendering of *anutsukāḥ* by "sorrowless." Neither of these two renderings are up to

[1] Prof. Max Müller was fully justified in making this observation with regard to the Hindu civilisation. Not that the Hindus have all ceased to fulfil the secular functions of human life. Nor that they have not developed secular Sciences and Arts in their extravagant zeal for the pursuit of the higher aspirations of religion. But that there is no other people on earth who have made so gigantic an effort to prepare their mind to 'dwell apart like a star' from all earthly good. And whatever their political status, so long as they are true to this spirit of their forefathers, they have a distinct place in the history of the world and they have a distinct message to impart to other peoples.

the mark. The substantives *utsuka* and *anutsuka* imply greed as a remote idea, their primary sense being connected with the Sk. *autsukya* or 'over-anxiety.' In Bengali the word *utsuka* is used in a good sense, to denote a person who is inquisitive, *e.g.*, eager to learn something.

Verse 5.—Viraneṣu averana=Pāli *verinesu averino.* The Prakrit forms are difficult of explanation, but no less so is the Pāli *verinesu.* M. Senart is of opinion that the Prakrit forms are derived from some words like *vira* or *vera*, phonetically=Sk. *vaira*, 'enmity.' These two words inculcate the Buddhist principle of stopping enmity by love.

Verses 6-7.—These are essentially, and even in expression, the same. The Pāli parallel to verse 7 contains a more striking moral, *viz.*, of feeding on joy like the shining gods. **Mu** corresponds to Pāli *no*, Sk. *naḥ.* Says M. Senart, "the form *mu*, *mo*=*naḥ* is known in the language of the Mahāvastu."

8 na ta driḍha ban(d)hanam aha dhira ya a(ya)[1]sa
daruva babaka va
saratacita manikunaleṣu putreṣu dareṣu ya ya
aveha (O)[2]
(C^{vo}, 31)

9 eta driḍha ban(d)hanam aha dhira oharina śiśila
drupamuchu
eta hi chitvana parivrayati anavehino kamasuhu
prahai (O)[3]
(C^{vo}, 32)

Cf. Dhammap., vv. 345-346 † (Taṇhāv., vv. 12-13):—

Na taṁ daḷhaṁ bandhanam āhu dhīrā yad āyasaṁ dārujaṁ pabbajañ ca
Sārattarattā maṇikuṇḍalesu puttesu dāresu ca yā apekkhā.

---

[1] The *ya* is supplied by us, according to M. Senart's suggestion (*q.v.* p. 80). The omission seems to be a mistake of the scribe.

[2], [3] The circles are supplied by us.

Etaṁ daḷhaṁ bandhanam āhu dhīrā ohārinaṁ sithilaṁ duppamuñcaṁ
Etaṁ pi chetvāna paribbajanti anapekhino kāmasukhaṁ pahāya.

Cf. Fa-kheu-pi-u, sec. XXXII. ("Lust"), pp. 179-180:—

"Hell, indeed, has its gyves and fetters, but the wise man regards not these as captivity; the foolish man who is immersed in cares about wife and child and their personal adornment, he it is who is in real captivity."

"The wise man regards lust as the imprisonment of hell, as the hard bound fetter from which it is difficult to escape, and therefore he desires to separate this and cut it off for ever, that being free from any such cares (or, desires), he may find rest and peace."

Cf. Udānav., ch. II. ("Desire"), vv. 5-6:—

"Look at those who are fondly attached to jewels, ear-rings, to their children (those are fetters); but iron, wood, and rope make not strong fetters, says the Blessed One."

"It is hard for one who is held by the fetters of desire to free himself of them, says the Blessed One. The stedfast, who care not for the happiness of desires, cast them off, and do soon depart (to Nirvāna)."

Notes.—This couple of verses seems rather out of place in the *Suhavaga*, as it serves to rob the optimistic reflections of their geniality. It has found its right place among the *Tuṣa*-verses in other recensions of the Dhammapada. However, looking the other way, it appears to form a logical sequel to the previous verses. In it we reach a point where we may expect to learn how to be free from attachment or what the fetters of attachment are. The reply is that a man can be free from attachment by getting rid of the pleasures of lust and walking out of the world after cutting the Gordian knot which is the affection for wives, children and wealth. There is no other way of escape than this.

Verse 8.—Aha dhira corresponds to Pāli *āha dhīrā*, an expression which would be grammatically incorrect. A reading *aha dhiro* or *ahu dhira* would have been quite correct. But it is not uncommon in the Prakritic languages to find a singular verbal form used along with a plural nominative and *vice versa* (see v. 15 *infra*). **Ya a(ya)sa**=Pāli *yad āyasaṁ*, 'that which is made of iron.' In M. Senart's opinion the metre proves that the error of the copyist does not consist in a simple inversion *yaasa* for *ayasa*, but, as the Pāli text indicates, in the omission of the second *ya*, *ya asa* for *ya ayasa*. For **daruva** and **babaka**, see M. Senart's notes (p. 80).

Verse 9.—**Drupamuchu**=Pāli *duppamuñcaṁ*, Sk. *duṣpramucyam*. The change of *duṣpra* to *drupa* may be viewed either as a case of inversion or as an instance of false analogy with *druracha drunivarana* (Citav., v. 5. pp. 142, 147).

10 ye rakarata anuvatati sotu saigata.........................
eta b(i)[1] ch(i)[2]tvana parivrayati anavehino
kamasuha prahai (O)[3]
(C^{vo}, 33)

Cf. Dhammap., v. 347 † (Taṇhāv., v. 14):—

Ye rāgarattânupatanti sotaṁ sayaṁkataṁ makkaṭako va jālaṁ
Etaṁ pi chetvāna vajanti dhīrā anapekhino sabbadukkhaṁ pahāya.

Cf. Fa-kheu-pi-u, sec. XXXII. ("Lust"), p. 181 :—

"The fool regarding the outward form as an excellency, how can he know the falseness of the thing, for like a silkworm enveloped in its own net (cocoon), so is he entangled in his own love of sensual pleasure."

Notes.—This verse sums up the teaching of the two previous ones and is differentiated from them by the simile of a spider entangled in its own net. The probable restoration of the second foot would be *saigata mrakaṭao*[4] *va jala*. In *rakarata*, *k* stands for *g*; cf. *kata* for *gata* (Magav. vv. 4-7, pp. 101-107). **Saigata**=Pāli *sayaṁkataṁ*, Sk. *svayaṁkṛtaṁ*, 'made by self'. The change is quite familiar—from *ya(ṁ)* to *i* (cf. *nai* for *nāyaṁ*, Apramadav., vv. 24, 25, pp. 138, 139) and from *ṅk* to *g* (cf. *paga* for *paṅka*, Apramadav., v. 23, p. 137).

---

[1], [2], [3] Supplied by us. [4] Also *makaṭako*.

11 ahivadanaśilisa nica vriḍhavayarino
catvari tasa vardhati ayo kirta suha bala ○

(C^{vo}, 34)

Cf. Dhammap., v. 109 † (Sahassav., v. 10):—

Abhivādanasīlissa niccaṁ vaddhâpacāyino
Cattāro dhammā vaḍḍhanti: āyu vaṇṇo sukhaṁ balaṁ.

Cf. Fa-kheu-pi-u, sec. XVI. ("The Thousands"), p. 108:—

"He who is ever intent on good conduct and due reverence to others, who always venerates old age, four happy consequences increasingly attend that man—beauty and strength, and life and peace."

Cf. Manu, II. 121 (quoted by Fausböll):—

Abhivādanaśīlasya nityaṁ vṛddhopasevinaḥ
Catvāri tasya vṛddhante āyur vidyā yaśo balam.[1]

Notes.—The Prakrit verse and its Pāli and Sanskrit parallels extol politeness and respect to the elders as the two cardinal social virtues, and inculcate that these serve to increase the life, fame, peace and influence of a man. They presuppose a common substratum which is no other than a popular maxim setting forth the general sense of Hindu society. The teaching thus inculcated is completely in accord with the Buddhist idea of discipline. Buddha promulgated respect to the elders as one of the seven conditions of national prosperity and communal well-being (Dīgha, II. pp. 74, 77). In his younger days he was unwilling to admit in theory any seniority by age, and as a matter of fact, he adhered to his theory throughout his life. The seniority of the Bhikkhus by age was determined by the number of Lents kept by them.

Ahi° stands for Pāli and Sk. *abhi°*. This is perhaps the only instance in our text where *h* corresponds to

[1] In Jolly's edition, the second line reads:
Catvāri tasya vardhanta āyuḥ prajñā yaśo balam.

bh. **Vridhavayarino**=Pāli *vaddhāpacāyino*, the same in meaning as the Manu *vṛddhopasevinaḥ*, a vowel sandhi (*vridha*+*arayarino*). The change of *c* to *y* is very common in the Prakrit of our text. For the anomaly in the *r*, see M. Senart's notes, p. 81.

12 d.l.bh. p.r.ṣ.?..
..................................yati viru ta kulu suhu modati O

(C^{vo}, 35)

Cf. Dhammap., v. 193 † (Buddhavagga, v. 15) :—

Dullabho purisâjañño na so sabbattha jāyati
Yattha so jāyati dhīro taṁ kulaṁ sukham edhati.

Cf. Fa-kheu-pi-u, sec. XXII. ("Buddha"), p. 132 :—

"To be born as a man is difficult; to attain to years (*i.e.* to live long) is also difficult; to be born when Buddha is incarnate is difficult; and to hear the preaching of the Law of Buddha is difficult also."

Cf. Mahāvastu, III. p. 109 :—

Dullabho puruṣâjanyo na so sarvatra jāyate
Yatra so jāyate vīraḥ taṁ kulaṁ sukhamedhati.

Cf. Udānav., ch. xxx. ("Happiness"), v. 29 :—

"An omniscient person is hard to find; he does not appear everywhere: 'tis happiness to associate with the steadfast, like unto meeting one's kinsmen; wherever such a steadfast person is born, that people finds happiness."

Notes.—The probable restoration of the Prakrit verse would be :—

d(u)l(a)bh(o) p(o)r(u)ṣ(ajaño na so sarvatra jayati
yatra so ja)yati viru ta kulu suhu modati O

—The verse is the utterance of an age when the Buddha was deified by his followers, and as such it cannot be dated earlier than the first century of Buddha's demise. The Mahāpadāna Sutta (Dīgha, II. No. 2) embodies the earliest specimen of the *Dhammatā* doctrine, corresponding to the Brahmanical theory of incarnation. This doctrine enumerates the general conditions of the advent of great men such as the Buddha, and it is in the light of this doctrine, as developed in the subsequent Jātaka literature, notably the Nidānakathā, that the significance of the expressions in the verse can be understood.

Dulabho poruṣajaño = Pāli *dullabho purisājañño*, 'the man of noble breed is hard to find'. *Poruṣajaño* is an instance of sandhi (*poruṣa + ajaña*). *Ajaño* = Sk. *ājanyaḥ*, is used of a horse of the finest breed; here it is used figuratively in the sense of 'best', referring to 'man'. The commonest Sanskritic expressions however to denote similar idea, are forms like *puruṣasiṁha*, *puruṣavyāghra*. As for the expression *dulabho*, 'hard to find,' some light on its significance is thrown by a passage in the Mahāgovinda Suttanta which expresses the following sentiment of the gods of the Thirty-three: 'Impossible it is that two supreme Buddhas should arise at the same time and in the same world system, far less to speak of three or four' (Dīgha, II. pp. 224-225, secs. 13, 14). Compare also Dhammap. v. 182 (Buddhav. v. 4):—

Kiccho manussapaṭilābho
Kicchaṁ maccāna jīvitaṁ,
Kicchaṁ saddhammasavanaṁ
Kiccho Buddhānam uppado.

The general sense of the verse quoted above is quite clear. We have only to note that looking more closely into it one can at once see that there is really a comparison involved: it is hard to be born as man, while it is far more difficult to see the advent of a Buddha who stands far above the level of common men. **Na sarvatra,** 'not in every place and family', *i.e.*, not in a country other than India, not in a province other than the Middle country and not in a family other than Kṣatriya and high class Brāhman (see Milindapañho, p. 225). **Suhu modati** has for its Pāli counterpart *sukham edhati*, 'attains happiness.' According to M. Senart, the Prakrit reading is a *lectio facilior* introduced through the unconstraint of the scribe or his predecessor. If the construction *suhu modati* be correct in Prakrit, *suhu* (= Sk. *sukhaṁ*) must be taken as an adverb, and the phrase would be idiomatic and mean '(he) delights uninterruptedly.'

13 (s)u[haṣino ye[1] kamaye[2] narethina v.][3].[.u.
suha śichi][4]tasavasa kici teṣa na vijati ○

(C^vo, 36)

Notes.—Neither the Pāli nor the Sanskrit counterpart of this verse has been traced. M. Senart's rendering of the second line—'The association with learned men is a blessing; they have no stain'—is hardly in keeping with the construction of the last pāda. *Kici teṣa na vijati* is apparently a Prakrit expression corresponding to Pāli *kicce tesaṁ na vijjati* or *kiñci tesaṁ na vijjati*, in which latter case *kici* must be regarded as a mistake for *kiji* (=*kiñci*), for everywhere in the Prakrit text *ñc* has been represented by *j*. Thus the pāda must be rendered *either*, (The happiness of an association with the cultured) does not exist in their line of action (*kici*); *or*, The slightest amount of happiness arising from association with the cultured does not exist among them.—Of these two renderings we prefer the second, as it seems more in harmony with the sense of the first line, so far as it can be made out from a tentative adjustment. We say *tentative* because the illegible traces of letters in M. Senart's reading—?????? *ya narethina v.*—have been read with the help of Frag. A. IV. (..............uhaṣino yo kama.e..................), which according to M. Senart's arrangement of plates, ought to have been adjusted in a verse included in one of the plates A[1], A[2], A[3], A[4] and B. As M. Senart says (p. 23), there are some fragments of A which find their proper places in B, *e.g.*, Frags. A. v and A. VI. Such was the disorder in which these fragments came into his hands that we should not be surprised if what he calls frag. A. IV. really belonged to his C^vo, 36, *i.e.*, the verse under notice. M. Senart rightly takes *narethina* as equal to *nariṭṭhīnaṁ*, 'of men and women,' although he has not been able to suggest any meaning of the first line taken as a whole. We admit that there is a great deal of uncertainty in our adjustment which can not, until the discovery of a

---

[1] M. Senart has *yokama.e.* We read the first syllable as *ye*, tentatively.

[2] Frag. A. IV., completing Frag. C. IXvo. There is a blank represented by a dot, in M. Senart's edition, for the *y* of *kamaye* in Fr. A.IV. The *ya* preceding *narethina* (Fr. C.IX^vo) perhaps makes up the last syllable of *kamaye*, though read without the stroke of *e*. Therefore, we do not read the *ya* apart, but have thrust it into the previous word which is thus constructed as *kamaye*.

[3] Frag. C. IXvo, 1.

[4] Frag. C. XVI^vo, 1.

parallel verse, be finally removed. In these circumstances we can only think of a restoration like the following :—

(s)uhaṣino ye kamaye narethina v(asu) (s)u(hu)
suha śichitasavasa[1] kici teṣa na vijati ○

—of which the Pāli counterpart would read :—

Sukhesino yo kāmaye naritthīnaṁ vāsaṁ sukhaṁ
Sukhaṁ sikkhitasaṁvāsā kiñci tesaṁ na vijjati.

14 [suha darśana ariana sa][2][vaso vi sada suho
adaśanena][3] balana nicam eva suhi sia ○

(C^{vo}, 37)

Cf. Dhammap., v. 206 † (Sukhav., v. 10) :—

Sādhu dassanam ariyānaṁ sannivāso sadā sukho,
Adassanena bālānaṁ niccam eva sukhī siyā.

Cf. Fa-kheu-pi-u, sec. XXII. ("Buddha"), p. 134 :—

"Oh, the happiness of seeing the Holy One! Oh, the happiness of being able to rely on him as present! Oh, the joy of the man who is able to avoid the company of the foolish, and act well and virtuously by himself!"

Cf. Udānav., ch. XXX. ("Happiness"), v. 27 :—

"To see the elect is happiness; to associate with the righteous is happiness; not to see fools is always happiness."

Notes.—This verse is appositely placed after v. 13 and its teaching is thrown into clear relief by the contrast implied between them. Moreover, this verse explains the expression *śichitasavasa* of the previous verse, and it praises association with the Āryas or the elect and condemns association with the fools. 'No friendship with a fool' (*n'atthi bāle*

---

[1] *Savasa* might, as in v. 15 fg., be taken as the Prakrit equivalent of the Pāli *saṁvāso*, in which case the expression *śichitasavasa* would be in apposition with *suha* preceding it, the sense being 'happiness which is association with the cultured'.

[2] Frag. C. IX^{vo}, 2. [3] Frag. C. XVII^{vo}, 2.

sahāyatā) is an emphatic pronouncement of the Dhammapada verse 330. The Prakrit reading agrees with that of the Udānavarga. We must note that the Prakrit verse slightly differs from its Pāli counterpart, and that with regard to the expression **savaso vi** (=Pāli *saṁvāso pi*), substituted for *sannivāso*. The addition of the particle (*a*)*vi* (=Pāli *api*) is necessitated by the exigency of metre. The expression **balana** (=Pāli *bālānaṁ*, 'of fools') denotes, when interpreted in the light of v. 13, persons who desire the pleasures of household life. **Nicameva**= Pāli *niccam eva*, a vowel sandhi (*nica+eva*).

15 [(ba)[1]lasagatacari u drigham adhvana śoyiṣu
dukha balehi][2] (sa)[3]vasu amitrehi va savrasi O

(C^{vo}, 38)

16 (dhiro ca)[4] [suhasavaso[5] ñatihi va ṣamakamo
dh][6][ira hi prañа i][7] bhayeya panito dhorekaśila
vatamata aria

(C^{vo}, 39)

[tadiśa sapuruṣa sumedha bhay(eya)] [8] [nachatrapatha va cadrimu O[9]

(A portion of C^{vo}, 40
completing C^{vo}, 39)

---

[1] Supplied by us, according to M. Senart's suggestion. [2] Frag. C. xvi^{vo}, 3.

[3], [4] Supplied by us, though the latter does not answer to the four dots of omission in M. Senart's edition, which are hardly in keeping with the metre.

[5] For the final *o*, see M. Senart's note *b* (p. 84).

[6] Frag. C. xxxvi^{vo}.

[7] Frag. C. xxxv^{vo}, 1. M. Senart reads *prañai* as one word.

[8] Frag. C. xx^{vo}; *eya* of the last word is supplied by us on the strength of a form *bhayeya* occuring in the self-same verse. The three dots of omission in M. Senart's edition appear hardly warranted, as they indicate that three letters are missing, whereas the metre proves that only one letter is wanting.

[9] Frag. C. xxxv^{vo}, 2. The bracket has not been closed after the circle as there remains a portion of the fragment, viz. *ra*, which belongs to the next verse; accordingly, the closing bracket is put after *ra* there.

Cf. Dhammap., vv. 207-208 † (Sukhavagga, vv. 11-12) :—

Bālasaṅgatacārī hi dīgham addhāna socati,
Dukkho bālehi saṁvāso amitten'eva sabbadā,
Dhīro ca sukhasaṁvāso[1] ñatīnaṁ va samāgamo.
(Tasmā hi :)
Dhīrañ ca paññañ ca bahussutañ ca dhorayhasīlaṁ
vatavantam ariyaṁ
Taṁ tādisaṁ sappurisaṁ sumedhaṁ bhajetha
nakkhattapathaṁ va candimā.

Cf. Udānav., ch. xxx. ("Happiness"), vv. 23-25 :—

"'Tis as great suffering to be in the company of fools as in that of enemies; he who associates with fools will repent him of it for a long time."

"'Tis happiness to see a virtuous man; to see one who has heard much is happiness; to see Arahats who are delivered from existence is happiness."

Notes.—There is, in the verses, nothing to comment upon, as they express, though in a somewhat different form, the very idea of v. 14. The first line of v. 16 is connected in the Pāli text with the counterpart of v. 15, a procedure which is hardly justifiable. The Prakrit text and the Udānavarga have rightly linked it with v. 16.

Verse 15.—**Śoyiṣu** = Pāli *socimsu*, an aorist form which is used, as M. Senart points out, in the sense of the present tense. Note that the verb is plural, though the nominative is singular (cf. *aha dhira*, v. 8 above). **Savrasi** = Pāli *sabbaso*, a form which is interpreted by M. Senart as due to Māgadhism. Nevertheless, he says that the reading might have been *savradhi*, in which case it would be = Pāli *sabbadhi*.

Verse 16.—**Dhorekaśila** = Pāli *dhorayhasīlaṁ*. *K* stands for *y*. **Cadrimu** occurs with a *u* which may tempt one to regard the word as an accusative form. But the sense is against such an interpretation. We do not venture to correct it to *cadrima* (for *candrimā*), because the very form *cadrimu* occurs again in I. B. 7 (p. 27) as nom. sing. All that we can say is that *cadrimu* is perhaps due to a false analogy with *suriu*, with which it goes hand in hand in common speech.

---

[1] Max Müller corrects the reading to *sukho ca dhīrasaṁvāso*.

17 [ra][1]dhakaro va camasa[2] parikica uvahana

(The remainder of C^vo, 40)

(yada)[3] [jahati kamana tadạ[4] samajati[5]][6] [s(u)[7]h(u)[8] sarva ca suhu][9] ichia sarvakama paricai O

(C^vo, 41)

Cf. Kāmajātaka, No. 467 (Fausböll, IV. pp. 172-3) :—

Rathakâro va cammassa parikantaṁ upāhanaṁ[10]
Yaṁ yaṁ cajati kāmānaṁ taṁ taṁ sampajjate sukhaṁ,
Sabbañ ca[11] sukham iccheyya sabbe kāme pariccaje.

Cf. Udānav., ch. II. ("Lust"), vv. 11-12 :—

"As the shoemaker, when he has well prepared his leather, can use it to make shoes, so when one has cast off desires, he has the highest happiness. If one longs for happiness, let him cast off all desires ; he who has cast off all desires will find the most perfect happiness.

Cf. Mahābhārata, XII. 174. 44-45 :—

Kiñcid eva mamatvena yadā bhavati kalpitam
Tad eva paritāpârthaṁ sarvaṁ sampadyate tathā.
Yad yat tyajati kāmānāṁ tat sukhasyâbhipūryate
Kāmânusārī puruṣaḥ kāmān anuvinaśyati.

---

[1] Continuation of Frag. C. xxxv^vo, 2.
[2] M. Senart reads *dhe arovacamasa.*
[3] Also, *ya ya* ; supplied by us.
[4] The interpretation may also be *ta da* (=*ta ta*)=*taṁ taṁ.*
[5] M. Senart reads *sa majati.*
[6] Frag. C. xx^vo, 3.
[7], [8] Supplied by us.
[9] Frag. C. xxxv^vo, 3.
[10] Fausböll wrongly connects this line with the previous verse in his work. We have followed the reading adopted by the Jātaka-Comy.
[11] Variant, *ce.*

Ibid, XII. 177. 48 :—

Yad yat tyajati kāmānāṁ tat sukhasyâbhipūryate
Kāmasya vaśago nityaṁ duḥkhameva prapadyate.

Notes.—This verse teaches, by the simile of a shoemaker fitting his leather by getting rid of its useless parts, that to be happy, truly happy, one must cast off one's desires.

Parikica = Pāli *parikantaṁ*, 'cutting' or 'fitting.' Phonetically the Prakrit form = Pāli *parikicca*, Sk. *parikṛtya*. To equate fitly with *parikantaṁ*, the form ought to have been *parikata* or °*katu*. **Paricai** = Pāli *pariccaje*, Sk. *parityajet*, 'should give up'. The elision of *j* in the Prakrit form presupposes an intermediate change to *y*. Note that we had *paricai* also for Pāli *pariccāgā* in v. 3 *supra*.

18 ....[nena yo atmano][1]............
[(ve) rasaṣaga][2]........?? so duha na parimucati O

(C^vo, 42)

Cf. Dhammap., v. 291 (Pakiṇṇakav., v. 2):—

Paradukkhûpadhānena yo attano sukham ichati
Verasaṁsaggasaṁsaṭṭho verā so na pamuccati.

Cf. Udānav., ch. xxx. ("Happiness"), v. 2 :—

"He who causes misery to others in seeking for his own welfare brings without distinction misery on friends and foes."

Notes.—The Prakrit verse might be restored, in the light of its Pāli counterpart, as follows :—

(para duhuvadha)nena yo atmano (suhamichati)
verasaṣaga(saṅsaṭho)[3] so duha na parimucati O

---

[1] Frag. C. XIX^vo, 1.
[2] Frag. C. XXXVIII^vo, not adjusted by M. Senart, who reads.........*rasa ṣaga*.........
[3] For the *ṅṣ* cf. *saṅsana* (for Pāli *saṁsanna*), Apramadav., v. 4, p. 123.

The interest of this verse lies in the fact that it makes clear the Buddhist position as to the pursuit of happiness on egoistic lines. It teaches that a man can not legitimately aspire for happiness so long as his pursuit injures the interest of others.

19 jaya v(e)[1]ra [prasavati[2] dukhu śayati parayitu
uvaśatu sohu śa][3]yati hitva jayaparayaa ○

(C^{vo}, 43)

Cf. Dhammap., v. 201 † (Sukhav., v. 5) = Saṁyutta I. p. 83 :—

Jayaṁ veraṁ pasavati dukkhaṁ seti parājito
Upasanto sukham seti hitvā jayaparājayam.

Cf. Udānav., ch. xxx. ("Happiness"), v. 1 :—

"From victory proceeds rancour; the defeated foe is in misery: if one casts off victory and defeat he will find the happiness of peace."

Notes.—Here at last we reach a verse which manifests the Buddhist transcendentalist view of happiness. To be happy in the absolute sense, a man must rise above the opposites, victory and defeat; the happiness resulting from victory is a relative feeling only.

---

[1] Supplied by us.

[2] M. Senart reads *prasahati*, but says that it is nothing but a gross mistake of the scribe, even though the *h* may be very clear. Our reading rests upon the Pāli *pasavati*.

[3] Frag. C. XIXvo, 2.

**

Prasavati=Pāli *pasavati*, 'begets', 'generates'. M. Senart reads *prasahati*, though he considers the reading as a gross mistake of the scribe. If the latter reading be adopted, the *h* can be said to have resulted from the hardening of a *y*, resulting from *v* of *prasavati.*

20 anica vata [saghara upadavayadhamino
upaji ti nirujhati][1] teṣa uvaśamo suho (○)[2]

(C^vo, 44)

Cf. Dīgha, II. pp. 157, 199; Saṁyutta, I. p. 158, § 6 :—

Aniccā vata saṅkhārā uppādavayadhammino
Uppajjitvā nirujjhanti tesaṁ vupasamo sukho.

Notes.—This verse which is very familiar to the student of Buddhist literature is chanted as a *mantra* or Pirit at the death of a person. It is the result of an after-thought proceeding from moralising upon the demise of a great man and teacher such as the Buddha. It teaches that the body is destined to perish, and that happiness results from the complete cessation of organic existence.

Although the colophon is missing from the extant Ms., we are confident that this verse formed a fitting conclusion to this chapter.

---

[1] Frag. C. xix^vo, 3.
[2] The circle is supplied by us.

ADDENDA

Containing certain additional parallels and notes.

The following Sanskrit parallels are quoted from the fragments of the manuscript of the Udānavarga in the collection of Pelliot and of Stein. The credit of noticing them belong partly to M. Sylvain Lévi and partly to M. de la Vallée Poussin. Here our references apply to Lévi's edition of the Apramādavarga (J.A., 1912, Vol. xx. p. 235 f,), and to Poussin's edition of some other chapters (J. R. A. S., 1912, p. 359 f.).

I. For the verses of the Apramadavaga, p. 119 ff. :—

Verse 1 = Lévi's Apramādav. v. 35 = Rockhill's Udānavarga, iv. v. 35 :

Uttiṣṭhen na pramadyeta dharmaṁ sucaritaṁ caret
Dharmacārī sukhaṁ śete hyasmiṁ loke paratra ca.

"Whoever has lived according to this law of discipline, in gentleness and purity, will, having cast off transmigration, put an end to his misery."—

Verse 2 = Lévi's Apramādav. v. 5 :

Utthānenâpramādena saṁyamena damena ca
Dvīpaṁ karoti medhāvī tam ogho nâbhimardati.

Verse 3 = Lévi's Apramādav. v. 6 :

Utthānavataḥ smṛtâtmanaḥ śubhacittasya niśamyacāriṇaḥ
saṁyatasya hi dharmajīvino hyapramattasya yaśo' bhivardhati.

Verse 4 = Poussin's Documents, Cittav. v. 32 :

Utthānakāleṣu nihīnavīryo (yuvā balī—⏑⏑)ko nirāśa (ḥ)
Sadaiva saṁkalpahatā kusīdo jñānasya mārgaṁ satataṁ
na vetti.

Verse 5 = Lévi's Apramādav. v. 21 = Rockhill's Udānavarga, IV. v. 21 :

Na tāvatā dharmadharo yāvatā bahu bhāṣate
Yastvihâlpam api śrutvā dharma kāyena vai spṛśet
Sa vai dharmadharo bhavati yo dharme na pramadyate.

"As many as you be, I declare unto you that those who, though they have heard but little of the law, have followed its commandments, have understood the law, they who follow the law have understood the law."[1]

Verses 6-7 = Lévi's Apramādav. vv. 1-2 :

Apramādo hyamṛtapadaṁ pramādo mṛtyunaḥ padaṁ
Apramattā na mriyante ye pramattāḥ sadā mṛtaḥ.
Etāṁ viśeṣato jñātvā hy apramādasya paṇḍitaḥ
Apramāde pramadyeta nityam āryaḥ svagocaram.

Verse 8 = Lévi's Apramādav. v. 10 :

Pramādam anuvartante bālā durmedhaso janāḥ
Apramādaṁ tu medhāvī dhanaṁ śreṣṭhîva rakṣate.

Verse 10 = Lévi's Apramādav. v. 4 :

Pramādam apramādena yadā nudati paṇḍitaḥ
Prajñāprasādam āruhya tvaśokaḥ śokinīṁ prajām
Parvatastha iva bhūmiṣṭhān dhīro bālān avekṣate.

Verse 11 = Lévi's Apramādav. v. 24 = Rockhill's = Udānavarga, IV. v. 24 :

Apramādaṁ praśaṁsanti pramādo garhitaḥ sadā
Apramādena Maghavān devānāṁ śreṣṭhatāṁ gataḥ.

---

[1] The translation is tentative.

" He whose speech exalts earnestness and who always despises heedlessness will be greater among the gods than he who has made a hundred sacrifices."

Verse 12=Lévi's Apramādav. v. 8=Rockhill's Udānavarga, IV. v. 8 :

Hīnān dharmān na seveta pramādena na saṁvaset
Mithyādṛṣṭiṁ na roceta na bhavellokavardhanaḥ

" Have nothing to do with false doctrines, have nothing to do with the heedless ; he who delights not in false doctrines shall not continue (in) the world."

Verse 14=Lévi's Apramādav. v. 37 :

Ārabhadhvaṁ niṣkramadhvaṁ yujyadhvaṁ buddhaśāsane
Dhunidhvaṁ mṛtyunaḥ sainayaṁ naḍâgāram iva kuñjaraḥ.

Verse 15=Lévi's Apramādav. v. 36 :

Apramādaratā bhavata suśīlā bhavata bhikṣavaḥ
Susamāhitasaṁkalpāḥ svacittam anurakṣata.

Add the following quotations just below tho Pāli verse quoted on p. 135 :

Lévi's Apramādav. v. 12 (Rockhill's Udānavarga, IV. v. II) :

Pramādaṁ nânuyujyeta na kāmaratisaṁstavam
Apramattaḥ sadā dhyāyī prāpnute ... sukham.

Verse 23=Lévi's Apramādav. v. 27 :

Apramāde rato bhikṣuḥ pramāde bhayadarśakaḥ
Durgād uddharate' tmānaṁ paṅkasanna iva kuñjaraḥ.

Verse 24=Lévi's Apramādav. v. 13 :

Nâyaṁ pramādakālaḥ syād aprāpte hy āsravakṣaye
Pramattaṁ Māra anveti siṁhaṁ va mṛgamātṛkā.

Cf. Therag. v. 30, 2nd line :

....

Ābādho me samuppanno, kālo me na pamajjitum̐.

Cf. Therig. v. 95 :

Appakam̐ jīvitam̐ mayham̐ jarā byādhi ca maddati
Purâyam̐ bhijjati kāyo na me kālo pamajjitum̐.

II. For the verses of the Citavaga. p. 140 ff. :—

Verse 1 = probably Rockhill's Udānavarga, XXXI. v. 9 :

"He who, thinking not of the body, lives in a cave, and wanders about all alone, does conquer this flighty mind, and is delivered of the greatest of terrors."

Verse 2 = Poussin's Documents, Cittav., v. 2 :

Vārija va sthale kṣipta okādoghāt samuddhṛta(ḥ)
Parispandati vai citta(m̐) Māradheyam̐ prahātavai.

One need not be surprised if the Prakrit expressions of the 2nd foot resembled those in Sanskrit and read somewhat like *ọkaogha samudhrata*.

Verse 3 = Poussin's Documents, Cittav, v. 28 = Rockhill's Udānavarga, XXXI. v. 28 :

A(nava)sth(itacitta)sya saddharmam̐ avijānataḥ
Pariplavaprasādasya prajñā na paripūryate.

"He whose mind is not stedfast cannot understand the holy law; he whose faith is fickle cannot acquire perfect wisdom."

Verse 5 = Poussin's Documents, Cittav., v. 8 :

Spandanam̐ capalam̐ cittam̐ dūrakṣam̐ durnivāraṇam
Ṛjum̐ karoti medhāvī iṣukāra iva tejanam̐.

Cf. The Jaina expression *cañcala-cavala-cita* (Leumann's Aupapātika Sūtra, s. 35, p. 46). Note that the Sanskrit verse is an exact counterpart of the Prakrit.

III. For the verses of the Sahasavaga, p. 154 ff. :—

Verse 1 = Pelliot Ms., Sahasrav., v. 3 (J.A., 1910).
Verse 3 or 5 = „ „ „ , v. 2 „

For the first half of each of vv. 6-11, cf. the first line of the Dhammap. v. 106 (Sahassav., v. 7) :

Māse māse sahassena yo yajetha sataṁ samaṁ

....

....

IV. For the verses of the Panitavaga, p. 169 ff. :—

Add the following notes on p. 172, just in the middle of the 6th line : cf. *pramajea*, Pāli *pamajjeyya* (p. 119). The Pāli counterpart *samayarea* (sing.) should be *samācarati* acc. to a Jātaka verse quoted below. For such optative forms standing for Present, as also for Past, cf. *adea* = Pāli *vyadheti*, *vyadhesi* (Balav. v. 4, p. 183). For instances where the final *a* corresponds to the Pāli suffix *tha* (3rd pers.) cf. *jaea* (Pāli *jāyetha*), Puṣav, v. 14, p. 152 ; *yaea* Pāli *yajetha*), Sahasav. v. 6-11.

For the first half of verse 4, cf. the first line in Poussin's Documents, Anityav. v. 24 :

[Narakaṁ pāpakar]maṇa(ḥ) kṛtapuṇyaṛstu svargatim

....

For verse 5, cf. Therag. v. 865 :

Sīlakkhandhe patiṭṭhāya satiṁ paññañ ca bhāvayaṁ
Pāpuniṁ anupubbena sabbasaṁyojanakkhayaṁ.

Note on p. 176 that acc. to Franke *cavadhi* = *cāpāt adhi*.

V. For the verses of the Balavaga, p. 179 ff. :—

Verse 1 = Poussin's Documents, Anityav. v. 41 = Rockhill's Udānavarga, I. v. 40 :

> Idaṁ (me kārya)ṁ kartavyam idaṁ kṛtvā bhaviṣyati,
> Ity evaṁ spantano martya jarā mṛtyuś ca mardati.

"Such and such actions are a source of felicity, which I, having performed them, will acquire. He who prepares himself in this manner, will overcome age, disease, and death."

The Sanskrit parallel and its translation quoted above fully bears out the general sense of the Prakrit verse as suggested by M. Senart: "by properly understanding one's duty, one crushes death and the pains of it." The meaning and the restoration suggested by us on p. 180 are rather based upon a verse of the Mahābhārata, quoted on p. 179. Although we are unable to understand the propriety of the inclusion of the verse under the Balavaga, if its sense be what is brought out by its parallel in the Udānavarga, we feel constrained to accept the explanation of M. Senart and restore the verse as follows :

Verse 2 = Poussin's Documents, Anityav. v. 38.

> Iha varṣaṁ kariṣyāmi hemantaṁ grīṣmam eva ca
> Bālo vicinta (yat)ī(ti) hy antarāyaṁ na paśyati.

Note that the first foot of the Prakrit verse corresponds to that of the Sanskrit, while its second foot is in accord with the Pāli. The Prakrit word at the end of the verse might as well be *paśati.*

Verse 3 = Poussin's Documents, Anityav. v. 39 = Rockhill's Udānavarga, I. v. 39 :

> Taṁ putrapaśusammataṁ vyāsaktamānasaṁ naraṁ
> Suptaṁ grāmaṁ mahaughaiva mṛtyu(rādāya) gacchati.

"Thou who art surrounded by children and flock, children are no refuge, nor are father, mother, and kinsfolk, thou art without a refuge."

For verse 6, cf. Poussin's Documents, Yugav. vv. 41-42 (=Rockhill's Udānavarga, xxix. vv. 45, 44:

> Akṛtaṁ kukṛtāc chreyaḥ paścāt tapati duṣkṛtaṁ
> Śocate duṣkṛtaṁ kṛtvā śocate durgatiṁ gataḥ
> Kṛtan tu (sukṛ)taṁ śreyo yat kṛtvā nânutapyate
> Nandate sukṛtaṁ kṛtvā nandate sugatiṁ gata(ḥ).

"It is better in both (this world and the other) if one has not done evil, for he who does it will suffer; it is good for one to do what is right, for he will have no affliction."

"He who has done that which is wrong, suffers for it, and when hereafter he will be in the evil way he will suffer; he who has done that which is right, is made happy, and when hereafter he will be in the happy way he will be happy."

Here is another instance where we find each of the two lines of a verse similar to the Prakrit or the Pāli has been expounded into one complete verse. The order of the two verses thus formed is inverted in the Udānavarga. This fact of inversion of verse-order and the discrepancy of verse-numbers suggest that the Turfan Ms. contains rather the text of an older compilation of the Udānavarga, *i.e.*, the original of the text portion of the Chuh-yau-king.

Verse 8=Lévi's Apramādav. v. 20=Rockhill's Udānavarga, IV. vv. 19-20:

> Yeṣāṁ tu susamārbdhā nityaṁ kāyagatā smṛtiḥ
> Akṛtyaṁ te na kurvanti kṛtye sātatyakāriṇaḥ
> Smṛtānāṁ samprajānānām astaṁ gacchanti āsravāḥ.

"He who comprehends the nature of the body, who reflects, and whose exertions are unceasing, does not what ought not to be done, and does what ought to be done."

"He, therefore, with memory and understanding will put an end to his misery, and when he has put an end to his misery (āsrava), he will find the untroubled state."

VI. For the verses of the Jaravaga, p. 186 ff. :—

Verse 3 = Poussin's Documents, Anityav. v. 29 :

Dhik tvām astu jare grāmye (varṇā)pakār(i)ṇ(i jaḍe
Ta)thā manoramaṁ bimbaṁ tvayā yad abhimarditam.

Verse 4 = Poussin's Documents, Anityav. v. 30 :

Yo pi varṣaśataṁ jīvet so pi mṛtyuparāyaṇaḥ
Anu hy enaṁ ja(rā yāt) i—· i mo- · i · vāntakaḥ.

Verse 5 = Poussin's Documents, Anityav. v. 34 :

(Par)ij(ī) rṇam idaṁ (rū)paṁ roganīḍaṁ prabhaṅguram
Bhetsyate pūtyasandehaṁ maraṇântaṁ hi jīvitam.

Verse 8 = Poussin's Documents, Anityav. v. 33 :

Yeṣāṁ rātridivâpāye hy āyur alpataraṁ bhavet
Alpodake ca matsyānāṁ kā nu (tatra rat)i(r bhavet).

For verse 12 cf. Poussin's Documents, Anityav. v. 32 and Rockhill's Udānavarga, I. v. 33 :

Āyur divā ca rātrau ca caratas tiṣṭhatas tathā
Nadīnāṁ (hi) yathā sroto (ga)c(cha)ti na nivartate.

"This life is fleeting away day and night; it is unstable like the stream of a great river; one goes on not to return again."

Verse 17 = Poussin's Documents, Anityav. v. 35 :

(Aciraṁ bata kāyo' yaṁ pṛthi)v(īm adhi)ś(e)ṣyati
Śūnya vyapetavijñāno nirastaṁ vā kaḍaṅgaram.

Verse 20 = Poussin's Documents, Anityav. v. 37 :

Anena pūtikāyena hy ātureṇa prabhaṅguṇā
Ni (   ) ? parāṁ śāntiṁ yogakṣemaṁ anuttaram.

Cf. Therig. v. 140 :

Iminā pūtikāyena āturena pabhaṅgunā

Verse 22 = Poussin's Documents, Anityav. v. 36 :

Kim anena śarīreṇa (visra)vāpūtinā (sa)d(ā)
(Ni)tyaṁ (r)og(ā)bh(i)bhūtena jarā-maraṇabhīruṇā.

Note that *nimedha* (p. 213) equates better with the Pāli *nmiddhaṁ*

Verse 24 = Poussin's Documents, Anityav. v. 28 :

Cīryanti vai rājarathā (ḥ) sucitrā hy ato
śarīram api ja(rām upe)ti
Sat(ā)n tu dharmo na ja(rā)m upeti santo hi
taṁ satsu nivedayati.

VII. For the verses of the Suhavaga, p. 218 ff. :—

Verse 3 = Poussin's Documents, Sukhav. v. 30 :

(Mā)trā (su)kha parityāgād yaḥ paśyed vipulaṁ sukhaṁ
Tyajen mātrāsukhaṁ dhīraḥ sa(ṁ)paśyaṁ vipulaṁ
sukhaṁ.

Verse 4 = Poussin's Documents, Sukhav. v. 43 :

Susukhaṁ bata jīvāmo hy utsukeṣu tv anutsukā(ḥ)
(U)tsukeṣu manuṣyeṣu vi(ha)rāma hy anutsukā (ḥ).

Verse 5 = Poussin's Documents, Sukhav. v. 47 :

Susukhaṁ bata jīvāmo vairikeṣu tv avairikāḥ
Vairikeṣu manuṣyeṣu viharāmo hy avairikā(ḥ).

Substitute *yeṣān no* for *yeṣāṁ no* in the Sanskrit verses oted on p. 222. Note that the Sanskrit verse quoted on p. 3 belongs to the Udānavarga (Sukhav. v. 44).

Cf. Mahābhārata, XII. 219. 50 :

Na khalu mama hi dahyate' tra kiñcit."

The ślokas corresponding to the Jātaka verses are not to e found in the existing texts of the Mahābhārata.

Verses 8-9 = Poussin's Documents, Kāmav. vv. 5-6:

(Na tad dṛḍhaṁ bandhanam āhur āryā yad āyasaṁ
dāravaṁ balbajaṁ
(Saṁraktacittā maṇikuṇḍaleṣu)p(u)treṣ(u) dāreṣ(u) ja
yā avekṣāḥ.
Etad dṛḍhaṁ bandhanam āhur āryāḥ sama(ṁ)tataḥ
susthiram duṣpramuñcaṁ
Etad api chittvā parivrajanti anape)kṣ(i)ṇaḥ
kāmasukhaṁ prahāya.

Verse 12 = Poussin's Documents, Sukhav. v. 29:

Durlabhaḥ puruṣo jānyo nāsau sarvatra jāyate
(Yatrâsau) jāyate vīras tat kulaṁ sukhaṁ edhate.

For the second half of verse 15 and the first half of verse 16, cf. Poussin's Documents, Sukhav. v. 24:

Duḥkho (bālair hi saṁvāso) hy amitre(ṇeva sarvadā)
Dhīrais tu sukhasaṁvāso jñātīnām iva samāgama(ḥ).

For verses 13-14 cf, Leumann's Daśavaikālika Sūtra Z.D.M.G.), viii v. 52:

Vivittā ya bhave sejjā, nārīnam va lave kahaṁ
Gihi-saṁthavaṁ na kujjā, kujjā sahūhi saṁthavaṁ.

Verse 17 = Poussin's Documents, Sukhav. vv. 11-12:

Rathakāra iva carmaṇaḥ parikartunn upānahaṁ
Yad ya(jja)hāti kā(m)ā(n)ā(natu)t tat sampadyate
sukhaṁ
Sarvaṁ cet sukham iccheta sarvakāmāṁ (pa)ri(tyaj)et
Sarvakāmaparityāgī hy atyantaṁ sukha(me)dhate.

ERRATA

		For	Read
p. viii. 1. 33	...	Order of chapter	Order of chapters
		Name of chapter	Name of chapters
p. ix. 1. 21	...	22 chapters	26 chapters
p. xlvii. f. n.	...	°Appra°	°Apra°
p. liii. 1. 21	...	Beugali	Bengali
p. 15	...	2 (verse-number)	12
p. 16. v. 14	...	śethi	śeṭhi
p. 72. v. 8	...	Dhammap. 195	Dhammap. 135(?)
p. 75. v. 17	...	stanza 321	stanza 32 (?)
p. 88 Frag. ix	...	fr. xv^{vo}	fr. xvi^{vo} (?)
p. 106. f. n.	...	translstion	translation
p. 129. v. 13	...	Majjhima, II. p. 103	II p. 104.
p. 134. (2)	...	mrabanana	marabanana
p. 141. v. 1	...	37	v. 37
p. 141. v. 2	...	34	v. 34
p. 141. v. 3	...	38	v. 38
p. 143. f. n.	...	oka	*eka*
p. 143. f, n,	...	(f, n, 11)	(f. n. 4)
p. 144	...	*āsine*	*āsīno*
p, 145, f, n, 2	...	cittasa	cittassa
p. 179. Mbh. Śloka		kṛtānta	kṛtāntaḥ
p. 196, f, n.	...	*kije*	*kiji*
p. 223	...	Cf. Mahābhārata, xii, 219-50	Cf. Udānav. (Pischel), v. 44,
p. 228. Manu-Śloka		tasya vṛddhante	sampravardhante

N. B.—Put.............ga 30 (A^{3}, 5) just below the Prakrit verse 30 on p. 116, Add (A^{1}, 4) under v. 22 on p. 136. Put... ga 17 (C,^{vo} 23) just below the Prakrit verse 17 (p. 167).